RESISTANCE AND THE STATE: NEPALESE EXPERIENCES

RESISTANCE AND THE STATE: NEPALESE EXPERIENCES

David N. Gellner

Berghahn Books
New York • Oxford

Revised edition published in 2007 by

Berghahn Books

www.berghahnbooks.com

©2007 David Gellner

Library of Congress Cataloging-in-Publication Data

A C.I.P. catalog record for this book is available from the Library of Congress.

British Library Cataloguing in Publication Data

A catalogue record for this book is available from the British Library

Contents

Section 2: The State and Ethnic Activism

Section 3: The State and Maoist Insurgency

List of Plates and Maps

COVER PHOTOGRAPH

Satirical comedy sketch 'Would you believe it?' (*esto pani hundo rahecha*) in Tansen, August 1999. Gai Jatra is the one day of the year when by tradition open criticism of figures of authority and respect is allowed. Here Prime Minister Krishna Prasad Bhattarai and his Secretary Kapila, played by Kiran Chitrakar and Narayan Kunwar of the Kalyan Kosh Samiti, dance to a popular Bollywood song in front of the Sital Pati, Tansen (photograph: Ian Harper).

List of Tables

Preface

The papers in this collection were initially presented (with the exception of chapter 10) at a day-long panel during the Modern South Asian studies conference in Edinburgh in September 2000. Most of the papers have been revised since that presentation, some substantially so, but these revisions were mostly done in early 2001 and—with the exception of two short passages (pp. 128–30 and 332–4)—do not cover the period since the declaration of a State of Emergency in November 2001. No collection of this sort can hope to be wholly up to date. What we, the contributors to this volume, have aimed for is ethnographically informed and historically grounded analysis. We hope that it will stand the test of time; but whether it does or not, is for readers to judge. We do not, of course, imagine that this is any kind of last word on the subject: It is, we hope, a useful contribution to the understanding of state and society in Nepal in particular and to discussions of the state in South Asia in general.

I thank the *European Bulletin of Himalayan Research* for permission to reprint from issue 19 (autumn 2000) revised versions of the papers which appear here as chapters 7 and 10. Many thanks also to William Douglas for help with the map on p. 23.

As editor I have, among other things, tried to impose a compromise between English euphony and Nepali usage: 'Nepali'—both noun and adjective—refers either to people or to the language, whereas 'Nepalese' is used only as an adjective in other, more abstract contexts (such as the sub-title of this book).

Many dates are given, in the Nepalese style, in Vikram Samvat or era (VS), which began in 57 BCE. No glossary of Nepali words or expressions has been provided, but the index should direct the reader to the place(s) where specialized terms are defined and discussed.

David N. Gellner, October 2002

For this edition, the opportunity has been taken to correct some typographical errors, to update the postscript to Judith Pettigrew's article, and to add to the list of recent references related to the Maoist insurgency on p. 357. On page 5 I have left the estimate of dead from the insurgency at 4,000 as it was in 2002. The figure today is 13,000 and rising. According to INSEC (inseconline.org) over 8,000 of these have died at the hands of the state. In the years since 2002 the state has indeed descended into increasingly futile and lethal authoritarianism. It has become all the more urgent to understand the background and context of the collapse of the state in Nepal.

D.N.G., Oxford, February 2006

List of Contributors

Ben Campbell has researched issues of development, environment, and indigenous knowledge and practice in Rasuwa District since 1989. He is lecturer in anthropology at Durham University and previously lectured at Edinburgh, Keele, Manchester, and Hull Universities. He has edited a special issue of *Conservation and Society* (2005, vol. 3 no. 2) called 'Re-Placing Nature', addressing anthropological encounters with and analyses of environmental protection. His book on the cultural politics of nature protection in Nepal, *Living between Juniper and Palm*, is in preparation.

William F. Fisher is Professor and Director of IDCE (International Development, Community and Environment Programs) at Clark University, Research Professor at the Marsh Institute, and Visiting Professor of Social Studies at Harvard University. He received a PhD in anthropology and MIA in international affairs from Columbia University. He is the editor of *Toward Sustainable Development? Struggling over India's Narmada River* (ME Sharpe, 1995), the author of *Fluid Boundaries: Forming and Transforming Identity in Nepal* (Columbia University Press, 2001), and the co-editor of *Another World is Possible: Popular Alternatives to Globalization at the World Forum* (Zed Books, 2003).

David N. Gellner is Reader in the Anthropology of South Asia at the University of Oxford. He taught in the Department of Human Sciences, Brunel University, west London, from 1994–2002. His most recent book (co-authored with Sarah LeVine) is *Rebuilding Buddhism: The Theravada Movement in Twentieht-Century Nepal* (Harvard University Press, 2005). Among his other books are *The Anthropology of Buddhism and Hinduism: Weberian Themes* (Oxford University Press, Delhi, 2001), *Nationalism and Ethnicity in a Hindu Kingdom* (with J. Pfaff-Czarnecka and J. Whelpton; Harwood, 1997), and *Inside Organizations: Anthropologists at Work* (with Eric Hirsch; Berg, 2001).

Krishna Hachhethu is a Reader at the Centre for Nepal and Asia Studies (CNAS), Tribhuvan University, and executive member of the Nepal Centre for Contemporary Studies. He has published widely on Nepalese politics. His books include *Party Building in Nepal: Organisation, Leadership and People: A Comparative of the Nepali Congress and the Communist Party of Nepal (United Marxist-Leninist)* (Mandala, 2002), (with L.R. Baral and H. Sharma) *Leadership in Nepal* (Adroit, 2001), and *State of Democracy in Nepal: Survey Report* (SDSA/N and IDEA, 2004).

Ian Harper trained as a medical practitioner, both in hospital medicine and general practice in the UK, before working for six years in public health and community health programmes in Nepal and India, subsequently 'retraining' in social anthropology. He is currently a lecturer in social anthropology at the University of Edinburgh where he is co-director of studies for the MSc in Medical Anthropology. His PhD in anthropology, 'Mission, Magic, and Medicalisation: An Anthropological Study into Public Health in Contemporary Nepal', from the School of Oriental and African Studies, London, was defended in 2003. His other publications include: 'Capsular Promise as Public Health: A Critique of the Nepal National Vitamin A Programme' *Studies in Nepali History and Society* 7(1): 137-173, June 2002; 'Relationships, Complicity and Representation: Conducting Research in Nepal during the Maoist Insurgency' *Anthropology Today* 20(1) (February 2004): 20-6 (with J. Pettigrew & S. Shneiderman); 'Interconnected and Interinfected: DOTS and the Stabilisation of the Tuberculosis Control Programme in Nepal' in D. Mosse & D. Lewis (eds) 2005 *Giving Aid: Ethnographies of Development Practice and Neoliberal Reform*, London & Ann Arbor, MI: Pluto); 'Anthropology, DOTS and Understanding Tuberculosis Control in Nepal *J. Biosoc. Sci.*(2006) 38: 57-67.

Karl-Heinz Krämer is affiliated to the Departmernt of Political Science at the South Asia Institute, University of Heidelberg (Germany) and is Nepal tutor for the InWEnt—Internationale Weiterbildung und Entwicklung (Capacity Building International), Germany. Since 1973 he has been engaged in research on modern history, politics, and society of Nepal. His books include *Das Königtum in der modernen nepalischen Geschichte* (VGH, 1981), *Nepal: der lange Weg zur Demokratie* (Horlemann, 1991), and *Ethnizitti und nationale Integration in Nepal* (Steiner, 1996).

Gisèle Krauskopff is 'Directrice de Recherches' at the CNRS and member of the 'Laboratoire d'Ethnologie et de Sociologie Comparative' of the University of Nanterre-Paris X (France). She has carried out extensive research among the Tharu of the Nepalese Tarai (see *Matres et possé dé s: Les rites et lòrdre social chez les Tharu (Né pal)* Paris CNRS, 1989; *The Kings of Nepal and the Tharu of the Tarai*, in collaboration with P. Deuel, CNAS, 2000–2001). She is currently working on the process of history-writing and rewriting, by ethnic or local leaders and on the sociology and formation of the intellectual elite, as well as on the structuration of their discourses.

Marie Lecomte-Tilouine, social anthropologist, is a member of the CNRS team 'Milieux, Sociétés et Cultures en Himalaya', Villejuif, France. Her publications, including her book (*Les dieux du pouvoir: Les Magar et lhindouisme au Né pal central*, CNRS, 1993), deal with religious strategies, mental representations, and the ethno-history of the Magars and caste groups in central Nepal.

Colin Millard received his PhD, entitled 'Learning Process in a Tibetan Medical School', from the anthropology department of Edinburgh University in 2002. He has carried out research on traditional medical practice in Ladakh and Nepal. His present research concerns are the politics of identity in South Asia, Tibetan medical practice, and the Bön religion of Tibet.

Judith Pettigrew is a Senior Lecturer at the University of Central Lancashire and a Research Associate at the University of Cambridge. She received her PhD in social anthropology from the University of Cambridge in 1995. Some of her previous publications include 'Living Between the Maoists and the Army in Rural Nepal' in *Himalayan 'People's War': Nepal's Maoist Rebellion*, edited by Michael Hutt (2004), 'Relationships, Complicity and Representation: Conducting Research in Nepal during the Maoist Insurgency' (with Sara Shneiderman and Ian Harper) in *Anthropology Today*, 2004, and 'Learning to be Silent: Change, Childhood, Mental Health and the Maoist Insurgency in Nepal' in H. Ishi, D.N. Gellner & K. Nawa (eds) *Nepalis Inside and Outside Nepal* (in press). She is presently writing a book on the impact of the Maoist insurgency on rural civilians.

Anne de Sales is 'Chargée de Recherches' at the CNRS and member of the 'Laboratoire d'Ethnologie et de Sociologie Comparative' of the University of Nanterre-Paris X (France). She has published widely on the Kham Magars, including the monograph, *Je Suis Né de vos Jeux de Tambours: La Religion Chamanique des Magar du Nord* (Nanterre: Société d'Ethnologie, 1991).

Christopher B. Tarnowski is Assistant Professor of Anthropology at Drew University, Madison, New Jersey. He has completed his doctoral dissertation entitled 'Forest Places, Political Spaces: The Social Implications of Community Forestry in Nepal' in 2002 (University of Georgia, USA).

Introduction: Transformations of the Nepalese State

• *David N. Gellner*

THE STATE

Humans have not always lived under states.[1] Non-state societies possess no specialized agencies of law-enforcement, taxation, or justice; disputes are settled largely by separating the warring parties (as among hunter-gatherers) or by feuding combined with mediation (as among pastoralists). As soon as there are inequalities and these are passed on from generation to generation by means of specialized roles in a specific territory, one can speak of incipient state-formation. In pre-modern times some people lived under states, others lived at the margins of states, and still others lived beyond the reach of states and even in ignorance of them. By contrast, everyone today lives under a state, at least nominally. States are all-pervasive. Marxist fantasies of a 'withering away of the state' and neo-liberal fantasies of 'rolling back the frontiers of the state' notwithstanding, the whole land-surface of the globe is divided up between different states, without remainder, in a way that would have been inconceivable several hundred years ago. The reach of state bureaucracies into people's lives is greater and more effective than ever before.

States can be defined in terms of economics, politics, or morality. Economically, they are organizations for extracting (and occasionally

---

[1]For useful comments on this introduction I would like to thank Krishna Hachhethu, Sharon Hepburn, Karl-Heinz Krämer, D.P. Martinez, David Washbrook, and John Whelpton.

redistributing) the surplus from those who produce it. Politically, they are organizations that dominate the means of coercion. Jurally or religiously they claim a monopoly of legitimate leadership, and therefore of the means of providing justice. It is characteristic of modern states to make monopolistic claims in all three areas: only the state may raise taxes, the state (in Weber's famous definition) must have a monopoly on legitimate violence, and only the state is sovereign (however it defines that sovereignty) within its territory (i.e., no other body can have jurisdiction without the state licensing it to do so). Weber himself deliberately defined the state in terms of its characteristic modern features:

> Since the concept of the state has only in modern times reached its full development, it is best to define it in terms appropriate to the modern type of state .... The primary formal characteristics of the modern state are as follows: It possesses an administrative and legal order subject to change by legislation, to which the organized activities of the administrative staff, which are also controlled by regulations, are oriented. This system of order claims binding authority, not only over the members of the state, the citizens, most of whom have obtained membership by birth, but also to a very large extent over all the action taking place in the area of its jurisdiction. It is thus a compulsory organization with a territorial basis. Furthermore, today, the use of force is regarded as legitimate only so far as it is either permitted by the state or prescribed by it ... The claim of the modern state to monopolize the use of force is as essential to it as its character of compulsory jurisdiction and of continuous operation (Weber 1968: 56).

This modern ideal type is, of course, subject to challenge in actual practice—by corruption, nepotism, mafias, ethno-nationalist secessionist movements, and so on.[2]

In all three of the domains that I have distinguished *pre-modern* states were not so ambitious, as Weber fully recognized. The king may claim ultimate ownership of all the land, but the effect of this in practice is often very limited. The king may be seen as the fountainhead of all ruling legitimacy, but in practice he has to acknowledge and accept the existence of numerous lords below him who have a considerable degree of autonomy in their own spheres. The king may wish to extract a greater surplus from his subjects, but he is likely to be restricted in so doing by their distance from his capital, by their ability to run away, by the fear of provoking a rebellion, and by his inability to persuade

---

[2]Pierson (1996) is a useful introduction to the sociology of the state.

the intermediaries to pass on to him any extra surplus that is extracted. In the terms of the old joke about Mussolini's Italy, pre-modern monarchical states were dictatorships tempered by inefficiency.

States and resistance go together. Wherever there has been some form of state organization, there has also been resistance to it. Resistance to the pre-modern state can take many forms which need to be distinguished. First, there are individuals and cabals within the elite who seek to take over the state for themselves (see Joshi and Rose 1966: ch. 3 for plots against the Rana regime). Second, there is the resistance of ordinary individuals. Despite the fact that this kind of regime, by its arbitrary and inegalitarian nature, encourages submissiveness in its subjects, they certainly adopted, as far as they could, the standard methods of the powerless, as described by James Scott in his classic study of class relations in a Malay village: 'foot dragging, dissimulation, desertion, false compliance, pilfering, feigned ignorance, slander, arson, sabotage, and so on' (Scott 1985: xvi).[3] But resistance consists of far more than just this; it is quite wrong to think of society as consisting of two and only two classes, with one holding power and the other resisting it (Ortner 1995, Gledhill 2000: 88–91). In so far as they could, ordinary Nepali people under the centralizing Rana regime (1845–1951) attempted to use the state for their own ends, by joining it, co-opting its personnel, bribing them, or morally coercing them. A third kind of resistance to the state occurs when there are pretenders from outside the elite who set themselves up as religious or religiously inspired leaders. The nineteenth-century rebel Lakhan Thapa (discussed by Marie Lecomte-Tilouine in ch. 7) is a good example. Fourth, when driven to desperation there were uprisings, 'peasant insurgencies' (Guha 1983). Nepal has seen few of these. Though Lakhan Thapa's movement is claimed by the Nepalese Maoists today as a forerunner of their own uprising which began in 1996, the Rana regime seems not to have treated it as such.

In modern times, there are analogous forms of resistance:

(1) struggles within the elite, when factions within political parties fight for dominance, or political parties themselves represent different sections of the elite;

(2) opposition to the activities of the state on the part of ordinary people, or exploitation of its mechanisms to personal advantage

---

[3] For examples in relation to the killing of cows in Rana Nepal, see Michaels (1997).

(this is often greatly enhanced, compared to pre-modern times, reflecting the much greater presence, or purported presence, of the state in people's lives);
(3)   opposition to the whole basis of the state based on explicitly political ideologies, expressed in underground movements and sometimes violent resistance;
(4)   full-scale and open rebellion, which happens only occasionally.

With regard to type (2) the observation of Fuller and Harriss (2001: 25) is worth repeating: 'given the obsession with "resistance" in much current scholarship, it is striking that the ordinary people described in this volume [Fuller and Bénéï 2001] are mostly not resisting the state, but using the "system" as best they can.' As for type (4), suffice it to say that authoritarian regimes may survive open rebellions if they are willing to suppress them ruthlessly; democratic regimes have great difficulty dealing with such insurgencies, if the rebels have genuine popular support.

NEPAL AS RURAL IDYLL

In the Western imagination and in the tourist literature that attempts to feed it, Nepal still stands for Shangri-la: an untouched, romantic, spiritually powerful, high-altitude backwater (as in the film 'Indiana Jones and the Raiders of the Lost Ark'). If the state features at all in this image, it is the theatre state, most famously theorized by Geertz (1982)[4]: the state exists, on this view, in order to perform complex rituals of power in which the King, either in person or represented by his sword or his Brahman, plays the central role.

It all should have happened in Tibet (Lopez 1998): Lhasa should have had Freak Street and Thamel, the trekking shops and pie shops, the courses on Mahayoga and shamanism, and the Up and Down Bar with Bob Seger and the Silver Bullet Band singing 'I'm going to Ta-Ta-Ta-Ta-Tibet'. But before the age of mass tourism could begin, one awkward fact got in the way. In 1959, following an uprising in Kham, the Chinese took full control of Tibet and caused the Dalai Lama, along with thousands of his followers, to flee to India. Subsequently, during the Cultural Revolution, many monasteries and monuments were destroyed. Western travellers were only permitted to visit Tibet

---

[4]But see also Kertzer (1988). I have discussed both of them in relation to Nepali examples in Gellner (2001: ch. 2).

much later and in small numbers. Many of the exiled Tibetans did indeed set up shop and monastery in the Kathmandu Valley. All this may explain why the imagery of Tibet is so often transferred to Nepal in the minds of Westerners ignorant of the region and why Westerners seeking Tibetan wisdom or the Tibetan experience come to Nepal. By contrast, it is impossible to understand how Nepalis view *themselves*, unless one first realizes that their self-image has nothing to do with Tibet, not even as a point of contrast. Tibet, for most Nepalis, is a faraway country of which they know nothing.[5]

Among those foreigners who actually travel to Nepal today, the arcadian image is often tarnished by the pollution, consumerism, and tourist overkill of Kathmandu. All the same, trekkers and other tourists have rarely had cause to doubt that rural Nepal was inhabited by cheery peasants, poor in material things, certainly, but well adjusted and hardy, trustworthy, peaceable, hospitable, and open. The stereotype might be argued to have reached its apogee (or nadir, depending on one's point of view) in the eulogies that successive generations of mountaineers have written about their Sherpa companions and assistants (Ortner 1999). Furthermore, in comparison to India, Nepal had, and to an extent still has, a reputation as relatively free of crime, violence, or ethnic hatred. The image of 'communal harmony' is even today still frequently invoked by Nepalese politicians and in Nepalese tourist literature. King Birendra took advantage of this image when he launched his diplomatic initiative to have Nepal recognized as a 'Zone of Peace' shortly after his coronation in 1975 (Shaha 1982: ch. 9). Nepalis themselves, while well aware that this picture is oversimplified, have none the less hoped that Nepal might be able to develop as a kind of Asian Switzerland: landlocked, mountainous, neutral, and prosperous.

The peaceful image of Nepal has suffered a rude shock since 1996 and the beginning of the so-called People's War (*jan yuddha*). Estimates of total deaths vary: official figures claim over 4000 killed and double that number injured; the real figure could be as much as twice as high. The government has seemed powerless either to capture the movement's leaders or to protect its own people, some of whom descended from the hills in September 2000 and staged a protest outside Singha Darbar, demanding to be treated as internal refugees

---

[5]The exceptions here are that minority of Nepalis who either are adherents of Tibetan Buddhism, or who possess oral traditions claiming an ultimate origin in Tibet, or who have traded in Tibet.

until the government could guarantee their safe return home.[6] The Maoists have targeted members of the Congress Party, policemen, and anyone identified as a 'class enemy' (usually landlords, opponents of Leftism, anyone working for US agencies).[7] So far they have not adopted a policy of taking tourists or Western aid personnel as hostages, but they (or in some cases robbers posing as Maoists) have held up tourist buses and made off with money and valuables.[8] They see their fight as justified by the inequalities of Nepali society, by the corruption of the government, and (as they see it) by its craven, pro-Western, pro-Indian foreign policy. Interestingly, the Maoists have explicitly denounced the view of Nepalis as peace-loving as a myth:

Even today any independent Nepalese would feel proud when they remember the fighting prowess, bravery and sacrifice of the Nepalese people in past history. It is a matter of no lesser pride that even Karl Marx, the proponent of communist ideology & the leader of the world proletariat, too, had appreciated the sacrifice, bravery and skill shown by the Nepalese people in those wars .... The reactionary propaganda that the Nepalese people are peace-loving and that they don't like violence is absolutely false. It is an incontrovertible fact that the Nepalese people have been waging violent struggle for their rights since the historical times.[9]

An even bigger shock to the idyllic and peaceful image of Nepal in the wider world occurred on the 1 June 2001 when, according to the official account, Crown Prince Dipendra mowed down most of his immediate family and close relatives in a drunken and drug-induced rage over his mother's refusal to countenance Devyani Rana becoming his bride. No coherent, empirically supported alternative

---

[6]Their list of demands is published as an appendix in Maharjan (2000), as is the 40-point ultimatum which the United People's Front presented to the government as a prelude to the Maoists launching their insurgency in February 1996.

[7]According to news reports, on 28 February 2001 Maoist guerillas shot dead Tikaraj Aran, a member of the Nepali Congress convention, in the village of Purana Gaon, Ramechhap. His son was quoted as saying, 'My father had given them funds [as] per their demands. He had been staying at the home as asked by them. But, I do not know why they killed him?' (www.nepalnews.com.np/contents/englishdaily/ktmpost/ 2001/mar/mar01/index.htm#8).

[8]The 1999 edition of the Lonely Planet guide to Nepal offered the following advice: 'Although they receive wide media coverage, the activities of the Maoists are not aimed at foreigners and so pose no threat to visitors to Nepal' (Finlay *et al.* 1999: 41).

[9]CPN-Maoist (1997). For further quotations from this document, see Lecomte-Tilouine, ch. 7, p. 245n.3, p. 246n.6, below.

account has emerged from the Palace, and consequently I, for one, feel obliged to accept the official story, at least in its main outlines. But the significant social fact is that the vast majority of Nepalis do not accept that Prince Dipendra did it. It is assumed that someone did it on behalf of the present king, Gyanendra, and his unpopular son, Paras. The facts that Gyanendra was out of Kathmandu at the time, that Paras was unhurt, and that Gyanendra's wife received only a minor injury, are all seen as highly suspicious. Inevitably, therefore, the events of 1 June have led to a big decline in the popularity of the monarch, if not in the legitimacy of the monarchy. Parliamentary democracy, in so far as it is tied up with monarch as head of state, has also been harmed. The Maoist demand for a republic has come to seem ever more cogent, and indeed, shortly after the events, Baburam Bhattarai, one of the principal leaders of the Maoist movement, declared that the republic had effectively been founded on 1 June.

Social scientists had predicted that the new Nepal, after the People's Movement (*jan āndolan*) or revolution of 1990, would face problems managing ethnic diversity (Bhattachan 1995, Raeper and Hoftun 1992, Gellner *et al.* eds 1997), but—with one major exception (Nickson 1992) and one minor one (Mikesell 1993)—no academic observer predicted that Maoism would cause such a problem. In fact the various governments, despite their weakness, have coped with the demands of ethnic activists fairly well. It is the more extreme ethnic activists who are wondering whether to throw in their lot with the Maoists. It is the violent Maoist movement that has caught the government out.

Important though the Maoist movement undoubtedly is, this volume does not focus on it to the exclusion of all else. Rather it attempts to encompass the whole context of the Nepalese state and to offer a cross-section of analyses of various resistances to it.

THE EXTRACTIVE STATE: THE RANAS

At the beginning of the twentieth century the population of Nepal was around 5 million (today it is over 22 million) (see Table 2, p. 16). Except in the Kathmandu Valley, the population was relatively sparsely spread, there was much uncut forest land, and it was government policy to encourage the settlement of virgin land with 5- or 10-year tax breaks, especially in the fertile Tarai strip bordering India. The government was not concerned to promote ethnic or national homogeneity, beyond a minimal respect for the dominance of Hindu norms. Indian peasants were welcome to come over the border and settle in Nepal.

The Rana family held all real power in its hands. The law of the land prescribed the hereditary roles that people of different castes could follow and the relationships between castes. In principle all land belonged to the king, and could only be held by individuals under various forms of conditional tenure. The state was effectively patrimonial: that is to say, it was considered to belong to the rulers (both the King and the Ranas) and the people only had what they held on sufferance and after supplying the needs of the rulers. The revenues of the state were used by the Ranas for their own private purposes: the ancient cities of Kathmandu and Lalitpur were surrounded with magnificent palaces housing numerous wives, servants, and concubines. The tax burden was severe, and the penalties for opposition or disobedience were harsh. Tax revenues were raised by contracting out to the highest bidder. There was a culture of subservience (*chākari*) to those in power. Caplan (1975: 222) lists three ways in which government jobs could be obtained: by using personal links to those already in post, by subservient gift-giving to the local governor, and by a straightforward payment of money (*ghūs*).[10] Higher posts in the civil service required moving around the country, and were not aspired to by lower-level bureaucrats. They were also rotated frequently in order to provide rewards for new courtiers and to prevent office-holders from building up a local powerbase. In short:

The Rana political system was an undisguised military despotism ... its main domestic preoccupation was the exploitation of the country's resources in order to enhance the personal wealth of the Rana ruler and his family ... any government revenue in excess of administrative expenses was pocketed by the Rana ruler as private income.[11]

The King's and the Ranas' positions were justified in Hindu terms:

[10]See also the much-read description of *chākari* and *āphno mānche* in Bista (1991); the concepts are applied to contemporary health-care bureaucracy by Levitt (1999).

[11]Joshi and Rose (1966: 38–9). The Rana regime was simply continuing, with greater efficiency, the practices of previous rulers (the contrast is with the period that followed). Whelpton (1991: 235) comments: 'Extraction of the maximum revenue without driving the population beyond endurance had always been the guiding philosophy of Gorkha administration ... Jang Bahadur did not so much innovate in these spheres, as display a greater finesse and determination in implementing them.' On the Rana regime's systems of control, see further Regmi (1978: ch. 2).

they were born to rule and ruled by virtue of a privileged relationship to the gods, which depended on their sponsorship of festivals, on their gifts to Brahmans and other Hindu holy specialists, on their own personal piety, and on their ordering of their domains in accordance with Hindu scriptural principles. Many ordinary people shared this definition of the country as the ruler's property. After the devastating earthquake of 1934 many refused to accept state aid, on the grounds that it was sinful to take the king's property (*rājasva*). (Hachhethu brings out how utterly this has changed within half a century when he writes, in chapter four, p. 165 in this volume, 'The state has long been perceived as the provider of basic necessities to the people...').

Nepal was and is landlocked and mountainous like Switzerland. But unlike Switzerland it has only one way out—via India. Nepal's geography, the secret of its independence from British India, has been a considerable hindrance in the modern period. All the natural lines of communication run north-south along the river valleys. In many regions of Nepal it is easier and more natural to head for India than to Kathmandu. In the Rana period the harshness and unpredictability of the state was ameliorated by its remoteness for many mountain villages. In the modern period the lack of roads and the general difficulty of communications have proved disastrous impediments to the spread of development as well as perfect terrain for guerilla warfare.

The Ranas did everything they could to prevent dissent. They discouraged the development of education so that literacy in 1951 stood at only 2 per cent. (Trichandra College, established in 1918, was open only to sons of the aristocracy.) They suppressed ruthlessly any attempts at political change and forbade conversion from one religion to another. They restricted the access of foreigners. But they could not prevent Nepalis working and studying in India; in the long run they could not isolate their population entirely. Had the Rana state been situated in eastern Europe fifty to a hundred years earlier than it actually was, historians—observing its use of modern means to shore up traditionalist privilege—would no doubt have labelled it 'absolutist'. Like the absolutist regimes of Europe, the Ranas set in motion changes which eventually undermined their own position.

THE DEVELOPMENTALIST STATE: THE PANCHAYAT REGIME

The overthrow of the Ranas in 1951 came about through a combination of factors: (i) the changed international situation (Indian independence); (ii) social change within the country (dissent from urban intellectuals who founded the Congress Party and were willing to launch armed resistance from India; they found support among disgruntled Ranas who had been excluded from power by their relatives); (iii) the support of King Tribhuvan, whose flight to the Indian Embassy and from there to Delhi precipitated the end of the Rana regime. There followed a period of manoevring and delay, including, finally, national elections in 1959, which were won overwhelmingly by the Congress Party led by B.P. Koirala. Approximately 18 months later, in 1960, the new king, Mahendra, Tribhuvan's son, threw Koirala in jail and established Partyless Panchayat Democracy. An ideology for Panchayat Democracy was gradually developed, which defined itself both by its opposition to the autocracy of the Ranas and by its opposition to the supposedly foreign ideology of political parties (see Table 2 below). The principal elements of 'Panchayatocracy' were as follows:

(1) Leadership of the king, as the bringer and guarantor of 'democracy'.

(2) A system of bottom-up representation on the basis of what were argued to be genuinely Nepali village-level councils (*panchāyats*), rather than through the supposedly foreign notion of political parties.

(3) Economic development (*bikās*), towards which aim all institutions were supposed to be subordinated.

(4) Equality of all citizens.

(5) Unity of the nation, as expressed in the slogan, 'One language, one dress, one country' (*ek bhāsā, ek bhesh, ek desh*) and the importance of 'building nationalism' (i.e., feelings of national identification).

(6) The banning of any non-governmental organizations (e.g., independent trade unions) that would represent sectional interests and increase internal conflict; they were replaced with official, supposedly non-conflictual 'class organizations' (*bargiya sangathan*) for youth, peasants, workers, women, students, and ex-soldiers (Joshi and Rose 1966: 406–10).

(7) Hinduism as the official state religion, with Buddhism, Jainism, and Sikhism seen as branches of Hinduism;

(8) Respect for traditional customs.[12]

---

[12]I have discussed this ideology further in Gellner (2001). For interesting discussions of the Panchayat period, see Joshi and Rose (1966), Borgström (1980),

The basic elements of Panchayat ideology were taught in school and pupils learnt by heart the reasons why political parties were unsuited to Nepal. The term that was introduced for 'democracy' and which entered the language was *prajātantra*, literally 'rule by subjects', and not the more challenging *ganatantra*, as was the case in Hindi and in India; *ganatantra* in Nepal was understood to imply republicanism.

Although the Panchayat regime was authoritarian, it was very mildly so compared to the Ranas. By the simple fact of aspiring to institutionalize equality, and by its attempt to bring education, health, and development to all corners of the country, the regime set in motion powerful forces of social change. Over several decades there were considerable improvements in levels of literacy, and in some indicators of health. The tax basis of the regime shifted from land to indirect taxes, mainly levied on imports. Increasingly the Panchayat regime relied on foreign aid to fund its day-to-day running. Large amounts of money concentrated in the capital, Kathmandu, so that both the elite and the less well-off who were based there certainly saw dramatic improvements in their standards of living and in their access to global culture. This meant that there was an equally dramatic gap opening up between the urban areas and the rest of the country, most of which was without electricity, let alone the consumer goods that were seen as evidence of progress in the towns.

Furthermore, not only was the gap between urban and rural areas growing larger because of the development of the towns, there is evidence that the standard of living in the villages was actually falling. Alan Macfarlane (1983; 1994: 108; 2001) has documented for the village of Thak how the quality of people's diet has declined as the purchasing power of a day labourer's wage has fallen, crop yields have declined, and the number of animals kept in the village has halved. Figures for Nepal as a whole apparently show that agricultural yields have indeed declined between the 1960s and the 1990s, whereas in other South Asian countries they have improved considerably (Panday 1999: 76). Large parts of Nepal suffer from long-term migration by men (and some women) to look for work outside: primarily in India, but increasingly in 'Arab' (the Gulf states and Saudi Arabia) and in East and South-East Asia. In short, if Macfarlane's detailed combination of quantitative and qualitative data over the last thirty years are typical, throughout the Panchayat period, and continuing into the 1990s, the

Gaborieau (1982), Shaha (1982), Seddon (1987), Pigg (1992), Pfaff-Czarnecka (1997), Whelpton (1997), Hoftun *et al.* (1999).

rural areas of Nepal have not only fallen behind the towns in *relative* terms, they have also, overall and taken in the round, experienced a gradual and *absolute* decline in their standard of living.[13]

This decline in the standard of living has occurred even in relatively favoured rural districts. But on top of this one must add that there are and have been considerable regional disparities within Nepal, with all the peripheral areas of the country having reason to complain that the government permits disproportionate benefits to flow to the central parts of the middle hills and especially to the Kathmandu Valley. Back in the 1970s Marc Gaborieau already pointed out that, of all the kingdom's different regions, the far west was the most disadvantaged:

... One has the impression of entering a vast back-country which is only slightly connected to the life of the nation and is little favoured by the central government ... [with few exceptions] there is nothing that reminds one of the modern world; anyone who climbs out of an aeroplane from Kathmandu feels as if they have gone back two centuries in time (Gaborieau 1978: 63).[14]

At least on paper the state attempted to reach out to all these districts and to bring them within the sphere of its formative institutions, especially the school and the health post. During the Panchayat period the close study of political subjects was not encouraged. None the less, a number of insightful ethnographic accounts of people's encounters with the state were published. Caplan's early ethnography of Limbu-Bahun interaction over land in east Nepal showed how literacy and contacts in the bureaucracy gave Bahuns an overwhelming advantage when land started to become scarce (Caplan 1970); a similar message, though focused more on competition for jobs, came from Borgström's (1980) study of a village at the southern end of the Kathmandu Valley. Judith Justice described the modes of working of the healthcare bureaucracy, so fixated on targets and seminars that what little healthcare reaches the villages is actually carried out by the one local functionary, the peon (a fact the bureaucracy itself could not admit) (Justice 1986). Ragsdale showed how education administered from the centre disadvantages village children, even when there are high levels of literacy because of local recruitment to the Gurkhas

[13]Other figures are not so unequivocal, and it may be that Thak (and possibly other villages with large numbers of Gurkha recruits?) is untypical; elsewhere the decline may have been only relative and not absolute (Seddon 2001).

[14]On the disadvantages faced by the Tarai, see Gaige (1975).

(Ragsdale 1989). Caplan's innovative study of a local district capital gave a vivid picture of 'the state' at local level. After a detailed case study, in which he examined memories of a demonstration through the bazaar by local supporters of the Gorkha Parishad party in 1953, he suggested that all participants 'attach positive value to: (a) acting "legally", (b) combating corrupt officials, (c) obeying the government; and (d) demonstrating loyalty to kin/village/district' (Caplan 1975: 170). It would be very valuable to have a follow-up study 30 years later. It is likely that there would no longer be wide agreement about either (a) or (c).[15]

PARLIAMENTARY DEMOCRACY, PEOPLE'S SOVEREIGNTY

As the 1980s progressed, the contradictions grew between the Panchayat state's rhetoric of national solidarity and all-round development, on the one hand, and the facts of corruption, stagnation, and decline, on the other. Although development had occurred, it was too uneven and was believed to have happened despite the regime, not because of it. Ethnic imbalances in wealth and power, though often understood in class terms (Gellner 1997, McDonaugh 1997), contributed to a decline in the regime's legitimacy. As the international situation became favourable, the banned Congress and Communist parties joined together in February 1990 for a programme of popular protest. The regime collapsed far more quickly than the opposition leaders had believed possible.[16] The King invited an interim government to stand in until a new constitution could be drawn up and elections held. The new constitution was ratified in November 1990 and vested sovereignty with 'the people' (but in the eyes of the extreme left it lacked legitimacy because it had been granted by the King, rather than voted on by a Constituent Assembly). Rather ambiguously the Constitution defined Nepal as 'a multi-ethnic, multi-lingual, democratic, independent, indivisible, sovereign, Hindu and Constitutional monarchical Kingdom'. The fact that the term 'multi-religious' was not included and that Nepal was still defined as Hindu was

[15]Some evidence for this comes from Borre *et al.* (1994: 158–9) whose opinion poll shows 56 per cent of respondents agreeing that a general strike against the government should be allowed. For a very useful survey of the ways in which academics have studied the Indian state since 1947, see Fuller and Harriss (2001).

[16]See chs 8 and 10 below. For detailed descriptions of the events of 1990, see Hachhethu (1990), Raeper and Hoftun (1992), Nickson (1992), Brown (1996), Hoftun *et al.* (1999).

immediately controversial, and in fact was the subject of considerable protests while the constitution was being drafted (see Hutt 1994, Gellner *et al.* 1997, Krämer, ch. 5 below). A summary of the parliamentary governments since 1990 is given in Table 1.

TABLE 1: GOVERNMENTS IN NEPAL 1990–2002

	PM	Parties	Length	Dates
1	KP Bhattarai	Congress +ULF interim	13 months	19/4/90–25/5/91
First general election (1991): Congress 110 seats (39.5% votes), UML 69 (29.3%)*				
2	GP Koirala	Congress majority	43 months	26/5/91–28/11/94
Second general election (1994): Congress 83 seats (34.5%), UML 88 (31.9%)				
3	MM Adhikari	UML minority	9 months	29/11/94–10/9/95
4	SB Deuba	Congress-NDP-NSP coalition	18 months	11/9/95–11/3/97
5	LB Chand	NDP-UML-NSP coalition	8 months	12/3/97–5/10/97
6	SB Thapa	NDP-Congress-NSP coalition	6 months	6/10/97–25/3/98
7	GP Koirala	Congress minority	5 months	26/3/98–25/8/98
8	GP Koirala	Congress-ML coalition	4 months	26/8/98–22/12/98
9	GP Koirala	Congress-UML-NSP coalition	5 months	23/12/98–26/5/99
Third general election (1999): Congress 112 seats (37.2%), UML 70 (31.6%)				
10	KP Bhattarai	Congress	10 months	27/5/99–9/3/00
11	GP Koirala	Congress	28 months	10/3/00–22/7/01
12	SB Deuba	Congress	14 months	23/7/01–4/10/02

*Percentages are calculated using valid votes only. Figures courtesy of Karl-Heinz Krämer

Nepali Congress Party: social democratic (founder, BP Koirala, influenced by Indian socialists, especially JP Narayan).

ULF: the United Left Front, formed to fight the Panchayat system in 1989, and dissolved when the three ULF ministers left the interim government in November 1990.

UML: Communist Party of Nepal (United Marxist-Leninist): originally revolutionary, now parliamentary leftist party.

NDP: National Democratic Party, 'right-wing' party of ex-Panchas, i.e., those politicians who had been active and accepted the pre-1990 Panchayat regime.

NSP: Nepal Sadbhavana ('Goodwill') Party: small regionalist party representing the Tarai region.

ML: Communist Party of Nepal (Marxist-Leninist): split from UML in March 1998, rejoined in February 2002.

The new multi-party parliamentary system pinned its hopes and its legitimacy even more firmly on development than the previous regime. It wrote the commitment to bringing about development into the Constitution, and it renamed village Panchayats (the word 'panchayat' now being taboo) as Village Development Committees (VDCs, or Gā-Vi-Sa in Nepali). But the new system faces exactly the same economic and demographic pressures, plus a whole raft of new political and ethnic ones (see Table 2). The contrast between the high hopes and euphoria of 1990 and, on the other hand, the political horse-trading, intra-party factionalism, and sheer greed of politicians in the 1990s has been stark. For many Nepalis parliamentary democracy (which is contrasted with the 'People's Democracy' proposed by the Maoists) has been thoroughly tainted (but one should note that participation actually went up in the general election of 1999). What was supposed to be the introduction of an entirely new system of government has in fact seen many of the same players return, and has led to much higher levels of corruption. Under the Ranas only the aristocracy fleeced the country, under guided democracy the elite fleeced the country, under parliamentary democracy the common man has the right to fleece the country (as represented by his fellow citizens)—such is the perception, at any rate. As Hachhethu describes in chapter 4, the state has become an empty husk, to be captured by whichever party wins elections under a Westminster-style winner-takes-all system that does little to encourage consensus-building or cross-party cooperation.

The state's prime method of legitimating itself is through development. The budget for development comes overwhelmingly from abroad, which involves (a) national dependency, and (b) numerous inefficiencies. Development involves the state trying to mobilize people and imposing new rules. Those relating to forests are amongst the most radical. The nationalization of the forests in 1959 is widely agreed to have been a disaster, and was reversed in 1978. More recent legislation to protect forests has been enacted and put in force without sensitivity to local conditions. Villagers have overnight been criminalized for doing what they had always done and have to do in order to survive (Harper and Tarnowski, ch. 1, Campbell, ch. 2). Harper and Tarnowski also show how discourses of decentralization often mask greater central control (as in Thatcher's Britain, one might add), and how discourses of democratization are rapidly mastered by local elites and used to preserve their own position through control of the crucial committees or 'user groups'. In the case of global medical initiatives

TABLE 2: RESISTANCE AND THE STATE BY PERIOD

Period	Nature of State	Problems	Responses
Rana (1846–1951) (population small: 5 million or less; Tarai region needs populating; modern nationalism weak and just beginning)	patrimonial	1. maintaining independence; 2. extracting surplus; 3. managing diversity; 4. (a) rules of succession; (b) pretenders and, later, principled dissent (encouraged by movement for Indian independence)	1. cooperation with British 2. 'feudal' contracts; repression; Hindu legitimation 3. construction of inclusive hierarchical Hindu tradition (Muluki Ain; Dasain festival; supporting Brahmans) 4. (a) poisoning, exile; (b) repression
Panchayat (1960–1990) (population growing rapidly; economic growth barely keeping up)	developmentalist, guided democracy (political parties banned)	1. maintaining independence; 2. development; 3. managing diversity; 4. opposition to regime	1. equidistance from India and China; presence in UN; 2. courting donors (India, China, USA); 3. nation-building through schools, Nepali language, symbols of the nation 4. imprisonment, exile, co-option, referendum
Multi-party (1990–) (population over 20 million and growing; many men go out to work: India, Persian Gulf, SE Asia, E Asia)	developmentalist, liberal democracy; weak multiculturalist	1. survival/legitimacy; 2. development; 3. managing diversity (explosion of ethnic movements); 4. armed insurgency	1. participation in international forums; 2. courting donors (now incl. Scandinavian countries, Switzerland, Canada, Japan); 3. symbolic acceptance of multiculturalism (languages on radio, in Constitution); 4. combination of repression and (till Nov 2001) offer of talks

Harper and Tarnowski also show how the state expects people to resist and how methods of ensuring compliance have to be built into projects. They document considerable resistance on the part of development workers themselves, sometimes open and vociferous and at other times more hidden, to the ever-increasing pressures towards documentation of targets attained. Medical and forest-related projects are two of the main ways in which the state impinges on ordinary villagers' lives (the imposition of National Parks is a third: see ch. 2). For many, government restrictions or demands appear—despite the language of empowerment and poverty-alleviation—as oppressive and authoritarian. Thus it is no surprise that, at a time of rural economic decline and rising expectations, there has also been what Baral calls an 'erosion of authority', both institutional and of leaders, as well as of prominent individuals (Baral 2000: 75).

The emergence of openly ethnic movements is a further challenge to the state, as described by Fisher, Krämer, and Krauskopff (chs 3, 5, and 6). Krämer tackles the unrepresentativeness of Nepal's political institutions. The dominance of Bahuns (Brahmans) has, if anything, got worse in the years following 1990. Interestingly, though, the respondents to the opinion poll he cites did not share the diagnoses of the ethnic activists, or did so only on some points. Gisèle Krauskopff takes up a very interesting case, that of the Tharus of the Tarai. The Tharus are in fact made up of a large number of groups who have only recently started to see themselves as one ethnic category. Several other groups, who might reasonably have amalgamated themselves with the Tharu appear determined to remain apart (the Rajbamsi of the eastern Tarai, for example). The Tharus can boast one of the earliest ethnic movements in Nepal, the Kalyankarini Sabha founded in 1949. Krauskopff convincingly shows that it was in fact a movement of a minority of well-off Tharu landlords that aimed at improving Tharu status by Sanskritizing their lifestyle (using Bahun priests, giving up pork and alcohol). (Anne de Sales in ch. 10 suggests that the same was true of the early Magar organizations set up by ex-servicemen.) The Kalyankarini Sabha belonged therefore to an older hierarchical world where ethnic uplift meant Hinduizing and Sanskritizing. It has been challenged in recent years by a very different organization, Backward Society Education (BASE), which is thoroughly modern in focusing on literacy and deriving its income from foreign donors. William Fisher's contribution, by describing the different ethnic or caste elements of a locality in Baglung, shows how the older, hierarchical communities are unravelling and a whole range of options are opening up, migration in search of work overseas being an increasingly popular one.

MAOISM IN NEPAL: A PERUVIAN MODEL?

The single greatest challenge to the state is undoubtedly the Maoist insurgency or 'People's War' as the Maoists themselves call it.[17] There is, for some, an inescapable logic to continuing the series of revolutions (1951, 1980, 1990) and carrying out one further revolution that would sweep away the rich exploiters altogether. Such thinking is certainly encouraged by the fact that the major opposition party, the UML (Communist Party of Nepal-United Marxist-Leninist), though espousing the parliamentary road, still makes use of the rhetoric of class war and revolution, as Hachhethu notes (ch. 4).[18] The UML's local cadres have often overlapped with Maoist sympathizers. The impact of Maoism at local level is described by Millard, Pettigrew, and de Sales (chs 8–10). A crucial point that emerges from ethnographic study is of course that its impact is different in different places. National political movements always work through, and are understood locally in terms of, pre-existing social relationships; that this applies also to the Congress Party and the UML, and that the political parties are frequently resorted to in people's negotiations with the state, is shown in Hachhethu's analysis (ch. 4).

Andrew Nickson displayed considerable insight in drawing attention to the potential for a Maoist uprising in Nepal, four years before it was declared and at a time when no other observer, either Nepali or foreign, took the threat seriously (Nickson 1992). Social scientists generally have a pretty poor record at predicting the future, so it is worth examining what Nickson had to say in some detail. Nickson pointed out that both Peru and Nepal were agricultural societies based on 'vertical ecology' (i.e., using gravity-fed irrigation), both had a history of warrior polities, both had a backward hill section inhabited by tribals suffering from ethnic and linguistic discrimination, on one side, and a lowland area favoured for development, on the other. Both had feeble economic growth combined with rapid educational advance. Educated Andeans, who had grown up in relatively authoritarian and violent rural areas, suffered significant discrimination in the capital Lima, and were attracted to the message of the Shining Path movement. Nickson suggests that a similar analysis may apply in the Nepalese case:

[17]For recent summaries, see Maharjan (2000) and Sharma (2000).
[18]Whelpton (1994: 55–7) documents the conflicting messages emerging from the UML about the degree and status of its commitment to political pluralism and to parliamentary democracy in the immediate aftermath of 1990.

Continued political, economic, administrative and military hegemony exercised by high caste groups from the 'middle hills' at a time of rapidly rising educational enrolment has strengthened the deep ethnic, regional and caste cleavages in Nepalese society as expressed through the job market. The Peruvian experience suggests that economic and social frustrations experienced by graduates from ethnic minorities and other low castes could well be translated into support for the all-encompassing political ideology of Maoism with its promise of a 'new republic' of equality and democracy (Nickson 1992: 381).

After continuing the narrative to include the Maoists' response to the elections of 1991, Nickson concluded:

The future prospects of Maoism in Nepal will similarly depend [as in Peru] largely on the extent to which the newly elected Nepali Congress government addresses the historic neglect and discrimination of the small rural communities which still make up the overwhelming bulk of the population of the country .... However, such a scenario is extremely unlikely .... The inability to effect structural reform through the parliamentary system and the continued deterioration in the economic well-being of the rural poor and urban youth, will encourage this process of political polarisation, even without any attempt by the monarchy to assert its power .... For these reasons, it would seem that, contrary to global trends, the medium-term prospects for Maoism in Nepal are by no means exhausted (ibid.: 383–4).

A similar, though much briefer, analysis by Stephen L. Mikesell appeared in the magazine *Himal* in 1993.[19] Mikesell's point of departure was the vociferousness of leftist demonstrations in Kathmandu against the Peruvian government after the arrest of Guzman, the leader of Sendero Luminoso. Mikesell went on to point out that

The School Leaving Certificate examinations [in Nepal] are designed so that an extremely low proportion of the population outside of the Kathmandu Valley succeeds. Nepali education simultaneously prepares the students for bureaucratic and managerial jobs and disqualifies most of them from these jobs. As is the case in Peru as well, the educational curriculum has not been built according to the situation and conditions of the rural population .... An immense class of people is presently being schooled in Nepal to despise their own rural background. The situation is ripe and ready for the rise of movements such as the Shining Path, which provide the population with an alternative and convincing-sounding 'true knowledge'. One form of absolutism and negation of social being thus can easily give rise to new ones as people become

---

[19]It is not clear whether Mikesell was aware of Nickson's article at the time.

disillusioned with the old unfulfilled promises of jobs, development, land reform, health for all, basic needs, etc. (Mikesell 1993: 32).[20]

He might have added that the formation of a new middle class in Kathmandu reproduced through English-language schools and oriented to the world market has meant that rural school and college graduates remain very much on the outside. The attractions of Marxism in such a situation, as well as the organizational advantages of having an undisputed leader, were analysed long ago by Donald MaCrae in an essay entitled 'The Bolshevik Ideology':

Marxism does not merely give access in tabloid form to western culture, it gives, at the same time, a feeling of superiority to it. The psychological oppression of the West is reversed by Bolshevism, and a felt inferiority can triumph in observing the inevitable judgment whereby the last shall be first, the first last .... The prestige of a science, the promise of a revelation, the hope of equality, are all seen against a succession of [Marxist] prophets and leaders .... [But] Marxism by its combination of ambiguity and theology offers a field for protracted internal argument .... As a result an infallible leader solves many problems. He maintains unity of thought and action and saves the ordinary party member many of the difficulties and dangers of thought .... (MaCrae 1961: 187, 193–4)

Much of this applied to Sendero Luminoso in Peru. Degregori (1997: 5) comments also on the violence of the language which Sendero documents use when describing the need to convert the peasants to the correct line. The particular local roots of violence in the Nepalese case, and the reasons why it may be experienced as a solution by the Kham Magars, are examined by Anne de Sales in ch. 10. More generally, a sombre psycho-cultural note is sounded by Pratyoush Onta in reflections on the anti-Indian riots of December 2000, which he links both to the Maoist insurgency and to the lynchings of suspected 'Mandales' in Kathmandu in 1990:

Anyone who cared to notice the rioters in Kathmandu were overwhelmingly young and male would have to ask whether being young and male are significant for an understanding of violence in Nepal today. They are. High levels of unemployment amongst semi-educated youth, easy circulation of

[20]A recent survey of insurgencies in Africa suggests that only those with educated leaders succeed in becoming organizationally effective (Clapham 1998: 9); the survey also suggests that Maoism is the pre-eminent model for such insurgency and that it may even 'be regarded as a "kit" which ... insurgent leaders can take over and apply to their situations' (ibid.: 8).

pessimism in college campuses, and the macho ways in which personal and societal problems are solved in the universe of Nepali and Hindi films, have given birth to a highly violent masculine imagination among this segment of the population .... The events of late December 2000 prove that Nepalis [are] a violent lot ... (Onta 2001: 14).

The launching of the 'People's War' and the growth of the Maoist movement have vindicated Nickson's and Mikesell's insights. Furthermore, both in Peru and in Nepal the leadership of the revolutionary movement has not come from the despised ethnic groups (McClintock 1998: 260–5). In Nepal the Maoist leadership is dominated by the Bahun caste which equally provides the leadership of both the major political parties.[21] The 'tribal' groups, especially the Kham Magars in whose territory the insurgency has been based, have provided many cadres, and a large proportion of the victims, but none of the leaders. On the other hand, the more southerly Magars have provided some important Maoist military commanders, and it may have been they who decided to attack the army in November 2001, thus precipitating the State of Emergency. While ethnicity has certainly played a role, it is by no means a simple, determining factor.

In the western hills it seems that the difference of ethnicity led state officials and police to despise and oppress the local population more than they otherwise would have done, both in the immediate aftermath of the Rana regime, and long afterwards.[22] This meant that these areas early on became a stronghold of extreme oppositional politics. A similar logic led to the towns of Kirtipur and Bhaktapur becoming strongholds of radical communist sympathies within the Kathmandu Valley, though they are far from being as remote and poverty-stricken as Rolpa or Rukum. The articulation of that resistance, however, has not been through ethno-nationalism but rather through violent revolt (as de Sales describes in ch. 10). The only, and partial, exception to this has been the town of Bhaktapur which is controlled

[21]Ramirez (1997: 60) suggests there is a connection between the Maoist cult of martyrs who will lead the people to their goal of conquering the 'filth and defilement' in society and the Brahmanical background of the Maoist leadership.

[22]Sharma draws attention to the fact that just one and a half months before the start of the People's War a fifteen-year USAID project, which spent $50 million, had come to an end in the Rapti zone which includes the most affected districts, and he speculates that this project had a role in raising people's consciousness and making them aware of inequalities (Sharma 2000: 35–6). Something similar is said to have occurred in Gorkha district (Judith Pettigrew, personal communication).

by the Nepal Workers' and Peasants' Party (NWPP), a parliamentary left communist party aligned with North Korea, which is, in effect, a party of Bhaktapur agriculturalists.

For their part, the Maoists have cleverly exploited the ethnic issue, by standing up for ethnic rights and holding out the prospect of autonomous regions. Many ethnic activists, disillusioned by the largely symbolic gains made since 1990, have been tempted to throw in their lot with the Maoists. Others, notably Gopal Gurung's Mongol National Organization (Hagen 1999), have rejected them, precisely because of the predominance of Bahuns in their leadership. The example and experience of Tibet seems to have little relevance here. Very few Nepalis have ever been to Tibet. They know little about it, except that it has roads and trucks and electricity. They feel no kinship with Tibetans, who are traditionally regarded as unclean cow-eaters (because of their consumption of yak). The fact that large numbers of Tibetan refugees have settled in Nepal is not taken as evidence of any fault in the political organization of the Chinese. There appears to be total ignorance, even on the part of intellectuals in Kathmandu, of the fact that autonomy for minority nationalities in the PRC exists only on paper.[23]

The great paradox is that, when China was interested in exporting revolution to the rest of world, Nepal did not seem likely to succumb: there were small groups of communist intellectuals in Kathmandu and Calcutta, but they had little support or organization in the country. Now that China has entirely lost interest in Maoism, a virulent and true-believing Maoist movement has arisen on its doorstep: it receives such outside support as it can muster from similar groups in India, and from sympathizers in the UK and USA, but no one even pretends that it comes from China (whereas their forerunners, the Indian Naxalites, did benefit from Chinese support).

THE MAOISTS AND THE NAXALITES

The Nepalese Maoists see the Naxalites of India as their forebears and maintain contacts with their contemporary Indian counterparts in Bihar and Andhra Pradesh. There are certain striking similarities, particularly the combination of an urban, educated leadership and a tribal base. But there are also several significant differences between

[23]Shakya (1999: 302) points out that the very setting up of the Tibetan Autonomous Region was a sign of China's 'final integration of Tibet'. On education in Tibet, see Bass (1998).

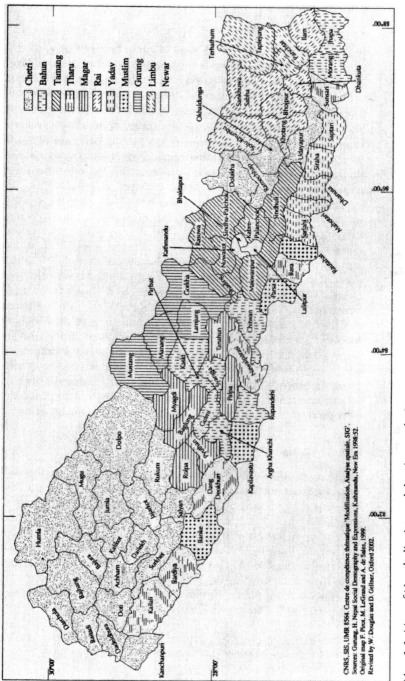

Map 1.1. Map of Nepal: districts and dominant ethnic groups.

CNRS, SIS, UMR 8564, Centre de compétence thématique 'Modélisation, Analyse spatiale, SIG'.
Sources: Gurung, H. Nepal Social Demography and Expressions, Kathmandu, New Era 1998:52.
Original map F. Picot, M. LeGrand and A. de Sales, 1999.
Revised by W. Douglas and D. Gellner, Oxford 2002.

their movement and that of the Naxalites in its heyday. First and most important, the state in Nepal is weak and its presence in the villages of the remote areas like Rolpa and Rukum was minimal, consisting principally of the schoolmaster and the (often unmanned) health post. The initial violence against policemen was reacted to by the state only after a considerable time and in a very counterproductive way. For a long time there was little sense of urgency. Every party at the centre was believed by its opponents to be providing tacit encouragement to the Maoists in order to discomfort its enemies. The movement was allowed to grow and spread as never happened in India.

The second difference with India has to do with the relative inaccessibility of the Maoist heartlands in Nepal. It was and is very difficult to get armed police in and out quickly. This led to a third difference, which is that the Maoist movement has spread much further and lasted far longer in control of its 'base areas' than the Naxalites ever did in India. Fourth, the international situation is very different today. Even China is 'revisionist' now. Support comes from small bands of true-believing revolutionaries in the West. Fifth, compared to Charu Mazumdar, if not to other Naxalite leaders, the Nepalese Maoists appeared for a long time to be more pragmatic. They carefully targetted their killings and skilfully won the support of local people, while exploiting the vacillations of the politicians at the centre. However, since November 2001 it has become clear that the Maoists themselves are split. While some of their leaders envision the possibility of compromise, others do not, preferring to fight to the bitter end.[24]

THE STATE AND THE FUTURE

Ordinary people's everyday experience of parliamentary democracy since 1990 has not been encouraging. Economically most people have felt very hard pressed by rising prices and a lack of employment. Politically there has been massive disillusionment with the new generation of leaders who came in on an unprecedented wave of optimism and hope in 1990, as Hachhethu describes in ch. 4. Far from ushering in a new kind of politics, the popular perception is that they have rushed to enrich themselves (and occasionally their parties) at the expense of the public. Competence and statesmanship have been conspicuously lacking, whether in relation to the Maoists, or in rela-

---

[24]On the Naxalites, see Banerjee (1984), Samanta (1984), and Duyker (1987), and on the movement in Andhra Pradesh, Sinha (1989).

tion to India and the key issue of water resources (Gyawali and Dixit 2000), or in the ordinary business of governing (Kumar 2000). Having said that, the electorate has shown considerable maturity, voting out of office at each election a large proportion of the incumbent MPs.

Popularly, *prajātantra* is supposed to have come to Nepal in 1951 with the fall of the autocratic Ranas. The establishment of parties occurred in 1990. So, though political and ethnic activists experienced a massive change for the better in the 1990s, this is not how many ordinary people see it: as far as they are concerned, democracy already existed; they thought that things would be better with political parties; now they know that parties are even worse than what existed before, and they would like to return to the Panchayat regime, with its relatively firmer leadership and more restrained opportunities for corruption. Others would like to go forward (as they see it) to the logical next step: a republic. Sometimes the benefits are seen in ethnic terms, at others in class terms.

Clearly much research remains to be done.[25] As Dhruba Kumar aptly observes, 'Perhaps, poverty, underdevelopment, destitution and deprivation are some of the ingredients leading to the creation of a revolutionary situation. But merely the creation of revolutionary situation does not necessarily lead to a revolution' (Kumar 2000: 31). In particular research is needed on local politics in order to explain adequately how the Nepalese hills became radicalized so fast. The excellent political anthropology of Philippe Ramirez (2000) shows how, at the local level, particular lineages become identified over time either with a Congress or with a communist, and ultimately, a Maoist position. He describes how the dominant lineage in a locality, controlling much land, and having many poor hill people as clients, can become identified as communist, though unfortunately his ethnography stops before the outbreak of the 'People's War'.[26]

The case studies in the present volume will contribute, we hope, to a better and more contextualized understanding of the revolutionary situation in Nepal. In general, this collection stands for more ethnographic grounding, both in studies of 'resistance' (Ortner 1995) and

[25]For comparison to India, see the case studies collected in Fuller and Bénéï (2001). There are several academic or quasi-academic studies of the Maoist insurgency in preparation.

[26]He has also contributed an important article analysing Nepali Maoist statements on religion (Ramirez 1997).

in studies of the state (Fuller and Bénéï 2001).[27] In resisting the state, the Maoists often make use of old methods commonly used in India under the British Raj. Thus the Maoist actions against landlords, and in particular the burning of mortgage deeds and other debt bonds, have a considerable pedigree in South Asia (and of course elsewhere) (Guha 1983: 141). On the other hand, the actual killing of landlords and other authority figures was relatively rare in the colonial period (ibid.: 162, 164). Guha argues that this was directly related to the hierarchical nature of the society: 'In a land where the peasant could wreck his superordinate enemy's prestige simply by walking past his house with an umbrella on his head or by substituting *tu* for *vous* in an argument with him, why should an insurgency need killing to make its point except in battle?' (ibid.: 166). Today, in Nepal, the violent destruction of landlords and of the agents of the state is very much a part of the Maoists' message, and the death toll is consequently much higher.

In certain areas the Maoists have effectively *become* the state; these they call their 'base areas'. Whether they conceive of their ultimate aim in terms of achieving a republican 'people's democracy' or in terms of more utopian Marxist notions of statelessness, the Maoists have in practice had to set up their own state within a state. Paradoxically they have reinstated many aspects of the Rana regime: rule by fear, taxes both in kind and in cash, forced labour on public amenities (paths, shelters, irrigation), arbitrary punishment of those suspected of opposition. The key difference is, of course, their egalitarian ideology, which includes a strong measure of gender-egalitarianism (the Maoists' transvaluation of conventional gender expectations and the impact this has on ordinary people is described by Pettigrew in ch. 9; see also Gautam *et al.* 2001).

If the Peruvian parallel still holds good, the government will organize local people into militias to resist the Maoists. Maoist exactions from the people will turn the people against them. A large number of locals will die, killed by both sides. However, crucial to the success of the Peruvian government against Sendero Luminoso was the capture

[27]As Harper and Tarnowski discuss in ch. 1, the topic of resistance in anthropology has become too popular for its own good: the concept has been stretched so far that it is in danger of becoming meaningless. The present contribution is concerned with resistance specifically in relation to the state; the theoretical advantages to be drawn from the discussion are likely to consist in greater clarity in understanding the state and people's relationship to it, not in refining a master trope with which to organize all future work in anthropology.

of their charismatic leader Guzman (Degregori 1997, McClintock 1998: 9–10). Whether the leaders of Nepalese Maoism will be able to evade capture forever remains to be seen (Kumar, 2000: 33, asserts that the government does indeed know where they are but does not dare to seize them). The problem for the Nepalese state is that, unlike the insurgents, it gains its legitimacy precisely from the contrast of its means of coercion with the Panchayat and Rana regimes. The key challenge it faces is to retain its authority, and fulfil its promise of development, without descending into authoritarianism.

REFERENCES

Banerjee, S. 1984. *India's Simmering Revolution: The Naxalite Uprising*. London: Zed Press.

Baral, L.R. 2000. 'Clash of Values: Governance, Political Elite and Democracy in Nepal' in D. Kumar (ed.) *Domestic Conflict and Crisis of Governability in Nepal*. Kathmandu: CNAS.

Bass, C. 1998. *Education in Tibet: Policy and Practice since 1950*. London: TIN/ Zed Press.

Bhattachan, K.B. 1995. 'Ethnopolitics and Ethnodevelopment: An Emerging in Nepal' in D. Kumar (ed.) *Domestic Conflict and Crisis of Governability in Nepal*. Kathmandu: CNAS.

Bista, D.B. 1991. *Fatalism and Development: Nepal's Struggle for Modernisation*. Calcutta: Orient Longman.

Borgström, B.E. 1980. *The Patron and the Pancha: Village Values and Panchayat Democracy in Nepal*. New Delhi: Vikas.

Borre, O., S.R. Panday, and C.K. Tiwari 1994. *Nepalese Political Behaviour*. Delhi: Sterling.

Brown, T.L. 1996. *The Challenge to Democracy in Nepal: A Political History*. London: Routledge.

Caplan, L. 1970. *Land and Social Change in East Nepal: A Study of Hindu-Tribal Relations*. London: Routledge & Kegan Paul.

_____ 1975. *Administration and Politics in a Nepalese Town: The Study of a District Capital and its Environs*. London: OUP.

Clapham, C. 1998. 'Introduction: Analysing African Insurgencies' in C. Clapham (ed.) *African Guerillas*. Oxford: James Currey; Bloomington: Indiana University Press.

CPN-Maoist 1997. 'Strategy and Tactics of Armed Struggle in Nepal (Document adopted by the Third Plenum of the CC of the CPN(Maoist) in March 1995)' *The Worker* 3 (Feb 1997). Also available at <http://www.maoism.org/misc/nepal/nepal.htm>.

Degregori, C.I. 1997. 'The Maturation of a Cosmocrat and the Building of a Discourse Community: The Case of the Shining Path' in D.E. Apter (ed.) *The Legitimization of Violence*. Houndmills: Macmillan.

Duyker, E. 1987. *Tribal Guerillas: The Santals of West Bengal and the Naxalite Movement*. Delhi: OUP.

Finlay, H., R. Everist, and T. Wheeler 1999. *Nepal: From Ancient Temples to Living Goddesses*. Melbourne: Lonely Planet.

Fuller, C.J. and V. Bénéï (eds) 2001. *The Everyday State and Society in Modern India*. New Delhi: Social Science Press and London: C. Hurst & Co.

_____ and J. Harriss 2001. 'For an Anthropology of the Modern Indian State' in Fuller and Bénéï (eds).

Gaborieau, M. 1978. *Le Nepal et ses Populations*. Paris: Editions Complexe.

_____ 1982. 'Les Rapports de Classe dans l'Idéologie officielle du Népal' *Purusartha* 6: 251–90.

Gaige, F. 1975. *Regionalism and National Unity in Nepal*. Berkeley: University of California Press.

Gautam, S., A. Banskota, and R. Manchanda 2001. 'Where There are no Men: Women and the Maoist Insurgency in Nepal' in R. Manchanda (ed.) *Women, War and Peace in South Asia: Beyond Victimhood to Agency*. Delhi: Sage.

Geertz, C. 1982. *Negara: The Theatre State in Nineteenth-Century Bali*. Princeton: University Press.

Gellner, D.N. 1997. 'Caste, Communalism, and Communism: Newars and the Nepalese State' in Gellner *et al.* (eds.)

_____ 2001. 'From Group Rights to Individual Rights and Back: Nepalese Struggles over Culture and Equality' in J. Cowan, M.-B. Dembour, and R. Wilson (eds) *Culture and Rights: Anthropological Perspectives*. Cambridge: Univ. Press.

_____, J. Pfaff-Czarnecka, and J. Whelpton (eds) 1997. *Nationalism and Ethnicity in a Hindu Kingdom: The Politics of Culture in Contemporary Nepal*. Amsterdam: Harwood.

Gledhill, J. 2000. *Power and its Disguises: Anthropological Perspectives on Politics* (second ed.). London: Pluto.

Guha, R. 1983. *Elementary Aspects of Peasant Insurgency in Colonial India*. Delhi: OUP.

Gyawali, D. and A. Dixit 2000. 'Mahakali Impasse: A Futile Paradigm's Bequested Travails' in D. Kumar (ed.) *Domestic Conflict and Crisis of Governability in Nepal*. Kathmandu: CNAS.

Hachhethu, K. 1990. 'Mass Movement 1990' *Contributions to Nepalese Studies* 17(2): 177–201.

Hagen, S.I. 1999. 'Making Mongols: Identity Construction and Ethnic Politics in Ilam District, Nepal' in R.B. Chhetri and O.P. Gurung (eds) *Anthropology and Sociology in Nepal: Cultures, Societies, Ecology and Development*. Kathmandu: SASON.

Hoftun, M., W. Raeper, and J. Whelpton 1999. *People, Politics, and Ideology: Democracy and Social Change in Nepal*. Kathmandu: Mandala Book Point.

Hutt, M. 1994. 'Drafting the 1990 Constitution' in M. Hutt (ed.) *Nepal in the Nineties: Versions of the Past, Visions of the Future*. Delhi: OUP.

Joshi, B.L. and J. Rose 1966. *Democratic Innovations in Nepal: A Case Study of Political Acculturation*. Berkeley: University of California Press.

Justice, J. 1986. *Policies, Plans, and People: Foreign Aid and Health Development*. Berkeley: University of California Press.

Kertzer, D. 1988. *Ritual, Politics, and Power*. New Haven: Yale University Press.

Kumar, D. 2000. 'What Ails Democracy in Nepal?' in D. Kumar (ed.) *Domestic Conflict and Crisis of Governability in Nepal*. Kathmandu: CNAS.

Levitt, M. 1999. 'A Culturally Appropriate Health Intervention in Conflict with Nepali Management Culture' in R.B. Chhetri and O.P. Gurung (eds) *Anthropology and Sociology of Nepal: Cultures, Societies, Ecology and Development*. Kathmandu: SASON.

Lopez, D. 1998. *Prisoners of Shangri-La: Tibetan Buddhism and the West*. Chicago: University Press.

McClintock, C. 1998. *Revolutionary Movements in Latin America: El Salvador's FMLN and Peru's Shining Path*. Washington DC: United States Institute of Peace Press.

MaCrae, D. 1961. 'The Bolshevik Ideology' in his *Ideology and Society: Papers in Sociology and Politics*. London: Heinemann.

McDonaugh, C. 1997. 'Losing Ground, Gaining Ground: Land and Change in a Tharu Community in Dang, west Nepal' in Gellner *et al.* (eds).

Macfarlane, A. 1983. *Resources and Population: A Study of the Gurungs of Nepal*. Cambrige: University Press.

——— 1994. 'Fatalism and Development in Nepal' in M. Hutt (ed.) *Nepal in the Nineties*. Delhi: OUP. (Originally published in *Cambridge Anthropology* 14: 1, 1990.)

——— 2001. 'Sliding Down Hill: Reflections on Thirty Years of Change in a Himalayan Village' (new preface to Macfarlane 1983) *European Bulletin of Himalayan Research* **20–1**: 105–10.

Maharjan, P.N. 2000. 'The Maoist Insurgency and Crisis of Governability in Nepal' in D. Kumar (ed.) *Domestic Conflict and Crisis of Governability in Nepal*. Kathmandu: CNAS, Tribhuvan University.

Michaels, A. 1997. 'The King and the Cow: On a Crucial Symbol of Hinduization in Nepal' in D.N. Gellner *et al.* (eds).

Mikesell, S.L. 1993. 'The Paradoxical Support of Nepal's Left for Comrade Gonzalo' *Himal* (May/April): 31–3.

Nickson, R.A. 1992. 'Democratisation and the Growth of Communism in Nepal: A Peruvian Scenario in the Making?' *Journal of Commonwealth Studies and Comparative Politics* **30**(3): 358–86.

Onta, P. 2001. 'Hate India, Love India: The Paradox of the Nepali Mindset' *Himal South Asia* **14**(2): 12–14.

Ortner, S. 1995. 'Resistance and the Problem of Ethnographic Refusal' *Comparative Studies in Society and History* **37**(1): 173–93.

——— 1999. *Life and Death on Mt Everest: Sherpas and Himalayan Mountaineering*. Princeton: University Press.

Panday, D.R. 1999. *Nepal's Failed Development: Reflections on the Mission and the Maladies.* Kathmandu: Nepal South Asia Centre.

Pfaff-Czarnecka, J. 1997. 'Vestiges and Visions: Cultural Change in the Process of Nation-Building in Nepal' in D.N. Gellner *et al.* (eds).

Pierson, C. 1996. *The Modern State.* London: Routledge.

Pigg, S. L. 1992. 'Inventing Social Categories through Space: Social Representations of Development in Nepal' *Comparative Studies of Society and History* 34: 491–593.

Raeper, M. and M. Hoftun 1992. *Spring Awakening: An Account of the 1990 Revolution in Nepal.* Delhi: Viking.

Ragsdale, T. 1989. *Once a Hermit Kingdom: Ethnicity, Education and National Integration in Nepal.* Delhi: Manohar.

Ramirez, P. 1997. 'Pour une anthropologie religieuse du maoïsme népalais' *Archives de Sciences Sociales des Religions* 99: 47–68.

_____ 2000. *De la disparition des chefs: Une anthropologie politique Népalaise .* Paris: CNRS.

Regmi, M.C. 1978. *Thatched Huts and Stucco Palaces: Peasants and Landlords in Nineteenth Century Nepal.* Delhi: Vikas.

Samanta, A.K. 1984. *Left Extremist Movement in West Bengal: An Experiment in Armed Agrarian Struggle.* Calcutta: Firma KLM.

Scott, J.C. 1985. *Weapons of the Weak: Everyday Forms of Peasant Resistance.* New Haven: Yale University Press.

Seddon, D. 1987. *Nepal: A State of Poverty.* Delhi: Vikas.

_____ 2001. 'The Contradictions of Rural Transformation in Nepal' (comments on Macfarlane 2001) *European Bulletin of Himalayan Research* 20–1: 117–23.

Shaha, R. 1982. *Essays in the Practice of Government in Nepal.* Delhi: Manohar.

Shakya, T. 1999. *The Dragon in the Land of Snows: A History of Modern Tibet since 1947.* London: Pimlico.

Sharma, S. 2000. 'Cār Jillā Maovādīko Hātmā' [Four Districts Controlled by the Maoists] *Himal* (16–30 July) 10(7): 30–40.

Sinha, S. 1989. *Maoists in Andhra Pradesh.* New Delhi: Gian.

Weber, M. 1968. *Economy and Society: An Outline of Interpretive Sociology,* G. Roth and C. Wittich (eds). New York: Bedminster.

Whelpton, J. 1991. *Kings, Soldiers and Priests: Nepalese Politics, 1830–1857.* Delhi: Manohar.

_____ 1994. 'The General Elections of May 1995 in M. Hutt (ed.) *Nepal in the Nineties.* Delhi: Oxford University Press.

_____ 1997. 'Political Identity in Nepal: State, Nation, and Community' in D.N. Gellner *et al.* (eds).

The State, Development, and Local Politics

chapter one

A Heterotopia of Resistance: Health, Community Forestry, and Challenges to State Centralization in Nepal

• *Ian Harper and Christopher Tarnowski*

INTRODUCTION

'Decentralization', 'democratization', 'participation', 'transparency', 'self-monitoring'—such are some of the terms of the continually shifting development discourse which is used to justify foreign interventions in Nepal. Decentralization, in and of itself, has become a primary goal in many different realms. Witness the very strongly contested battle within parliament over the terms of the Decentralization Act, one that ended in acts of physical violence between politicians. Witness the importance placed on decentralization by the development discourse in all its mutations, the emphasis on 'civil society' and its perceived greater flexibility, and independence from centralized government and bureaucratic structures, in a time when it seems that capitalism, with its attendant need for free markets and liberalized economies rules triumphant. These are troubling and confusing times, and Nepal, as everywhere, is caught up in the winds of powerful global changes.

As we were thinking through how to approach writing a paper on 'resistance to the state' we were faced, we soon realized, with several not inconsiderable problematics. Firstly, to talk about the state, we had to know what was meant by this frequently over-determined term, this fetish, that the anthropologist Taussig says is filled, overfilled, with 'soulstuff' (Taussig 1997), to say nothing of its links with the idea of the Nation. We realized that we had to write a prior and previous paper, to set up the problematic, before we could even begin to write on resistance. Deferred as we are, we have to briefly describe our albeit speculative thoughts for this other text.

We realized that in these two apparently unrelated areas of research—and those working in these separated aspects of the development industry rarely if ever communicate—namely those of health and forestry, there are some apparent overarching points of similarity. Both rely heavily on 'decentralization' and as we attempted to articulate the actual modalities, the practices that were necessary for this to occur, we discerned marked points of contact. Within both sectors this involves the formation of quasi-agreements by local people, groups, patients, with the government sectors, the formations of committees, holding regular meetings and particularly strict reporting and recording formalities. Paradoxically, or so it seems to us, despite enunciatory claims to decentralization, these programmes are producing an entire apparatus through which the state is able to govern its people, its health and management of resources, in an increasingly centralized manner. As we read some of the proliferating literature (and a weakness of our analysis is that we have done this only in English) emerging within Nepal on the research being undertaken on decentralization, and the focus on its failure to occur, this dependence on textual forms of communication, and the apparatus necessary to undertake it, is completely effaced. What is blamed for the failure to decentralize—and such is the importance now of this concept, that to fail to do so becomes diagnostic of Nepal's 'backwardness'—are all the usual suspects: Hinduized bureaucracy, caste, stubborn adherence to tradition, pre-modern feudalism, 'source and force', '*chakari*'.[1] We pose the question as a strategy to enter into the on-going debate: Is it not time to step outside of 'culture', particularly those reified 'pre-modern' culprits, and to focus more closely on these textually mediated forms of practice?[2] In short, are not the problems

[1]'Source and force' is the local Nepali-English term for using personal connections; *chākari* in Nepali denotes subservient behaviour aimed at winning favours from a superior. This has been described in the health sector by, amongst others, Judith Justice (1986), and more generally in bureaucracies by Bista (1991). An interpretation of the links between these modes of behaviour and discourses of corruption in modern politics has been written by Adams (1998).

[2]Stacey Leigh-Pigg's innovative analyses similarly question how Nepal is constituted through discourses of health and development: for example, the idea of 'belief' and its circulation within cosmopolitan discourses on 'traditional healers' (1996), or the manner in which ideas of tradition and culture circulate at trainings and in the planning process in relation to traditional health practioners (1997).

with decentralizing (which we agree is a laudable goal) in fact a consequence of 'modern' forms of discourse in themselves, and the need for information? In this perspective it becomes startlingly ironic that poverty of information is yet another layer of 'poverty' to be added to all Nepal's other woes, as charted by so-called development experts.

Having set up the architecture of centralization in this way, as a structural analysis (and buildings are constantly deemed to be an important pre-requisite for many a development intervention), and a necessarily simplified suggestion of some of the processes of state formation, we can now turn to this paper, to meditate on some of the movement within this framework: the contestations, manipulations, appropriations, acquisitions, and manoeuvres that occur within and around these state formations, questions, in other words, of agency and resistance, or so they are for this collection.

To do so, this text is divided into three major sections. The first, on the historical shifts of Nepal's community forestry programme, 'elites' articulated as a problem, and theft, is written by Tarnowski. The second, a more discursive examination of the global and Nepal's tuberculosis programme, and following the strategies of its implementation to more peripheral sites, is written by Harper. For both these sections we use the pronoun 'I'. For the final section we merge to become 'we' again as we are for this introduction. Although stylistically different and emphasizing differing aspects of these programmes we hope that these two narratives act in the form of a 'dialogue', as we bring them together to pose questions around an anthropological, and our own, engagement with 'resistance'.

COMMUNITY FORESTRY IN NEPAL

Spread across a remarkably varied landscape, Nepal's forests have always been considered a vital resource; to the majority of the populace, more than 90 per cent of whom are classified as subsistence farmers who continue to be dependent on forest products for their livelihoods, and to the state, which has sought to control and exploit forests as a source of revenue for more than a century. However, Nepal's current forest policies, and the considerable changes, reformulations, and permutations they have undergone, are reflective of a great deal more than the value of forests as a resource to be exploited. In particular, the history of the Community Forestry Programme reveals the rise (and plateau) of environmentalist concerns, shifts in development theory, and the ever-increasing role of foreign donors and bi-laterally funded development projects in shaping Nepal's forest policies. Yet Nepal's forest policies are not only products, but also productive. Obviously, forest policies are a means to directly shape how forests are managed and used. But perhaps not so apparent, forest policies in Nepal have become a means to introduce institutional change far removed from the natural resource management sector. Whereas forests once served primarily as a source of fuelwood, fodder, or timber, or as a source of revenue for the state, they have become, through a multi-faceted history, sites of and for development.

Throughout the 1950s, 1960s and early 1970s, a bias towards forest protection was paramount (Gilmour and Fisher 1991). Prior to the 1950s there was little in the way of formal forest policy in Nepal. The state was content to issue *birtā* land grants and exploit Tarai (and some accessible Middle Hills) forests for the sale of timber to generate revenue (Mahat *et al.* 1986). *Birtā* land grants were issued to local nobles, most often located in the Middle Hills, in lieu of having to pay a salary for particular services, giving to the holder the whole of the produce of the land, and functioned as an incentive to bring previously forested land under cultivation. Then in the early 1950s, when forest policy began to take shape, a distinct separation between Tarai and Middle Hills forests began to emerge. In contrast to the hill forests, where inaccessibility afforded few opportunities for industrial forestry and where environmentalist concerns were being directed, 'protection' of Tarai forests was a product of their immense commercial value (Gilmour and Fisher 1991). Indeed, in the early 1960s, when the Forest Resources Survey was established, its main purpose was to map and inventory the country's forests, with particular attention to providing an assessment of the commercial exploitability of forest resources (Bajracharya 1983). (Even today, while Community Forestry policy is meant to apply to all areas of the country there remains a strong bias against 'handing over' Tarai forests as community forests.)

Prompted by a perceived decline in the condition of the nation's forests (and strongly advocated by donor agencies), the Nepal government introduced the Forest Nationalization Act, 1957, and the Birta Abolition Act, 1959. In eradicating the *birtā* system of tenure—believed to be a hindrance to effective forest management—these Acts sought to 'protect, manage, and conserve the forests for the benefit of the entire country' (Bajracharya 1983: 234). Under the Act's guidelines, all forest land was to be placed under the control of the Forest Department, which would perform a policing and licensing role to ensure an adequate system of protection and maintenance of forest resources. But given the extremely limited capacity of the department's four professional foresters, such a mandate was highly unrealistic. Most important, these Acts were designed to establish forest legislation with respect to government ownership and assert control over most forest land as well as to define limitations on individual forest holdings (Mahat *et al.* 1986).

Shortly thereafter the Forest Preservation (Special Arrangement) Act, 1967 was introduced. Its purpose was to strengthen the 'enforcement role' of the Forest Department by defining forest offences and prescribing penalties (Gilmour and Fisher 1991). To assist the Forest Department in the conservation of forest resources and in its policing functions the Forest Preservation Special Courts were created. Not only did the Forest Preservation Act prove to be of limited use, its implementation was at times somewhat selective. According to Mahat *et al.*, in actual practice 'it was only the weaker section of society which was brought under the purview of this law enforcement activity and powerful individuals involved in offences often escaped through influence and manipulation' (1986: 230).

By the early 1970s, both at the international and national levels there emerged a series of concerns surrounding the overlapping problems of deforestation, environmental instability, and meeting local needs. At the international level a series of conferences and policy statements elucidating the new social role for forestry in the promotion of community development was led by the Food and Agriculture Organization (FAO), with support from the Swedish International Development Authority (SIDA [Arnold 1991]). The new focus was to become 'forestry for local community development' (FAO 1978). It was also in 1978, that the World Bank issued its influential Forestry: Sector Policy Paper signalling a major shift in its forestry activities away from industrial forestry towards environmental protection and meeting local needs (Arnold 1991: 2). Hence, it is apparent that this new approach to development, referred to as 'Community Forestry', emerged, not out of the forestry sector as would be expected, but rather had its roots in rural development.

The first concerted effort by Nepal to assess the problems of deforestation, soil erosion, and landslides came following the UN Conference on the Human Environment in 1972 (Mahat *et al.* 1988). Later, in 1974, a Task Force on Land Use and Erosion Control was established within the Planning Commission. One of the first recommendations of the Task Force was to suggest separate measures for the Mountain, Hill, and Tarai regions. The Mountain Region was perceived as an area where resources were under-used and intensive development efforts were needed. The Hill Region was believed to be the area with the greatest problem. The scarcity of usable land and the simultaneous deterioration of land resources (specifically forest resources) meant that a more 'conservation-oriented land-use pattern' was considered appropriate. This resulted in renewed efforts (at least in writing) to crack down on deforestation, especially due to 'illegal' product collection and conversion to agricultural land. In the Tarai the problem was held to be a choice between agricultural land expansion, made possible by the success of the malaria eradication programme, and forest area preservation. The adopted solution was a contradictory mix including a resettlement programme (moving people to the Tarai), protecting valuable sal forests from encroachment by locals, and an increase in commercial felling by the government.

Finally, in 1975, a conference was convened in Kathmandu to discuss issues related to forest management in Nepal. Attended by District Forest Officers (DFOs) from throughout the country as well as senior members of the Forest Department and Ministry of Forests and Environment, the meeting, although scheduled for only three days, lasted a full twenty-three. Out of the conference, a working group was formed with the task of formulating a plan to guide the future development of forestry in Nepal. The result was the National Forestry Plan, 1976, Nepal's first step in the formulation of policies to address forestry development in the Hills, and which introduced the rhetoric of involving the rural populace in forest management for the first time (NAFP 1979: 13).

Together with the desire for forests to contribute towards national development, the new forest policy touched upon a variety of issues. One of its initial objectives was to reverse the negative attitudes and actions (such as deforestation for land entitlement) that were produced by the nationalization of forests in 1957. It identified the conservation, management, and development of forests as requiring 'a collective effort of all people in the country' (NAFP 1979: 13). While issues related to wildlife management, grazing, the forest industry, and the like were discussed, the government initiated improvements in forestry education and training through the Nepal Forestry Institute, an improved organizational system within the Forest Department. According to government accounts (HMG/N 1991, 1992) it was hoped that the new Forestry Plan would provide greater flexibility and allow local people more involvement in the control and management of forest resources. This was to be accomplished through a new approach to forest management: 'Instead of adopting a blanket approach all over the Kingdom, a suitable forest management system will be adopted for each zone on the basis of its geographical peculiarities as well as social priority' (NAFP 1979: 16). According to Bajracharya (1983), it was the first time that a plan was to be carried out in accordance with the socio-economic realities of the nation, through people's participation, collectively and individually, and with the government providing the necessary technical and extension services.

Following the policy base established by the National Forestry Plan, the Panchayat Forest, Panchayat Protected Forest, and Leasehold Forest Legislation was passed in 1978. These rules were issued as part of the First Amendment of the Forest Act and were intended to involve communities and private interests in the management of forests. It was under this new legislation that the rules and regulations governing the handing over of government forest land—virtually all land not cultivated or otherwise under private ownership—to the control of *gaun* (village) *panchayats* were specified. These areas were to be operated under an official management plan with the objective of supplying the forest produce needs of the people living in the panchayat.

In contrast to previous forest policy, both the National Forestry Plan and the legislation passed in 1978 have been considered to represent a more progressive—even radical—approach to forest management. However, despite the rhetoric of people's involvement in forest management, the approach suggested by the National Forestry Plan was suspiciously similar to the development models of the 1950s and 1960s. In other words, 'people-oriented' forest and land-use policies had yet to materialize (Gilmour and Fisher 1991). It was understood that this legislation would formally recognize the rights of villagers to manage their own forest resources with technical assistance (where necessary) being provided by the Forest Department. Although the government recognized the necessity of incorporating local people in forest management, the persistent bias of forest policy was towards 'protection, production, and proper utilization', primarily in accordance with the desire to halt environmental deterioration and ensure that forests contribute to development of the national economy (NAFP 1979: 14–16). Within the newly designated panchayat forest areas, villagers were restricted from clearing, cultivating, or settling in the forests. Rather than increasing villagers' involvement in management activities, the policy imposed greater restrictions on use, not to mention, making 'unauthorized' collection of products a criminal offence. And in addition to a lack of support for fostering local initiatives and participation, villagers still lacked authority to make decisions regarding the management and use of their forests.

During the 1980s, the government's efforts were directed to the issues of local level 'empowerment' and 'decentralization' of control. While under the National Forestry Plan forests were 'considered as social property' (NAFP 1979: 22), it was not until the passage of the Decentralization Act 1982 that forest legislation finally recognized the legal rights of villagers to control the management of forests. According to the Act, village panchayats were empowered 'to form people's consumers committees [what are now referred to as "user groups"] to use any specific forest area for the purpose of forest conservation and through it, conduct such tasks as afforestation, and forest conservation and management on a sustained basis' (Gilmour and Fisher 1991:14).

The momentum gained during the 1970s and especially the 1980s as the government moved in the direction of 'maximizing community control' culminated in the preparation of the Forestry Legislation Reform and the Forestry Sector Policy Statement (Master Plan) 1989. The Master Plan for the Forestry Sector (MPFS) institutionalized the programme approach to guide forestry development by introducing six major Forestry Sector Programmes, the largest of which is the Community and Private Forestry Programme (HMG/N 1992: 6).[3] The central focus of the Master Plan is for forest resources to be managed through the active participation of individuals and communities to meet *their* needs. It stresses 'people's participation' in forest management, and provides the legal and organizational framework needed to increase the contributions of communities to forestry development. The basic strategy of the Master Plan involves the (1) the 'handing over' of all accessible hill forest areas to communities to the extent that they are able and willing to manage them, (2) the formulation and implementation of simple operational plans, and (3) the retraining of all Ministry of Forests and Environment (MFE) staff for their new role as advisors and extension workers (HMG/N 1992: 6).

The most significant outcome of the Master Plan was the Community Forestry Programme. 'Community Forestry', as defined by forestry legislation and policy in Nepal, refers to the forest manage-

---

[3]It is estimated that investment in community forestry would amount to 47 per cent of total forestry sector investment over the next two decades (Gilmour and Fisher 1991: 15).

ment strategy whereby forests are protected, managed, and utilized by the local forest users. Its main emphasis is on the involvement of 'local people' in planning, implementing, and decision-making in all aspects of forest management: development, production, protection, and use. As the Master Plan states, the goal is 'to encourage communities to be increasingly more self-reliant. The challenge of community forestry is indeed to mobilise the vast manpower and other resources of rural communities for forest development and management to meet their own needs' (MPFSN 1988: 145; quoted in Burch and Messerschmidt 1990).

The process by which the local community acquires formal authority begins with the recognition and establishment of 'Community Forest User Groups' (CFUGs) at the community/local level. The CFUG refers to those members of the local community who make use of the forest and its various products. As emphasized by the government, it is crucial that the CFUG be carefully identified to include 'the poor and landless, and all who depend directly on that forest' (HMG/N 1991: 6). From among these members, a committee is selected and charged with the responsibility and authority to make and enforce decisions regarding access to the forest, collection and use of products, the collection and use of funds generated by the user group, prescribing fines and penalties for infractions of the rules, making amendments to the operational plan, etc. The committee includes the senior positions of chair, vice-chair, secretary, and treasurer, as well as several general members who together total from 11 to as many as 17 members (depending often on the number of household in the user group). Following deliberations among the CFUG committee and general members, an 'operational plan' is drawn up to formalize the management and strategies and to officially recognize the members of the user group. Once an agreement between the user group and the Department of Forests (DoF) is reached with respect to the operational plan, the (formal) responsibility for management is passed from HMG to the user group (HMG/N 1992).

More recently, the 1990s have witnessed an unprecedented increase in the influence by donor agencies in shaping forest policy. In stressing 'people's participation' in forest management, donor agencies have propelled policy makers to shift policies towards the construction of the legal, organizational, and institutional framework needed to increase and strengthen the contributions of local communities for 'sustainable forestry development'. In fact, the greatest efforts to improve the implementation of community forestry have centred around increasing the 'participation' of disadvantaged groups (DAGs, usually taken to include the poor, landless, women, and low-castes or *dalits*) through, in the latest 'development speak', 'institutional capacity building', creating and strengthening local 'democratic' institutions, fostering 'good governance', and improving livelihoods and eradicating rural poverty.

'Democratic institution building' is the latest, and most ubiquitous, feature of the several bi-laterally funded community forestry projects, the most influential of which are the Nepal-United Kingdom Community Forest Project (NUKCFP), the Nepal-Australia Community Resource Management Project (NAUCRMP), and the Nepal-Swiss Community Forestry Project (NSCFP). Its incorporation into community forestry policy and practice has come on the heels of the 'democracy movement' of 1990 and the subsequent 'democratization' of—or proliferation and penetration of 'democratic discourse(s)' into—all spheres of Nepali life. Indeed, 'democratization' has become a major 'centralizing' concept around which a vast array of development projects (whether in the natural resource sector or elsewhere) are now designed and implemented.

In community forestry, whether from the standpoint of formal forest policy, the perspective of projects, or as considered by many villagers at the local level, 'democracy' has come to stand as both an overarching (if not vague) end in itself and as a means to foster other objectives: these include greater 'participation' in project activities, 'empowerment' of DAGs and women, and more equitable and egalitarian 'participation' in all areas of community forestry, such as decision-making in meetings, representation on committees, attendance at trainings, and benefit sharing. Perhaps more importantly, the infusion of 'democratic institution building' into policy is an attempt to combat inequality, particularly an imbalance in the number of 'elites' involved in community forestry at the local level.

DEMOCRACY IN RESISTANCE

Turning away from my historical narrative of community forestry policy, I now wish to explore how 'elites'—not the conventional subjects of writings on 'resistance'—are involved in resisting community forestry policies and project strategies. The preponderance of local 'elites' occupying positions of authority (such as chair, vice-chair, secretary, treasurer) on community forestry user group committees is identified in project documents and by project staff as 'elite domination' and is considered one of the most notable 'problems' of the Community Forestry Programme as it is implemented at the local level.

During a 'Community Forestry Awareness Workshop' I attended in March 1999, I became acutely aware of the number of VDC politicians (perhaps the most influential of local 'elites') involved in community forestry. The workshop was held by the District Forest Officer of a certain district for the purpose of 'raising awareness' about the community forestry process among local VDC politicians in the district. The one-day workshop was attended by 44 of the 50 VDC chairs in the district. During a break in the programme I took the opportunity to ask those in attendance if they were members of a CFUG committee. I was astonished to discover that 18 were committee chairs, 8 were vice-chairs, and another 12 were general members of a user group committee in their respective VDCs. It was ironic that such a workshop should be organized to 'raise awareness' among such a group. I later raised this issue in interviews with the staff of several community forestry projects, and was told that such a situation was extremely common in the districts in which their respective projects operate. These figures clearly justify the concern that community forestry is providing a means by which 'elites' are able to consolidate and legitimate their existing positions of authority within local arenas of power.

That 'elite domination' is such a common 'problem' is a major concern where community forestry policy claims to accomplish the exact opposite; that is, to benefit and empower the 'poor, landless, and women'. According to several community forestry project staff, this is a case where 'well-intentioned policy simply fails in practice', and where 'it will merely take time for the intended social changes to become institutionalized'. While it might be easy to dismiss this situation as an 'implementation problem', I have been most intrigued by how so many local 'elites' have managed to accomplish this in the face of such explicit policy prescriptions. According to community forestry policy, they are to be elected 'democratically'. Yet, the same policy prescriptions that stress the institutionalization of 'democratic' principles and processes also strive to privilege disadvantaged individuals and women, though apparently with little success.

Consider Thulo Ban (a pseudonym), the VDC where I conducted research. Every local politician, including the VDC Chair, Vice-Chair, and all of the nine ward members, were also members of one of the four community forest user group committees in the VDC. The Chair of the Thulo Ban community forest user group was arguably one of the most powerful individuals in the village. In addition to being the chair of the community forest users group committee, he was the Vice-Chair of the VDC, and a member of the school committee, drinking water committee, and seed improvement committee. He was by no means exceptional in this regard, as several of his contemporaries, the other members of the community forest users group committees, were also represented on these other committees. Indeed, that the dozen or so members of each of these committees are nearly identical is a striking, and perplexing, feature of local 'development' efforts that strive to increase 'participation' of the disadvantaged, poor, and women through 'democratic' means. How is it that 'elites' manage to acquire and maintain control of the user group committees? And what do they do with their control?

The Thulo Ban committee Chair's (s)election illustrates the contradictory nature of 'democracy' as practised within community forestry. Accounts of the Thulo Ban committee chair's 'election' range from vague descriptions suggesting that elections were bypassed completely (he simply 'stole his position', one elderly user group member claimed), that it was the result of collusion with the local forest ranger, and that he was 'elected to the committee democratically ... by majority vote.' The scepticism of collusion or 'stealing' the chair position is not entirely groundless. Because of the Chair's 'knowledge' and involvement in other 'village works', I was told, his 'nomination' as Chair of the user group committee was strongly endorsed by the Forest Ranger who assisted the user group in acquiring control of their community forest. As it turned out, the Chair was the only one who was nominated for that position. And in addition to a lack of choice of candidates, those in attendance were asked to indicate, by a show of hands, if they disagreed with his selection. Despite this process, many of the committee members consider the Chair to have been 'elected unanimously' and 'democratically'.

While this process of 'electing' members to committees is arguably less than ideal, there is more to this entrenchment of control than merely running for office uncontested. The tendency for a small group of 'elites' to maintain their control of user group committees is in large part the result of a number of their personal qualities, and of shared ideas about what constitutes 'good leadership', which, when combined with the standards established by community forestry legislation, make it difficult for anyone other than an 'elite' to hold the position. The daily operations of community forestry involve adherence to the rules and procedures as specified in operational plans, organizing regular (usually monthly) committee and general user group meetings, record keeping, and attending a variety of workshops and meetings at the range post and district level. These are the kinds of activities, so I've been told, that only 'good leaders' can be actively involved in. Such leaders are of course literate, have experience in meeting with other leaders, whether from other VDCs or at the district level, and have the time and money to spend on such activities. Not surprisingly, people (usually, though not excusively men) who are already experienced politicians are ideal candidates for committee membership on community forest users groups. But more than anything else, these individuals—such as the Thulo Ban committee's Chair—are the ones who 'come forward' to lead, and through their positions of leadership come to be most influential in shaping and dictating the future of community forestry at the local level.

The authority, power, and influence that elites wield is particularly apparent within the context of the general operations of community forestry, when meetings are held, decisions made, and records kept. While claims are made that the monthly committee meetings, and the decisions made in them, adhere to 'democratic'—or more precisely, 'participatory'—principles, committee meetings are more typically venues within which the chair imposes unilateral decisions (made prior to the meeting) under the guise of acting on behalf of the user group members. A meeting held in April 2000, by the Thulo Ban community forest users group committee, is illustrative of this. The meeting began with the chair introducing the issues to be covered in the meeting: when the forest would be open for collection of fodder, the repayment of loans, the use of the user group's funds, and the payment of fees for products, and who would attend an upcoming workshop to be held in the district centre. Rather than open up the topics for discussion, however, the Chair proceeded to inform everyone in attendance of the decisions he had reached on these issues. One of his unilateral decisions involved the selection of a group of four user-group members (which included himself, his brother, and two other relatives) to attend the community forestry workshop. Two of those selected, however, only learned of being selected at the meeting and could not attend because of previous, conflicting commitments. Rather than ask those present if they were interested in attending, the Chair chose two others, telling (rather than asking) them to attend. Another of his decisions, perhaps more indicative of his sentiments and priorities, was the 'donation' of Rs 40,000 for the construction of a community forest user-group office in the VDC. Although two of the other three user groups contributed to the construction costs, this amount far exceeded the others' contributions. More importantly, however, it meant that funds (Rs 10,000–12,000) that were intended to go towards purchasing goats for a poor household, as part of an income-generating scheme that several committee members were in favour of, ultimately would not occur. In this instance, the Chair's decision was not only his own, but went against the sentiments of other members of the committee, members who apparently share power, or so the rhetoric of a 'democratic' community forestry would have us believe.

The significance of community forestry, and the role of 'democracy' as a central (though slippery) concept, is that it has opened up a new space within which individuals can further accumulate social capital, political and economic influence, and other forms of power and control at the local level. Consequently, 'elites' are able to utilize their social capital within the local context—as good leaders, experienced, knowledgeable, etc.—to acquire and/or entrench their privileged positions within the community through means (democratic elections) sanctioned, even valorized, by community forestry policy in order to counter other community forestry policy prescriptions (i.e., those that attempt to empower the disadvantaged and women). 'Elites' are able to manage this through a discursive shift, or an inclusiveness, whereby 'democracy' is evoked as a gloss to envelope the malleable electoral processes of 'democracy' as local practice, combining it with the 'participatory' and emancipatory intentions of community forestry policy. And yet 'elite' engagement with the community forestry process doesn't end with a 'resistance' to policy prescriptions in an effort to get and keep control on community forestry committees. It extends throughout village politics such that 'elites' are able to use their authority to make decisions that serve their own interests and resist the attempts made by other members of the community to improve their own positions, whether in terms of greater political involvement, or 'participation' in community forestry or other village affairs, or even something as seemingly simple and mundane as acquiring sufficient forest products.

Before moving on to another case of resistance in community forestry, I wish to pause to highlight my uneasiness with the categorization of 'elites'. Despite the frequency with which the term 'elite' is deployed, it is frequently used uncritically as if it were a politically

neutral term. (The same can be said for many other such terms—
'participation', 'community', 'democracy' ...). If 'elite domination' is
a 'problem' afflicting the implementation of community forestry, as
many project staff, bureaucrats, and other scholars would have us
believe, it is critical that we recognize that the category 'elite' is a highly
politically charged term concealing, rather than revealing, numerous
intersecting subject positions. These include the advantages afforded
by wealth, educational background, gender, and the accumulation of
other forms of social capital, such as experience in village activities
that are political- and/or development-related, that form major com-
ponents of what it means to be an 'elite'.

FOREST PRODUCT 'THEFT' AS RESISTANCE

'Theft' (or pilferage, etc.), as Scott (1985, 1986) has observed, is a
common, and directly beneficial, form of resistance employed by the
oppressed to combat shortages, inequitable access to resources, and
the like. But 'theft', not surprisingly, was also an activity that was a
difficult subject to investigate at the village level. In order to adequately
examine 'theft' as a form of resistance in the context of community
forestry in Nepal, I need first to say a few words about my attempts to
raise this issue within my overall examination of community forestry
policy and practice, and with my engagement with both the general
members of local community forestry user groups, and the committee
members. My understanding and documentation of particular cases
of 'theft' in Thulo Ban began with my early attempts to understand
the general workings of community forestry at the local village, or
'community', level.

Early generations of government forest management (through
to the late-1970s and early-1980s) defined the role of the Department
of Forests as one of 'policing' the forest; i.e., forest staff—forest rangers,
guards, and watchers—were charged with the duty of patrolling forests
in order to protect them from local villagers who, it was argued, were
encroaching on the forest by illegally harvesting and clearing forests
for agricultural land. Similarly, much of the literature on indigenous
forest management systems, and common property resources more
generally, has been overly preoccupied with how access to resources
are restricted and how the restrictions are operationalized and
enforced. In the case of community forestry, one form or another of
direct monitoring or 'policing' is still employed, either through hiring
local villagers to serve as forest guards or watchers (*ban pāle*). What

emerges from this preoccupation is a sense of threat to forests by local villagers whose tendency is to disobey rules. This 'threat' is compounded by posters, educational videos, and tales of corruption depicting caricatured local 'elites', bureaucrats, and often Department of Forest staff (including District Forest Officers and more senior staff) as environmental villains.[4] Complementing these portrayals of powerful, greedy, sinister local 'elites' are those of images of poor villagers driven to decimate forests because they have large families, own little or no land, are uneducated and unemployed, as if by some social-environmental law. The result is a powerful imagery of villainy at the village level whereby the theft of resources, if left unchecked, leads to environmental crisis.[5]

The frequency with which such images are evoked suggests that such theft, corruption, or however it is labelled, is a commonplace occurrence and easily observable if one only looks for it. But raise the question with members of a user group committee, as I did, and one is met with a silence that all but erases this issue from purview. Over the course of two months involving interviews with a total of 40 (out of 43) committee members from three community forestry user groups, only in three instances did anyone admit to incidences of 'theft' or even 'rule-breaking'. And these instances were simply dismissed as 'going to the forest when it is closed' for collection. Over the course of several months my knowledge of 'theft' was limited to only these three specific cases, all of which took place within the previous two years. Nevertheless, it was not uncommon for the committee members I interviewed to state, rather vaguely, that 'theft' was 'common in the past', because 'before, the people did not know the rules. But now people know [the rules] and go to the forest only when the forest is open.' In a context where three CFUGs included a total of 340 households (131, 75, and 134, respectively), I was astonished, if not

---

[4]One of the interesting features of these depictions is that they are evoked not only by development practitioners, project staff, and environmentalists, but with an equal frequency by local 'elites', bureaucrats, and Department of Forest staff located in Kathmandu and at the district level.

[5]There is a powerful point of contact between these narratives and depictions in print and film and those in the health sector. 'Health' is frequently portrayed, for example in promotional posters, in terms of the number of children that families have, such as in many health posters, shown to have a direct bearing on the environment; in the case of 'healthy' and happy (but small) families, ensuring a flourishing, healthy, resource-rich environment, or in the case of larger, 'sick' families, producing a devastated, barren landscape.

also suspicious, to learn of such near-total compliance with the forest management rules. Even the few cases that were admitted to were explained away with the same justification: 'It is only those people who do not know the rules who break them,' I was told repeatedly.

Despite more than three months of probing this issue I couldn't induce anyone to give me the name of a single person who had been caught stealing forest products. It was only through chance that I learned of a couple of cases of recent 'theft' that led me to question what I had been told previously and to rethink the causes of 'theft' and rule-breaking. During a visit to the home of Krishna P., a member of one of the user group committees whose home is located within a two-minute walk above the community forest, we stopped our conversation to watch three women and a teenage boy walk by carrying *doko*-loads of fodder from the community forest. After the group had passed, Krishna told me how he had caught one of the women who had just walked by 'stealing fuelwood from the forest during the off-season'.

The individuals/households in question were caught collecting fuelwood 'illegally', I was told by a forest guard. A week or so later I approached Kumari P. to ask her about the incident, but was told that it didn't happen, that it was a misunderstanding and that she has never broken the community forestry rules. I asked her if she knew of anyone else who had been caught stealing forest products or breaking the rules, but she replied that she didn't know of any such cases. My initial interview with Kumari took place in early 1999, but it wasn't until eight months later while I was interviewing her about the situation with her husband being away for long periods of time (as a soldier in the Indian Army), that I had the opportunity to ask her again about being caught stealing that she explained the circumstances surrounding the incident. She provided several reasons for 'stealing' fuelwood from the forest while it was 'closed for collection'. This was recorded in the committee's records as amounting to one *bhāri* of fuelwood, or approximately 20 kg, enough to provide about four days worth of cooking fuel. She first explained that she wasn't able to collect enough fuelwood during the period in which the forest was open because her husband was away and she was the only household member able to provide the labour. This was added to her lacking other sources of fuelwood, such as trees on private land, and her inability to afford to purchase fuelwood from someone else. When I asked her about breaking the rules, and her being punished by the committee/user group— which amounted to a fine of Rs 15—she felt that the punishment was unfair. 'Why must I pay a fine for fuelwood that is mine already?' she asked me. 'The forest products belong to all the members' of the user group. The forest doesn't belong to the government anymore. They [the committee members] say it is ours to protect and use. If I don't collect fuelwood from the forest, how can I cook food to eat? How can I feed my children?'

I also asked Kumari if she had gone to any of the committee members to ask for more products and if she felt that the rules about forest collection, such as when the forest is open for collection, should be changed. Not surprisingly, she said she felt she has no other means of getting the products other than collecting them 'illegally'. 'I don't agree with the rules. They should be changed so that others like me can get fuelwood when they need it, not just during the season when the forest is "open". Many people cannot collect enough when the forest is "open". But what can we do? I have to take fuelwood from the community forest when I need it.' But when I asked Kumari if she had raised the issue in a user group meeting or with committee members, it was apparent that she feels disempowered within the context of 'formalized community forestry'. She explained, 'I have not talked to any committee members. What can I say to them? Even if I tell them that I need more fuelwood or that the rules are not good for people like me, the committee will not change the rules. They do not listen to people like me.' What other means does she have but to defy the rules imposed upon her by her by the members of the user group committee, the local arm of power produced by the Community Forestry Programme?

RESISTANCE AND THE TUBERCULOSIS CONTROL STRATEGY IN NEPAL

Tuberculosis is an appalling disease, and as a medical practitioner working in east Nepal in the early 1990s I saw hundreds of people with this debilitating, and biomedically treatable, affliction. The (unnecessary) deaths of many haunt my humanist imagination, and the memories of these dead do not leave me as I write this paper. The tuberculosis discourse that I analyse, and place within a broader political economy, is an attempt to address the problem of tuberculosis, and assist those with this disease. It too is haunted by the spectres of the tuberculosis dead, and is driven by a global humanism. Let us not forget this, nor that this most apolitical of politics, the attempted reorganization of human behaviour around invisible micro-organisms, may be one of the most powerful, totalizing, yet effaced, tools of global politics in the world today.

Globally deaths from TB number 1.9 million per year and are more than the combined total of those caused by diarrhoea, malaria, AIDS, tropical diseases, and leprosy, according to a 1994 WHO document, quoting 1990 global figures. How can we ignore a germ that infects more than a third of the world's population? Is it possible that no one really cares whether 30 million people die in the next decade from TB? A desperate cry from the World Health Organization, this followed the 1993 declaration of the problem of tuberculosis as a 'global emergency'. The WHO proposed a global plan to control the disease, which it named Directly Observed Therapy Short-course (DOTS). Directly Observed Therapy Short-course was introduced into Nepal as national policy in 1995.

A global problem, then, and like so many other aspects of globalization, Nepal is particularly affected, as the greatest burden falls on the 'developing' world. 'Tuberculosis is one of the most significant health problems facing Nepal, infecting over 60 per cent of the adult population. Every year 44,000 people develop active TB, of whom 20,000 have infectious pulmonary disease' (NTP and HMG 1999: ii). In this text, the Nepal National Tuberculosis Programme strategy, Nepal's statistics—population; population growth rate; infant mortality rate; life expectancy; adult literacy; urban population; urban growth rate; per capita GNP; GNP growth rate; population in poverty (all the important indicators, internationally defined categories of progress, requirements for the world development league tables)—are placed alongside the figures for TB. Nearly 90,000 currently have TB in Nepal. Over 220,000 people will develop TB in the next five years, the equivalent to the entire population of a hill district, we are informed.

What is this entity that wreaks so much havoc, and against which so many health workers, institutions, nations, are attempting to battle? The intent of the bacillus which causes the disease tuberculosis is to destroy humankind. Reading the literature produced about this entity it soon becomes apparent that it is endowed only with the capacity to perform absolute evil. The bacilli's reign is one of 'terror' alone, we are told by a medical historian, as he sets the scene for medicine's historic and heroic battle against this disease that even today remains as 'baffling and menacing as ever' (Ryan 1992: 3). The agency attributed to it is not unlike some of the local forces that afflict people in the hill district where I lived and researched between October 1998 and March 2000, and which have remained the fascination of many, particularly foreign, anthropologists of Nepal.

TB is absolutely real, socially constructed, and the product of discourse at one and the same time (Latour 1993a).

The single most important and problematic aspect of this entity is one of 'resistance'. The *tubercle bacillus*, as a bacterial entity, has the ability to evolve and mutate and thus resist and defy attempts to battle it. This capacity to resist human kind's attempts to combat them is a direct response to human intervention, to antibiotic use and the 'irrational' use of antibiotics. The acquired resistance that results is due to a gene transfer, which then allows the resistance to be transferred from one bacterium to another (Sleigh and Timbury 1982). In her huge and popular tome *The Coming Plague: Newly Emerging Diseases in a World Out of Balance*, Garrett has a chapter dedicated to 'The Revenge of the Germs'. The 'mutability of bacteria, coupled with their ability to pass around and share genetic trumps in a microscopic game of cards, seemed to increasingly leave *Homo sapiens* holding the losing hands' (Garrett 1994: 411). We are dealing with 'resistance' here at the very source of life itself. These areas being charted are, as the American philosopher and feminist historian of science Donna Haraway points out, where 'life itself' replicates through information transfer, within that realm of pure being—that realm purified and transmitted socio-politically, epistemologically, technically as nature becomes biology, and biology becomes genetics, charted cartographically by scientists in their cultures of technoscience (Haraway 1997: 131 ff). No wonder there is nervousness and a sense of desperation if 'resistance' occurs in this (scientifically defined) realm of pure being.

The *tubercle bacillus*' potential for resistance was noted soon after the discovery and trials of its first anti-microbial agent, streptomycin, in the 1940s (Ryan 1992). Tuberculosis, unfortunately, is only curable biomedically by combination therapy lasting at least six months. Much of the research following this realization of its resistance to antimicrobials, has been into looking at combinations of agents to both cure tuberculosis and, at the same time, to prevent the occurrence of resistance. Discussion and debate in Nepal in the early 1990s was on the modes and possibilities of changing the then standard regime, which required a daily injection of the drug streptomycin, for the initial two months, to a shorter, entirely oral combination, with the drug rifampicin included. A key worry amongst a transnational public health 'community' has been that the uncontrolled introduction of particularly rifampicin will result in 'resistance' to the drug emerging, resulting in the loss of this key drug in the war against tuberculosis. If we lose rifampicin, then we lose the fight against tuberculosis, is a 'bottom line' statement I have heard numerous times over the last few years. However, in 1995, Nepal adopted a short course regimen, with rifampicin, and the strategy for its introduction is the DOTS (Directly Observed Therapy Short-course) policy pushed by the WHO. This strategy involves the following key points: political commitment, reliable drug supply, microscopy services, use of short-course drug regimens, direct observation of therapy (DOT)—that is, the tablets must be seen to be swallowed by someone accountable to the health service, the most controversial aspect of the strategy—and systems of monitoring (WHO 1997).

How did this strategy evolve? Till the late 1980s tuberculosis as a disease had virtually disappeared as a public health threat from much of the 'developed' world, although it remained a large problem in much of the rest of the world. It re-emerged to centre stage in international health programmes for three reasons. First, there was its association with HIV and AIDS and its re-emergence as a problem in the 'West'; second, economic research demonstrated that treating tuberculosis was amongst the most cost-effective health interventions at a time when value for money was demanded of all health interventions (World Bank 1993); finally there was the growing threat of multi-drug resistant tuberculosis (MDR-TB).

The combination with HIV has resulted in a 'vicious partnership', as discussed in 'Working together against us' (WHO report on the tuberculosis epidemic, 1995), and termed an 'alliance of terror' (Ryan 1992: 389). A recent editorial of *The International Journal of Tuberculosis and Lung Disease* (IJTLD) evokes the situation thus: 'The towering twin threats to global tuberculosis control are the continual explosion of HIV-related tuberculosis and the increasing prevalence of drug resistance. The former threatens to overwhelm treatment capacity in many parts of the world, while the latter raises the spectre of incurable disease that can be transmitted to the community' (Chaisson *et al.* 1999). This evocation of a sense of pending doom and crisis is a common stylistic device in many scientific journals on the subject of tuberculosis. 'Drug-resistant strains of TB increasing world-wide ... super-deadly TB strain is spreading' reads a recent WHO press release on their web site, a result of the international survey of MDR-TB started in 1996 by the WHO and the International Union Against Tuberculosis and Lung Disease (WHO 2000).

This 'nightmare of resurgence', as the health economist Gill Walt called it, has resulted in the realignment of a number of 'actors' including the WHO, the World Bank, the pharmaceutical industry, bilaterals, national governments, government services and health workers and patients (Walt 1999). Since 1999 tuberculosis control programmes have been funded by both the Gates Foundation and George Soros' Open Society. Tuberculosis was the subject of an entire conference at a ministerial level held in Amsterdam in March 2000, as well as being on the agenda for at the G8 Summit in Japan in 2000. Its global political visibility is on the rise.

In this context it is worth looking at some of the texts produced in recent years in a particular way, focusing on lines of blame, of accusations, as to the cause of, and the reasons for drug 'resistance'. It seems that sources of resistance are twofold, according to a global transnational professional class involved in the research into tuberculosis. Firstly, as Small (1999) states in an editorial in the IJTLD, sizeable clusters of disease are often attributable to single sources of infection, which has been proven by the use of molecular fingerprinting techniques used in epidemiology. Yet another editorial in the same journal states: 'A single unchecked case can foster mini epidemics .... Until we address the challenge of the long term completer, prolonged and interrupted therapy will remain a countervailing force of effective TB control, and TB elimination will remain a hope beyond our reach' (Chaulk 1999). The second source of the growth of MDR-TB is clearly articulated by the WHO: 'Poorly-managed TB control programmes are the primary source of multi-drug resistance' (WHO 1994). Articulate the 'cause' of the problem, and the necessity for strategies to address the causes follow: in this case, individual adherence to treatment and the strengthening of national efforts to control the disease.

But the bacilli are also 'airborne killers'. 'Tuberculosis bacilli are collecting frequent-flier miles', as increasing global mobility becomes another problem for tuberculosis control (Panos and WHO 2000). 'It is hard to imagine how any nation can protect its citizens from potentially infectious visitors .... TB bacteria are global stowaways, sneaking free rides into new locales by hiding undetected inside millions of unsuspecting people' (ibid.: 94). More tuberculosis is found in refugees, who have less access to treatment than other groups, and remain more vulnerable: 'Their mobility makes them more difficult to treat' (Wares 2000). 'The history of TB in the world is one of crossing borders', an article on the Johns Hopkins web site proclaims, in an article that refracts the peculiar reversals that I wish to highlight (Coberley 2000). During colonialist expansion tuberculosis was spread to many parts of the world, but it is now being re-imported, as migration is reversing, and spreading back to Europe and North

America. Overall, Coberley informs us, 36 per cent of all cases in developed countries are seen in the foreign-born and the percentage is increasing, perhaps because of regular revisits to their countries of origin. Studies from the Netherlands, we are told, show that 17 per cent of all cases are transmitted by the foreign-born. Using a cost-benefit analysis that estimates the treatment of tuberculosis to be 1000 times more expensive in the US than in LDCs (Less Developed Countries), it is both cheaper and more humane to root out tuberculosis in the country of origin than to treat it in host countries (Coberley 2000). These views are shared by the WHO: 'It is no longer possible to eliminate an infectious disease in one part of the world and allow it to run rampant in another. In short, it will be impossible to control TB in the industrialised nations unless it is sharply reduced as a threat in Africa, Asia and Latin America' (WHO 1994).

These fears are echoed inside international health and aid institutions in Nepal, and in the Nepal press. There are dozens of articles in the Nepal press (both in Nepali and in English) about tuberculosis and the DOTS strategy. In the *Himalayan Times* of 31 October 1999, in an article entitled 'Tuberculosis can be more dangerous than AIDS', it is stated that 'Mainly men between the ages of 15 and 60 get the disease, those of a productive age and if they stop taking their medicine, after a while the bacteria digests [Np. *pachāi*] the medicine and they can become more dangerous than AIDS, says Bishwaram Shrestha of the National Tuberculosis Control Programme' (my translation). In the *Rising Nepal* of 28 November 1998, Sanat Kumar Sharma writes of the widespread use and misuse of antibiotics leading to resistance of bacteria, and asks 'What we can do to prepare for the great epidemic that may occur in the days to come?' echoing the fear of much of the public health discourses above. In the *Kathmandu Post* of 22 December 1998: 'One in every five Nepalese suffering from tuberculosis is an international migrant'; the article quotes Dr Dirgha Singh Bam, Director of the National Tuberculosis Centre, as saying 'TB is moving freely across our borders. It doesn't need visa or passport.' At the 1998 SAARC meeting in Kathmandu on tuberculosis it was said: 'TB snowballing into a serious threat'. These reports, chosen at random, reflect a considerable outpouring in the press on the tuberculosis problem within Nepal.

At a national level, to narrow my analysis down further within Nepal, where does blame lie for the high levels of drug resistance? In Kathmandu the reasons are as follows, as reported in *Tubercle and Lung Disease* in 1996: 'TB drugs are freely available on the market;

private practitioners treat patients using insufficient regimes, without motivational training for them nor any observation of therapy. Other reasons for this number of many advanced and problematic cases may be the high illiteracy rate of 74 per cent ... the existence of many traditional healers, who were contacted first; a lack of trust in the basic health service (ethnic barriers, high absence rate of health post staff) and religious reasons' (Neher *et al*. 1996: 305). Notice how the forces ranged against the control of TB have now broadened to include social 'barriers', a barrier always being a fairly solid metaphor not just for resistance, but anything that causes an abrupt termination on a particular trajectory. A year previously another article had highlighted drug reactions and side effects, poverty and thus no money to buy medicines (a major argument for the availability of free medicines, as specified with DOTS) as factors leading to patients 'defaulting' from treatment. Resistance may increase because of the free movement across the border with India, it is suggested (Onazaki and Shakya 1995).

RESEARCH SITE: AN INTERNATIONAL CONFERENCE IN KATHMANDU

The DOTS strategy has allowed, or rather attempted to facilitate, a realignment of forces. Resistance is anticipated. Strategies are developed: it makes economic sense (tuberculosis affects adults and therefore the GNP: World Bank 1999); treating TB is the most humane thing to do in times of limited funding; treatment of people with TB leads to the elimination of poverty. These are the issues that need to be addressed to get tuberculosis control on the agenda within the fiercely competitive world of health-related programmes (malaria, polio and immunizations, vitamin A, mother-child health, safe motherhood, to name a few, are all competing for space within Nepal's evolving health services).[6] DOTS, as a strategy, has allowed the tuberculosis discourse to be inserted into other on-going processes. As a consequence 'social mobilization' becomes crucial, and the health worker's task becomes one of being able to persuade politicians, the media, NGOs, businesses, local groups and others that DOTS is the

[6]Little has changed since Judith Justice described and analysed the interactions and competition between government and agencies each with their own priorities and agendas in the late 1970s (Justice 1986).

best thing to do. At a three-day conference in Kathmandu on 'TB and Human Rights' in February 1999, organized by tb.net (a loosely defined transnational virtual organization of which I am also now on the steering group) the attendees (over 120 in all), many from Nepal but also from a number of other countries, were introduced to this concept. It is the 'process of bringing together all feasible and practical inter-sectorial allies to raise awareness and demand for a particular programme'. 'Social mobilization is most effective when it involves a mix of advocacy, community participation, partnerships and capacity building activities' (Conference Handout, but see also WHO 1998). We were organized into role play groups by the two facilitators, one from the WHO and the other from UNAIDS. This style of conferencing, a favourite ritualized activity of many development workers in Kathmandu, but here more participatory, was not met with the enthusiasm that the organizers had hoped for. They were surprised to learn that such group dynamics and styles of training are not part of the learning style of many of the more senior-level health workers in Nepal.

There were other forms of resistance too. A journalist from India used her role-play forum—a group supposed to be acting as advocates for DOTS, to persuade the media that DOTS was the thing to do—as a forum for a sustained attack on DOTS. She accused them of bulldozing DOTS, of stifling debate on other ways, of ignoring larger questions around integrated health service delivery. It doesn't work in India she argued, in the more rural areas, it just places a greater burden on the already sick. And, she asked, what happens when the interest in TB diminishes and the funding disappears? In her comments at the end of the conference she further questioned why the voices of the DOTS doubters were not present. She also doubted the 'magic bullet' approach and the dependence on medicines as the answer to the TB problems. She was disappointed by the absence of debate and stated that, as she had wandered among people during the three days, many had felt that they were just being told what to do. In the official conference proceedings, her voice is also absent. 'She was so negative,' one WHO official told me, exasperated. 'She came in with these anti-DOTS prejudices and left with them, she hadn't changed her mind at all.' A salutary warning perhaps to all those who attempt to manipulate the media to their own ends.

Resistance to the DOT component of DOTS was allowed, in the form of a debate, in which two people, both working in tuberculosis control in Nepal, defended and attacked the motion 'We believe that mandatory DOT infringes personal liberties.' The abstraction meant that the personal convictions of the two presenters were irrelevant. Style and force of argumentation were important here to persuade the audience one way or the other.

For the motion: What are the links between Coca Cola, sex, and DOTS? They are all cool, sexy and selling! They are all sold as bigger and better than they really are. They all have a good image supported by a powerful media machine and are examples of good marketing. The speaker quoted John Porter from the London School of Hygeine and Tropical Medicine: 'Interventions for infectious disease control like DOTS embody the imbalance of power and capacity between the public health profession and infected person and lead to a moral debate between civil liberties and public health.' DOT—definitely over the top. 'There is no scientific evidence to support that DOT is effective,' he told us, quoting a number of recent trials. DOT is designed to make patients compliant and ignores the failings of the system. He then went on to talk about the ethical dimension, arguing that it breaks many ethical conditions, and contravenes human rights.

Against the motion the argument went along these lines: It works, is effective, and supports the patient. It reduces deaths, reduces relapses, prevents drug resistance. There is increased survival in people with HIV. It is cost effective, we cannot afford not to do it; it is necessary as no low-income country has achieved the WHO targets (finding 70 per cent of all active cases and curing 85 per cent of them); it is supportive: 'tough love', 'the human bond'. What are the alternatives? Socio-economic development will take too long. BCG vaccination does not decrease the prevalence. Unfortunately, unsupervised treatment does not produce the outcomes we desire. It is the normal sensible patient who defaults: Who would want to take eight months of treatment for a disease when you feel better in a few weeks? He drew on some trials: one that the previous speaker had used as an example providing evidence that DOT doesn't work he criticized on methodological grounds. He drew on article 29 of the Universal Declaration of Human Rights, stating that everyone has a duty towards their communities. Since it is concerned with the protection of the individual and the community, DOTS is not dissimilar to banning smoking, wearing crash helmets, making drugs illegal. Anyway the majority of people will accept voluntary DOT. At close, with the vote, the motion was lost, by a narrow margin.

TO THE PERIPHERY ...

I wish to shift my narrative away from the centre now to the district, where I spent much time researching my interests. Shortly after I arrived in the field, on visiting a village outside of the district centre, I was asked to see an old woman who was being treated for tuberculosis. She was being treated with the standard regimen and she died later from a severe drug reaction to the drug thiacetazone. I was told that she had swelled up, that her eyes and mouth had blistered red, and then she had died. In the early 1990s I worked in east Nepal with an international NGO in a tuberculosis control project and I had seen several people die of this awful side effect. It was with great relief that we introduced short course chemotherapy (SCC), and I was delighted when shortly after my arrival this time short course was also introduced into this district, even if it did come with DOTS, as part of a trial, supported by the Nuffield Institute, looking at ways that DOT—the 'directly observed' component of the policy—was being introduced. The district had been randomly assigned as a 'community' DOTS district, in which the local ward level Female Community Health Volunteers were to do the observation of the first two months of treatment. The point of the trial was to compare this method with 'family' DOT, where the patient chooses their supervisor (NTC internal document 1999: 'Randomized Control Trials (RTCs) to compare different TB delivery strategies which may be appropriate for areas where access to health services is poor—Protocol for training and monitoring'). I became intimately bound up in the introduction of this trial, the training involved, was asked to become a member of the district DOTS committee, and could not shake off my previous identity as a doctor or my biomedical knowledge of tuberculosis.

For much of the time I was deeply uncomfortable with this dual subjectivity, researcher in anthropology/ public health worker and the tensions that this produced as it seemed to lead to considerable ethical and moral ambiguity. My training in anthropology had introduced me to Foucault's notion of biopower, of the intimate connections between the state and the introduction of medical and public health practices as part of the production of disciplined bodies (I did not need to read Osborne 1997 to know that Foucault's work is of little use to policy dialogues). Here it seemed we had a perfect example, of increased surveillance, of the need for disciplined patients—internationally defined perhaps, but state-implemented. I was acutely aware of a literature which tends to emphasize the negative, repressional aspects of the state, and the links with certain dominant groups or interests (the most famous and controversial in Nepal being Dor Bahadur Bista's *Fatalism and Development*, 1991, in which he links the formation of the bureaucratic state apparatus with 'Hinduization'). I was also aware of writings that tend to analyse the introduction of biomedicine as a threat to the 'traditional', and the loss of indigenous ways of being and healing. This includes much anthropological writing and this powerful negative portrayal of biomedicine reveals, I would suggest, the 'trace' of anthropology's previous concerns, of its tendency to reify and romanticize the 'traditional' contra the 'modern', and is as much a question of metaphysics and method. I was aware too of the growing criticisms by many Nepali anthropologists particularly of 'foreign' anthropologists for the lack of a practical aspect in their work and their tendency to reify difference, which runs against the project of national integration and development (see, for example, Regmi 1999). These were battles of abstraction, and over-determinations, which none the less came to possess me and generate an existential anxiety that rarely left me. I hope that I do not lose that ambiguity as I continue to write here on 'resistance' and ask you, the reader, to follow me further to my next 'sites'.

When I arrived in the district, there were a number of public health initiatives going on. The major ones, I was informed by the District Health Officer, who had been recently transferred here from the far west, were the DOTS programme, the pulse polio campaign, the vitamin A project, and the permanent sterilization camps, part of the family planning programme. All these vertical projects were associated with considerable extra funding and support from a number of bilaterals, multilateral, INGOs and each seemed to be evolving in directions that went against the other major thrust of 'health sector reform' which involves the push towards the 'sector wide approach' to health management, decentralized planning, and the involvement of local people in defining the health problems and strategies to address them (Tarnowski in the previous section has traced the discourses of democracy, decentralization etc., through community forest policies, strategies and discourses: a similar process could be traced for the health sector). Suffice it here to say that the sheer numbers of forms, reports, and meetings generated seemed phenomenal to me. The fact that often double sets of figures had to be filled out, one for the vertical project and their often international surveillance systems, and another for the Ministry of Health, was truly confounding. I have little doubt that many of these shifts, away from the integrated primary healthcare projects of the 1980s, represent the fractured, vertical agendas of internationalist discourses, of which the strategies around tuberculosis are only one, and the need for quantitative figures for evaluations, in order to assess progress towards targets. Paradoxically also it leads to greater control and centralization.

The first major 'resistance' I encountered was to my very presence and interrogations! This was not just within the District Health Office, but other organizational settings too, and I found myself actively ignored on more than a few occasions. How many times did I need to be told to come another time, that someone was busy, and would see me another day before I realized that my presence was not welcomed? How much was my frustration related to the shadow of an ESRC grant, the pressures to get my PhD and to say something original, but based in plenty of 'evidence'? Some people were decidedly hostile. I tried to work out why, but was left only with hunches, and a feeling of increasing paranoia. I wondered if it had to do with my own declared links with health activists also known to be associated with leftist parties? Silences seemed to be feeding the possibility of conspiracy theories, and not just mine.

However, there was antagonism to the presence of the District Health Officer too, who had also just arrived in the district. He told me of the difficulties of remaining outside of politics (he himself was also rumoured to be attached to the UML), and how tasks like hiring new peons was so difficult, or of selecting new mother-child health workers. Asking rhetorical questions was one method of explanation he used: 'Why do you think that 65 per cent of all peons in this district come from one VDC?' he once asked me. There was a lot of resistance to him selecting new peons from the Village Development Committees that they came from. Certainly it transpired after a long while, and as I got to know a few people better, that there seemed to be certain interests at stake with a core of people in the office, many who were closely linked to the accountant. 'In Britain, the accountant probably doesn't have much status, but here in Nepal they have the highest status of all,' I was told somewhat cryptically by one informant. I didn't like how suspicious I had become; there seemed to be too many secrets floating around. I came to doubt people's motives for things, just as many were no doubt suspicious of mine. A friend of mine, who runs a health post and clinic, was accused of stealing public funds in a local paper. Another friend, an expatriate, was accused of misappropriating funds and was under investigation. I asked one group of health workers where the truth was to be found, on reading some of the local papers. 'Truth!' was the exclaimed response: 'In Nepal! You will only find politics!'

Towards the end of my stay I had a long conversation with the tuberculosis supervisor for the district about his work and the office. We had had a difficult relationship and had argued once or twice about the introduction of DOTS, and the eligibility of several patients to receive treatment. 'How would *you* like to work in that office?' he had asked me. 'How often do you see any of us doing any work?' The promise of a trip to Bangalore had been taken away from him and given to a relative of the Minister of Health, he told me. He had suddenly, and inexplicably, been transferred to another district after being rewarded by the then District Health Officer and given a pay rise. 'They thought I was a communist because of that, and they took offence', he said, although he only hinted at who the 'they' were. He had managed just to stay where he was and ignore the order. Fortunately the person he had wanted to be transferred with didn't want to move either, so they had just stayed put (almost everyone I spoke to regarding transfers, saw them as motivated entirely by party-political considerations). Such regular and repeated transfers are articulated by many working in the international aid sectors as a severe constraint to the further development of the health sector. 'And we get paid nothing', he continued. 'How can we survive without doing a little private practice? Would *you* care in an environment like this?'

I realized that I was a considerable problem for him, as he was attempting to manage his superiors. 'We have to let them know what it is they want to hear', he said, on one of our many days together when I suggested that some of the problems and ambiguities be highlighted to the central-level policy makers at the National Tuberculosis Centre (NTC). His focus on getting the reports right seemed to override the interests of the patients at times (at an analytical level I would suggest that this reflects the central/institutional concerns with the need for surveillance, for detailed and accurate information, upon which evaluation and planning are dependent). At one point he pleaded with me not to tell anyone anything, not to rock the boat, and yet my fear always lay with the implications for further DOTS policy. I was heartened that so many staff were able to adapt and ignore central directives that their experience told them couldn't work, and let their bosses know otherwise, but I feared that these somewhat mediated 'truths of survival' (as I shall call them) would be translated into national policy. He managed to take supervision teams only to the 'best' health posts every time that they came to the district. 'But', I would reason, 'they should really be taken to Y, where something quite different is happening.' 'Next time,' he assured me, but the next time too, it was back to the regulars. One VDC in this district has a continual stream of foreign and other visitors, a symbol of hope, of the possible, in a range of development activities.

The 'DOTS—Defaulter creation system', laughed the Health Post in Charge at health post Y, a way out from the district centre on one of the roads sneaking through the district. He had a thriving private clinic as well, and of all the health staff I spent time with his clinical and diagnostic skills were the best. (It was impossible for me, trained in medicine, and the years of work I have had training and working with health workers not to judge this aspect of many health workers' work. The numbers of poorly trained and inexperienced community health workers emerging from the increasing numbers of private technical training colleges, is truly worrying.) 'It is a system that just won't work', he told me. 'What do we do with someone who has tuberculosis but the ward Female Community Health Volunteer (FCHV) is not interested, or is away, or thinks that TB is a filthy disease of the impure and won't have anything to do with it? I just give them their medicines, and we haven't had anyone not take their medicines yet.'

A new nurse who had just been transferred from another nearby district agreed. 'It won't work up here', she said, 'so we just give the patients their medicines.' 'Do you mind if I tell people this?' I asked. 'Not at all', she said. 'They should know how unworkable the programme is.' She had worked in a 'model' DOT district in the Tarai before coming here. There, though, they had additional assistance from JICA (the bilateral aid arm of the Japanese government), with supervision vehicles available too, and that had made all the difference. 'It is easy to say "Mobilize the FCHVs" ', she told me, 'but it is not so easy to do. They are not aware, and many feel that it is unsafe to go too near a TB patient. But they also have to do more and more work these days [they are being burdened with family planning, administering polio, vitamin A capsules, etc.], but they do not get paid.' Indeed, at almost all the DOTS orientation training that I had been too, FCHVs had complained about not being paid for their work, although they all received a small stipend for attendance at training sessions. 'The ill are sincere and afraid', she told me. 'Is it not possible to trust them and give them their medicines? It is not the solution to have DOTS committees, but to support the ill in the "field".' She supplies weekly DOT, because the FCHVs are not around and lack interest. If they don't come back then she will follow them up.

She did bring this up at one of the regular two-day seminars for health workers (held every four months) when each health post reported back to the district centre, part of the system for ordering the drugs and allowing the flow of information back to Kathmandu, and beyond, to Geneva for global programme evaluation. At a meeting in which much of the discussion had resulted in mud-slinging between the district office and the health posts over filling out forms correctly, she asked about FCHVs not supervising patients, and there was murmured agreement. I was surprised at this openness, and the response from the DTLA was that it was 'community' DOTS policy, so the answer is more training and further motivation. When I interjected and said that I thought that this was a trial, it produced an angry response from the regional supervisor, that this is not a trial. It is simply that the supervision by the FCHVs has to work, they are the backbone of the programme. It is a matter of their honour (Np. *ijat*), working in the community and they need encouragement. Motivation starts from the 'grass roots' and works towards the centre. He had visited nine districts now and it was the health workers' job to motivate the people. 'This is an infectious disease and DOTS is the last chance for the people that there is', he told us. He recounted the progression from receiving a category 1 treatment regime, through to a category 2 treatment for treatment failure, and then all that is left is MDR-TB. (There are three categories for treatment: (1) New sputum-smear-positive patients (2) Treatment failures and retreatment cases (3) All other types of tuberculosis.) 'We should not forget that we are a part of the community too and it affects us as well', he continued. 'In the model DOTS district in the Tarai, the DOTS committee is active and hostels have been built by some communities, sub-committees have been formed. DOTS acts as the way to further mobilize the FCHVs.' He sighed that he was not interested in local problems and politics, only in getting the policy implemented, and he was disappointed with this district, that it was not as forward-thinking as others he had visited. Another healthpost worker mumbled that the local leaders in his area were not interested in forming vitamin A committees and they certainly are not going to be interested in forming DOTS committees. Quite a display of resistance.

The District Tuberculosis Supervisor perceived most of the problems with the implementation of DOTS at the district level as being because of the lack of knowledge, and the answer to this was more training, from the centre. He also recognized problems in the sub-centres, those designated as DOTS treatment centres. In the year and a half I was in the district several of the sub-centres were struck off the list because the staffing levels were not up to the NTP (National Tuberculosis Programme) guidelines. These were, of course, the ones in the remoter, less served areas. Anyway, he said, it is no good just blaming the FCHVs for not doing the work. He listed the programmes that were going on at present, as we sat drinking tea on a bench in the warm January sun, sitting outside his office: Family planning, malaria, immunization, AIDS and sexually transmitted diseases, tuberculosis, leprosy, polio, vitamin A, the FCHV programme, the traditional birth midwife-training programme, the primary health care outreach programme, health education, mother-child healthcare, safe motherhood, each with separate training. 'How many is that?' he asked, as I wrote them all down. 'Now the healthpost staff only work from ten to two, it should be five, but that never happens. When do they get a chance to do all this work? Then there is the poor training of staff in the technical line, that many people have false certificates. As we are close to the border with India it is easy to buy them,' he continued. (One such case had occurred in the district centre. A practitioner was exposed in the national press for being in possession of a false (Np. *nakalī*), MBBS certificate.) Family 'source' remains a problem, which has also now moved into the private sector training too. On top of this, understanding about TB and DOTS is low. It is no good looking just at TB, but at all the problems. All these vertical programmes coming from Kathmandu are reflected in the District Health Office, and in the health posts, he concluded. I asked him what he suggested doing about it. 'Commitment from the staff is necessary first, but nobody really cares. There needs to be more teamwork, more sense of purpose. But the pay is too low. It seems that adding more staff is the answer, but in fact we need fewer staff, more responsibility and more pay. And central supervision should be compulsory.'

He went on: 'Look at DOTS, there are ten major criteria that need to be met before short-course chemotherapy is introduced.' (There is a quasi-agreement between the NTP and the district prior to the introduction of DOTS to a district, with strict minimum criteria for inclusion. Again it is the more remote districts that often do meet the criteria.) 'Why not implement short-course chemotherapy first— rather than enforcing all these criteria, like staffed treatment centres, microscopy services—and monitor the outcomes? Also orientation for everyone should be compulsory, not just those doing the work.' We went on, till he suggested that decentralization is what is required, at least to the district. 'But that will never happen in Nepal,' he told me. 'Why?' I asked. 'The worship of power (*shaktiko puja*),' he said. 'Power, if those at the centre let go, then there will be no value to them, people would stop needing them to solve their problems, and they would feel empty. It is like this: "First it is difficult to understand, after understanding it is difficult, and the more you understand the more difficult it becomes." There is a saying in Nepal: it's like learning a language. "At first it is difficult to learn the alphabet, then it is harder to learn words, making a sentence more difficult still, it is always more difficult." But', he added, somewhat bitterly it seemed to me, 'I am the only one who knows the difficulties of the post, but no one ever asks me; they just tell me what to do. And people moan all the time that in Britain and America everything is fine, that there are no problems, but how can they know? They haven't been there, after all. It's like marriage', he said, 'we cannot know what it is like until we are in it'. With this he was returning to his more immediate concern, that of his own marriage, which was arranged for a few weeks hence. 'Ah, now that is really not too bad', I said, and we laughed ....

WHAT OF THOSE WHO HOST THE TUBERCLE BACILLUS?

And finally I turn to the patients themselves, those unfortunate enough to host the *tubercle bacillus*, although we have arrived at them from a long and tortuous path. As I re-read my notes, the dozens of interviews with those suffering with tuberculosis, I find it extremely difficult to push 'resistance' into what they expressed to me. I could imagine it into one or two places at a push, but the weight of death, a not uncommon consequence for not taking the drugs, is a high price to pay for this resistance. I should also note here that methodologically my subject position, as a doctor and a foreigner, did not perhaps place me in the best position to collect material on the subject of resistance. I remember a young man who died in east Nepal in the early 1990s, who swore that he took his drugs, who got sicker and sicker, and only after he died did his desperately distraught wife tell us that he never took his drugs, he didn't believe in them. Most frequently by the time someone presents to the health services and receives a diagnosis they are desperate, and their contact with a bureaucratic medical system is an avenue of hope, the flip side of despair, in the negotiation of the diagnostic maze in search of a cure.

Of the few who were labelled as 'defaulters' with whom I spoke, the attitudes of health staff and the difficulties erected by the health bureaucracy seemed to be the most obvious resistance to people getting the drugs they needed, and often demanded. The stipulations and process for getting those with tuberculosis to receive their drugs from as close to their homes as possible were considerable. At one health post I attended, the two people diagnosed with tuberculosis who arrived from the district centre that day, neither had the requisite referral forms, and both were sent back, a round trip of some six hours on the bus. If, that is, they ever went back. Both received the news in stoical silence. In the past the healthpost worker informed me he would have started them on treatment anyway, but now they are so closely scrutinized because of the new drug-ordering system that he cannot get away with it. During the monsoon of 1999 I walked with one health worker to the far west of the district, through the pouring rain, to follow up a man who had delayed coming to the designated treatment sub-centre with the local female community health volunteer. When we arrived at his home we were informed that he had just died. He had been too busy to visit the health post a second time immediately, as he had to work in his fields.

It was a genuine surprise to me, the relief that many people expressed on receiving a diagnosis of tuberculosis. Most seemed to know that it was curable, had known someone else who had it, and had recovered. It used to be known locally as *khapate*, a disease that dried you up before you died, but now the name 'TB' has passed into everyday usage, and it is treatable with medicines, I was told repeatedly. The district that I was in also had a large and well-established mission hospital and in the 1960s and 1970s one of the early missionaries had spent much time seeking out tuberculosis sufferers and treating them, and was very fondly remembered by people locally. Indeed some, particularly from India, just referred to this as the TB hospital. One person I got to know well expressed great relief that it was not *gyāstrik*, another condition expressed locally that usually necessitates a life-long change in dietary patterns. Certainly people complained about the standard of health care in the healthposts, saying that they had little faith in certain practitioners, or government medicines; some even preferred to pay for their medicines privately than receive them for free. When the mission hospital aligned itself with the DOTS programme and started to refer those with tuberculosis back into the government public system, many just came back and paid for their drugs.

Others wished to keep the diagnosis quiet, were worried of the reactions of neighbours or friends, of what others would think of behaviours that could have led to this condition, widely regarded to be tainted with impure habits, such as drinking and smoking. Several of those suffering had profound struggles with their own ideas as to the causes of the disease, once they had been labelled with the diagnosis. Several people had pleaded with me that they had never smoked, drank, eaten impure foods, so how could they have possibly got the disease? Occasionally I had heard comments of the problem of tuberculosis being within others; the porters who hang out in the district centre; with the Magars, as they are the ones who migrate to India and then bring it back (it is implicit that they smoke and drink). A diagnosis like tuberculosis will always feed into existing, albeit shifting lines of division, as it does in the internationalist discourses I articulated earlier.

When I asked specifically about the possible causes for their condition, I don't think that anyone mentioned the *tubercle bacillus*, although all would have received some form of health education. Hanging on to the trace of tuberculosis, the biomedical category, is becoming harder now as it dissolves into a sea of explanations, rationalizations, conflicting ideas, experiences, judgements, and convictions. Almost everyone I talked to visited a range of practitioners, before and during treatment. Explanations given to those with tuberculosis would be multiple, confounding, revealing. People's reactions to differing advice would be diverse, nearly always based on personal evidence, not abstractions. Rumours about different practitioners, allopathic and others, swirled, shifted. This one is good for children, that one for this particular condition of spirit attack, such as *moc* or *masān*.[7] Many people had a clearly defined idea as to how clusters of symptoms may relate to a particular condition. Many people with tuberculosis in the district, and from outside, who developed jaundice visited an old woman, who was renowned for 'sweeping' jaundice into oil. One health worker with whom I was discussing this laughed and said that it was like the specialization that occurs in medicine! One young man who had nearly died before he received his tuberculosis treatment described in great detail his visits to a number of *lāmāharu* (the generic term used for a wide range of local practitioners of healing, often elsewhere referred to as *dhāmī-jhānkrī*), hospitals, private practitioners, and

---

[7]See Maskarinec (1995) for a beautifully written book addressing a variety of local diagnostic treatment categories in and around Jajarkot (but not categories like tuberculosis).

his frustration with differing diagnoses from witchcraft (Np. *boksī lāgyo*), to *'gyāstric'*, and liver disease to tuberculosis. He was convinced after he had a 'video x-ray', the local term for an ultrasound and could see the lesions in his abdomen. (The mission staff were wondering at a virtual epidemic in the demands for these diagnostic procedures.) Another man told me of how he did not have any faith in *lāmāharu*, until he got tuberculosis and his medicines only started working after they were empowered with a blown mantra. After a long conversation with a local Ayurvedic practitioner, and his subtle theorization as to delicate humoral balance, and how mismatching climate, certain behaviours and foodstuffs could tip the body towards developing what I would call tuberculosis, resonated much more with what people were telling me was often the cause of the disease, or at least a significant influence impinging upon it. Many health staff were absolutely adamant that fish should not be eaten if someone had been coughing up blood, as it heats the body too much. This advice didn't conflict with the giving of medicines, and is perhaps another example of the 'hybrid' practices and advice which seem to be being adopted.

I could go on with a long and detailed composite study of the complexities of this 'interface' (a very poor metaphor to describe this space) between the allopathic and indigenous, as related to healing activities. Indeed the often bewildering complexity of adaptations, shifts, movements, both on the part of those suffering from illness and those who practise healing would fill a book that I may one day wish to write. At this point, though, I should say that any insistence on giving primacy to 'resistance' would be what Ortner (1995) has called an 'analytic by-product' and would do violence to the empirical evidence that I have.

A FINAL ANECDOTE OF RESISTANCE

On a cold winter's day in January 2000 I returned to health post Y. A huge mural advertizing Panther Condoms greets the traveller on the way into this small dusty town that has grown up at a junction in the road. Over sweet tea, I asked the shop owner how the recent 'polio day' had gone, part of the international thrust to eliminate polio, this being the third year of the three-year initiative. During this time each polio day has been declared a national holiday and there is a strong sense of national pride that Nepal has been so successful in reaching its targets for this programme, as reflected in much of the media, a balance to Nepal so often finding itself near the bottom of the development indicator league tables. Every child registered in the VDC had received their drops I was told. There were two women who 'did not understand' at first, the need for the polio drops, but they did later. They had not turned up voluntarily to bring their children for the drops so at the end of the day the healthpost in charge and the FCHV had gone down to their house to find out why. As they reached their house I was told they had run down the hill, pulling their children behind them. They had been found hiding behind a clump of bamboo. They then had to be coerced up the hill to the healthpost, threatened by the police, told that they would never be examined by a doctor again if they did not have their drops before they consented. At the follow-up polio day six weeks later they were first in the queue: 'They had come to understand.' I heard this story at least four times: the women were the butt of quite a few jokes locally. Radha, assisting with my research, went to visit them, to ask why they had not wanted their immunizations. Maile, one of the mothers, phrased it in this way: 'However many immunizations children have, they still get ill. What is the point? All my children have been fully immunized, but my first son coughs at night and is restless. I also had tetanus, after the family planning operation, but I developed lumps in my abdomen. I went to the hospital twice for that but nothing happened. I had to argue with the doctors. Also, the health workers, responsible for these polio drops threatened me: "What are you going to do if your children get ill? You will have to come back to us". Nothing happens without money. If I have money I can go to the town, there are plenty of doctors there.' Had she ever had any negative experiences with the immunizations themselves? 'No, but there was a rumour that a child who had the polio vaccine had died.' Did she have any faith in the vaccines? 'No'. So why did she take her children for them? '"If you don't take your children to the immunization centre, then we will send the police to take you to the centre", the female community health volunteer said. I replied, "I have not done anything wrong: how can you call the police?" And the health post "in charge" just laughed. The health workers keep bothering us, so we do it.'

There is a powerful image, an image of resistance, of defiance, common in post-1990 Nepal, found frequently on the covers of magazines and papers, of groups of protesters marching together, fists held high, banners aloft. It is to be found on a polio flyer that was handed out from this health post as well, the banner proclaiming 'Let's eliminate polio'.

POSTSCRIPT

This is the first time that we have written for an international audience of this kind. It is a new experience for us, and one that we approach with a sense of both uncertainty and anxiety. We are at the point now as researchers being trained in anthropology, when we are asked to do this, to write, to represent, to integrate in certain ways aspects of our empirical data with certain modes of theory. Our training has alerted us to the 'crisis of representation', to anthropology's problematic history, to the links between anthropological research and fundable interests (how much anthropological research is funded now from development industry sources, and how much is the increasing utilization of anthropologists linked to more sophisticated means of planned social behavioural change, as it was in colonial times?). These are a few of the core issues to our evolving discipline which we inherit, and are forced to address. Our point here is to admit that our own position as writers is fraught with complexity and contradiction. There are certainly a variety of ways to 'see' or 'read' resistance, as we discuss below, and we feel it is important to stress that how resistance is viewed, read, and interpreted, is contingent on a positionality. Hence, the reason for our choice of title, a Heterotopia of Resistance, as we discuss the myriad forms of resistance and the manner in which it has been, and continues to be, theorized.

Perhaps unlike other ethnographers/writers we did not set out to investigate diffuse forms of 'resistance' or quotidian responses to 'power'. Indeed, it was not until we learned of this session, at this conference, that we set out to reflect upon our field experiences (which were ongoing at the time) and piece together this paper. Indeed, neither of us either arrived in Nepal to study a particular reified group (for example the 'Newar', the 'Tamang'), or locale, but were instead more interested in modalities and practices relating to the implementation of one of the overarching idioms of globalization, namely 'development', as practised through the health and forestry sectors. Although all anthropological approaches possess their presuppositional difficulties and political implications we believe that different 'traces' inflect our writing, ones we wish not to elide.

In preparation for the conference on which this book is based, we read much that had been written on resistance, and for us it really was a turning away. We turned away from our original research concerns, away from our locales of research, from our commitment and work with groups working in development in Nepal, and our gaze alighted (back) onto the dominant screen upon which our research findings are to be projected. Despite a few exceptions, this movement, away from the local, away from Nepal, towards a transnational stage, must be the predominant trajectory of most research performed in Nepal by 'bideshi' (foreign) researchers. The translations that take place, linguistically, epistemologically, politically, form perhaps the last great effaced space in the process of the generation of knowledge on, and about, the 'other'—in this case Nepal. Should we not attempt to turn our gaze onto some of these translations, to unpack them a little? A transnational surveillance system that charts those who have tuberculosis, how forests are managed, and how the various actors 'resist' these machinations of the state may be more closely related and intertwined than we would like to admit. Michael Taussig, always a challenging, if not polemical, transnational academic posed the following question, at a keynote address at a conference on 'Violence and resistance in the Americas' in 1989, and it is a question whose force we acknowledge:

At which point I feel it is fair to ask about us. What do we do from this point on? Carry out more studies of other people's resistance? Surely not. For while it is crucial that the whole world be informed of injustice when it occurs, and makes injustice its concern, surely part of the concern should be with the whole Western project of self-fashioning through constructing the Third World Other as an object of study? Surely it is this project that has to be radically rethought and refunctioned? ... Resistance—always by the poor and the powerless, strikes me as running the risk of continuing the early colonial project under liberal guise made all the more deceitful ... by the appeals for an ethnographic practice that strives to grasp the natives' world view and point of view ... (Taussig 1992: 51).

Many writers now, and over the last twenty years, have started to grapple with 'resistance'. James Scott's *Weapons of the Weak* is credited as foundational for its role in highlighting the myriad ways that peasant farmers in Malaysia resist and confound supposed hegemonic formations, particularly with their 'hidden transcripts'. Scott's class analysis has been led in a number of interesting directions by a variety of scholars across disciplines: cautions against the tendency to essentialize and romanticize resistance have been added, as well as cries to add gender relations to more class-based ones (Moore 1988) as well as regionalism, ethnicity, state control—sites of intersection of power and difference where oppositional identities are articulated (Tsing 1993). Space and place are also powerful metaphors for the articulation of resistance, which always has to occur in a given time and place (Pile and Keith 1997).

There has also been a proliferation in the use of the writings of Michel Foucault in the social sciences, and the use of his notion of the micropower and biopolitics. With the discursive production of 'modern' bodies, to which the state is central, the body itself becomes the site of 'resistance' to discourses attempting to prescribe certain subjectivities, indeed it is the body that becomes the 'other' of discourse where resistance is played out (Turner 1992). It has also led to the questioning of the need for consciousness for resistance to take place. The theorist Homi Bhabha has suggested that resistance can be read as much as an effect of discourse as the conscious articulation of political intent (Bhabha 1994). This has become particularly relevant to medical anthropology and sociology where Foucault's ideas have become central in theorizing health and related fields (see for example Petersen and Bunton 1997). Of more general significance, Abu-Lughod (1990), in reversing the maxim, 'where there is domination, there is resistance', suggests that we treat resistance as a 'diagnostic of power'. This has stimulated many writers to simultaneously write about resistance and its counterpart, dominating power.

To turn to our narratives above, both the example of the theft of forest products, and the resistance of bacteria, can certainly be articulated as the direct creation of discourses. Theft would not be theft without the changed legal definition of the collecting of firewood. Without the relationship of warfare that we, as moderns, have adopted towards micro-organisms, there would be no resistance: this can only be the effect of discourse, as micro-organisms do not have consciousness. The strategies that 'elites' adopt in locales where forest user groups are set up can be seen as acts of resistance/compliance towards the state's manipulations, as can the manoeuvring that occurs by health-workers who in the process of having to closely scrutinize the outcomes of ill patients, also come under closer scrutiny themselves (not least by anthropologists). At the complex level of patients' 'compliance' with treatment, as presented in the narrative above, we doubt the usefulness of the analytic of 'resistance', and would rather not use it. In one sense behaviour that does not involve the taking of tuberculosis medicines could be 'resistance', certainly as the effect of an imposed discourse, occasionally consciously articulated. Adding to many of the cautions articulated above, if anything 'existence' rather than 'resistance' would be a more meaningful term (Scheper-Hughes 1992: 533). Certainly we are troubled by the example of the two women coerced into having to vaccinate their children with the polio vaccine, and to the possibility of coercion in taking medicines, but that is perhaps an inevitable effect of the totalizing, totalitarian objectives of any global campaign that necessitates compliance for the general and global good.

Resistance might well have appeared more salient if Harper had been researching with (or on) a reified 'ethnic' group, and if that group had perceived the health service to be controlled by another group. Then the DOTS programme might easily have been interpreted as reflecting the interests of the dominant group. Thus in a special issue of *Contributions to Nepalese Studies* in 1998 dedicated to fertility transition in Nepal—and there are a number of questions that should be asked around the political economy of the large surge of funding that has gone into researching questions around population and its control in Nepal, as much by anthropologists as demographers and others—Neidell *et al.* suggest that the 'Moslems' amongst whom they were researching tended to disregard messages around family planning as they perceived it as an arm of the Hindu state, as a way for Hindus to perpetuate their political and social dominance by limiting Moslem reproduction. The authors admit that the information they were given may indeed be the consequence of the researchers being perceived to be an arm of the state (Neidell *et al.* 1998). As a doctor, with his commitment to tuberculosis programmes, and as a foreign researcher, we feel that Harper may have been poorly placed to elicit information on 'resistance' to taking tuberculosis treatment, indicating the highly contingent and relational nature of knowledge generation. There is also a considerable difference between taking a medicine when being seriously ill, and the imposition of a practice when feeling well, as with both contraceptive uptake and vaccinations.

The situation with 'elites' in community forestry is confounding, if not also troubling, for the limitations it poses for the emancipatory aims of community forestry policy. If 'elites' have managed to position themselves so as to administer community forestry at the local level, then they have also been able to administer a silence in which the space where the 'politically disadvantaged' (the poor, landless, women, uneducated, low castes) resist their dominating power is erased, made vacuous. Meanwhile, 'theft' in community forestry provides an opportunity to explore the multiple intersections of power; where differences based on education, wealth, gender, and political/social capital overlap. 'Theft' is not just a reaction to shortage of fuelwood and other forest products. It is a product of a process of regulation of behaviours in which Kumari and others like her are marginalized from political involvement and in which their voices are silenced. In this case, 'theft' may be treated as a 'diagnostic of power', of the new space opened up for power by community forestry. In this sense community forestry produces 'theft' and has criminalized behaviour because it has the power to do so. But 'theft' is not only a resistance to a structural process of disempowerment or silencing, it is also a form of 'resistance' directed at the dominating power exercised by local 'elites' on a daily basis. It is a relational politics between those in positions of authority and power and those who are not. Local 'elites', as user group committee members making decisions about forest access, product collection, use of the user groups' considerable funds, occupy a privileged position within the realm of local politics. Nevertheless, this dominating power does not go unchallenged, even if it only takes the form of anonymous visits into the forest to 'steal' products.

As Nordstrom and Martin (1992) point out, the 'cultural logics' used in repression may be co-opted in rebellion. While local political 'elites' power is being eroded—or attempts are being made to erode their power—through the infusion of community forestry with 'democratic' institutions, 'elites' have managed to co-opt the discourse of democracy to strengthen their power. This is despite a concerted effort by several community forestry projects to stimulate a transformation of 'traditional' political processes, which are identified as corrupt, based on nepotism and favouritism, etc. In this sense, 'elite' resistance could also be interpreted as a form of 'contestatory dialogue' in which the form and product of resistance is 'made, unmade, and remade dialogically, in social, historical processes' (Kaplan and Kelly 1994: 128).

In her examination of Bedouin women's resistance to dominating power Abu-Lughod stresses that 'one way power is exercised in relation to women is through a range of prohibitions and restrictions which they both embrace ... and resist' (1990: 43). Community forestry is quite similar in this respect. Both 'elites' and the Department of Forests exercise power through setting 'prohibitions and restrictions' (defining what are and are not 'appropriate' management practices, rules, when and how much forest products can be collected, and so on). These are embraced, in support for a development programme that provides a clear advantage over the alternative—government control—and is resisted, for example, by not complying with the rules set out in operational plans (unilateral decisions made by committee members, 'misuse' of the user group's funds, 'theft'). Similarly, women and other DAG members both resist and support the systems of power within community forestry. For example, even though they recognize particular individuals as possessing a dominating power, the disempowered continue to vote for these same individuals, perpetuating their own subordination. But is this merely a form of false consciousness? To consider such an explanation, however, 'dismisses their own understanding of their situation' (Abu-Lughod 1990: 47), some of whom are more aware of it than others (or all too aware of it, perhaps).

Like Abu-Lughod (1990), we are troubled by the issue of intentionality/consciousness in acts of resistance. How can we acknowledge certain forms of resistance—such as the incidences of forest product theft described above—'without either mis-attributing to them forms of consciousness or politics that are not part of their experience ... or devaluing their practices as pre-political, primitive, or even misguided?' (Abu-Lughod 1990: 47). For example, it is difficult to interpret Kumari's 'theft' of forest products as an intentional act of resistance against the dominating power of user group committee members, or a declarative act to proclaim her marginalized/subordinate gendered status. And what of instances where TB patients resist taking their medication? How do we make sense of 'resistance' where the outcome is greater illness and certain death? As Bhabha reminds us, 'Resistance is not necessarily an oppositional act of political intention' (1985: 153).

By reading our narratives as indicative of resistance, to fit it into existing theory, as 'elites' ourselves, we also can perhaps be read as strategizing to enter into the highly competitive, and patrolled, arenas of academia. Is this what we are doing? Perhaps methodologically it is important to apply one set of analytic methods to ourselves as to others? This leads to the greatest difficulty we have with accounts of resistance, that of the privileged positionality involved as the anthropologist 'discerns the hidden meaning behind the informant's statements and practices' (Nordstrom and Martin 1992: 7). Does this lead us to adopting a position akin to Gramsci's mythical conscious elite, a superconscious revolutionary vanguard? But what are the alternative ways of conceptualizing such acts? Either it isn't 'resistance' unless consciously done, or highly/overtly 'organized', or we're left with the paralysis derived from a 'crisis of representation'. Ortner (1995) criticized many writers of and on resistance for what she calls 'ethnographic refusal', the need for more attention to detail, to holism, to thickness. She says that there is a tendency to refuse to see any internal conflict in groups reified as being dominated, which leads to a tendency to romanticize. Culture is often ignored, particularly religion. Subjects also tend to be dissolved as complex questions of agency are sidelined as the 'analytic by-product' of resistance. Although we may agree with many of her points, indeed her criticism can be turned around onto us, she never questions her own access, as an anthropologist, to knowing the deeper meaning within the uncritical reification of the groups she studies. For much of our research we were marginal (how could we be otherwise?): how, therefore, can we claim some kind of privileged access to wholeness, or to the truth of resistance, or anything for that matter?

Anthropological texts on 'resistance', and its counterpart 'power', have proliferated in the last twenty years in a transglobal anthropological literature—mostly written in English, it should be noted. From our reading of literature on resistance, 'resistance' has come to occupy its position(s) in theory through a shift from its initial articulation in terms of large-scale, highly organized movements of political resistance, to include a more nebulous, more all-pervasive facet of human experience. Lately, or so it seems to us, almost any reaction to change of any kind could be construed as resistance, such that the meaning of the term has diffused into an essentialized component of human nature, allowing nearly any researcher (including ourselves, here) the opportunity to document it. But what are the consequences when 'resistance' becomes a commonplace in our research? What happens when, as Latour writes, 'There is no difference between the "real" and the "unreal", the "real" and the "possible", the "real" and the "imaginary". Rather, there are all the differences experienced between those that resist for long and those that do not, those that resist courageously and those that do not, those that know how to ally or isolate themselves and those that do not' (Latour 1993b: 159). A similar shift has occurred with regard to human rights and the tendency to treat nearly everything as a fundamental human right (for example, we have recently read in a newspaper in Nepal that access to development should be viewed as a fundamental human right). The movement to reading almost everything as resistance seems to us to make the term all but meaningless. This leads us to wonder on the proliferations on the writings on resistance, which seems to have arisen around the same time as the 'crisis of representation'. Dare we suggest that this represents a tendency to redemption within anthropology, an atonement for our past sins? We note the ease with which the movement towards resistance has occurred after a number of criticisms of the discipline. Could this not be the path of least resistance for the most resistant of all, namely us as anthropologists? Is this movement all too comfortable and easy?

Where does that leave us? Had we approached the subject of resistance to the state through a particular reified group, through the politics of identity, or language, which has become so fashionable within the sciences of the social, then undoubtedly our perspective would be quite different. Our point is not to say that this is wrong, or that it is not complete, only that there remains the trace of any previous engagement, of the history of a discipline, that has tended to ignore the state as an entity; when it is introduced, the state brings with it, we would suggest, a negative metaphysics of power, of repression, and there may be a tendency to overdetermine this. After all, we never just reveal the facts as they are, without them being defracted through our methods, including the theoretical. We are as wary of overdetermining the boundaries of theoretical terms like 'resistance' and the 'state', as we are of concepts such as 'caste' or other groups. We would like to be wary, as Derrida warned, although he was talking of approaching philosophy armed with certain concepts (in our case, with 'resistance' and 'state') that have been '... determined or overburdened with reminiscences of a long problematical tradition, but also with a speculative grid in which the classical figure of an antagonism is apparent from the start, then the operative debate which one prepares to undertake from within this philosophy, or on the basis of it, is in danger of appearing not to be not so much an attentive scrutiny as a putting into question, that is, an abusive investigation which introduces before hand what it seeks to find, and does violence proper to a body of thought. No doubt to treat a philosophy by introducing the foreign substance of a debate may be efficacious, may surrender or set free the meaning of a latent process, but it begins with an aggression and an infidelity. We must not forget this' (Derrida, 1997: 154).

Where, though, such a deconstructive turn will lead us, we are unsure. Unfortunately not to stable ground, and certainly to more politicized spaces. These are certainly challenging times to become involved in anthropology.

REFERENCES

Abu-Lughod, L. 1990. 'The Romance of Resistance: Tracing Transformations of Power through Bedouin Women' *American Ethnologist* 17(1): 41–55.

Adams, V. 1998. *Doctors for Democracy: Health Professionals in the Nepal Revolution*. Cambridge: Cambridge University Press.

Arnold, J.E.M. 1991. *Community Forestry: Ten Years in Review*. Rome: Food and Agriculture Organization of the United Nations.

Bajracharya, D. 1983. 'Deforestation in the Food/Fuel Context: Historical and Political Perspectives from Nepal' *Mountain Research and Development* 3(3): 227–240.

Bhabha, H. 1985 'Signs taken for wonders: questions of ambivalence and authority under a tree outside Delhi, May 1817,' *Critical Inquiry* 21(1): 124–55.

——— 1994. 'Signs taken for Wonders' in Bhabha *The Location of Culture*. London and New York: Routledge.

Bista, D.B. 1991. *Fatalism and Development: Nepal's Struggle for Modernization*. Calcutta: Orient Longman.

Burch, W.R.J. and D.A. Messerschmidt 1990. 'An Assessment of the Master Plan for the Forestry Sector, Nepal' (IOF Project Discussion Paper No. DP90/1). Nepal: Office of Agriculture and Rural Development.

Chaisson R., J. Coberly, and K. De Cock 1999. 'Editorial: DOTS and Drug Resistance: A Silver Lining to a Darkening Cloud' *Int J Tuberc Lung Dis* 3(1): 1–3.

Chaulk, P. 1999. 'Editorial: Tuberculosis Elimination and the Challenge of the Long Term Completer' *Int J Tuberc Lung Dis* 3(5): 363–4.

Coberly, J. 2000. 'We Cannot Eliminate TB on One Continent: TB Crosses Borders' www.hopkins_tb.org/tb_conf/tb_conf_4.html

Derrida, J. 1997 [1978]. '"Genesis and Structure" and Phenomenology' in Derrida *Writing and Difference*. London: Routledge.

FAO 1978. *Forestry for Local Community Development* (FAO Forestry Paper No. 7). Rome: Food and Agriculture Organization of the United Nations.

Foucault, M. 1978. *The History of Sexuality. Vol. 1: An Introduction*. New York: Random House.

Garrett, L. 1994. *The Coming Plague: Newly Emerging Diseases in a World Out of Balance*. Penguin.

Gilmour, D.A., and R.J. Fisher 1991. *Villagers, Forests and Foresters: The Philosophy, Process and Practice of Community Forestry in Nepal*. Kathmandu: Sahayogi Press.

Haraway D. 1997. *Modest_Witness@Second_Millenium.FemaleMan_Meets_OncoMouse*. New York and London: Routledge.

His Majesty's Government, Nepal 1991. *The Community and Private Forestry Pragramme in Nepal*. Kathmandu: Ministry of Forest and Environment, Forest Department, Community Forestry Development Division.

——— 1992. *Operational Guidelines of the Community Forestry Programme*. Second edition. Kathmandu: Ministry of Forest and Environment, Forest Department, Community Forestry Development Division.

Justice, J. 1986. *Policies, Plans, and People: Culture and Health Development in Nepal.* Berkeley: University of California Press.

Kaplan, M. and J. Kelly 1994. 'Rethinking Resistance: Dialogics of 'Disaffection' in Colonial Fiji' *American Ethnologist* **21**(1): 123–51.

Latour, B. 1993a. *We Have Never Been Modern.* New York: Harvester Wheatsheaf.

——— 1993b. *The Pasteurization of France.* Cambridge and London: Harvard University Press

Mahat, T.B.S., D.M. Griffin, and K.R. Shepherd 1986. 'Human Impact on Some Forests of the Middle Hills of Nepal. Part 1: Forestry in the Context of the Traditional Resources of the State' *Mountain Research and Development* **6**(3): 223–32.

——— 1988. 'Human Impact on Some Forests of the Middle Hills of Nepal. Part 5: Comparisons, Concepts, and Some Policy Implications' *Mountain Research and Development* **8**(1): 43–52.

Maskarinec, G. 1995. *The Rulings of the Night: An Ethnography of Nepalese Shaman Oral Texts.* Madison: University of Wisconsin Press.

Moore, D.S. 1997. 'Remapping Resistance: "Ground for Struggle" and the Politics of Place' in Pile and Keith (eds), pp. 87–106.

Moore, H. 1988. *Feminisism and Anthropology.* Cambridge: Polity Press.

NAFP 1979. *Nepal's National Forestry Plan 1976 (2033)* (unofficial English translation). Kathmandu: Nepal-Australia Forestry Project.

Neher, A., G. Breyer, B. Shrestha, and K. Feldmann 1996. 'Directly Observed Intermittent Short-course Chemotherapy in the Kathmandu valley' *Tubercle and Lung Disease* **77**: 302–7.

Neidell, S., B. Niraula, S. Morgan, and S. Stash 1998. 'Moslem and Non-Moslem Fertility Differences in the Eastern Terai of Nepal' *Contributions to Nepalese Studies (Special Issue on Fertility)*: 109–28.

Nordstrom, C. and J. Martin (eds) 1992. *The Paths to Domination, Resistance, and Terror.* Berkeley: University of California Press.

NTP and HMG/N 1999. 'Tuberculosis Control in Nepal 2055–2060 (1998–2003): Long Term Plan'.

Ogden, J., S. Rangan, M. Uplekar, J. Porter, R. Brugha, A. Zwi, and D. Nyheim 1999. 'Shifting the Paradigm in Tuberculosis Control: Illustrations from India' *Int J Tuberc Lung Dis* **3**(10): 855–61.

——— 1999. 'Compliance versus Adherance: Just a Matter of Language. The Politics and Poetics of Public Health' in Porter and Grange (eds).

Onazaki, I. and T. Shakya 1995. 'Feasibility Study of a District Tuberculosis Control Programme with an 8-month Short-course Chemotherapy Regimen Utilizing Integrated Health Service Network under Field Conditions in Nepal' *Tubercle and Lung Disease* **75**: 65–71.

Ortner, S. 1995. 'Resistance and the Problem of Ethnographic Refusal' *Comparative Studies in Society and History* **37**: 173–93.

Osborne, T. 1997. 'Of Health and Statecraft' in A. Petersen and R. Bunton (eds).

Panos and WHO 2000. 'Airborne Killers' (adapted from WHO report 1996) in K. Dixit, A. John, and R. Gupta (eds) *TB Do or Die: Journalists Take a Look at how Asian Countries are Fighting Tuberculosis.* Kathmandu: Panos and WHO.

Petersen, A. and R. Bunton (eds) 1997. *Foucault, Health and Medicine.* London and New York: Routledge.

Pigg, S.L. 1996. 'The Credible and the Credulous: The Question of Villagers Beliefs in Nepal' *Cultural Anthropology* 11(2): 160–201.

_____ 1997. '"Found in Most Traditional Societies": Traditional Medical Practitioners between Culture and Development' in F. Cooper and R. Packard (eds) *International Development and the Social Sciences: Essays on the History and Politics of Knowledge.* Berkeley: University of California Press.

Pile, S. and M. Keith (eds) 1997. *Geographies of Resistance.* New York: Routledge.

Porter, J. and J. Grange (eds) 1999. *Tuberculosis: An Interdisciplinary Perspective.* London: Imperial College Press.

Regmi, R. 1999. *Dimensions of Nepali Society and Culture.* Kathmandu: Modern Printing Press.

Ryan, K. 1992. *Tuberculosis: The Greatest Story Never Told.* Bromsgrove: Swift Publishers

Scheper-Hughes, N. 1992. *Death Without Weeping: The Violence of Everyday Life in Brazil.* Berkeley: University of California Press.

Scott, J.C. 1985. *Weapons of the Weak: Everyday Forms of Peasant Resistance.* New Haven: Yale University Press.

_____ 1986. 'Everyday Forms of Peasant Resistance,' in J.C. Scott and B.J. Tria Kerkvilet (eds) *Everyday Forms of Peasant Resistance in South-east Asia.* London: Frank Cass and Co.

Sleigh, J. and M. Timbury 1982. *Notes on Medical Bacteriology.* Edinburgh: Churchill Livingstone.

Small, P. 1999. 'Tuberculosis in the 21st Century: DOTS and SPOTS' *Int J Tuberc Lung Dis* 3(10): 855–61.

Taussig, M. 1992. *The Nervous System.* London: Routledge.

_____ 1997. *The Magic of the State.* New York and London: Routledge.

Tsing, A. 1993. *In the Realm of the Diamond Queen.* Princeton: Princeton University Press.

Turner, B. 1992. *Regulating Bodies: Essays in Medical Sociology.* London and New York: Routledge.

Walt, G. 1999. 'The Politics of Tuberculosis: The Role of Process and Power' in Porter and Grange (eds).

Wares, F. 2000. 'Have TB will Travel' in Dixit *et al.* (eds). (See Panos, above).

WHO 1994. 'TB: A Global Emergency—WHO Report on the TB Epidemic' WHO/TB/94.177

——— 1995. 'WHO Report on the Tuberculosis Epidemic 1995' WHO/TB/ 95.183

——— 1997. 'WHO Report on the Tuberculosis Epidemic 1997'. WHO/TB/ 97.224

——— 1998. 'TB Advocacy: A Practical Guide 1999' WHO/TB/98.239

——— 2000. www.who.int/inf-pr-2000/en/pr2000-19.html.

World Bank 1993. *World Development Report 1993: Investing in Health*. Oxford University Press.

——— 1999. *Entering the 21st century: World Development Report 1999/2000*. Oxford University Press.

chapter two

Resisting the Environmentalist State

• *Ben Campbell*

INTRODUCTION

With the growth over the last thirty years of international environmental concerns in practices of governance, programmes designed to address environmental degradation have become increasingly important dimensions of statecraft and civil society mobilization. In Nepal it has perhaps been through environmental programmes that the intervention of the state into rural communities of the periphery has been most directly experienced, generating conflicts and debate over appropriate management regimes. Communities and state institutions have had to respond in this time to the effects of changing national and international environmental policy paradigms (Ives & Messerli 1989, Gilmour & Fisher 1991, Fisher & Gilmour 1999, Guthman 1997). There has been a shift from top-down, heavy-handed, 'government knows best' conservation approaches, such as forest nationalization in the 1950s, and national parks since the 1970s, to the adoption of seemingly people-friendly approaches, partly inspired by an international mood more favourable to perceptions of indigenous environmental wisdom. But, apart from the question of how much things have really changed on the ground as a result of policy shifts (in terms of both bio-physical conditions and participatory inclusion), many fundamental anthropological issues of environmental governmentality have hardly been raised, despite decades of social-scientific research on the environment. This chapter raises two main questions. What transformations in concepts of agency and legitimate domains of intervention are entailed in the state inserting itself in aspects of everyday rural society that historically were of little or no interest to it? And, second, are the models of human-environment relationships in Himalayan communities that have been offered up to now adequate to explain these communities' resistance to the state's environmental surveillance?

Since the 1990s a series of studies from across Nepal have documented socio-economic, political, and cultural impacts of nature conservation regimes on various communities (Brower 1991, Cameron 1995, Shrestha and Conway 1996, Diemberger 1996, Ghimire 1992, Graner 1999, Müller-Böker 1995, Stevens 1993). These studies have for the most part focused on the political economy of class and ethnic differentiation regarding land shortage, on conflict with environmental security forces over customary entitlements to forest produce, and on disruptions to local resource management systems caused by state intervention. As yet there has been little attempt to apply new theoretical directions in ecological anthropology to environmental management in Nepal. One strand of theory taken up here is Ingold's 'dwelling perspective' (Ingold 1992, 1996, 2000) which approaches human-ecological engagement in a way that moves beyond the nature/society separation inherent both in the conventional anthropological concept of 'culturally constructed environments', and in strict protection policy. It will be argued here that the modernist opposition between nature and society introduced through environmental programmes is resisted through a variety of everyday practices and counter-discourses. The problem with Ingold's dwelling perspective is that it does not easily lend itself to contexts of conflict and resistance. The other strand of theory referred to in this chapter is a Foucauldian critique of discourses of environmental governmentality. Rutherford argues that '[r]egulatory ecological science does not so much describe the environment as constitute it as an object of knowledge and, through various modes of positive intervention, manage and police it' (1999: 56). This latter approach has been developed primarily in relation to the role of expert knowledge in the regulation of environmental problems of industrialized countries, but with significant modification it is clearly relevant to the context of global conservation rationales in countries, like Nepal, that presume certain credentials for the state as an authoritative environmental actor.

RESISTING THE ARTIFICE OF NATURE

In contrast to the passion for resistance that the Himalayan environment has inspired among social movements and academics in India,[1] the environment in Nepal has occupied a very different discursive and political field. Whether for reasons of political history, relations of environmental capital extraction, or conditions of agrarian society, the environment in Nepal has not constituted a focus for generalized socio-political critique, around which diverse social forces have found a rallying cause. There is nonetheless a story of resistance to tell that is not so much about a visible public resistance of tree-hugging against logging, as a dogged persistance of the marginalized poor in continuing to live and act as much as possible away from visibility and environmental surveillance. In response to Ortner's call for ethnographic complexity in accounts of resistance (Ortner 1995), I attempt here to present perceptions from the dominated to explain why environmentalist credentials claimed by state institutions are resisted, and to explore alternative formulations of 'a group's locally and historically evolved bricolage' (Ortner 1995: 176) in respect to understandings of the state's legitimacy in environmental affairs.

In 1976 the Langtang National Park was created, straddling Rasuwa and Sindhu-Palchok districts to protect a representative section of the central Himalaya. The immediate effect on local communities was the criminalization of subsistence skilled practice in the production and exchange of forest products, hunting, pasture burning, and swidden (shifting agriculture). In Rasuwa District the predominantly Tamang-speaking population's semi-autonomous traditions of political society have historically had to accommodate and service the state's presence and demands. Recent research by Holmberg, March, and Tamang has discussed Tamang resistance to extractive state labour and natural resource provision through their socio-ritual complex (Holmberg *et al.* 1999, Holmberg 2000). Here I want to emphasize the practical ontologies of Tamang dwelling and oral accounts of historical memory that counter, tacitly and explicitly, the current regime of nature protection.

There is not the space here to wander in much detail along the forest pathways (*ri gyam*), crags (*blee*), pasture openings (*kharka*), and treeless upland ranges (*naangye*) that the Tamang communities

[1]See Guha (1991) and Shiva (1989) for classic positions, and Linkenbach (2000) and Sinha *et al.* (1997) for critical reviews.

of the Langtang National Park know as 'our own place' (*nyang ki lungba*). It is lived in as a highly mobile criss-crossing of repeatedly shifting residence in animal-human shelters *godi* (Np. *goth*). Territorial vertical extensivity rather than settled intensity is the pattern of productive livelihoods. The vertical axis is a common leitmotif of songs and ritual chants that draw on themes of biotic polarity, as between the yak and water buffalo, or the juniper and the palm. Most villagers spend little time in their houses, which are used mostly as stores and for ceremonial entertainment. Movement and dispersal in the surrounding environment of scattered field-holdings of different altitudes in conjunction with livestock gives a constantly shifting quality to social emplacement and displacement.

When I discussed with a senior lama of Tengu village his memory of swidden cultivations (*mrangshing phyeeba*), he rolled off a series of place names indicating their location above the altitude of the majority of current permanent terraced fields. He said where there were tall trees on sites selected for swidden, these would be cut down and when dry the branches were set fire to. He remembered mostly potatoes being planted for two or three years in succession before leaving the site to fallow. He went on to talk about ownership of the forest:

In olden days this forest was called 'Kalo Ban'. Then afterwards it became national forest. It was called 'Kalo Ban' because it looked black ['dark']. There were not many people in those days. There was no Forest Department. In olden times the king had not made it government forest. It was all private (*niji*) forest.

He recalled, as evidence of local control of the forest, that around the time of the election in VS 2017 (1959) a dispute occurred with the community of Yersa over possession of high boundary pastures which was won by the chiefs of Dhunche. Fights and livestock raiding from both sides are remembered by the older generation. Chiefs (*mukhiyā*) defended boundaries, and used their coordination of collective cattle transhumance as a means of asserting territorial rights, regulating seasonal pasture access, and protecting standing crops. But although open access to forest resources for village community members was reported, the state did have a significant presence in the form of royal dairy cattle herds that passed through the high pastures every year, and villagers were called on to supply corvée labour for manufacture of equipment, shelter, and porterage. Holmberg *et al.* (1999) have calculated the demands of the state for this labour alone on households of a Tamang village in Nuwakot, just a few miles away on the western slope of the Trisuli river, to have been roughly 90 days annually.

Small-scale commercial timber processing went on into the lama's early adulthood in the 1960s. Wood contractors came from Kathmandu who offered specific wage rates for loads carried by Tamang villagers all the way to Sorakhutte (on the northern edge of Thamel, Kathmandu), some four or five days' walk. Categories of *kānchi, sāili, māili,* and *jethi* loads gathered Rs 9, 10, 12, and 15 respectively in VS 2025/6 (1968). Children and women would carry four wooden planks at a time, really strong men could manage seven. The Tamang were also involved in the production and porterage of pine resin (*tangshing ki tango*). They cut sections of the pine treetrunk with an axe and gathered the resin over three or four days into tins of four *pāthi* volume. Back then one such tin would be worth Rs 15 or 16. The lama had heard these days the value is more like Rs 1000.

Forest and alpine plants were important medicinal resources for exchange in the merchants' shops of Trisuli Bazaar (a well-known entrepot for trade in Ayurvedic medicine). I was given a list of seven principal plants which were sold there, before the park's ban on such trade. In addition, a barter system exchanging equal measures with husked rice operated for *thulo ohodi* (*astilbe rivularis*), *breḷ* (*bergenia ciliata*), and *takpa* (Himalayan paper birch, *betula utilis D. Don*).

With this historical background of both market-led and state-enforced forest utilization, the turn-around of state policy toward conservation, that involves banning forest product exchange, and instituting bureaucratic licensing of forest resources even for subsistence reproduction, is deeply resented, and evaded when the need arises. Under contemporary park regulations for domestic timber provision a cubit system of value calculation is made, well beyond the means of most families' financial capacity. The key Tamang idiom and tactic for regulatory evasion is *amrangnale*, 'without being seen': for instance waiting till after dark to drag bamboo loads downhill from sites with difficult access unlikely to be frequented by park officials; and secreting precious items out of view. The risk of jail is part of this defiant provisioning, but informed knowledge of officials' daily practice and their habit of never wanting to stray beyond the main trails makes entrapment a low probability. Even when formal procedures are followed by villagers for licensed timber felling of substantial quantities, it has been my experience that the officials complain vociferously if villagers have identified a suitable tree more than a short stroll away. *Ma māthi jāndaina!* ('I'm not going up there!') I heard one of the officials say.

Another incident was particularly instructive of the manner in which forest provisioning has now to be presented in an appearance of legal conformity. In a village not far from park headquarters, a passing senior park official noticed a Tamang carrying a solid section of a whole tree trunk on his back. The man and his load were impounded at the headquarters, with accompanying threats of severe justice. The offender was a hired herder from outside the park limits, unfamiliar with the necessary presentational skills of surviving park surveillance. Dead and fallen branches are permitted for fuelwood collection, but this case of evident felling was too blatant to be seen in public. The culprit's employer, a local village lodge-keeper, would have to pay several thousand rupees fine and was incensed that his herder had not chopped and split the tree trunk into unremarkable logs. The lodge-keeper's own brother-in-law fortunately had good relations with the park hierarchy and negotiated for a reduced fine, along with a promise of such an event not being repeated. People with such connections and financial resources are far more able to circumvent the letter of the law for conservation enforcement.

Apart from forest products, it is the impact of increasing numbers of wildlife that most concerns villagers of the entire national park. The extent of crop damage and livestock predation by a wide range of animals can severely affect harvest yields, and the limited opportunities for cash sales of surplus potatoes and domestic animals. Extra demands are put on stretched family labour to guard the dispersed locations of ripening crops, which tends to impact most on the poor who cannot sustain large household sizes or afford hired herders. The combative relationship with thieving wildlife is a prevalent feature in Tamang oral narratives of animal characteristics and behaviour (Campbell 2000).[2] Revisiting my fieldwork diary entries, I am reminded of the

[2]The injustice of protecting animal species that threaten underprivileged communities' livelihoods is not simply a matter of clammering, unfed mouths. There is a profound cultural violence performed by elevating animal over (specific groups') human rights in this version of nature/society opposition. During my research on crop and livestock losses it became clear that though conservation measures were indeed experienced as punitive and unwarranted given their indiscriminate protection of all species, there was more at stake than the criminalization of livelihood practices (hunting, burning, and exchange of forest products). This could be seen as a denial of the very 'phenomenological unity' (Viveiros de Castro 1998) across the animal-human divide that sustains notions of identity, meaningful difference, and relationship. Extra-human sociality is a theme that has characterized recent ecological anthropologists' thinking (Descola's 1996 and Bird-David's 1999 reassessment of animism, Rival 1998, etc.). Relations between species (as between clans, and castes) are characterized

frequency with which at the end of a day visiting dispersed herding encampments, people made use of my return to the village settlement to inform a neighbouring fieldowner of wild boars eating their finger millet, or similar dangers. Once, leaving an encampment in mid-December moonlight after a meal, I asked my host if I should worry about encountering bears on the track. No, he said, the bears were not around any longer as they had gone off into forest caves, having finished all the finger millet.

As a measure for helping villagers against wild boars invading croplands, hunters from the Department of National Parks and Wildlife Conservation periodically stay in villages of the park. However, their hunting competence is not highly rated (compared to their capacity for food and drink), and when I asked them if they also cull the large numbers of monkeys, they simply replied 'Do you eat monkey meat?' The hunting is thus more a continuation of game pursuit for privileged kinds of meat than a systematic operation for control of agricultural pests. Choice animal parts (thighs and head) are distributed to park officials and army personnel, the remainder being partitioned equally among villagers. Development programmes are available to the villagers for agronomic development designed to offset the subsistence costs of nature protection, such as in 1997 through a Danish-backed NGO. Yet, the project workers professed inability to address the key issue of animal damage, when this was raised as the main cause of low yields. Direct compensation for animal damage has been ruled out as a policy. During a discussion of balancing the interests of park and people, a Nepali worker from another NGO supporting a buffer zone initiative informed me that at the levels of park hierarchy such as ranger there was simply no interest in local people's concerns, just the one 'ideology' of protection.

Advocates of global biodiversity protection might argue that the regulatory measures discussed above are necessary to halt the loss of species and threatened habitat, and that the Tamangs' unseen defiances ought to be extinguished. However, the arguments and accounts of events articulated by Tamang park residents do not suggest a picture of an environmentally (or politically) conscious institutional culture within the park organization, or indeed of any active gathering of

---

in Tamang oral narratives and mythical accounts by communicative dispute over their difference. The Tamang make this explicit, in contrast to the dis-engaged, de-socialized vision of nature held by conservationists (Campbell 1998).

biodiversity relevant knowledge. There is in fact no 'scientific' facil-
ity within the park (IUCN 1993). An American Peace Corps soil
conservationist working in the district commented that the park
was 'a dead loss, they don't do anything'. It was 'all political'. Talking
with a local supplier of food and stores to the park administration, I
enquired whether kerosene was used by its officials to reduce wood
consumption. 'They don't use kerosene, *nikunja*! ('the park')', he
replied, in a self-explanatory way. They preach but don't practise conservation. Villagers have limitless stories of unwarranted officiousness,
harrassment, and bribe-seeking. One, a former peon employee of the
park, told me of patrolling with the warden and being sent to find
local girls for him. However, the extreme rarity of seeing park patrols
off main trails means that knowledge of local biodiversity distribution is probably far greater among villagers than officials. Non-Tamang
park officials couldn't even identify the commonest weeds. When I
asked if anyone had seen the rarest mammal in the park, the red panda,
villagers were able to describe it with evidence of directly observed
knowledge. They said the *upi* does not damage crops or livestock. It
stays around bamboo groves, climbs trees, and is mostly nocturnal.
They thought that the park is not aware of it being about in their
forest, for if this was known, high herding encampments of *chauri*
(Tm. *yaa godi*) would probably be prohibited.[3]

At the time of writing (2001), it is three years since I have been
back to find out if satisfactory negotiations have been conducted to
set up village management committees to take on legitimized usufruct
rights over forest 'buffer zones' under the UNDP's Park-People programme. The strategy for this attempt at 'participatory conservation'
is, however, skewed towards a bureaucratized form of stakeholder
inclusion. This programme assumes that constitutions, management
plans, and revenue incentives will be perceived as conferring state-
recognized access rights that will bring on board disgruntled villagers,
and put an end to age-old practices of direct engagements with what
Ingold calls 'environmental affordances'. That such a mediation of
people's environmental interactions has, in the communities familiar
to me in the park, been met with non-compliance suggests 'resistance',
but strategies for opposition are not so much directly confrontational.
Rather they involve manoeuvres in the field of state complexity and
its lack of coordination. In 1998, the first discussions about user group

---

[3]Yonzon's study of the red panda was conducted in the northern section of
the park (see Fox, Yonzon, and Podger 1996).

constitutions within the park had brought up the problem that villagers wanted to register not with the park warden but with the Chief District Officer, seen as more democratically accountable. This clearly illustrates how manipulating the institutional departmentalization of the state can be an avenue for resistance against organs of the state less disposed to negotiation, and reflects the fact that local people have to face up to institutionally heterogeneous aspects of the state's presence in peripheral areas. Contradictory messages are given out by offices for the competing national interests of biodiversity protection, tourism, dairy development, agriculture, and health.[4]

In Rasuwa District this diversity of state officialdom only become part of the local scene in the early 1970s when Dhunche became an administrative centre after the division of Nuwakot into three separate districts. Prior to this, older villagers speaking of occasions when *sarkār* came through their locale conveyed a sense of central authority appearing in either almost magical or dramatic incidents. Jang Bahadur killed a tiger at Bokhajunda; the army kept a weapons store at Godam field; huge rope hunting-nets were ordered to be made for trapping live game to carry off to Kathmandu. The older generation all said that as children they were instructed by their parents to run away at the first sight of approaching state officials. Resistance to contemporary state environmental policies has to be set against this background of local memory and evasionary skills learnt from childhood, and yet the regulatory regime derives its rationale from decontextualized global agendas for biodiversity conservation. The model for participatory conservation being prepared for the mountain regions of Nepal has been piloted first in the Tarai since the mid-1990s. Its source is a global generic design of the Park-People programme for giving poor people some access to the revenue benefits of protected areas. Within this intervention policy, histories of state-community relations affecting particular regions, countries, or for that matter colonial legacies, do not feature in how the politics of biodiversity are being thought of, favouring a de-politicized environmental managerialism (Brosius 1999b). It is necessary to turn to historical and cultural analyses to appreciate how state institutions and representatives have made claims to and imagined what is now perceived as the dilemma of 'the environment'.

[4]See Saberwal (1999) for an excellent historical account of conflict between the Forest and Revenue Departments in Himachal Pradesh over evidence for degradation, and associated policies towards Gaddi shepherds.

DEALING WITH 'THE DILEMMA' IN NEPAL

Julie Guthman provides an insightful deconstruction of the contradictory emergence of the Nepalese state's environmentalism. Reminding us of the pre-modern polity's project of selective forest politics, she recalls that '[a]t least as far back as the sixteenth century, the state created incentives to convert hill forests to agriculture in order to reap land taxes, but protected the *Terai* (fertile lowlands) forests as military security until the late nineteenth century' (Guthman 1997: 47). Till around 1973, right up to the end of the 'modernization' era of development regimes in Nepal, 'natural resources existed primarily to be exploited' (ibid.: 53). When the theory of Himalayan environmental degradation ('The Theory') came to the fore as the primary perceptual filter of rural realities in Nepal, linking population growth with deforestation, it was as a hugely effective legitimizing discourse for state eco-intervention. As Guthman points out, though, the formulation of the theory 'did not particularly inspire a *more adequate conceptualization of human-environmental interactions*, but instead created a compelling polemic to justify certain interventions' (ibid.: 47; my emphasis). The structures of the state were not brought into question by Eckholm's (1976) account of crisis, who instead 'saw the state as a critical architect of the necessary solutions .... The "fact" of systematic environmental destruction gave one more way for development agencies to intervene under the aegis of meeting basic needs' (Guthman 1997: 57). The crisis was not so much to do with biophysical reality but was socially constructed, or, in the words of Thompson, Hatley, and Wharburton, 'generated *by* institutions *for* institutions' (1988). The kind of environmental 'knowledge' produced under the crisis was inherently an exercise of power in bringing into perception generalized causal linkages between demographic growth, forest depletion, and poverty, while making invisible the attendant power relations. The Theory supported 'a slew of preservation and conservation (such as afforestation) measures, many of which were at best ineffective and, at worst, wrested control from local resource users to the detriment of the very resource base they were designed to protect' (Guthman 1997: 63).

The subsequent responses to the inadequacies of paradigmatic environmental knowledge contained in the theory of Himalayan environmental degradation have been, at least in rhetoric, searching among the fragments of theoretical fallout for essentially pragmatic solutions. In the heyday of The Theory peasant ignorance was paramount. Since the mid-1980s, however, peasants have been regarded as the unavoidable vehicles of meaningful change in paradigms for environmental protection through various versions of 'co-operation', whether as community forestry user groups, or as committee-coordinated conservation area residents.[5] Participation, process, plurality of stakeholders, and buffer zones are the key words in the post-Theory fumbling for eco-legitimacy. While local environmental knowledge is lauded in principle, power—except the opportunity to emulate bureaucratic procedures for specified rewards—remains fundamentally non-negotiable (Campbell forthcoming b).[6]

In the absence of manifest state environmental competence, a space presents itself to be filled by new anthropological thinking on human-environmental relations. For decades the cultural diversity and/or relative village autonomy of Nepalese rural society have been commented on. For some this has been a cause of regret: that, for instance, national economic integration has been thereby impeded (Schrader 1988). Perhaps, though, the environmental implications of discrete rural universes have been little appreciated. In the literature on Nepal the issue of autonomous community organization has been most explicit in discussions of the east Nepali form of communal land tenure known as *kipat*, which was abolished formally in the early 1960s at the time of Land Reform (Caplan 2000: 197–212).

A recent article by Ann Forbes, based on material from the Yamphu, a Rai sub-group, continues this debate with considerable insights for theorizing environmental articulations with power and the politics of place more generally. Forbes gives an account of a land dispute that invokes narratives of community history and agency.

[5]Critics of community forestry in Nepal include Elvira Graner (1999) who has identified property-based exclusions from claims to user group membership in Sindhu-Palchok. Meanwhile Bina Agarwal (1997) notes how in India committee membership is replacing citizenship as the defining criterion for establishing rights in the commons.

[6]Gilmour and Fisher comment that 'there are serious questions about bureaucratic culture and power that throw doubt on the viability of implementing community forestry through the bureaucracy' (1991: 181). Despite the participatory rhetoric, the 'traditional' forestry paradigm continues in many places. '[T]here are fundamental differences in the institutional framework (or culture) within which the bureaucracy operates, and the institutions which are the framework of action and decision making in villages.' Government officials and professional foresters assume 'a vacuum of knowledge and institutional capacity in rural communities', and that local social organization can only be recognized in the form of committees (1991: 182).

According to one of the protagonists 'kipat meant that the Kiranti could do what they wanted on their own lands; it meant having their own wish (*aphno kushi*) ... holding on to kipat thus came to mean holding on to the power of autonomy' (1999: 115). Although apparently seen as a threat to national integrity, the loyalty to the kingdom and the payment of taxes depended on the power that headmen could exercise over their tenant farmers. These headmen were left alone in the nineteenth century because the king was 'too busy to intervene'. 'According to the Yamphu headmen and subjects with whom I spoke, the most important features of the kipat system included unmarked boundaries around fields and a system of land tenure based on the categorization of people, not land' (ibid.: 116). '[R]ights to kipat lands depended more on the relationship among users and on the resource in question than they did on any fixed rules of tenure' (ibid.: 118).

Forbes locates her narrative in discussions about the weakening of national boundaries in the globalization of culture, which 'may allow for a resurgence of local identities attached to local places' (ibid.: 116). Her interpretation of the continuing meaning of *kipat* in contests over land is one that involves 'the relationship between identity and the land' (ibid.: 117).

[T]he passion the Yamphu feel about their land and the anger that propels them through the disputes has to do with more than securing a livelihood. Holding on to inherited land is a way of carrying on a father's legacy, a way of remembering ancestors' labor on the land, a way of upholding their place in the family lineage. Land rights express the web of social relations in time and space, and the land itself expresses the character of the household members through the quality and care with which they farm. The hours and energy invested in the soil are evident in the harvest. This time and labor is invested to provide enough food for one's family, but land is also a way of securing one's place in the social and physical landscape, literally, a foothold in the world. It is the one place where villagers can do things their own way on their own land, where they can still be kings on their own land .... It is this agency and autonomy that the Yamphu express in the concept of kipat (Forbes 1999: 122).

The transition from collective *kipat* to private *raikar* tenure entails a shift from being able to hold as much land as can be made use of, to a situation where only what is surveyed and registered in individuals' names holds weight. Forests and pastures in particular thus came to be considered government land.

For the time being, villagers continue to use these lands according to previous conceptions of ownership, but individuals no longer have any legal claim to them. Through the recently created Makalu-Barun National Park and the Department of Forests, the central government (not neighbors and other users of the resource) is now the community that will determine the conditions under which these individuals will be able to continue to use these unsurveyed resources (Forbes 1999: 129).

This account neatly expresses the problem of distinguishing ownership and control. A parallel regime of practice operates in a fragile countering to the new formal arrangements of legality. Control in the sense of use and engagement is technically de-legitimized but not effectively displaced. Yet the compelling ontology of 'natural' rights to land derived from ongoing practices of social life and collective identity remains, according to Forbes, a matter of continuing enactment

because of the way villagers use and conceive of the land in the present, not because of some inherent relationship between identity and land .... In the process of securing their claim to the land, disputants also create a particular 'phenomenological property of social life, a structure of feeling that is produced by particular forms of intentional activity and that yields particular sorts of material effects' (Appadurai 1996: 182) .... While a 'structure of feeling' may have strengthened the relationships between Yamphu and the land, this very feeling was often antithetical to the project of the nation-state (Forbes 1999: 130; original emphasis).

In exploring these concepts of phenomenological qualities in the relationships people of eastern Nepal hold with their permanent fields, shifting cultivations, forests and pastures, and their understanding of themselves and their history of being in these settings, Forbes opens a way to seeing how resistance to state classifications of the environment can be located in the ontological realities of livelihoods pursued according to their own momentum of being of their place and in their world. Ortner (1995) similarly emphasizes the importance of identifying 'structures of feeling', contradictory subjectivities, and the enactment of autonomous projects in considering the 'authenticity' of resistance.

Forbes claims that eighteenth- and nineteenth-century governments of Nepal constructed national identity by severing links between ethnic identity and local place, *kipat* being the exception to this process. As someone without deep ethnographic knowledge of eastern Nepal, it has always seemed to me that the uniqueness of *kipat* status has been overworked,[7] certainly if it is offered up as contrasting to a 'generalizable mode of belonging to a wider territorial imaginary' (Forbes quoting of Appadurai), if such is the contingent, alienable quality of belonging attributed to identities among other rural communities of Nepal. Who among them do not also share in a compromised autonomy of livelihood, and partake in an awareness of their distinctive cultural identity contributing to their economic underdevelopment? To give adequately weighted ethnographic significance to the 'phenomenological properties' entailed in the production of Himalayan social livelihoods it is necessary to contextualize this 'autonomy' in multiple claims to independence and incorporation, in which different kinds of identities and scales of legitimation are likely to interact, from sacred landscapes to international migrant labour networks. In these multiple incorporations, though, the matter of agency ought to be assessed, which Forbes defines well as 'the ability of some individuals to attach their boundaries around people and the land, while others are forced to act within lines created by others' (1999: 133).

RESISTANCE AND ECOLOGY

The historian Richard Grove argues that colonial forms of land designation interrupted customary interactions with forests, pastures, and soil by inserting public/private categorizations of tenure. These 'have exercised the most intimate and often oppressive impact on the daily lives and ways of production of the rural majority throughout much of the world' (1998: 180). As a counter to studies such as James Scott's *The Moral Economy of the Peasant* emphasizing agrarian rent extraction, Grove points to the synchronicity of many instances of resistance to colonial regimes with their introduction of environmental policies. In India 'episodes of coordinated popular resistance to colonial rule ... were, almost barometrically, preceded by phases of vigorous resistance to colonial forestry policy' (Grove 1998: 206). He notes that the effects of conservation structures were as destructive to the poor as the appropriation of environments by private capital (ibid.: 183).

---

[7]In many studies *kipat* appears not to have operated in terms of its own birth-right account of its working, but rather by the politics of wealth in people (e.g., Caplan 1991).

Ignoring often long-evolved relationships between people and nature, the effects of 'conservation' have tended to profoundly threaten traditional mechanisms of subsistence and thereby to threaten and alienate whole cultures from their environmental contexts (Grove 1998: 222).

As colonial administrations developed soil and forest conservation measures from the middle of the nineteenth century those who experienced the force of such measures were frequently communities whose subsistence practice transcended simple private-public ownership principles: 'the activities of shifting cultivators presented a much softer target than the far more damaging activities of timber operators with their allies in high places' (ibid.: 192).

Resistance to interventions in human-environmental relationships in the name of nature conservation needs to be interpreted not only in terms of appropriated material resources but also as displacements to particular dwelling ontologies effected by the radical separation of people from their surroundings, objectifying nature as bordered off from society. This allows for a positioned, motivational level of human-environmental relationality beyond a mere calculated reckoning of costs and benefits of conservation, which more economistically oriented accounts of human behaviour rely upon. It is an approach that differs epistemologically from mention of 'expressive dimensions' of ecological resistance (Guha and Martinez-Alier 1997: 13).

Tim Ingold's writings on the dwelling perspective of ecological engagement offer an alternative to nature/culture dualism (1992, 2000). He argues that people do not primarily interact with their environments through culturally mediated filters of classificatory categories. This opens up important new ways of thinking about the anthropology of nature conservation. In most contexts conservation entails an enforced disengagement of people from relatively unregulated access to their environments. It inserts the same disengagement of conceptual model (pure nature) from lived-in environment identified by Ingold (1992) in the logic of cultural construction. He persuasively argues we cannot understand human ecology by using as terms of analysis the categories of separate nature or biophysical reality so particular to the perceptions and technological regimes of urbanized modernity. Only in such conditions does the possibility of cultural construction conferring meaning to a separated environment come into being. Instead it is the dwelt-in ontology of direct engagement with environmental 'affordances' that should be the starting point for human ecology.

Whether people now living under conservation regimes in Nepal can be said to have previously enjoyed wholly 'unmediated' relationships to the affordances of their environment can be questioned, or at least the language and implications of the term 'mediation' need clarification. At what point, for instance, do the differentiating systems of property, class, ethnic identity, and community organization common in Nepal need to be considered as cultural mediations of direct engagement? I take it that the existence of institutions which regulate differential resource access between persons, genders, and groups does not necessarily question the phenomenological dimension of the dwelling perspective, but the mediations of social control, the hierarchies of authority, and the exclusions of property and inheritance need a politics of environmental engagement to complement the phenomenology. Himalayan societies, after all, make many kinds of interruptions to people's routine direct ecological engagements, such as prohibiting ploughing on full-moon days. Indeed ritualized temporality may offer insights for analysing the state's environmental surveillance. The state's environmental competence has to be questioned when it often seems that control measures are enacted arbitrarily in terms of periodicity, visibility, and the offences targeted. State controls often act more to define hierarchical relationships of power towards subordinate communities than to enact eco-regulation. I would argue that the enforcement of conservation policies is often a ritualized form of social control, and that ethnographers need to be aware of what governmentally communicative effects are achieved in their implementation.

STATES OF BEWILDERMENT AND ALTERNATIVE PATHS TO
ENVIRONMENTAL KNOWLEDGE

Transnational institutions allocating global funds for environmental protection like UNDP clearly hold a pragmatic stance straddling biodiversity alarmism and poverty alleviation agendas, yet they are at the forefront of 'eco-cracy' (Sachs 1993) and the regulation of biopolitics. In my attempts to theorize the interrelations of local, national, and transnational levels of eco-regulation in a Himalayan valley, Paul Rutherford's (1999) discussion of biopolitics within metropolitan governmentality has been helpful in identifying what is and is not going on. For a start he suggests specialized scientific discourse on ecology is identified as providing the intellectual machinery of government 'whereby social relations with nature are thematized and brought into the domain of conscious political calculation through the formation of programmes of government' (ibid.: 59). Governmentality, though, is not exclusive to the state in the systematic shaping of individuals', groups', and populations' conduct (ibid.: 60). '[T]he development of programmes of environmental security can be understood as drawing on [a] ... complex, open and unstable "politico-epistemic configuration" ... [composed of] fragile and mobile relationships between non-state professionals, intellectuals and social movements, and state agencies' (ibid.: 50). This aspect of openness has only in the last decade been acknowledged in Nepal, where previously national and international scientists and monarchical government effectively inhibited civil society input. Rutherford draws attention to Foucault's analysis that the complexity of modern society appears to engender an increasing reliance on liberal techniques of government which depend on governing at a distance, in a 'regulated autonomy' of locales, entities, and persons.

When considering the shift from coercive state protectionism to buffer zone negotiation of give and take in national park policy, it is possible to discern an effect of convergence between global neoliberal de-regulatory policies and pragmatic expediency within post-panchayat Nepal (i.e., from 1990). For Foucault liberalism 'dissolved the immediate unity between knowledge and government, and consequently the equation of maximized governmental effectiveness with maximal regulation' (Foucault cited in Burchell *et al.* 1991: 138–9). Yet it has to be said that as far as a politico-epistemic configuration of environmental regulation in Nepal is concerned, there is a need to recontextualize theories of ecological governmentality developed in relation to science, state, and resources in the West. How is it possible to think of ecological governmentality other than in terms of a scientized process of normative self-regulation? What epistemic configurations, forms of knowledge and dialogical possibility, cultural registers, and perceptions of agency are necessary for an ethnographic problematization of ecological governmentality?

In previous writing on the ecological injustices of national park administration I have tended to formulate the problem simply as an external imposition of nature-society dualism on a people and an environment in mutual engagement (Campbell 2000). This conjures up an all too familiar dis-articulation of the local and national that obscures historical, political, and cultural structures of coexistence.

Critics of national park conservation policy such as McNeely assert that

> By ... establishing national parks that have no management, the authority of governments tends to be spurious. While many governments have claimed power over resources, they lacked the capacity to implement their responsibilities, thereby creating among indigenous peoples a lack of confidence in the capacity of either state or local institutions to regulate access to local resources. (McNeely 1997: 178–9)

Similar comments about state disarticulation with conservation and the development process in general have been made regarding Nepal, for instance by Thompson *et al.*, claiming the levers of administrative power were not necessarily connected to anything 'out there' (Thompson, Hatley, and Wharburton 1986).[8] This kind of statement ignores the possibility that though governments may not have effectively exercised direct control over remote situations, *other relationships of sovereignty rather than control*, may have existed in culturally distinctive ways not visible if notions of modern nation-state competency are presumed as the norm.[9] The fact is that over the centuries various

[8]Other studies of the environmentalist state in India have far more sceptical critiques (including of course Arundhati Roy's passionate essay 'The Greater Common Good'). Subir Sinha (2000) highlights some of the yawning gaps in knowledge and effectiveness among Indian forest officials. Their experience is often of being sent on 'hardship' posting, knowing very little about the conditions they find themselves in, and having little impact on trade in illegal natural commodities: 'Centralised control does not translate to the everyday acts of monitoring and sanctioning, of surveying and stock-taking that state actors pursuing conservationist and preservationist agendas need to perform. Stated intent in international fora does not eradicate rampant corruption at lower levels of the state. In the event that the centralised state has asserted its authority ... [in India] there have been backlashes ranging from local mobilisations to nationalist and subnationalist demands. States seem to have fragile, or at least contested, authority, incomplete knowledge and control over factors that militate against prudent resource use ...' (2000: 199).

[9]Haripriya Rangan's (1997) attempts to counter the convergence of neo-liberals and eco-populists in their shared view (though from very different starting points) that 'the state must withdraw from the sphere of environmental protection and natural resource management' (1997: 71). Rangan has mounted a defence arguing that in India the state is a heterogeneous rather than monolithic entity, and not 'uniformly despotic' in relation to environmental management regimes. More specifically, the property or ownership status of natural resources, whether belonging to the state, individuals, or commons is claimed not to determine how they are used. Rangan suggests that forms of control under the state, separated out from issues of property, have been flexibly and responsively altered through negotiation with civil society.

states have exerted influence over the context of local environmental practice and discourse in areas such as the Langtang National Park.

More recently I have come to examine this formulation in the light of the regional Himalayan scholarship on mountain cults (Blondeau and Steinkellner 1996). Rather than understanding the environmental role of the state as a series of sorry stories of inept conservation practice, a broader appreciation of how local and hegemonic traditions have historically coexisted in areas like the Himalayan chain allows a more culturally nuanced approach to state agency.

Studies of mountain cults in the Himalaya and Tibet can appear arcane and hermetically sealed off from issues of contemporary, engaged livelihoods and development processes, but buried within them lie hidden cultural treasures, as yet seemingly untouched by the political science of resource use. One of these is a suggested link between mountain verticality and notions of fertility. Ramble offers a suggestion that 'it is the vertical axis itself, rather than any particular god or class of supernatural beings inhabiting the landscape, that is linked to notions of fertility' (1996: 150–1). I will discuss this idea giving it a dwelling perspective slant. But there are also conceptualizations of the relationship between place, commmunity, the state, and hierarchies of knowledge, that can be lifted from their philological framing and turned to problematize theories of state competence in the development of policies of nature protection. There are important tools here that can be used for thinking about cultural dispositions for agency in intervening in local affairs. The discourses of development and nature conservation are for their part equally hermetic in defining terrains of knowledge, and pay scant attention to issues of cultural or political significance in their managerialist approaches to human-environmental activity.

Does ritual attendance to mountain verticality express an indigenous theory of cosmic fertility? The Tamang of Rasuwa District are, to recap, transhumant agro-pastoralists living in shifting residence between fields, forest, and pastures at different elevations and times of year, taking fertility from crop cultivations and diverse biotic habitats up and down the mountainside. Creation mythology stresses the natural foundation of human life between the extent of where the juniper and palm grow. Movement of families and animals between the variety of environmental affordances (fodder, wild fruit, fungi, bamboo) extending over a range of three and a half thousand metres, is the basis of livelihood and social reproduction. Stillness is only achieved in the marking of a twice annual centering when families' movements bring them back to dwell momentarily and symbolically as residents of a permanent village for festivals in spring and autumn. At these times, people and spirits are ritually reminded by shamans and Buddhist lamas to remain in their 'own places'. Clan and village hierarchies are renewed by animal sacrifices, emulating state rituals of legitimation.

In mid-winter and mid-summer, by contrast, pilgrimage to regionally incorporative sites of the most powerful gods of place at polarized high and low points of the mountain (Gosainkund lake at the top and Shikar Besi cave at the base of the massif) are undergone to renew powers of reproductive fertility for crops, animals, children, health, and money, in a procreative understanding of life welfare (as a pilgrim, you have to decide between these which it is you have come for). On pilgrimage, ethnic and religious groups marked by conspicuous difference find terrains of mutual accommodation sharing in a single source of ritual focus. At these times animal sacrifice is forbidden, and the ethnic heterogeneity of the communities that depend on the fertility of the mountain and its waters is celebrated, with little sense of overt political hierarchy characterizing relations between the various participating communities. The sense of proximate access to magical sources of fertility at these vertical poles is experienced directly as simultaneously sacred, erotic, and violent. People return to their villages animated by encounters with strangers, danger, and the unknown, carrying pots of water blessed at the shrines and springs, with their thoughts focused on whether their wishes for a calf, a child, a pot of gold, a good harvest, or long life will come true.

There is a clear homology of agro-pastoral transhumance between ecological extremes of village territory, and accessing fertility at the regional shrines of sacralized verticality. The basis for Tamang villagers' engagement with the pilgrimage is ontologically compelling through the experience of ecological verticality, but the pilgrimage also involves people coming from Kathmandu and further afield, who are not transhumant agro-pastoralists, and for whom the mountain sites and the water sources connect to much larger models of sacred landscape. Subterranean water courses supposedly bring the water from the holy lake to temple pools within the Kathmandu Valley, and the Hindu monarchy has historically considered it a duty to support the pilgrimage.

The Nepali state participates in what the theorists of the mountain cult refer to as a 'mandala' model of sacred geography, with different sites of local worship linking up into a regional map of power places that can be identified within Hindu mythology. I suggest that it is more at this level of encompassing, hierarchized eco-cosmology that the authorities of the National Park historically claim territorial administrative dominion in the area, and express the cultural legitimacy of their environmental sovereignty. The Park's official display board explains the pilgrimage only in terms of Sanskritic myth. For the authorities, the drummings of the shamans, and the vigorous, if not quite ecstatic, libations of herders' milk at the shrine are tolerated, though regulated, by an equally intimidating policeman restricting passage into the cave to just a few people at a time. Pilgrims are not expected to conform to an orthodoxy of ritual practice, but an officially condoned diversity of worship is held as encouraging recognition for the sacred geography that sustains state sovereignty. According to Gingrich, this would be a classic example of 'hierarchical merging', whereby 'tribal elements' are encompassed by 'scripturalism' into layered cosmological strata (Gingrich 1996: 260). It matters not that the Tamang have a 'pathway' rather than mandala model of geo-cosmic reproduction (Höfer 1999).

Returning to my earlier comments on how divorced the literature on the mountain cult appeared to be from people's lives of engagement, the dwelling perspective helps to understand how rituals, livelihoods, and political relations can be thought of in mutual articulation, with fertility and verticality being part of engaged Tamang experience. The mountain cult literature seemed to ignore these connections (with the exception of Diemberger 1996), but in spite of its discursive closure on the contemporary world, it has offered something quite powerfully suggestive for environmental cultural theory. Moving across from one field of research to another, could the idea of 'hierarchically merged' modes of environmental relationship be applied to thinking about the politics of nature protection? Tamang practices of environmental engagement run counter to modernist categorical impositions of nature-culture dualism introduced through conservation. Now I am led to think about the translation of global environmental protection regimes across cultural contexts in terms of political hybridity. What the global perspective on conservation has failed to address is the variability in the cultural rootstocks of political history onto which environmental governmentality has been grafted.

As mentioned earlier, several commentators have pointed out that by establishing national parks that effectively have no cultural infrastructure for their control and management, the authority of governments claiming power over resources is spurious when it comes to implementing responsibilities (Stevens 1997, McNeely 1997).[10] In this scenario the levers of institutional power seem virtually unattached to the conditions they are meant to influence, leaving room for the continued, if often furtively resistant, engagements of local communities with the resources of biodiversity around them. Rather than a total vacuum of consensus and control operating in these circumstances, it is perhaps more culturally convincing, and less patronising, to discuss the relationship between governmentality and environmental resources in countries like Nepal as characterized by sorts of 'hierarchically merged' responsibilities, that ritually assert authority and pragmatically tolerate autonomy. In the areas where national parks tend to be set up, beyond the pale, outside the extent of intensive central administration, sovereignty and control separate out. Where concepts of democratic process are absent or embryonic (as in Nepal) ecological management and notions of injustice are perhaps more likely to find expression through ritual non-compliance with hierarchy rather than through political instrumentality.

Kay Milton's thoughtful comments on global environmental discourses emphasize the poverty of cultural theory among both advocates and opponents. Advocates of global solutions to ecological habitat and biodiversity loss reproduce standardized management regimes and policies around the world. Environmental governmentality under global management continues to depend on nation-states being seen as the principal regulators of human activity (Milton 1996: 187). The global level of conservation organizations' operation makes it difficult for groups ignored by national authorities to find outlets for their voices, when democratic norms of representation are presumed. 'It is also difficult for those whose understanding of the environment differs fundamentally from the global model to influence a debate which takes that model as its starting point' (ibid.: 179).

Opponents of globalism, on the other hand, see the framing of environmental problems in a global context as 'a deliberate move

[10]It is important to recall the history of the Nepalese state's relationship to areas now exhibited as examples of biodiversity conservation. Ghimire points out that 'the Ranas were able to impress their British counterparts by taking them hunting in the Tarai forests, and these areas still remain as one of the important centres for entertaining foreign dignitaries. Indeed, many national parks, particularly in Chitwan and Bardia, were initially developed in order to satisfy and protect the game and recreational interests of the aristocracy, rather than for wildlife conservation' (1992: 190).

by Northern interests to ensure that only global agencies will be considered competent to deal with them' (Milton 1996: 191). In this view globalism centralizes control of resources, but, as I have argued for the Tamangs in the Langtang National Park, 'it also destroys the ways in which local communities understand their environments' (ibid.: 192). Local perspectives are authoritatively replaced by scientific ones, and local knowledge is denied the status of systematic knowledge. Knowledge gained from looking at the environment is privileged over knowledge gained from living in it. Western science continues to dominate debate of how to conserve the environment. 'Knowledge derived from scientific surveillance and monitoring of the Earth is seen as a more reliable basis for environmental management than knowledge derived from local experience' (ibid.: 193).

For Milton, both globalists and anti-globalists rely in the end on inadequate understandings of culture. Both positions in their own ways embrace the 'myth of primitive ecological wisdom'. Whether signed up to global conservation treaties or resisting them by asserting rights to territory, autonomy and self-government, the realities of political hybridity as I have tried to sketch for the context of Nepal remain invisible. As anthropologists we can understand the environment as a discursive purification (Latour 1993), and as a cultural tool of strategic essentialism (Fairhead and Leach 1995), that takes its power from shading out mediating relationalities. The issues emerging from looking ethnographically at ecological resistance draw attention to ontological repercussions of environmental appropriation, and responses to the criminalization of subsistence livelihoods, that call for an understanding of layered historical relationships between communities and the state in interpreting strategies adopted to negotiate the reproduction of livelihoods in the face of regulatory authority.

CONCLUSION

As the institutions that are formulating policies for global environmental protection depend to a large extent on working through nation-states, it is important to ask on what assumptions of agency and capacity this dependence is founded. The turn by conservationists, away from relying on assumptions of protected area implementation by state agencies, towards communities as vehicles for delivering conservation policy, follows the general trend in decentralizing development practice encouraged by neo-liberal state deregulation and the evidence of counterproductive state interventions (Adams and Hulme 1998). But what assumptions of 'community' are thereby mobilized?

Simply devolving environmental responsibility from state to community is unconvincing in view of the unequal political relations between local communities and the centre that persist behind the rhetoric of decentralization. It further substantializes 'communities' in ways that deny heterogeneous networks of communication and resource exchange with outsiders (Sivaramakrishnan 1998). People's resistance to being co-opted into conservation programmes as 'communities', even in supposedly community-friendly projects, demonstrates continuing *de facto* top-down managerialism. If 'communities' have arrived in conservation policy intentions, they tend not to be the argumentative and fissiparous realities known to ethnographers. It is not possible to overcome ecological underprivilege by transferring roles, rewards, and duties to an ideal construction.

Conservation measures can have enormous effects on formal and informal local power structures, such as through requirements to form precise memberships of resource user groups (Agarwal 1997), or through expropriating the distribution of environmental entitlements from processes of local accountability, as described by Forbes. Problems of communication with conservation authorities, and of negotiating between groups of unequal power have been highlighted by Blaikie and Jeanrenaud (1996), identifying difficulties facing conservation agencies in achieving the 'new conventional wisdom' of consensual agreements with local communities:

A plurality of understandings along with a variety of competing interests (some of them decidedly anti-conservationist) begs the question of whether negotiations can be equal. The former have their scientific agendas, and the latter have all sorts of contingent interests in biodiversity conservation. The usual case is that there is disagreement between the two parties and also between local people themselves (Blaikie and Jeanrenaud 1996: 70).

A very common perception in Nepal is of conservationists belonging to a historical succession of intervening outsiders. There is, I suggest, a fundamental misapprehension of appropriate agency in the common identification of ecologically framed intervention imperatives. The recent history of environmental governmentality in Nepal demonstrates an incomprehension of what it is to live in everyday terms of environmental intimacy, mirroring the account of 'two worlds in mutual ignorance of each other', given in Ramirez's

(2000) analysis of political relations between the centre and rural social realities. The engineering of conservation-minded subjectivities internalizing civic environmental goals is a fantasy given the active memory of how the state has compelled forest resource extraction in the not so distant past, and fails to implement environmental governance beyond symbolic interventions, however forceful, currently. For the Tamangs of the Langtang National Park, the environment is irredeemably political. Local headmen once derived legitimacy from transhumant coordination and allocations of land, a role that the park has removed but not effectively replaced, taking away the territorial, pastoral, and redistributive *raison dêre* for local leadership. The vacuum of management on the ground resulting from community disempowerment is consequently filled in the regulatory breach by subjectivities practising low visibility eco-provisioning, and feigned myopia of others' infringements: a cautiously circumspect and politically mute version of Ingoldian dwelling.

In the long term, productive appropriation of environmental discourse may become part of collective identity formations in Nepal, as has occurred for instance among fisher people of the Rapti river. It may happen that national and transnational frameworks of conventions and rights will be taken up as avenues for political action by collectivities and alliances of various orders. In other words, Nepalis may move beyond a simple 'counter-identity' of oppressed subaltern groups expressing antagonism and 'reactive oppositional discourses' (Gledhill 1994: 92), which do not in themselves challenge power structures. Escobar's work (1999) on the autonomous take-up of the biodiversity agenda by Colombian social movements, and Baviskar's (1995) study of the Narmada Dam conflict show growing confidence, and also desperation, among such groups to do so. That it might be politically expedient for indigenous people to present themselves as 'responsible guardians of the Earth's resources', and ally themselves with environmentalists (Milton 1996: 202), is a contemporary dynamic that anthropologists have to investigate, and which in Nepal is only just emerging.[11]

What I have attempted to do in this chapter is to show how ethnographers can give distinctive accounts of the ways people interact with rather than simply represent their environments, and how they

[11]See for instance the 1995 'Resolution Supporting the Struggle of the Indigenous Peoples of Nepal for the Recognition of their Rights to the Forest' in IAIP 1997.

interact with a diversity of relationships and discourses of sovereignty regarding their environments. Current formulations of eco-globalization are singularly unhelpful in imagining this hybrid motivational complexity. Static two-dimensional portrayals of state versus community, produced under the problematically accountable, interventionist environmentalist state, are understandably resisted through an unpublicized, opportunistic disregard, as the cultural history of a variety of dialogues and claims to environmental control and sovereignty (coercive, consensual, and commercial) are erased in the discourse of conservation governmentality. Motivations for resisting the environmentalist state come from this discourse's entrenchment of mutually opposed positions which set the *jangali* (uncouth) rural peasant reactively defending livelihood strategies against the eco-enlightened state official acting on behalf of global regulatory science. People on the ground know this opposition does not describe the world they live in.

REFERENCES

Adams, W. and D. Hulme 1998. 'Conservation and Communities: Changing Narratives, Policies and Practices in African Conservation'. Working Paper 4, *Community Conservation in Africa*. Manchester, IDPM.
Agarwal, B. 1997. 'Environmental Action, Gender Equity and Women's Participation' *Development and Change* 28: 1–44.
Appadurai, A. 1996. *Modernity at Large: Cultural Dimensions of Globalization*. Minneapolis: University of Minnesota Press.
Baviskar, A. 1995. *In the Belly of the River: Tribal Conflicts over Development in the Narmada Valley*. Delhi: OUP.
Bird-David, N. 1999 'Animism Revisited: Personhood, Environment, and Relational Epistemology' *Current Anthropology* 40: 67–91.
Blaikie, P. and S. Jeanrenaud 1996. 'Biodiversity and Human Welfare' in K. Ghimire and M. Pimbert (eds) *Social Change and Conservation*. London: Earthscan.
Blondeau, A.-M. and E. Steinkellner (eds) 1996. *Reflections of the Mountain: Essays on the History and Social Meaning of the Mountain Cult in Tibet and the Himalaya*. Vienna: Verlag der Österreichischen Akademie der Wissenschaften.
Brosius, P. 1999a. 'Green Dots, Pink Hearts: Displacing Politics from the Malaysian Rainforest' *American Anthropologist* 101(1): 36–57.
―― 1999b. 'Analyses and Interventions: Anthropological Engagements with Environmentalism' *Current Anthropology* 40(3): 277–309.
Brower, B. 1991. *Sherpa of Khumbu*. Delhi: Oxford University Press.

Burchell, G., C. Gordon, and P. Miller (eds) 1991. *The Foucault Effect: Studies in Governmentality.* London: Harvester Wheatsheaf.

Cameron, M. 1995. 'Biodiversity Conservation and Economic Development in Nepal's Khaptad National Park Region: Untouchables as Entrepreneurs and Conservation Stewards' *Himalayan Research Bulletin* 15(2): 56–63.

Campbell, B. 1994. 'Forms of Cooperation in a Tamang Community of Nepal' in M. Allen (ed.) *Anthropology of Nepal: Peoples, Problems and Processes.* Kathmandu: Mandala.

—— 1998. 'Conversing with Nature: Ecological Symbolism in Central Nepal' *Worldviews* 2(2): 123–37.

—— 2000. 'Animals Behaving Badly' in J. Knight (ed.) *Natural Enemies: People-Wildlife Conflicts in Anthropological Perspective.* London: Routledge.

—— Forthcoming a. 'Introduction: The Politics of Environmental Engagement' in B. Campbell (ed.) *Re-Placing Nature: Ethnographies of Connection and Administrations of Distance.*

—— Forthcoming b. 'Nature and its Discontents in Nepal' in B. Campbell (ed.) *Re-Placing Nature: Ethnographies of Connection and Administrations of Distance.*

Caplan, L. 1991. 'From Tribe to Peasant: The Limbus and the Nepalese State' *Journal of Peasant Studies* 18: 305–21.

—— 2000 [1970] *Land and Social Change in East Nepal: a Study of Hindu-Tribal Relations* (2nd ed.). Lalitpur: Himal Books.

Descola, P. 1996. 'Constructing Natures: Symbolic Ecology and Social Practice' in P. Descola and G. Palsson (eds) *Nature and Society: Anthropological Perspectives.* London: Routledge.

Diemberger, H. 1996. 'Political and Religious Aspects of Mountain Cults in the Hidden Valley of Khenbalung: Tradition, Decline and Revitalisation' in Blondeau and Steinkellner (eds).

Eckholm, E. 1976. *Losing Ground: Environmental Stress and World Food Prospects.* New York: W.W. Norton.

Escobar, A. 1999. 'Whose Knowledge, Whose Nature? Biodiversity, Conservation, and the Political Ecology of Social Movement' *Journal of Political Ecology* 5: 53–82.

Fairhead, J. and M. Leach 1995. 'False Forest History, Complicit Social Analysis: Rethinking some West African Environmental Narratives' *World Development* 23(6): 1023–35.

Fisher, R.J. and D.A. Gilmour 1999. 'Anthropology and Biophysical Sciences In Natural Resource Management: Is Symbiosis Possible?' in R.B. Chhetri and O.P. Gurung (eds) *Anthropology and Sociology of Nepal: Societies, Cultures, Ecology and Development.* Kathmandu: SASON.

Forbes, A. 1999. 'Mapping Power: Disputing Claims to Kipat Lands in Northeastern Nepal' *American Ethnologist* 26(1): 114–38.

Fox, J., P. Yonzon, and N. Podger 1996. 'Mapping Conflict between Biodiversity and Human Needs in Langtang National Park, Nepal' *Conservation Biology* 10(2): 562–9.

Ghimire, K. 1992. *Forest or Farm: The Politics of Poverty and Land Hunger in Nepal.* Delhi: Oxford University Press.

Gilmour, D.A. and R. J. Fisher 1991. *Villagers, Forests and Foresters.* Kathmandu: Sahayogi Press.

Gingrich, A. 1996. 'Hierarchical Merging and Horizontal Distinction: A Comparative Perspective on Tibetan Mountain Cults' in Blondeau and Steinkellner (eds).

Gledhill, J. 1994. *Power and its Disguises: Anthropological Perspectives on Politics.* London: Pluto.

Graner, E. 1999. 'Forest Policies and Access to Forests in Nepal: Winners and Losers' in R.B. Chhetri and O.P. Gurung (eds) *Anthropology and Sociology of Nepal: Cultures, Societies, Ecology and Development.* Kathmandu: SASON.

Grove, R. 1995. *Green Imperialism: The Colonial Expansion, Tropical Island Edens and the Origins of Environmentalism, 1600–1860.* Delhi: OUP.

—— 1998. 'Colonial Conservation, Ecological Hegemony and Popular Resistance'. Chapter 6 in his *Ecology, Climate and Empire.* Delhi: OUP.

Guha, R. 1991. *The Unquiet Woods: Ecological Change and Peasant Resistance in the Himalaya.* Delhi: Oxford University Press.

—— and J. Martinez-Alier 1997. *Varieties of Environmentalism: Essays North and South.* London: Earthscan.

Guthman, J. 1997. 'Representing Crisis: The Theory of Himalayan Environmental Degradation and the Project of Development in Post-Rana Nepal' *Development and Change* **28**: 45–69.

Hatley, T. and M. Thompson 1985. 'Rare Animals, Poor People, and Big Agencies' *Mountain Research and Development* **5**(4): 365–77.

Höfer, A. 1999. '*Nomen est numen:* Notes on the Verbal Journey in some Western Tamang Oral Ritual Texts' in B. Bickel and M. Gaenszle (eds) *Himalayan Space: Cultural Horizons and Practices.* Völkerkundemuseum Zürich.

Holmberg, D. 2000. 'Derision, Exorcism, and the Ritual Production of Power' *American Ethnologist* **27**(4): 927–49.

——, K. March, and S. Tamang 1999. 'Local Production/ Local Knowledge: Forced Labour from Below' *Studies in Nepali History and Society* **4**(1): 5–64.

IAIP. 1997. *Indigenous Peoples, Forest, and Biodiversity.* London: International Alliance of Indigenous-Tribal Peoples of the Tropical Forests (with the International Work Group for Indigenous Affairs, Copenhagen).

Ingold, T. 1992. 'Culture and the Perception of the Environment' in D. Parkin and E. Croll (eds) *Bush Base, Forest Farm: Culture, Environment and Development.* London: Routledge.

—— 1996. 'Hunting and Gathering as Ways of Perceiving the World' in R. Ellen and K. Fukui (eds) *Redefining Nature.* Oxford: Berg.

—— 2000. *The Perception of the Environment: Essays in Livelihood, Dwelling and Skill.* London: Routledge.

IUCN 1993. *Nature Reserves of the Himalaya and the Mountains of Central Asia.* Oxford: Oxford University Press/International Union for Conservation of Nature and Natural Resources.

Ives, J. and B. Messerli 1989. *The Himalayan Dilemma: Reconciling Development and Conservation.* London: Routledge.

Latour, B. 1993. *We have never been Modern.* Cambridge, MA: Harvard University Press.

Linkenbach, A. 2000. *Appropriating the Himalayan Forests: Ecology and Resistance in Garhwal (North India).* University of Heidelberg. Habilitation thesis.

McNeely, J. 1997. 'Interaction between Biological Diversity and Cultural Diversity' in S. Büchi *et al.* (eds).

Milton, K. 1996. *Environmentalism and Cultural Theory.* London: Routledge.

Mosse, D. 1994. 'Authority, Gender, and Knowledge' *Development and Change* 25: 497–526.

Müller-Böker, U. 1995. *Die Tharu in Chitawan: Kenntnis, Bewertung und Nutzung der natürlichen Umwelt im südlichen Nepal.* Stuttgart: Franz Steiner Verlag.

Ortner, S. 1995. 'Resistance and the Problem of Ethnographic Refusal' *Comparative Studies in Society and History* 37: 173–93.

Ramble, C. 1996. 'Patterns of Places' in Blondeau and Steinkellner (eds).

Ramirez, P. 2000. *De la disparition des chefs:une anthropologie politique népalaise.* Paris: Editions CNRS.

Rangan, H. 1997. 'Property vs. Control: The State and Forest Management in the Indian Himalaya' *Development and Change* 28: 71–94.

Rival, L. (ed.) 1998. *The Social Life of Trees.* Oxford: Berg.

Roy, A. 1999. 'The Greater Common Good' in A. Roy *The Cost of Living.* London: Flamingo.

Rutherford, P. 1999. 'The Entry of Life into History' in E. Darier (ed.) *Discourses of the Environment.* Oxford: Blackwell.

Saberwal, V. 1999. *Pastoral Politics: Shepherds, Bureaucrats, and Conservation in the Western Himalaya.* Delhi: OUP.

Sachs, W. (ed.) 1993. *Global Ecology: A New Arena of Political Conflict.* London: Zed Books.

Schrader, H. 1988. *Trading Patterns in the Nepal Himalayas.* Saarbrücken: Verlag Breitenbach.

Shiva, V. 1989. *Staying Alive: Women, Ecology and Development.* London: Zed Books

Shrestha, N.R. and D. Conway 1996. 'Ecopolitical Battles at the Tarai Frontier of Nepal: An Emerging Human and Environmental Crisis' *International Journal of Population Geography* 2: 313–31.

Sinha, S. 2000. 'The "Other" Agrarian Transition: Structure, Institutions and Agency in Sustainable Rural Development' *Journal of Peasant Studies* 27(2): 169–204.

———, S. Gururani, and B. Greenberg 1997. 'The "New Traditionalist" Discourse of Indian Environmentalism' *Journal of Peasant Studies* 24(3): 65–99.

Sivaramakrishnan, K. 1998. 'Modern Forestry: Trees and Development Spaces in South-west Bengal, India' in L. Rival (ed.) *The Social Life of Trees*. Oxford: Berg.

Stevens, S. 1993. *Claiming the High Ground: Sherpas, Subsistence, and Environmental Change in the Highest Himalaya*. Berkeley: University of California Press.

_____ (ed.) 1997. *Conservation Through Cultural Survival: Indigenous Peoples and Protected Areas*. Washington: Island Press.

Takacs, D. 1996. *The Idea of Biodiversity*. Baltimore: Johns Hopkins University Press.

Thompson, M., T. Hatley, and M. Wharburton 1986. *Uncertainty on a Himalayan Scale*. London: Ethnographica.

Viveiros de Castro, E. 1998. 'Cosmological Deixis and Amerindian Perspectivism' *Journal of the Royal Anthropological Institute* 4: 469–88.

For further discussion of environmental protection in Nepal, and a consideration of some effects of the Maoist insurgency on conservation projects, see my article 'Nature's Discontents in Nepal' in *Conservation and Society* 2005, 3(2) (available online at www.).

chapter three

The Politics of Difference and the Reach of Modernity: Reflections on State and Society in Central Nepal

- *William F. Fisher*

C hanges in Nepal over the past decade—most dramatically, the 1990 overthrow of Nepal's Partyless Panchayat system of government, the writing of a new democratic constitution, the burgeoning growth of politically vocal, national ethnic and religious associations, and the persistence of a class-based 'People's War' since February 1996—have highlighted various forms of resistance to the state, emphasized the fluid and malleable character of the discourse underlying the Hindu Kingdom of Nepal, and drawn attention to the ongoing process of forming and transforming a society. Within Nepal images of an imposed order with unequal benefits, a dark threatening political and social chaos, and an uncertain confusion run through the heated debates about national culture and order. Since 1990, dissatisfaction with the status quo and with the inability of the government to respond effectively to economic and social concerns have sustained and fueled a variety of ethnic, regional, and class-based challenges to the dominant or official view of the nation that range from calls for the establishment of a republic to calls for territorially and ethnically based autonomous zones.

At the heart of these disputes are competing views of the nation of Nepal. One portion of the population mourns the apparent demise of a harmonious Hindu kingdom often described as flower garden of four *varnas* (estates) and 36 *jāts* (castes) which collectively share a heroic past, speak a common language, follow a common religion, and are led, at least symbolically, by a divine and benevolent king.

Others dismiss this view as an excessively romantic misrepresentation and describe instead a Nepali past of internal colonization, Hindu oppression, and forced assimilation of non-Hindu minorities into a hierarchical system. In their view Nepal is not a nation rendered asunder by recent strife but a 'nation in the making' that can fulfill its potential only if it finds a way to recognize itself as a culturally and religiously plural society.

Since 1982, there have been widespread disagreements about the seriousness of Nepal's ethnic and class problems, the threat they pose to national integration, and the causes of unrest.[1] How do we explain and account for contemporary conflict in Nepal? Depending on the speaker, the current unrest in Nepal is attributed to a variety of causes. Some attribute it to two hundred years of Hindu oppression, growing awareness of this history among affected social groups, and the political freedom since 1990 to talk about it freely. Other analysts attribute it to rural poverty, political neglect, caste prejudice, or a general frustration with the post-1990 governments. But less charitable views portray ethnic and class protests as a misunderstanding and misuse of new democratic processes and political freedom to promote what are essentially communal claims. Many observers characterized it as rabble-rousing by a few ethnic and class activists who are out for personal gain, and some point to the complicity of foreign scholars in essentially ethnic identities and promoting a critical view of the two-hundred-year history of nation-building in Nepal.

These disagreements about causes are also linked to assessments of their importance. In the 1990s, an increasing number of observers had come to acknowledge that the Janajati problem was one of the most serious problems faced by Nepal at the moment—one that some analysts thought would take but a single match to set off a conflagration.[2] But other analysts have questioned how far these ethnic discourses penetrate to the villages and the impact they have on different portions of the rural population. Meanwhile, in 1996, class-based unrest in western Nepal did manifest itself in a violent revolt or 'People's War' that has spread to most of the 75 districts of Nepal

[1]My research in Nepal has followed ethnic revivalist discourses in Nepal since 1982 with the formation of the Thakali Sewa Samiti, and more widely since 1990 with the formation of the Janajati Mahasangh.
[2]Among others: Padma Ratna Tuladhar, 1993 interview; Krishna Bhattachan (1995).

in varying degrees and resulted in the death of hundreds of police, Maoists, and bystanders caught in the crossfire.[3]

The variety of positions echoes familiar academic debates about conflict between class and ethnic groups and a state. These debates contrast those who focus on the influence of economic and political disparities against those who stress the primordial and ascriptive features of social collectivities. State-centric analyses tend to view movements based on identity politics as a threat to the state, rather than part of ongoing historical processes of nation-building.[4] Approaches that privilege some primordial sentiment, at least have the merit of according with the diagnoses of the ethnic nationalists themselves. After all, contemporary ethnic calls for a better deal or for regional autonomy in Nepal are all linked to culture, rooted in history, and tied to territory. But this approach tends to essentialize culture, failing to account for the ways in which there is often less to these claims to tradition than meets the eye. While early studies in Nepal tended to analytically isolate ethnic groups and cultures and thus inadvertently contribute to the perception of them as bounded and timeless entities, more recent studies in Nepal have recognized that ethnic boundaries emerged in tandem with the development of the Nepali state and that these boundaries were and remain fluid (see, for instance, Fisher 1987, Levine 1987, Holmberg 1989). Explanations that highlight the inherent fragility of multi-ethnic states, uneven regional

[3]The body count rose dramatically in 2001–2. By the end of May 2002, it was estimated that nearly 4,000 individuals had died due to the Maoist insurgency. The accuracy of this estimate is hard to assess.

[4]Another analytic approach, acknowledging that activism is unevenly distributed through ethnic communities, focuses on the manipulative activities of ethnic elites who seek to promote their own careers and status by acting as ethnic entrepreneurs, seeking benefits for themselves and their communities by using ethnic nationalism to mobilize their ethnic clientele and using the threat of secession as a bargaining chip. This approach partially illuminates the historical role of marginalized ethnic elites in Nepal in encouraging their communities to assimilate to the national culture (or more precisely, to the culture of the national elites) and their acquiescence in the current attempts of these marginalized groups to emphasize their differentness from elite or 'national' culture. This perspective is shared by high-caste Hindu elites who attribute ethnic activism to leaders who are out to serve their own self-interests. But while the Nepali case suggests the value of a mobilizing elite for the development of an inchoate minority or ethnic consciousness into a politically salient ethnic nationalism, this approach makes too much of this role and overemphasizes the passivity of the masses.

development, the resilience of primordial sentiments, or the instrumental actions of selfishly motivated ethnic elites are not sufficient
to account for the contemporary movements in Nepal where ethnic
and community identities are crosscut by class and unequal access
to resources, and the potential for violent confrontations is fueled by
both ethnic loyalties and class.[5]

Does the Maoist insurgency or the past decade of anti-Hindu-elite
activism on the part of ethnic 'minorities' indicate that what some see
as a two-hundred-year process of nation-building in Nepal has failed?
In Nepal, what is the relationship between social divisions based on
religious, ethnic, linguistic, and class lines, and the visions of a national
culture that holds the country together? Does the reassertion of ethnic
and class identities amount to a rejection of the nation or is it better
understood as a part of what has elsewhere been identified as
'modernism in the streets'?[6] To answer these questions and to assess
the outburst of ethnic and class anger that has emerged in Nepal
since the People's Movement of 1990, one must not only understand
the diversity of contemporary political expressions but also examine
the historical bases and structural conditions for these expressions.

This paper reflects on the impact of contemporary ethnic and class
debates at the village level, focusing on the perspective from a rural
area in Myagdi District in central Nepal. It examines how people
see themselves and their relationship to the state as they strive to
adjust to changing circumstances. The analysis draws primarily upon
interviews with Thakali, Magar, Chantyal, Newar, Bahun, Chetri, and
Dalits conducted at five intervals, each approximately five years apart–
in 1982, 1987, 1992, 1997, and 2002 (with emphasis on interviews
after 1990).[7] Most of the interviews were conducted in Myagdi District,
but since 1992 I have also conducted interviews among migrants from
Myagdi in Kathmandu, as well as locations in Japan, Hong Kong, the
United Kingdom, and the United States. The discussion here draws

[5]Versions of these theories are used by elites in Nepal as well as by foreign
scholars to question the legitimacy of political activists by portraying elite
behaviour and values as separate from 'mass' perception and behaviour. Elite
behaviour is characterized as instrumental, manipulative, and rational while
that of the masses is portrayed as either irrational or primordial.

[6]Lionel Trilling quoted in Lash and Friedman (1992: 33).

[7]I use the term 'Dalit' here as if it were synonomous with the Sano Jats (*sāno
jāt*, literally 'small caste'), the set of groups treated as lower status by all other
groups within Myagdi. Prior to the early 1990s this term was not used in Myagdi
and, as will be clear later, its use still has political connotations.

primarily from interviews with two distinct groups of informants. The first are primarily from landowning families with education up to but generally not exceeding grade ten. The second are wage labourers, with little or no land, very low levels of education, and without family traditions of overseas labour migration.[8]

The discussion in this paper treats only a small part of the ongoing processes by which a Nepalese nation has been and continues to be moulded as individuals and groups confront changing social realities and attempt to adapt to them and reform them.[9] I argue that, over the last twenty years, there has been a complex pattern of relationships between individuals in or from Myagdi, on the one side, and the state and the vision of national culture that it actively promotes, on the other. These relationships have been characterized at various times by resistance, engagement, circumvention, and accommodation.

MYAGDI AS A LOCALE AND AS A SET OF SOCIAL NETWORKS

Myagdi is a particularly interesting and appropriate case for the discussion of state and society relations in Nepal: it is a hill region that, by the early 1980s, was relatively well integrated into national life, both symbolically and geographically; it has had active ethnic associations (including the Thakali Sewa Samiti since 1983, Magar and Chantyal associations since the early 1990s, and Dalit organizations since the mid 1990s); it borders areas affected by Maoist activities since the beginning of the insurgency though it has been affected

---

[8]These two groups are taken as illustrative for the purposes of this paper. They are not comprehensive of all points of view in Myagdi, and many of my informants would not fit easily into either one. Nevertheless they are two particularly significant categories and the difference between these two categories became clearer in looking back over my notes of the past twenty years. In general the first might be called 'middle-class' and reflects the views of families who generally have enough land to produce sufficient food for their yearly needs. The second group may own some limited land but spend a good portion of their time dependent on employment by the first group. The two groups crosscut ethnic or *jāt* distinctions, though some groups fall more within one category than the other. The first category would include almost all the Thakali while the second would include almost all the Sano Jats.

[9]This paper is part of a larger project which examines the volatility of contemporary ethnic and class conflict in Nepal and examines the changing conditions, opportunities, and constraints under which interrelated sets of agents forge histories, visions, and procedures for organizing, and the potential for conflict as people (re)construct identities and communities through innovation, resistance, and accommodation.

directly only since 2001; and globalization has made its residents both consumers and labourers in a broader economic marketplace. All of these factors have had an effect on the changing consciousness of individuals in the area and contribute to changing notions of the nation, the role of the government, class, and ethnic relations.

In the areas of Myagdi District where I have lived and conducted interviews, villagers have responded differently to four competing discourses since the 'restoration of democracy' in 1990. These discourses—of nationalism, ethnic difference, class, and modernization—are not exclusive: depending on their own structural position within Nepali society villagers are variously receptive to these discourses. To some extent they pick and choose elements from each, and the varying orientations of villagers to contemporary Nepal are influenced by their views of nationalism through the prism of one or more of the other three discourses. Over the past twenty years these discourses have entered the local scene at different times and with varying impacts on portions of the local population. The discussion below considers the impact of these discourses as they arise at different times.

In my discussion of Myagdi, I follow the practice of my informants in treating it only partly as a geographical space or as a political district in Dhaulagiri Zone in central Nepal. By referring to someone as 'of Myagdi' individuals highlight a set of social networks and relationships that extend beyond the borders of the district. These relationships not only extend across district borders but also cut across *jāt* and class membership in significant ways. This sense of Myagdi as a social network to which one belongs is particularly common among migrants outside of the geographic boundaries of the political district of Myagdi, that is, for example, in Kathmandu, or in British Army camps, in Hong Kong, Tokyo, and in Cambridge, MA. 'Being from Myagdi' provides a social connection sometimes more important than those formed by class or ethnic membership, than being Thakali or Pun, for example. This identification is not without limits, however, and it does not apply immediately or equally among all categories of residents or migrants from the district. It is less applicable, for instance, between Dalits and those from other *jāts*. Nor is it always important between Bahuns and other *jāts*. The connection is strongest among those from the middle set of *jāt* categories.

MYAGDI IN 1982

Myagdi lies south of the Dhaulagiri massif and west of the Kali Gandaki river. The area is encompassed by a large drainage system that flows into the Kali Gandaki and a series of ridges that rise to altitudes exceeding 11,000 feet. Copper mining was important in the area until the 1930s but in 1982 the economy of the area was primarily agricultural and pastoral. On the edge of the region are several large Newar bazaars but, within the area itself, commerce is conducted by Thakalis, Chetris, and Gurungs. In 1982 (and until the mid-1990s) the area was accessible only by foot from two roadheads near Pokhara and Naudanda. These trails converged near Kusma, the capital of Kaski district. Within a short distance along the Kali Gandaki are two other district capitals: before the road was constructed in the mid 1990s, Baglung was a half-day walk north of Kusma, and Beni, the district centre of Myagdi, another half-day walk further north. From Beni a major trail follows the Myagdi River to the bazaar of Darbang where numerous routes diverge to reach villages on the surrounding ridges: one route heads over the Jaljala pass to Dhorpatan. Another trail leads south through Baglung to Riri Bazaar.

Myagdi is a multi-ethnic area with significant numbers of Bahun, Chetri, Magar, Thakali, Newars, Gurungs, Chantyal, and Dalits. *Interjāt* relationships in Myagdi are generally described in terms that echo the hierarchy established in Nepal's nineteenth-century legal code, the Muluki Ain. But in practice, while *jāts* maintained their distinctiveness, their relationships in 1982 (and, in fact, throughout the last half of the twentieth century) have been characterized by a modified *jāt* hierarchy wherein significant hierarchical distinctions between *jāts* are generally drawn only between three categories of peoples. This modified hierarchy positions Bahuns at the top and Sano Jats (or Dalits) at the bottom while the middle category encompasses the bulk of the population including Magars, Thakuris, Chetris, Thakalis, and Chantyals. In some instances, particularly with respect to marriage, these endogamous groups maintain ritually marked boundaries. In general, these boundaries were loosely maintained in the early 1980s and seemed to be breaking down. Moreover, while individuals within these groups will make claims about the relative hierarchy of these groups, there was no consensus on this issue either within or between groups.

Of these groups Thakalis have the smallest population, constituting a tiny percentage of the total population of Myagdi District in 1982 (about 1.5 per cent of the total population and never more than 3 per cent of the voting population in any single VDC). Though they are widely dispersed, they are far more visible than their proportion of the total population would make them. This is due to their presence in large numbers in central bazaars, the high number of political leaders and other prominent Thakali elites (moneylenders, landlords, etc.). Chantyals are also a small group; more concentrated in rural villages than the Thakali and relatively less successful economically. Magars are by far the most populous group in the region. Dalits are diverse and geographically spread throughout the region with long-distance social networks.

By 1982 the discourse of nationalism had been ongoing in Nepal in one form or another for two hundred years and its dominant mode had had considerable influence in Myagdi. The three traditional pillars of Nepali nationalism—the monarchy, Nepali language, and Hinduism—had been well established in this area. Though a multi-ethnic area, the monarchy was generally revered (or at least not openly disparaged), Nepali was well established as the predominant language, and Hindu influence was widespread and major Hindu holidays widely celebrated even though many participants within all four *jāts* treated them more as national than religious events. Local political debates or discussions about caste, class, and identity contained little that would suggest the class and ethnic discourse that would emerge in the late 1990s. The first ethnic association appeared in 1983 but there was little hint of the impact these kind of associations would have after 1992. There were lingering ideological divisions from the debate prior to the 1980 referendum on the Panchayat system and some local elite families remained strong supporters of then banned Nepali Congress Party. But the principal concern of the first group of landowning informants remained 'development' (*bikās*) and efforts to get the government to initiate and follow-up on development efforts in the region. Landless informants were split in their responses during this period: some aspired to improve their economic position by emulating the practices of the rural middle class, while a large minority were cynical about their role within the local structure and pessimistic about their chances of changing their conditions.

The integration of Myagdi in the national culture prior to 1982 had occurred despite the relative isolation of the area and the limited presence of government agents and agencies outside of the district capital. In 1982, when I first went to the district, there were many individuals who had never seen, let alone ridden, in a motor vehicle. There were no roads, no electricity, and no telephones in the district. Outside of Beni, the district capital, itself two days walk from the nearest roadhead, there were very few government offices, and those that did exist had been recently established and were generally poorly staffed.

In some significant ways, however, the area was not as isolated as this description might appear to suggest. For many of the middle-class landowning Myagdi residents, connections with outside worlds are longstanding and have had an important bearing on the way new discourses about identity and modernity are integrated. One source of evidence for these connections was readily viewed in the photo albums owned by nearly every middle-class family in the main bazaars. These revealed stories of kin or neighbours serving in the British or Indian army and posing in India, Hong Kong, Belize, and England. Not only soldiers, but also wives and occasionally parents, made these trips overseas. These albums stimulated many long discussions among villagers about other parts of the world, modernity, the relationship between Nepal and other countries, overseas economic opportunities, and the relative merits of democracy and socialism. The historical depth of these connections was evidenced by the narratives of family histories that spanned as many as five generations.

MYAGDI IN 1987

From 1982 to 1987, the observable changes in Myagdi were incre-mental and not particularly dramatic. There was a significant growth in the number of government agents and agencies represented in the outlying bazaars, an increased number of development projects (though these had little discernible impact on the well-being of most villagers), and a noticeable rise in cynicism about the government's capabilities or the sincerity of its agents. At the same time there was a drop off in recruitment by the British Army that fueled concerns among Magar and Thakali populations whose lifestyles had become depend-ent upon remittances from sons serving in the army about what new options might be available to the younger generation.

Thakali ethnic revivalism had bloomed during the 1980s and Thakali awareness of and presentation of their own ethnic solidar-ity had become quite noticeable in the area by 1987. Other groups, particularly Magars, Bahuns, and Chetris, had taken notice of it. It is not that there was no resentment of the Thakali prior to this period, especially among their political and economic rivals, but this resent-ment became more widespread in the late 1980s. As a small but very prominent population in Myagdi, the increased solidarity of the Thakali and the advantages of their national association became in-creasingly visible. By the late 1980s there were local backlashes against Thakali politicians as Magar political candidates successfully rallied support from portions of the Magar population that had previously supported the Thakali candidates. Basant Bahadur,[10] a Thakali in the bazaar of Darbang, commented on this to me in July 1987:

As you know, around here [in Myagdi], everyone used to support Thakali candidates for the [village] panchayat. Magar, Chantyal, Kami, Sarki, Damai, Chetri, everyone used to support the Thakali candidates. But this last election the Magars decided to support only those candidates who were Magar. They came down into the bazaar from all the surrounding villages and until late at night they paraded up and down the street shouting slogans. My family huddled in the house and was afraid to go out. We were all afraid to go out and vote.

Previous political supporters of Thakali candidates, on their part, felt fully justified in switching their support to new political candidates. As Mani Lal, a Pun Magar from Okarbhot explained:

We had always supported leaders from other *jāts*. Why should we continue to do this? Now we could see that the Thakali were organizing to push for their own interests. Why shouldn't we stand up for our own needs? Why should we help them to get richer and more powerful?

MYAGDI IN 1992

Between 1987 and 1992 changes were much more significant, both in Nepal as a whole and in Myagdi. These changes were brought about by ideological conflicts like the People's Movement and ensuing debates about democracy, ethnic difference, and national unity, as well as material changes like the construction of roads into the area, and the emergence and growth of a new pattern of transnational labour migration.

The 'restoration of democracy' and the overthrow of the Panchayat system dramatically raised people's hopes and expectations. With democracy many expected a fast track to *bikās* and modernity. But instead of modernity, the aftermath of 1990 produced doubt and uncertainty. In 1992, two years after the establishment of a democratic government, villagers in Myagdi were still unsure about how to respond to the promises of democracy and continued to express a great deal of support for the monarchy.

After 1990 the debates about ethnic difference begun by intellectuals in Kathmandu slowly infiltrated into the rural areas. Initially

[10]All names have been changed to preserve anonymity.

these issues were seen as urban concerns and political factions seemed unchanged in the rural areas of Myagdi. In the villages these issues arose in two ways: one was through the anti-Hindu rhetoric of the Janajati movement which sought to forge an ethnic majority out of what were minority groups within the hierarchy codified by the earlier legal codes of Nepal. The second emerged from the more specific ethnic revivalist rhetoric and activities of new social organizations like the Nepal Magar Sangh and the Nepal Chantyal Sangh that began in Kathmandu but spread quickly to Myagdi villages.[11] The second form of ethnic revivalism has had the stronger influence in the district and by 1992 had not yet fed into a pan-Janajati consciousness. Instead, at least in the Myagdi case, these ethnic revivals put groups in competition with one another as they increasingly emphasized and celebrated their differentness rather than their similarities.

The Janajati intellectuals in Kathmandu set out not only to oppose what they describe as a state-created and maintained system of social hierarchy but also to demarcate and shape a new social system, one that is non-hierarchical and non-discriminatory. They set out to do this through a number of interrelated strategies. First, ethnic intellectuals challenged state-imposed symbols of the nation, subversively appropriated and recodified signs, and looked within their own groups' history and traditions for symbols of unity around which their community might be imagined and mobilized. Through this effort they sought to turn social groups into political entities: nationalities, which could begin to bargain with the state for increased social, political, and economic rights of their citizens. The ethnic activists legitimized their actions by citing a history of subordination, land theft, and slavery at the hands of the ruling elite. Foremost in this process was a reconception of their community histories and a demand for a reconceived national historical narrative. They also subversively embraced previously despised characterizations and reinterpreted them with positive attributes. And finally they set up or re-emphasized a number of disturbing dichotomies—janajati and jati, indigenous and non-indigenous, Hindu and non-Hindu, flat nose and aquiline nose—all of which called attention to ongoing processes of discrimination.

Most significant of these innovative strategies was the attempt to create under the rubric 'Janajati' a new ethnic majority by bringing

[11]These two and the Thakali Sewa Samiti are three of the twenty-two ethnic groups associated with the Janajati Mahasangh (see Fisher 1993).

together in one forum what have always been marginalized minorities.[12] In the post-1990 environment, rising minority consciousness
generated many ethnic, religious, linguistic, and regional associations.
Groups where communal consciousness had been focused locally
or on kinship groups showed some signs of a growing sense of pan-
ethnic solidarity. In some cases, linguistic and cultural distinctions
previously used by the ethnic communities and the state to mark
differences between such groups were reinterpreted as minor variations within a broader community. The boundaries of this emerging
community are still in flux, still in the process of being imagined.
Ethnic intellectuals are in the process of facilitating the imagining of
their communities by inventing or resurrecting myths of origin identifying themselves as 'pre-Aryan' peoples of Mongoloid origin.

During the early 1990s, this intellectual activity at the centre had
limited effect in the rural areas and among some of the so-called
'janajati' groups. The Thakali, for example, continued to wrestle with
the question of whether they were truly 'janajati' or whether they belonged to the high-caste Thakuri category, as was suggested by the
widely repeated story of the their alleged descent from the Thakuri
prince, Hansa Raja (Fisher 1987, 2001). Despite this general ambivalence about their status, many Thakali and Magar did express a heightened awareness of their ethnic difference, and could cite examples
of ethnic inequality and prejudice. Without mounting a full-scale
boycott of the Hindu religious holiday of Dasain, many of the Thakali
did publicly downplay the religious significance of a holiday they had
previously accepted unquestioningly. Gyan Prakash expressed his
understanding of this to me in November 1992:

[12]Until 1990 the term 'Janajati' (*janajāti*) was not part of the common national
political vocabulary. It became popular in the late 1980s among a small group
of ethnic activists as a term to describe the largely Tibeto-Burman hill groups of
Nepal. Deliberately translated into English as 'nationalities' rather than the more
common 'tribal' or 'ethnic group', the term was used to draw attention to their
conviction that Nepalese society consists of a number of different but equal
nationalities that collectively constitute the nation. The translation of the term
reflects resentment and rejection of the historical treatment of people in Nepal
as social entities (i.e., *jāts*) and a reassertion of their identities as territorial bodies
(*deś*). The ambiguity of the dictionary definitions for 'nationality' is also consistent
with the different claims and strategies that characterize the Janajati movement.
Nationalities may refer simply to 'groups of people, each of which has a common
and distinguishing linguistic and cultural background and form one constituent
element of a larger group (as a nation)', or it may also be taken to suggest that
each of these aggregations of people is 'potentially capable of forming a nation-
state' (see the OED).

We used to celebrate Dasain without thinking about it. But this is actually a holiday for Bahuns and Chetris. Before we didn't pay much attention to this and so we celebrated it with everyone else. Our Thakali holiday is Torongla, as you know. This [Dasain] is not our holiday. So we continue to visit our families and friends but we don't to recognize [the rituals] as the Bahuns and Chetris do. They are also welcome to celebrate Torongla with us.

For some groups, particularly within the younger generation, economic opportunities mattered more than political and ideological change. So, when democracy failed to bring development and modernity, they went to seek it elsewhere. By 1992 a new transnational labour migration had begun to attract many young people from Myagdi. In increasing numbers young men went overseas for wage labour in Korea, Hong Kong, Singapore, and Japan. Within a few years after this pattern began, wives, single women, and even men in their 50s followed. This pattern continues today with some slight shifts over the years concerning the preferred country of migration. Migrants have gone overseas for periods ranging from one to nine years. They save as much as $1,000 per month and send the money back through friends and family for the purchase of land, the construction of houses in Kathmandu, and the education of their children. This travel has involved large numbers of Thakalis, some Magars, and smaller numbers of other *jāts* from Myagdi. A small, but equally significant, wage-labour migration of low-status groups to the Persian Gulf also continued through the 1990s allowing these individuals to send back much smaller amounts for the purchase of marginal farm land and small huts within Myagdi district. Overseas migration costs money and, paradoxically, poorer individuals had to draw loans from established local patron-client ties to make these journeys that would help them to reduce their future dependence on their patrons.

MYAGDI IN 1997

By 1997, there was more overseas migration, increased ethnic consciousness, growing scorn of the post-1990 government, and a marked rise in the class awareness of service *jāts*. Nearly every extended family I encountered that year along the Myagdi and Kali Gandaki river valleys had stories to tell of friends and family members now residing—at least temporarily—in Kathmandu or abroad. News, new ethnic histories, and a loose sense of Janajati solidarity flowed easily from one place to another along with people and foreign remittances. It seemed as if there was no 'there' in Myagdi that wasn't intimately connected to Kathmandu, and also to Tokyo, the Persian Gulf, or the United States. In this new bustle of interconnectivity, these networked communities were consumers more than producers of ethnic ideology. They selectively consumed the new ethnic ideology even as they had become avid consumers of modernity, drinking Coca Cola, replacing local alcohol with bottled beer, or better yet, moving to Kathmandu where life could be eased with electric rice cookers and running water.

Within these networked communities, the focus on becoming modern was striking and the common mode of expression was through consumption, buying, eating, and possessing modern things. Attitudes toward the faltering democratic state bordered on indifference and individual assessments of the government reflected far lower expectations than at any point since the restoration of democracy in 1990. There was a growing doubt that the government had the capacity to address the enormous economic problems facing Nepal or the political will to redress growing inequities. The enormous disparity between overseas wages and the amount that could be earned locally encouraged ongoing outward migration and discouraged many individuals from making capital investments in the district. In the urban enclaves of Myagdi-centered communities of Kathmandu, issues of ethnic identity and difference were still current but less enthusiastically discussed than the monthly wages of friends and kin in Tokyo and Los Angeles.

In Tokyo in 1997, I met old friends from Myagdi at the temple at Hamamatsucho, where more than two hundred acquaintances from villages in central Nepal—most from Myagdi—had gathered on their day off from work. Through the discussion at this and other gatherings during my stay in Japan, I came to see it as they did, that the villages I had known in Myagdi were expanding to take in isolated parts of Kathmandu, Tokyo, and Cambridge, Massachusetts. Far from their geographic home, my Myagdi acquaintances clung to every remembrance of their villages and were sympathetic to and even active in efforts to revitalize their ethnic and regional traditions. Fundraising to support local shamans was as successful as fundraising to upgrade the village schools.

The identities that they carried with them and employ through these journeys were as much place-specific, *jāt*-specific, and Janajati, as Nepali. This was made clearer during a meeting held at the Yeti Restaurant in Shinjuku. Here, amidst the gleaming modernism of Tokyo I was presented with the two most recent issues of the Thakali ethnic magazine of Japan, and heard long animated discussions contrasting the lamentable failure to form an all-Nepal association in Tokyo with the existence of thriving local Newar, Thakali, and Gurung social organizations. Pressed to explain why there were difficulties in forming a more broad-based Nepal association, they stressed ethnic differences that became increasingly apparent in the migrant context. 'Bahuns do not consider us their equals. It is the same here as it is in Nepal. You know our history well,' my acquaintances argued over and over again, 'and will understand that just because we are Janajati and have flat noses we should not be treated as lesser citizens of our own country.'

In the years since the passage of the constitution, groups and individuals in Nepal have defined themselves in opposition to Hinduism in increasing numbers. Since the early 1990s, many of the ethnic associations have continued to persuade their constituencies to stop observances of the Hindu holiday of Dasain. Over the past years there has been a proliferation of new historical accounts of ethnic origins that take the inverse form of previous 'Sanskritized' accounts. In the new charter myths, groups no longer trace their origins to a long-forgotten Hindu past, but instead trace their origins to some long-forgotten Buddhist, indigenous, or autochthonous past, explicitly citing their differences from Hindu populations in Nepal.

It was readily apparent in 1997 that the new ethnic categories and narratives had made equally deep inroads among the Magar, Chantyal, and Thakali populations in Myagdi and in their extended networked communities. The term Janajati, more puzzled over than understood in 1993, now rolled off everyone's tongue more fluently; Magars sought me out to recount their newly learned lore of ancient Magar kings and hastened to tell me that 'we found that Hinduism wasn't really our religion'. There remained clear differences between urban and rural populations, just as I had recorded when the Thakali first organized fourteen years earlier (Fisher 1987), but these differences were more muted than before, in part by the astonishing increase in mobility in and out of the area.

As much as they valued their territorial and cultural ties and identities, the Myagdi migrants, in particular, were realistic. They placed great emphasis on both the maintenance of their ethnic identity and the skills they identified with modernity but they recognized the attraction overseas labour held for their children. 'Personally', my friend Mahen explained, 'I think we must all give our children a good education, encourage them to be doctors and engineers. But in Nepal a doctor or engineer makes only 4,000 rupees per month [US$80], while a boy can make Rs 15,000–20,000 [a month] as a *lahure* [serving in the British Army] and 50,000 [US$1,000 a month] in Japan. How can I convince my son to stay in school?'

Politically, those from middle-class Myagdi families were both highly critical of what they saw as an ineffectual state and at the same time unsympathetic to the Maoists. Their criticisms of the state reflected the view that the government was dominated by urban, high-caste Hindus who used their positions to exploit Nepal for their own advantages. They accepted the need to rework both state and society to give them a more equitable chance for government positions and development benefits. However, in the Maoists they saw a more fundamental threat to Nepali society. In their criticism, they rarely acknowledged the ideological stance of the Maoists, or the validity of their class-based analysis of Nepal's problems. Instead, they tended to dismiss them as bandits and troublemakers.

The second group of informants from Myagdi, those from wage-labouring, landless families were in a very different position by 1997. Lower-caste groups (a few now identifying themselves as Dalits) had particularly picked up both the anti-Hindu discourse of the Janajati movement and the class discourse of the Maoists. Of all the groups resident in Myagdi, these lower-caste groups felt they had the least invested in any notion of a Nepali nation. As Dalit informants described it, their oppressors were everywhere: high castes, the Janajati, and agents of the state were all equally dangerous adversaries. Their resentment was expressed against categories of people—landlords, moneylenders, and elites—even as they remained dependent upon specific individuals and families from these categories for their day-to-day welfare. For them, the Maoist discourse that explained the need to eliminate, not the people who filled the categories, but the categories themselves, resonated with their simultaneous and apparently paradoxical hatred of and reliance on (and even affection for) specific individuals within those categories.

MYAGDI IN 2002

By 2002, a number of events—the massacre of the royal family in June 2001, the increase in Maoist activity in Myagdi, the involvement of the army in the suppression of the Maoist insurgency, and the imposition of a State of Emergency within the country—further transformed life in the rural areas of Myagdi.

The royal family—King Birendra in particular—had continued to retain the loyalty of the vast majority of informants in Myagdi throughout the 1990s. No one from that region appears able to accept the official explanation of the massacre, a fact that, coupled with a widespread dislike and distrust of the current King and his son, fuels numerous theories about conspiracies and creates a great deal of dismay and uncertainty. Without a trustworthy benevolent monarch and with a widespread Maoist insurgency and a government led by bickering and inept political parties, people from Myagdi find it difficult to be optimistic about the immediate future. Within the district, the Maoists became an undeniable presence in 2001: they regularly asked for contributions from landowners, shopkeepers, and schoolteachers, their requests often coupled with thinly veiled threats. All government agents were withdrawn from the district except for those in the district centre of Beni. And many landowners and others moved, at least temporarily, into Pokhara and Kathmandu. 'It's very frightening in Myagdi now', my friend Birendra explained in June 2000, 'we are afraid to leave the village after dark and have to be very careful even in daylight. The Maoists come in and promise people guns and clothes if they will join them. With these guns, they are nothing more than thieves, robbing from people whenever they like.' Lal Bahadur, in charge of a police station along the Myagdi River, argued that 'they [the Maoists] are pressuring people to think in a negative way, motivating them with anti-government slogans'. 'But the big problem is', Jyoti, a former policeman from Baglung District said to me, 'that the police don't know who is a Maoist and who is not. Most of them are not from the area and they are young and frightened because so many police have been killed.' Outside of Nepal, people from Myagdi expressed considerable concern about the Maoist activity in the area and voiced their fears about returning. They felt they would be readily identifiable as individuals who had worked overseas and targeted by the Maoists if they were to return.

For some poorer families in Myagdi the basic message of the Maoists resonates with their own frustrations and the claim that militancy is a necessary strategy has appeal for the younger generation. Indeed, it would seem that many of the poor in Myagdi needed little outside motivation to think negatively about the government. For some, the Maoists offered a model of how they could act on their frustration in an effective way. Listening to them over the past five years, it would appear that, at least in Myagdi, a growing government presence in the late 1980s and early 1990s helped fuel anti-government sentiment by providing demonstrable evidence of ineffective, arrogant, caste-biased, and corrupt government. As Lal's comment (and those of many other informants) suggest, many of the agents of the state in Myagdi act without apparent sympathy or interest in local social dynamics. This fact has helped to fuel anti-government sentiment has grown not only among the poor but also among the middle classes.

CONCLUSION

Four distinct but interdependent discourses—those of nationalism, ethnic difference, class conflict, and modernism—were all in play in different ways among Myagdi's population by the year 2002. In varying ways the latter three all play off of and affect the concept of Nepali nationalism and the villager's perceptions of the Nepali state.

The discourse of both the Maoists and the Janajati movement offer encouragement to those who are frustrated with the status quo and want to change it. But they offer different strategies for effecting that change. For many residents in Myagdi the frustration with the government gives a boost to the multi-ethnic discourse that proposes a new vision of a Nepali nation, while Maoists appear threatening— easy to dismiss as nothing more than poor bandits without ideology.

Migration offers another way to respond to the frustrations of poor government and a stagnant economy by allowing the labour migrants to sidestep the inefficiency of the present government by going overseas, moving beyond the limited opportunities of Nepal to take advantage of those provided by globalization. In this context, modernity is seen as education, learning English, secularization, transnational connections, and individual freedom. And, perhaps ironically, it means the freedom to travel overseas while choosing to keep your own identity (as Nepali but also as Thakali, Janajati, etc.) and social networks.

But the options of migration and multi-ethnicity are not attractive to everyone. Dalits note that the multi-ethnic ideology continues to exclude them. Furthermore, the discrepancy in overseas opportunities puts poorer individuals from Myagdi further behind in a local economy stimulated by foreign remittances. For some members of these groups, the direct action of the Maoists offers a more immediate release of frustrations—particularly for people who feel they have little left to lose.

In Myagdi individuals have had access to numerous dimensions of identity—those based on class, ethnicity, kinship, locality, religion, for example—some of which become more important at certain times. Historically in Nepal, as is true elsewhere, it has been moments of political or economic crisis that have often been the catalyst which brings forth aspects of group and individual identity. Looked at over time, the interactions within and among groups, and the conflicts between the national identity and other identities reveal a changing set of relationships. Ethnicity, for example, is not simply an ad hoc or random social construction but a re-creation using the past (albeit partially or wholly imagined) to construct a present with an eye toward the future (Fisher 1987). Ethnic boundaries are fluid and flexible but not infinitely so. They move in response to economic and political opportunities and constraints, and vary within the community depending on such factors as class, gender, age, locale, occupation, education, etc. (Fisher 2001, Foster 1991, Williams 1989). In Nepal, as elsewhere, these constraints are and have been affected by the changing nature of the state.

While it would be inaccurate and premature to characterize the process of nation-building in Nepal as a failure, it is important to acknowledge that the very process of building a nation leaves in its wake seeds of resentment that later come to threaten national unity. The ethnic and class contestation that has resulted in the creation of new identities and alliances is itself not new but is instead the contemporary manifestation of a process that has been going on for at least two hundred years

What do the local adoptions of one of these three contemporary forms of actions—the adoption of a multi-ethnic vision of the nation, transnational labour migration, and supporting a direct insurgency— mean for the state? In a significant way the three new discourses that compete with nationalism—ethnic revivalism, Maoism, and modernism—are all brands of Nepali nationalism. The Myagdi case suggests that there is an apparent paradox in the contemporary attitudes of Nepali citizens towards the notion of a Nepali nation: in spite of all the disputes about national culture, there is an almost unquestioned agreement that a Nepali nation exists. It is the content of that sentiment of nation that is openly contested. While the dissonant voices heard in Nepal sometimes call for varying degrees of autonomy, in Myagdi they are not usually put forth as ethnic nationalisms—for example, as Magar nationalism, Dalit nationalism, or Thakali nationalism—that compete with Nepali nationalism. Instead, they represent differing visions of Nepali nationalism: calls for a nation that allows for plural identities, religions, languages, and cultures. The moderate, and at the moment more dominant, ethnic activists see their expression of nationalities not as the rejection of nation but as the only viable basis for it.

As nationalism evolves through a contested process, the outcome is by no means predetermined. What may begin as a move for multiple moderate goals including greater cultural independence, a fairer distribution of resources, or access to power, may take on a more radical or assimilated direction depending on the interaction with the apparatus of the state. Intellectuals play but one of the roles in the process and villagers another. The point is not whether or not the choices and arguments of intellectuals in Kathmandu reflect the masses but under what circumstances the villagers find it in their interest to adopt a more radical or moderate direction.

What is demonstrated by the Myagdi material is that, whatever their choices, villagers do have agency. They are not passive recipients of ideology, discourses, or values from leaders or political elites. They choose to act according to understandings they construct themselves. Of course they set out to make their own lives under circumstances not of their own choosing and their social and material conditions do influence how they see and respond to their options. In other words, poverty and caste membership do matter. What matters even more is the perception that opportunities are not equal: that some possess opportunities to improve their conditions while others lack any other means but violence to effect a change in their circumstances.

REFERENCES

Bhattachan, K. 1995. 'Ethnopolitics and Ethnodevelopment: An Emerging Paradigm in Nepal' in D. Kumar (ed.) *State, Leadership and Politics in Nepal*. Kathmandu: CNAS.

Fisher, W.F. 2001. *Fluid Boundaries: Forming and Transforming Identity in Nepal*. New York: Columbia University Press.

_____ 1993. 'Nationalism and the Janajati' *Himal* (March/April): 11–16.

_____ 1987. 'The Re-Creation of Tradition: Ethnicity, Migration, and Social Change among the Thakali of Central Nepal'. PhD dissertation, Columbia University.

Foster, R. 1991. 'Making National Cultures in the Global Ecumene' *Annual Review of Anthropology* 20: 235–60.

Gellner, D.N., J. Pfaff-Czarnecka and J. Whelpton (eds) 1997. *Nationalism and Ethnicity in a Hindu Kingdom: The Politics of Culture in Contemporary Nepal*. Amsterdam: Harwood.

Holmberg, D. 1989. *Order in Paradox: Myth, Ritual, and Exchange Among Nepal's Tamang*. Ithaca: Cornell University Press.

Lash, S. and J. Friedman (eds) 1992. *Modernity and Identity*. Oxford and Cambridge, MA: Blackwell.

Levine, N.E. 1987. 'Caste, State, and Ethnic Boundaries in Nepal' *Journal of Asian Studies* 46: 71–88.

Rosaldo, R. 1989. *Culture and Truth: The Remaking of Social Analysis*. Boston: Beacon.

Williams, B.F. 1989. 'A Class Act: Anthropology and the Race to Nation Across Ethnic Terrain' *Annual Review of Anthropology* 18: 401–44.

chapter four

Nepali Politics: People-Parties Interface

• *Krishna Hachhethu*

AN OVERVIEW OF POST-1990 POLITICAL DEVELOPMENTS

N epali political parties have entered a new phase after the
success of the *jan āndolan* (People's Movement) of 1990.
Political parties in Nepal began as a symbol of opposition
to the century-old Rana oligarchy in the early 1930s and 1940s and
they led an armed revolution against the Ranas in 1950–51. They
had evolved as movement organizations and, except during the first
experience of a multi-party system between 1951 and 1960, continued
as such against the Partyless Panchayat system from 1960 to 1990.
The restoration of democracy in 1990 was therefore a milestone for
the revival of party politics in Nepal.

The Nepali Congress (NC) and the United Left Front (ULF, consisting of seven communist parties) together launched the People's
Movement in February 1990 which terminated successfully in its
objective of overthrowing the Panchayat regime in April of the same
year. The enactment of a new Constitution—framed by representatives of the NC and ULF as well as by the King's nominees to the
Constitution Recommendation Commission—attempted to translate
the spirit of the People's Movement into a legal document which would
become the supreme law of the country. By this Constitution, the
sovereign power of the state was transferred from the palace to the
people for the first time. The Constitution attempted to ensure the
stability of the newly established democratic regime by stating categorically that popular sovereignty, constitutional monarchy, the multi-

party parliamentary system, and fundamental rights of the citizen are unamendable. The avowed commitment to the fundamental principles of the new Constitution by the rightist Rashtriya Prajatantra Party (RPP) (National Democratic Party, NDP, in English)—a party formed by the followers of the dismantled Panchayat system—as well as by several leftist splinter groups, including the Communist Party of Nepal, Unified Marxist-Leninist (UML), irrespective of their ideological stands in the past, demonstrates the assimilation of the major ideological and political forces of the country into the mainstream of the parliamentary process.

The 1991 general elections for the 205 members of the House of Representatives (HOR)—the first parliamentary elections held after the restoration of democracy—had its own significance in introducing the democratic process based on a popular mandate. The 1991 general elections created a two-party system with the NC in government and the UML as the major opposition party. This is generally considered an ideal situation for political stability and the institutionalization of democracy. The second parliamentary elections held in 1994 produced a hung parliament, bringing a reversal in the parties' positions. The UML moved from the opposition to the Treasury bench as the largest party in the HOR and the NC was relegated to the opposition as the second-largest party. The NC, however, has regained its original position with a comfortable majority in the HOR after the third parliamentary elections 1999. Table 4.1 presents the positions of the political parties in the last three parliamentary elections.

In its initial phase the political transition—the demolition of the Panchayat structures and the setting up of democratic institutions—was smooth and the political parties won some of the credit for that task. But the parties were soon blamed for the rapid emergence of political instability and the erosion of democracy in its functional attributes. The first elected majority government of the NC led by Girija Prasad Koirala collapsed before the end of its prescribed five years' tenure due to internal conflicts in the ruling party. The same reason eventually led to the defeat of the NC in the 1994 mid-term elections, which produced a hung parliament. The UML, as the largest party of the parliament, formed a minority government, but it also fell from power after nine months due to internal dissension over the choice of a coalition partner. During the second parliament (November 1994–May 1999), Nepal experienced eight governments of different types. The frequent changes of government led people to believe that Nepali politics had degenerated into a naked struggle for power. The

TABLE 4.1: PARTIES' POSITIONS IN THE FIRST, SECOND, AND THIRD PARLIAMENTARY ELECTIONS

Parties	Number of Seats Elected			% of Popular Vote		
	1991	*1994*	*1999*	*1991*	*1994*	*1999*
NC	110	83	112	39.5	34.5	37.2
UML	69	88	70	29.3	31.9	31.6
ML	–	–	0	–	–	6.6
RPP	1	20	11	5.6	18.5	10.4
RPP (Chand)	3	–	0	6.9	–	3.4
NSP	6	3	5	4.3	3.6	3.2
NPF	–	–	5	–	–	1.4
NeWPP	2	4	1	1.3	1.0	0.6
UPF	9	0	1	5.0	1.4	0.9
CPN (Democratic)	2	0	0	3.2	1.7	0.05
Independents	3	7	0	4.4	6.4	2.9
Other small parties	0	0	0	0.5	1.0	1.75
Total	205	205	205	100	100	100

ML = Communist Party of Nepal (Marxist-Leninist), NSP = Nepal Sadbhavana Party, NPF = National People's Front, NeWPP = Nepal Workers' and Peasants' Party, UPF = United People's Front, CPN = Communist Party of Nepal.
Sources: EC (1991, 1994, 1999)

problem of government instability remains as before in spite of the fact that the 1999 general elections brought a return to a two-party system. Krishna Prasad Bhattarai was compelled to resign after holding the post of Prime Minister of the NC majority government for ten months. Long before he finally resigned in July 2001, G.P. Koirala had to face endless speculation that he would face the same fate as his predecessor. In fact, the party system in the post-1990 period is dominated by intra-party conflicts over access to power as well as by unhealthy inter-party competition, which has created a sort of political crisis, impeding the consolidation of the newly achieved democracy.

The study of political parties is the least-developed area in the literature on Nepali politics. The pioneer authors (Gupta 1964; Joshi & Rose 1966; Chatterji 1967; Chauhan 1971) give a comprehensive picture of Nepal's first experience of democracy in 1951–60. The literature on Nepali politics that was published between 1960 and 1990 concentrates either on the patrimonial system under the Panchayat regime (Shaha 1978, 1982) or on the parties' oppositional politics (Baral 1977, 1983; Chatterji 1977, 1980, 1982; Parmanand 1982). With the restoration of democracy in 1990, studies on Nepali politics increased and diversified both in content and in methodology. Empirical and quantitative studies in areas like elections, public opinion, leadership, government, and parliament have been carried out by different institutions and authors (POLSAN 1991, 1992; NOSC 1993; IIDS 1993; SEARCH,1994; Borre *et al.* 1994; Chalise 1995; CCD 1996; Sharma & Sen 1999). A number of books in a more qualitative, descriptive, and analytical vein have been written both by Nepali (Baral 1993; Kumar 1995; Sharma 1998) and by foreign scholars (Hutt 1994; Brown 1996; Hoftun *et al.* 1999); these focus on problems of democracy, development, and governance in Nepal in the post-1990 period. Most of such scholarly works concentrate on the description of political developments and on the analysis of major events and trends in Nepali politics. Though political parties have a prominent place in research and studies on post-1990 politics, the authors do not treat political parties as the central unit of their study. Furthermore, research on political parties at the local level is completely lacking in the literature on Nepali politics and parties so far.

This paper makes an attempt to explore party-people relations in Nepal in the post-1990 period. For conceptual clarity I have borrowed from 'linkage theory' which defines political parties 'as agencies for forging links between citizens and policy makers' and suggests two general modes of linkages: through penetration in society and through reaction to public opinion (Lawson 1980). In addition, I have used the 'party transformation' approach (Panebianco 1988) to comprehend the changing nature of party-people relations. Party-people relations are shaped by the interaction of respective interests. People's involvement in party politics is generally motivated either by personal gain or by public benefit or by both. An individual seeks, in return for his or her vote, the favour of the party in order to fulfill their personal interests, i.e. money, jobs, or other opportunities. The interest of public benefit, another motivational factor, relates to the people's adherence to the party's ideology, goals, policies, and programmes, and their trust in the party's ability to deliver service to society in terms of development. The interest of the party is to maximize its votes through the distribution of collective incentives (identity, solidarity, ideology, policies, and programmes) to the people in general as well as through selective incentives (power, status, money, jobs, and other material rewards) to the party's clients. In India, political parties have also achieved popularity among the people through the parties' local leaders' non-political activities (Weiner 1967; Kohli 1991). This paper is mainly based on primary data collected through review of the parties' documents and through field study in the course of my PhD. The fieldwork was carried out in six districts (Dhankuta, Dhanusha, Kathmandu, Tanahu, Bardiya, and Bajhang) over a period of seven months between February 1995 and May 1996. These districts were selected taking into consideration the need to make it broadly representative of different development regions, ecological zones, caste/ethnic/tribal groups, and political parties. The paper covers only the NC and the UML, the two dominant parties representing two different ideologies: the NC is a liberal democratic party but with a socialist trademark and the UML is a communist party but with allegiance to multi-party democracy. I examine party-people relations at both the central and local levels under four major headings: the setting of ideological goals, the formulation of public policy, development-related performance, and the distribution of patronage.

PARTY-PEOPLE RELATIONS AT THE CENTRE

Ideological Platforms and People's Preferences

The initial period after 1990 was a euphoric phase followed by mass enthusiasm for joining political parties. Individuals with vested interests had different considerations in joining a political party, but the choice of party by most ordinary people was largely determined by two factors: the result of the People's Movement and ideological preferences. Though the People's Movement was mainly an urban middle-class movement, the people at large, including the rural masses, had retained the habit of Nepali society, namely 'follow the victor', when choosing a political party. A large section of the people, therefore, was attracted either to the Congress or to the Communist parties, the perceived winners of the 1990 Movement. In choosing between them, the party's policy and performance in terms of social change and economic development was the least important factor in the formative phase of democracy, because parties and the interim coalition government (April 1990–May 1991) were overwhelmingly preoccupied by specific political objectives, viz. constitution-making and general elections, rather than by establishing socio-economic programmes. Thus, the people's emotional and sentimental attachments to a broad ideological identity—to the NC as democrats or to the UML as communists—worked as the guiding factor in their choice of party.

NEPALI CONGRESS

The NC is closely associated with the main achievement of 1990: the restoration of multi-party democracy. Because of its long struggle, since its inception, for the parliamentary system and for a constitutional monarchy, the NC has long been considered as the main protagonist of democracy in Nepal. Thus the party was ideologically in an advantageous position against the UML's non-conformist stand on parliamentary system in the initial phase of democracy. As was suggested by NC propaganda during the 1991 parliamentary elections: 'Vote for RPP: vote for partyless system; vote for communist: vote for one-party dictatorship; vote for NC: vote for democracy' (IIDS 1993: 36).

When defining the party's ideology of democratic socialism, almost all Congress leaders and workers refer to what the late B.P. Koirala said and did. Some policy measures taken against the feudal landlords, i.e. the abolition of *birtā*, *jāgirdārī*, *jamindārī*, and *rājarājouta* forms of land tenure by B.P. Koirala's NC government in 1959–60, were used to project the NC as a bona fide socialist party. B.P. Koirala equated socialism with a mixed economy, different both from the Western capitalist system as well as from a communist state-controlled and centralized economy (Koirala 1979). He encapsulated the party's socialist goals in the slogans 'rural development' and 'upliftment of

TABLE 4.2. IDEOLOGICAL PLATFORMS OF NC AND CPN(UML)

Contents of Ideology	NC	UML
Party represents	People of all classes and castes	Proletariat and working class
Nepali state, at present	Poor and developing country	Semi-feudal and semi-colonial
Goal	Democratic socialism	Communism
Political system	Parliamentary democracy	People's multi-party democracy
Economic system	Mixed but open economy	Mixed but protected economy
Monarchy	Constitutional monarchy	Republic
Religion	Freedom of religion	Secular state
Language	Nepali as national/ official language	Equal status for all languages
Main slogan	Peace, stability, and development	Food, clothing, and shelter for all

Sources: NC (1990), UML (1993)

the poor'. In order to convince people that the NC's socialist ideology is for the cause of the poor, NC leaders and workers frequently quoted a famous conversation that B.P. Koirala had with King Mahendra:

Each and every Nepalese family should at least have a house like mine; like me they should have plenty of food to eat; their children should go to school like my children; and when sick, they should be able to get medical treatment, and further, let them have cows and buffaloes in their courtyards. (Koirala 1979)

The NC's socialist image was exclusively personalized with the image of B.P. Koirala to the extent that most party leaders and workers were found to be unaware of how their own party's election manifesto defined democratic socialism in terms of a 'mixed economy', 'equitable distribution of national product', 'participation of labour in production management', 'equal dignity and rights to all the people', 'government's service to the oppressed and poor people', and 'social security for the old, disabled and helpless people' (EMNC 1991). Without the symbolic figure of B.P. Koirala the NC appeared ideologically an orphan in so far as the party's vision about its proclaimed goal of democratic socialism was concerned. Due to a lack of clarity in thought and vision on its avowed goal of democratic socialism, the NC was unable to put forward any radical policy or programme for the development of the country.

On the political front, too, the NC seemed to be heading away from the centre and towards the right. Though the objective of the People's Movement was not for a republic, it was a fight against the King for the transfer of sovereignty to the people. The palace was, therefore, generally perceived to be hostile to the spirit of the Movement. The NC has revived and reaffirmed its policy of reconciliation with the King. Its reconciliatory stance appeared the moment the ban on political parties was lifted in a remark of the party's President, Ganesh Man Singh: 'His Majesty is a very gentle person. His liberal disposition and his love for his people is truly deep. That is why he accepted our request for multi-party system' (*Rising Nepal*, 9 April 1990). The popular sentiment immediately following the Movement was against the NC's reconciliation with the King.

The change of political regime through a mass uprising naturally raised the people's aspirations for change in other areas also. The advent of democracy in Nepal raised in its wake the voices of different groups of people who had hitherto been silent. The demands of the minority and disadvantaged sections of society became increasingly apparent soon after the restoration of democracy. But the NC supported the retention of Nepali as the national and official language, which could be considered as a realistic and a pragmatic step. Its principle of 'freedom of religion' was reduced to the affirmation that Nepal should continue as a 'Hindu state'.

Though the NC made an outstanding contribution to the transformation of the political structure towards parliamentary democracy and constitutional monarchy, at the same time it resisted pressures for radical change, preferring to retain some of the old symbols and traditional structures. It is therefore generally considered to be a liberal and centrist party, but oriented towards the right in the political spectrum of the country. This ideological identity has both advantages and disadvantages in mobilizing public support.

Communist Party of Nepal (UML)

The UML officially designates Nepal as a 'semi-feudal and semi-colonial' (*ardha-sāmānta* and *ardha-upanibesh*) state. Its declared objective is 'to abolish feudalism, comprador bureaucratic capitalism, and imperialism.' With adherence to Marxism and Leninism as the guiding principle of the party, the UML identifies itself as the 'representative of proletarian and working class.' Nationalist capitalists, the middle class, intellectuals, etc., are its allies (ML 1991, UML 1991).

The UML stands on the left of the political spectrum of the country. In the Nepali understanding this means to advocate radical change and greater equality among the people. The party appeared broadly successful in symbolizing itself 'as a party of new ideas' (POLSAN 1991: 14) espousing 'rapid and radical change', and also in projecting its image as a champion for the cause of the poor and the disadvantaged sections of the society.

The projection of Nepali communism as 'radical, nationalist, and pro-poor' is nothing new. Such credentials had long been established since the foundation of the Communist Party of Nepal in 1949. The UML, the most dominant of several splinter communist groups, acquired a new identity as a supporter of the multi-party system. It actively participated in the 1990 Movement and spoke out for the consolidation of its achievements. Despite the party maintaining its communist identity, the UML, immediately after the promulgation of the Constitution, took a decision to endorse the system of multi-party competition as the means to achieve its goal of *naulo janbād* (New People's Democracy). It has tried to convince the people that the ideologies of communism and the multi-party system—generally conceived as two antagonistic principles—could become complementary and supplementary. Its communist trademark has remained valuable in attracting the majority of the poverty-stricken people of Nepal, particularly in the early days after 1990 when the national psyche was yearning for rapid and revolutionary change.

The transition to democracy in Nepal came to a logical conclusion: the restructuring of the polity on the basis of constitutional monarchy and a parliamentary system. But mere change of political regime, though concrete and substantial, did not satisfy the people at large. The popular feeling that political reform on its own was inadequate came to the surface in different ways. The interim period was featured by mobs manhandling some *mandale* (notorious henchmen of the Panchayat regime); there were squatters' movements which forcibly took over public places; ethnic activists demanded a secular state and equal status for all languages; industrial workers and government and corporation employees went on strike and demonstrated for increases in their salaries and other facilities. All segments of society demanded a better situation and quick benefits after the demise of the Panchayat system (Hoftun *et al.* 1999).

The UML fuelled the people's resentments arising from their frustrations at the slow pace of change. It tried to give the impression that whatever had been achieved during and after the People's Movement, was less than it wished for. The UML also instigated movements to radicalize social needs and interests. It projected itself as a quick provider of 'bread for the hungry, jobs for the unemployed, land for the landless, and shelter for the homeless'. The party machinery, local leaders/workers, and the party-run news media in particular, actively sought the confiscation of land from landlords and redistribution so there would be 'four *bigha* per family'. Such populist slogans and propaganda raised the hopes of the poor and disadvantaged sections of society. The UML tried to combine the class interests of the poor with the ethnic interests of the minorities while generally radicalizing both people and society.

Policy Platforms and the People's Choices

NEPALI CONGRESS

Though ideological factors predominated in the people's choice of party in the initial phase of democracy, the NC and the UML provided separate policy platforms in order to sustain and expand their support base in society. Since the 1991 parliamentary elections, they have brought out their policy platforms related to social change and economic development to win the support of a larger number of people. The

NC's policy position on several areas of development, i.e. agriculture, industry, social security, foreign policy, etc., are spelled out in its documents (speeches, statements, resolutions, etc.). But the key points included in its election manifestos and in the Congress government's first annual policy statement (presented to the Parliament) have been primarily considered to map out its policy position on the overall development of the country. The highlights of the NC's policies and programmes are presented in Table 4.3.

TABLE 4.3. THE NC'S POLICY COMMITMENTS

Areas	Election Manifestos, 1991, 1994, and 1999	Government's Annual Policy Paper, 1991
Democratization	Protection/promotion of democracy Free and impartial elections Impartial administration Independent judiciary Decentralization Political stability**	– Protection/promotion of democracy – Decentralization
Agricultural Development	Provide right to tiller^x End of dual ownership in land Expansion of irrigation Establish fertilizer industry^x Provide all facilities to farmers Agricultural revolution**	 – End of dual ownership in land – Irrigation to 38,000 hectares of land – Establish fertilizer industry^x – One window system in providing facilities for farmers
Industrial Development	Emphasis on small-scale, agro-based, labour-intensive and cottage industries Industrialization**	– Emphasis on small-scale, agro-based, labour-intensive and cottage industry
Infrastructure Building	Link roads to all 75 districts Postal service to each village and expansion of phone services Rural electrification	– Road on districts having link with highway – Postal service to each village – Rural electrification
Privatization, Liberalization	Encourage private sector mainly in industry, commerce, tourism, hydro-electricity, tele-communi-cations$^+$	– More emphasis on private sector, joint venture, and foreign investment – Small hydro-electricity through private sector

(contd...)

(Table 4.3 continued)

Areas	Election Manifestos, 1991, 1994, and 1999	Government's Annual Policy Paper, 1991
	Encourage and protect joint ventures and foreign investment Liberal economy** Privatization**	– Hand over of unwanted public owned industries to private sector
Social Service and Welfare	Pure drinking water for all Free education up to secondary level Radical change in education** Health care in each village Price control Free legal services to poor Abolition of bonded labour system Distribution of land to squatters	– Provide pure drinking water – Free education up to secondary level – Primary health service to all – Price control – Special programmes for women, children, disabled, and people of remote areas – Distribution of land to squatters
Minority and Backward Communities	Primary education in mother tongues Consideration of minority languages in state-run electronic media Special consideration for ethnic groups and backward communities+ Special concessions for women in education, health, and employment Increase women's participation in politics and in decision-making+ Equal right for women to inherit parental property**	
External Relations	Based on principle of democracy, human rights, and world peace Greater friendly relations with both neighbours, India and China Foreign assistance in accordance with national priorities	– Based on principles of democracy human rights, and world peace – Greater friendly relations with both neighbours, India and China – Foreign assistance in accordance with national priorities
Others	70% national investment for rural development^x Human development+ Employment and poverty alleviation+	– More national investment

Key: (+) = added in 1994; ** = added in 1999; (x) = omitted either from the 1994 or from the 1999 manifesto or from both

An overview of the NC's policies embodied in its election manifestos suggests that the party covered wide areas of development, including the protection and promotion of the newly established democracy through free elections, impartial administration, an independent judiciary, and decentralization. Rural development was its priority and the party therefore proposed to invest 70 per cent of the available resources in this area. In the agricultural sector, unlike its own policy in the 1950s and unlike the communists' on-going campaign for the redistribution of land, the NC's proposed land policy at this time appeared growth-oriented: it focused on providing irrigation and other facilities. The end of the dual ownership of land remained as one of the targeted goals of the Congress government, but the protection of the rights of the tiller (mentioned in the 1991 election manifesto) was missing from its annual policy statement when in government as well as from the party's 1994 and 1999 election manifestos. The party gave emphasis to agro-based and labour-intensive small and cottage industries in conformity with B.P. Koirala's thought. The same words, if not in spirit, were copied in the Congress government's annual policy paper. The NC's election manifestos and its government's annual policy promised to provide relief for the people from price rises and assured a number of social welfare programmes to the disadvantaged sections of society. The distribution of land to squatters was a top priority. But the party withheld its earlier promise to end the bonded labour system. In foreign affairs, the NC and its government kept its stand on the principles of 'democracy, human rights, and world peace', and improving friendly relations with Nepal's neighbours, India and China.

On minority problems, the NC promised to grant citizenship certificates on the basis of enrolment in voter lists of the 1980 referendum, in order to appeal to the *madise* communities of the Tarai belt. Besides, it undertook to consider enabling the use of minority languages in primary schools and in the government-run media to some extent. Its promise to grant concessions to women in the fields of education, health, and employment was upgraded later to include endorsing the need for greater female participation in politics, administration, and the decision-making process. The party committed itself to equal inheritance rights for women in its 1999 election manifesto. But none of these commitments found a place in the Congress government's annual policy paper, though the issues related to citizenship and minority languages were implemented. The NC had only a few policy commitments relating to the interests of minorities and backward communities. An observer, therefore, rightly remarked: 'A noticeable shortcoming of the [NC's] manifesto was that it failed to highlight the issues related to regional disparities and ethnic problems' (Upreti 1993: 58).

The NC's approach to development underwent some change. Instead of rural development, the NC election manifestos of 1994 and 1999 adopted the concept of human development as the central thrust. Emphasis was given to employment, poverty alleviation, and the harnessing of hydro-electricity. A distinct change appeared in its privatization policy. Previously, the NC election manifesto in 1991 simply considered the role of the private sector under the purview of its mixed economic policy. After the party assumed power the Congress government adopted the policy of privatization and liberalization with great enthusiasm on the grounds that it was imperative to integrate the Nepali economy into the global wave of market competition (BS 1992; NC 1992). The Congress Party endorsed the government's new economic policy stating the need of 'redefining of socialism to make economic policy of the NC dynamic' (NC 1992). The Congress government wanted more investment to come from the private sector, from joint ventures, and from foreign investments, and it wanted the areas of such investments expanded from industry, commerce, and tourism to hydro-electricity, tele-communication, education, health, etc. Government-owned industries and enterprises which were running a deficit were to be transferred to the private sector. The Congress government's policy of privatization and liberalization was followed in both the 1994 and the 1999 election manifestos.

COMMUNIST PARTY OF NEPAL (UML)

In its 1991 election manifesto the UML made a number of policy commitments for restructuring Nepali society, economy, and politics. The issues of infrastructure building and social services dominated the UML's election campaigns, just as they did those of the NC. However, the UML gave more emphasis to land reform aimed at ending 'feudal land ownership' by reducing the current ceiling on land holding, ending dual ownership of land, and safeguarding the rights of the tiller. This was continued in their manifestos for the 1994 and 1999 elections. Another issue the UML emphasized in all three parliamentary elections was that of the minority and disadvantaged sections of the society. The proposal for reservations for the backward community and another to make the Upper House of Parliament an assembly of ethnic minorities and disadvantaged groups were unique to the UML's election manifestos. The UML's policy commitment to bring about a fundamental change in relations with India through the abrogation of the 1950 treaty was designed to attract the mass. Its policies on social security and welfare included measures such as the abolition of untouchability, distribution of ration cards, etc. In the industrial sector, the UML, like the NC, stressed the need for the establishment and expansion of agriculture and forest-based and labour-intensive small and cottage industries. Indeed it characterized its industrial policy as aiming at bringing about a 'self-sufficient nationalist economy'—in apparent disregard of its simultaneously expressed policy on privatization. A summary of the UML's policy commitments is given in Table 4.4.

TABLE 4.4. UML'S POLICY COMMITMENTS

Areas	Election Manifestos, 1991 and 1994	Government's Annual Policy 1994
Democratization	Commitment but amend- ment in Constitution Distribution of voter identity cards[+] Replace title of 'His Majesty' before 'Government' Total restructure in admini- stration[x] Independent judiciary Decentralization Political stability and good governance**	Consideration of multi- party democracy
Agricultural Development	End of feudal land owner- ship Land ceiling Land to the tiller Protection of rights of tiller End of dual ownership in land Expansion of irrigation Provide all facilities for farmers	Land reform

End of dual ownership in land |
| Industrial Development | Self-sufficient economy Classification of industry on the basis of ownership: public, private and foreign investment | Development of all kinds of industries Single-door system for facility in industrial sector |

(contd...)

(Table 4.4 continued)

Areas	Election Manifestos, 1991 and 1994	Government's Annual Policy 1994
	Emphasis on small-scale, agro and forest-based, labour-intensive and cottage industries Facilities through one-window policy	Expansion of tourism industry
Infrastructure Building	Road facility to all 75 districts Expansion of telephone services Rural electrification	Link-road to district headquarters Rural electrification
Privatization Liberalization	Expansion of private sector[+] Selective privatization and liberalization, i.e. trade, commerce, industry, tourism, and urban development[+]	Follow policy of privatization Encourage private-sector and foreign investment in industries based on indigenous raw materials, export promotion, import substitution, water power projects Transfer of unwanted public-owned industries into private sector, priority to national investors
Social Security and Welfare	Pure drinking water to all Free education up to secondary level Expansion of health facilities Price control Distribution of ration cards Abolition of bonded labour system Distribution of land to squatters Special programmes for women, children, old, disabled, and backward communities	 Free education up to secondary level Expansion of health service to VDC level Price control Abolition of bonded labour system Distribution of land to squatters Programmes for children, old, and disabled
Minority and Backward Communities	Abolition of untouchability End of constitutional provisions retaining discrimination on the basis of caste, language, and religion	

(contd...)

(Table 4.4 continud)

Areas	Election Manifestos, 1991 and 1994	Government's Annual Policy 1994
	Make Upper House an assembly of ethnic and disadvantaged groups Reservations for the people of backward community/areas in education, health, and employment Primary education in mother tongue Gender equality Equal property rights to women^x	Uplift womenfolk
External Relations	No ideology in foreign policy$^+$ Equal relations with both neighbours, India and China Repeal unequal treaty with India Foreign assistance in accordance with national priorities	Close relations with both neighbours, India and China Solution to Bhutanese refugee problem
Others	Rural development Balanced regional development Employment and poverty alleviation**	Build Your Village Yourself campaign

Key: (+) = added 1994; ** = added in 1999; (x) = omitted either from the 1994 or from the 1999 manifesto or from both.

Though the contents of the UML's policy platform in the areas of land reform, industrial development, infrastructure building, social security, and minority groups were retained in its 1994 and 1999 election manifestos, some new dimensions appeared which indicated a shift in its policies and its election agenda. Its previously stated republicanism and its slogan for restructuring the administration were now omitted. Its call for amendments to the Constitution was reduced to one point, directed against state protection for the Hindu religion and the Nepali language. Support for privatization—though in restricted areas only, i.e. trade, commerce, finance, industry, tourism, and urban development—was a new departure for the UML, allegedly adopted in order to satisfy Western donor countries. The party stated categorically that there would be 'no ideology in the formulation of foreign policy'. Its high-pitched demand for the abrogation of the 1950 treaty with India was toned down to a need for review and modification of the treaty.

Interestingly, the UML government's annual policy paper appeared to be a rather conservative document. The contents under the index of social security, infrastructure building, and industrial policy embodied in its election manifestos were translated into its government's annual policy paper. However, its promised land reform was confined to a programme to end dual land ownership and its several policy incentives, made through its election manifestos, to the minority and disadvantaged groups were completely forgotten, except for the phrase 'uplift the womenfolk', in its government's annual policy paper.

On economic policy too, the UML government's annual policy paper took the line of a liberal market economy pledging greater investment by the private sector, joint ventures, and foreign investment and pledging to continue the transfer of sick public enterprises to the private sector. But in practice the policy of liberal market economy and privatization was frozen during the UML government. If the UML government's annual policy statement was taken as a guideline one could conclude that it had espoused a conservative, reformist, and liberal economic policy. Prime Minister Man Mohan Adhikari, in an interview with a correspondent of *Newsweek*, pledged to 'take cautious steps, with a minimum reform, a minimum change .... Our economic and political program is adjusted to the present reality' (*Newsweek*, 28 November 1994).

Both the UML and the NC were similar in essence and substance so far as their policies relating to land reform, social service, minority problems, infrastructure building, and industrial development were concerned. Differences between them were much more noticeable in their different ways and styles of communicating. This led to alternative policy platforms in some areas. The NC put more stress on peace, stability, and democracy, whereas the UML campaigned for rapid, radical, and revolutionary change. The NC's proposed land reform gave more emphasis to the growth of agricultural production whereas the UML stood for the redistribution of land. The NC supported privatization; the UML was against it. The NC was less sensitive to minority problems whereas the UML, at least in its rhetoric, appeared more sympathetic to ethnic demands. The NC was in favour of continuing and consolidating close relations with India whereas the UML advocated change through a review of the 1950 treaty. The NC wished for bilateral cooperation with India to harness Nepal's hydro-electric potential whereas the UML emphasized multi-lateral cooperation in this sector. The NC made area/sector (i.e., rural, agricultural, electricity) the thrust of its development approach whereas the UML made class and community (i.e., poor, peasant, minorities, backward groups, etc.) the targets for development.

Performance

NEPALI CONGRESS

G.P. Koirala, in his capacity as the first elected prime minister after the restoration of democracy, envisaged building a 'new Nepal' by eradicating aberrations left behind by previous regimes, by bringing political stability and sustainable economic development, and by providing immediate economic relief and essential needs to the people. But when he left power after three and a half years in government, many things had not changed at all; in other fields things were better in some sectors but worse in others. Table 4.5 provides an evaluation by the Congress government itself on its own performance.

The data given in Table 4.5, which are meant to demonstrate the NC government's achievements, in fact demonstrate its poor performance, except in the areas of infrastructure-building and social service. It takes the credit for providing one or more of these facilities—drinking water, health posts, schools, post offices, roads/bridges, electricity, or telephone—to the people at the grass-roots level. The expansion of infrastructure facilitates the lifestyle of the people but it does not necessarily raise the living standard of poor people. People need an ever-increasing income to pay for the ever-increasing charges of public utilities, i.e. drinking water, electricity, telephone, transportation, etc. The income of the people at the mass level largely depends on the economic growth of the country and equitable distribution of the fruits of development.

The NC government claimed the growth of national economy by 5 per cent during its tenure. For the benefit of the larger number of population, the growth in the agriculture sector is very important since the livelihood of more than 80 per cent of the population depends on agriculture. But the production of principal food crops, cash crops, and others increased only marginally, leading to a constant decline of exports and increase in imports of food items during the

TABLE 4.5: THE PERFORMANCE OF THE NC GOVERNMENT (1991–94)

Areas	Self-assessment of NC Government (May 1991–November 1994)
Democratization	Institutionalization of democracy at local level through local elections 1992 Granting more power and authority to local elected bodies
Agricultural Development	Drafting of a bill related to land ceiling and end of dual ownership in land Irrigation facility to 93,737 ha of land
Industrial Development	Formulation of new industrial policy and foreign investment policy
Infrastructure Building	Construction of 2197 km of roads Post offices in all VDCs Telephone facilities provided to 142,000 lines Hydro-electricity produced: 2,350 kw
Privatization and Liberalization	Commitment to invest Rs 40 billion in joint ventures Transfer of several public industries/corporations to the private sector
Social Service and Welfare	Free education up to grade 8 Provided drinking water to 165,600 people Establishment of health care centres in 1,300 VDCs Land provided to 15,000 squatters
Minority and Backward Communities	Constituting Language Recommendation Committee Eight major languages used in the public electronic media (for news broadcasts) Scholarships for 41,000 girl students Appointment of 1,400 female teachers
External Relations	Additional trade facilities from India
Others	Economic growth rate 5%

Sources: NC (n.d.), EMNC (1999)

Congress government (ES 1995). Another question relating to land reform was distributive justice. The NC showed some concern over this issue but it largely appeared insensitive in this matter. Its ideological commitment to democratic socialism, which stressed justice and equitable distribution of resources, was diluted by the priority the Congress government gave to liberalization and privatization.

In this context the Congress government carried out a number of policy measures, especially in areas of trade, commerce, industry, and joint ventures. Consequently the number of industries increased and the capital flow committed was Rs 40 billion in joint ventures. In addition to the sale of some sick public enterprises to the private sector, the effect of liberal economic policy could be seen in an unprecedented growth of financial institutions and commercial banks. But most of them were confined to urban areas, and had little impact in the rural and agricultural sectors where the overwhelming population of Nepal is to be found. The question that has to be asked is: Who benefited from the growth of national economy as the result of the privatization and liberalization policy?

The immediate cost of the Congress government's liberal economic policy was high for the people. Privatization, increase in charges of public utilities, and the withdrawal of subsidies are some of the major conditionalities tied to the post-cold war foreign aid/loan flows from donor countries. The Congress government totally failed to resist the flat conditionalities of the donors. Against the government's promise to provide economic relief to the people, the prices of public utilities, i.e. drinking water, electricity, telephone, petroleum products, fertilizer, etc. increased sharply. Besides, the ever-increasing price rise in food-grains, consumer items, and other essential commodities made the day-to-day life of the people harder. In essence, the Congress government largely failed to link the growth of national economy with the basic needs of the people.

COMMUNIST PARTY OF NEPAL (UML)

The UML succeeded the NC and formed a minority government after the November 1994 general elections, which lasted for 9 months till early September 1995. The economic condition of the country and the people largely stagnated despite the change in actors and some changes in the approach to development.

By reintroducing the subsidy system the UML government con-trolled price rises, even if they could not reduce them. The govern-ment was credited with stabilizing the prices of essential goods and consumer items. Besides, the UML government launched a populist programme, the Build Your Village Yourself (BYVY) campaign, under which each Village Development Committee was entitled to receive a direct grant of Rs 300,000 from the central government. The UML government also initiated some social service/welfare programmes, including a pension of Rs 100 per month to senior citizens and the distribution of land to 58,000 squatters. The UML government was criticized for its populist economic policies focusing on the distri-bution of limited resources rather than on the growth of the economy.

TABLE 4.6: THE PERFORMANCE OF THE UML GOVERNMENT (1994–95)

Areas	Self-assessment of the UML Government (November 1994–September 1995)
Democratization	Consolidation of democracy
Agricultural Development	Constitution of Land Reform Commission
Industrial Development	15% industrial growth
Infrastructure Building	Construction of 100 km. motorable roads
Privatization/Liberalization	
Social Security and Welfare	Providing free education up to grade 10 Land distribution to 58,000 squatters Pensions for old, widowed, and disabled
Minority/Backward Communities	[No achievement claimed]
External Relations	Initiating package deal on Mahakali river Proposed to review the 1950 treaty with India
Others	Implementing Build Your Village Yourself programme

Source: EMUML (1999)

In the fiscal year of 1994/95 (seven out of the total nine months' tenure of the UML government was during this fiscal year) agricultural production declined; the import of food-grains increased; and foreign aid also decreased to Rs 7,542 million from 12,877 million in the preceding fiscal year (ES 1995). The registration of joint venture industries declined from 38 in the previous fiscal year to just 18 in 1994–95 (DW 1996). The real estate business and the share market both went down sharply, suggesting economic stagnation and recession. This suggested that the UML government deliberately ignored the long-term economic interest of the country when taking up populist distribution-oriented programmes.

In fact both the NC and the UML were engaged either in in-fighting within their respective parties or in inter-party confrontations on emotional and sentimental issues. As a consequence, the two major parties gave most of their time to unproductive issues of intra-party and inter-party conflict. They could neither forward their own agenda nor could they properly address the problems of the people. It is suggested that both the NC and the UML were moving closer to becoming a part of the state rather than consolidating themselves as 'people's organizations'. As they were aware of their failure to deliver 'public goods' to the people, both the NC and the UML seemed to be preoccupied with the alternative methods of party-building through granting 'selective incentives' to their own party clients.

The Distribution of Patronage and the Emergence of Power-brokers

One of the ways the NC and the UML tried to sustain and expand their own support base was through the distribution of patronage. This is a system of establishing links through rewards to party clients for a variety of services—donations, mobilization of voters, and others—to the party. The mass is generally excluded from such benefits since political parties, by their patronage functions, seek the loyalty of the affluent sections of society who will thereby mobilize public support in their turn. This is, therefore, like a market-exchange system— 'votes for favours' and 'favours for votes'—between the power-brokers and the party. The power-brokers may be varied: relatives and friends of party leaders, party workers, intellectuals, local notables, and other affluent sections of society who wish to use the party as an instrument to achieve their own personal interests.

One of the main reasons for the emergence of both the NC and the UML as parties of patronage was that most of their rank and file leaders have tended to see power, position, and privileges as a deserved pay-off for their struggles and sacrifices in the past. A number of other factors have pushed the parties in the same direction, e.g. the erosion of ideology and leadership quality, in-party factional competition for organizational control, increasing election expenditure, candidates' promise to fulfil particular individual interests of voters, and so on. Of course, favours for party clients is a *sine qua non* irrespective of the party's ability to attract the mass through its ideology, policy, and performance, but as the party's dependency on patronage distribution increases so its capacity to distribute collective incentives decreases.

NEPALI CONGRESS

The appeal of the NC as the protagonist of democracy, which was strong immediately after 1990, lessened over time for three reasons: the poor performance of the Congress government, the absence of a serious threat to parliamentary democracy, and the change of its immediate rival's ideology in favour of the multi-party system. Along with the poor performance of the Congress party and its government, internal power conflicts among its troika of leaders—Ganesh Man Singh, Krishna Prasad Bhattarai, and Girija Prasad Koirala—led to a considerable erosion of their popularity, because it made them appear selfish and power-hungry in contrast to their earlier image as as men of principle. Thus the personalities of the Congress troika leaders, which had been used as assets by almost all Congress candidates in attracting the voters in the 1991 parliamentary elections, figured low in the party's campaign strategy in the 1994 and 1999 general elections. So the NC's capacity to attract the mass through its ideology and its leaders decreased. Consequently, Congress relied increasingly on the other main method of party building, i.e. patronage.

Patronage is guided by the personal interest of power-holders to consolidate their influence in their own electoral constituency. Realizing what they needed to do in order to be re-elected next time, Congress parliamentarians and ministers did strive to provide services to the power-brokers in their own electoral constituency. Since the NC is a mass-based party, party activists were not the sole beneficiaries of patronage by the Congress government. Others who were relatives, friends, or had personal connections with the Congress leaders, benefited more in grabbing opportunities from the state and the government. Each of the Congress leaders, MPs, and ministers (those interviewed) had records of providing jobs and other favours to several hundred persons during the three-and-a-half years' rule of the Congress government. Ram Chandra Poudel, Minister of Local Development in the G.P. Koirala government of 1991–94, said: 'Soon after the NC formed the government, party workers from all over the country flowed to Kathmandu seeking personal benefits and recommendations for jobs and other services to their relatives and friends' (interview, 15 October 1996). Another minister of the same government, Bir Mani Dhakal, had a similar experience: 'Inter-personal relations between ministers and party leaders were largely dominated by a tendency of the party leaders to insist on using government resources for their personal and political interests and more so in the distribution of patronage, i.e. for appointments, transfers, and promotions, and for granting *thekkā* (contracts) to persons they wished to favour' (interview with Bir Mani Dhakal, 25 September 1996). Despite this, the party was defeated in the 1994 mid-term elections. This suggests two things. First, political awareness among the Nepali people is increasing, and so the influence of power-brokers among the voters is declining. Second, the 'selective incentives' which a political party provides through distributing patronage cannot be a substitute for 'collective incentives', i.e. the mobilization of public support through ideology, policy, leadership, and performance.

COMMUNIST PARTY OF NEPAL (UML)

The replacement of Congress rule by the UML minority government brought in its wake massive changes in executive posts at all levels not only in the bureaucracy but also in other public institutions, i.e. corporations, hospitals, educational institutions, etc. Since the UML is a cadre-based mass party practising a strong levy system, the pressure from party-run clienteles was very strong. The UML tried to institutionalize the government's patronage distribution functions. It tried to use the party as an active and powerful state organization through party-run clienteles under the purview of the party's State Affairs Department. The logic behind the formation of the State Affairs Department at both central and district levels was to prepare a profile of civil servants and to control the appointment, transfer, and promotion in bureaucracy and corporations from the lowest to the highest posts. Recommendations from the party, at least from the party District Committee, became mandatory in taking decisions regarding recruitment, transfer, and promotion in government service.

Thus, once the UML got to power, it bluntly manipulated the state resources for patronage purposes. The formation of the Commission for Landless at the central and local levels was another lucrative avenue for party clients. The UML government distributed land to 58,000 squatters within a short span of time acting on the party's recommendations. The transformation of party loyalists to the posts of Local Development Officer with the power of dispensing funds allocated to the BYVY programme and a provision of all-party committee at the Village Development Committee level to spend such funds was one of the several instances which suggested that the UML government even used development resources in this way. The overall impact of the UML's manipulation of state resources and distribution of patronage exclusively to party clients had not yet come out clearly. But the party claimed that it was able to recruit 10,000 new members during the tenure of the UML government (UML 1996). Its rank and file leaders, however, felt that as selfishness, opportunism, and individualism increased among party leaders and workers, there would be a negative impact on the UML's capacity to distribute collective incentives to the people in general.

PUBLIC RELATIONS AT THE LOCAL LEVEL

Party-people relations in Nepal at the macro level is generally determined by multiple factors, such as ideology, policy, development, power, and patronage. The ability of the NC and the UML to attract the masses through their own ideology and leadership declined over time because the parties' and the leaders' behaviour largely deviated from their own proclaimed goals and policies. Instead, the question of development and patronage distribution came up as the main content for negotiation between the party and the people. This general trend was reflected in party-people relations at the micro level as well. The nature of the functions to be carried out by the party local unit is not generally different from those of its central organization, though there is a clear demarcation in boundary (place) of their jurisdictions. There are, however, some distinctions.

The higher units in the hierarchy of the party structure engage more in state affairs, whereas the lower-level units are involved more in people's affairs. Unlike the party's central leaders, who generally devote more time to power politics, the local leaders and workers have to get involved in the day-to-day life of individual members of the society, e.g. in social, cultural, judicial, developmental, and other matters, in addition to political work. So, the local unit of a political party constitutes a key link in maintaining regular contact with the people. It is the main channel by which the party penetrates into society and through which society interacts with the party. An attempt is made here to explore relations between parties (NC and UML) and the people at the micro level in the sample districts in a triangular perspective: transmission of party's identity, people's expectations, and the party's responsive functions.

Transmission of the Party's Identity

The identity of a political party is generally shaped by a combination of two factors: on the hand hand its proclaimed goals, objectives, and principles, and on the one the character and behaviour of its leaders and workers. Ideology plays a vital role in building a party's image. The local units do not set the party's ideology nor do they formulate the party's general policies or programmes. They usually receive these from the party's central organization and leaders, and then transmit them to the people. So the local units have a crucial role in injecting the party's norms, values, goals, policies, and ideology into society and thereby mobilizing public support.

NEPALI CONGRESS

Being the oldest party in Nepal the NC does not have an identity problem. But in the changed context after the restoration of democracy in 1990, the party has renewed its relations with the people in a new light, largely through its newly constituted local organizations. Its local leaders and workers stress the party's ideology, history, and leaders' personalities. In all six sample districts—from the eastern hills of Dhankuta to the western Tarai of Bardiya—they equated the party with the achievements of the People's Movement, claiming that 'Congress means multi-party system' and 'multi-party democracy means Congress'. The NC's credentials as synonymous to the multi-party system is based on its long history of struggle for democracy. Party workers never failed to mention the events of the Congress's armed struggle in 1950–1 against the Rana oligarchy, its long fight against the Partyless Panchayat system, and the role of its supremo Ganesh Man Singh as commander of the 1990 Movement. Congress activists all over the country, including the sample districts, emphasized the image of the leaders of the party (Ganesh Man Singh, Krishna Prasad Bhattarai, and Girija Prasad Koirala) as the *nāyak* (hero) of the country. The popularity of Ganesh Man Singh and interim prime minister K.P. Bhattarai peaked after the restoration of multi-party democracy. Singh's refusal of the offer of the prime ministerial post and the widespread coverage given to the simplicity of K.P. Bhattarai's life-style—he shifted to the prime minister's official residence with just one *chātā* (umbrella), one *surāhi* (an earthen waterpot), and one *tinko bakas* (a tin trunk)—were invariably mentioned by the NC's leaders, workers, and sympathizers. The general pattern was described by an NC leader in Tanahu:

Soon after the restoration of democracy in 1990, the NC Tanahu District Committee launched a year-long campaign of party building through distributing party membership at mass scale and constituting party's grass-roots level organization down to the village level. Over the year of the interim period, the party organized victory rallies and mass meetings in each village of the district. The speakers in mass meetings had almost the same content. They recalled the long history of the party's struggles against the dismantled Partyless Panchayat system. They equated Congress with the newly achieved multi-party democracy. They highlighted the *nāyak* image of the party's three top leaders, Ganesh M. Singh as *lauhā purush* (iron man), K.P. Bhattarai as *shānta purush* (symbol of simplicity), and G.P. Koirala as *krānti purush* (revolutionary person). They promised peace, prosperity, stability, and development under democracy and the Congress rule. There was a wave of people joining the Congress party. (Interview with Dhruba Wagle, 19 April 1995).

COMMUNIST PARTY OF NEPAL (UML)

The UML has projected multiple identities. It has acquired new credentials as a supporter of liberal democracy. In the changed context, it has gradually given up some conventional communist rhetoric, i.e. class war, armed revolution, republicanism, the one-party system, and the dictatorship of the proletariat. However, it still retains its communist trademark as a party of the proletariat and as strongly nationalist. The party's history and its ideological ambiguity in the post-1990 period have limited its ability to appeal widely. The UML's rather ambiguous support for the multi-party system seemed more pragmatic and less normative. A survey conducted prior to the 1991 elections found that majority of communist workers and voters, most of them belonging to the UML, thought that the party's proposed idea of *bahudaliya janbād* was qualitatively different from the existing multi-party system. They subscribed to fundamental change in the political structure in the future and considered support for the multi-party system to be a pragmatic and realistic first step (Hachhethu n.d.). Moreover, most of the UML's local leaders and workers understood the proposal of *bahudaliya janbād* as the party's immediate and tactical goal until it was formally endorsed by the party Fifth National Congress in January-February 1993. So, in the early phase of democracy, the UML cadres penetrated into the society as communists rather than democrats, but without attacking the newly achieved multi-party system.

After the restoration of democracy in April 1990, the UML had launched a year-long national campaign or 'party introduction programme' organizing rallies and mass meetings all over the country. In all the sample districts the party activists introduced the UML to the people using its key slogans: 'food, housing, and clothing for all', 'land to the tillers', 'confiscation of land from landlords', 'redistribution of land to the landless and a low ceiling on landholding', 'end of feudal exploitation', 'uplifting poor, women, and other disadvantaged groups'. They addressed the social, economic, and other problems of the country in a revolutionary manner, which helped to sustain the UML's image as a relatively radical party in comparison to the NC. The UML's populist slogans and propaganda matched the radical situation of the country in the early post-1990 period. The end of the

People's Movement was, in fact, the beginning of a new revolution: a revolution of the people's rising expectations in which different segments of society asserted themselves in pursuance of their own interests. The people's aspiration for change had come to the surface in different ways, ethnic resurgence being one of the most prominent.

In the eastern hills, the advent of democracy was followed by Rai and Limbu assertion of an independent ethnic identity with a campaign for the boycott of the national Hindu festival, Dasain. A local leader of the UML in Dhankuta said that his party emphasized its stand for a 'secular state' and 'equal status for all languages' in order to gain support from the Rai-Limbu communities, who form a majority in the eastern hills (interview with Bishnu Maden, 21 May 1995). Similarly in the western hills, in Magar-Gurung dominated areas, the UML projected itself as a protector of minority rights for hill ethnic groups. In the Kathmandu Valley, the party put more stress on the language issue and anti-India feeling to cash in on the sentiments of the Newars. More than one fourth of the population of Bajhang is constituted by Dalits (low castes) and most of them, according to a local Dalit leader of the UML, were attracted to his party's high sounding slogan for the abolition of the caste hierarchy (interview with Govinda Nepali, 12 December 1995). In the Tarai districts of the mid and far western regions (Dang, Banke, Bardiya, Kailali, and Kanchanpur) the UML launched a one-point campaign against the bonded labour system in gaining support from the majority community of these districts, the Tharu, a plains tribal group. The case of Bardiya, as told by most local leaders of both the NC and the UML, could be presented as a case study to show how the UML gained a new identity associated with the minority and backward community's resurgence when its local organization launched a *sukumbāsi* (squatter) movement on behalf of the local Tharu community:

Tharus constitute a majority in the total population of Bardiya district. Most of them are landless and work as bonded labourers. They had long hoped for land from the state's policy of land distribution to *sukumbāsi*. Their hope revived when political change occurred. The UML-Bardiya cashed in on this sentiment after the restoration of democracy in 1990. Engineered by some local leaders of the UML, the *sukumbāsi*s, mostly Tharus, forcibly captured public land in an organized way covering 37 plots. The biggest was Kandara where 3,900 families settled illegally. The local organization of the NC and the UML took opposite stands on this problem. The former was against illegal settlement of *sukumbāsi*s, whereas the UML protected them, organized them, and finally turned them into its vote bank. The Congress-*sukumbāsi* hostility was heightened by the Congress government's forcible demolition of all *sukumbāsi* settlements in this district in 1992 but the UML-Bardiya compelled the government, after non-stop picketing for 29 days, to settle these *sukumbāsis* temporarily in different areas of the district. Later, the UML government (November 1994–September 1995) distributed land to 6,000 of the total estimated 18,000 *sukumbāsi* families in the district. In this way, Bardiya became a stronghold of the UML, not because of its ideology, nor because of its organizational power, but because the party mobilized the squatter movement and a campaign for the abolition of bonded labour, which deeply touched the interests and sentiments of local Tharus.

Thus the UML's local organizations in different districts adopted area- and community-specific strategies in order to cash in on much-increased ethnic and backward assertiveness, which contributed to the development of the party's multiple identity. The UML was, therefore, projected as a multi-faced party, best suited to all segments of the pluralistic society of Nepal. For the majority community—the hill caste groups—it was and is a party constituted mostly by Brahmins (Bahuns) in terms of the composition of the party's rank and file leaders; for religious minority groups, it was a secular party; for the hill ethnic groups, it was a party championing equal status for all languages; for the Tharu community in the Tarai districts of mid-west and far-west regions, it was a liberator from the bonded labour system; for what in India are called scheduled castes, it was a party for the abolition of the caste system.

PEOPLE'S EXPECTATIONS

The role of the NC and the UML's local organizations in transmitting their own respective party's normative identity into the society declined gradually. After the end of the interim period, ideological and policy matters were raised only when the party needed mass mobilization for rallies, protests, mass meetings, elections, etc. In normal times other issues, i.e. the use and abuse of power by leaders, the individual and collective interests of specific groups of people, development and underdevelopment, etc., have dominated party-people communications. Particularly after the 1991 general elections and the 1992 local elections, the activities of local organizations right down to the district level were mostly confined to the internal business of their respective party; this was particularly so, of course, for the internal elections of representatives to the party's National Convention and for the selection of the party's executives. The grassroots organizations of these parties became virtually defunct except during elections. In between elections only a few local party leaders were found to be active in their individual capacity and without a formal committee to support them. After the 1992 local elections, most active local leaders captured important posts at various levels of the state's elected bodies. They had new responsibilities which involved keeping in regular touch with the people. It is the parties' representatives to elected bodies who have to interact more with the people than the office bearers of party organizations. The party's elected wing enjoys formal power, authority, and resources. The decline in the parties' local organization increases the elected wing's role in party-people relations. This is reflected in people's needs and expectations from political parties. The major content of the people's expectations from political parties, reported by the NC and the UML's district leaders of the sample districts are given in Table 4.7.

TABLE 4.7: PEOPLE'S DEMANDS AND EXPECTATIONS FROM POLITICAL PARTIES ACCORDING TO PARTY LEADERS AT DISTRICT LEVEL

Expectations	NC	UML
Individual Interest		
Dispute settlement	6	7
Favour for job and other opportunities	7	6
Favour for work related with government offices	9	7
Collective Interest		
Party affairs	3	4
Development	4	3
Others	2	2

Score: maximum 10, minimum 1. N = 179. Data collected by structured interview.
Source: Hachhethu (2001)

Nepali Congress

The data presented in Table 4.7 illustrate how local NC leaders came under heavy pressure to become involved in matters of individual interest to the voters rather than in work for the collective interest of the society. The NC representatives to the District Development Committee of Dhanusha, Kathmandu, Tanahu, and Bajhang, said that issues relating to the general interest of society, i.e. governance, development, party affairs, etc., were articulated only by persons elected to Village Development Committees, not by ordinary people. In urban areas local organizations sometimes exerted pressure on political leaders for development in areas such as the supply of drinking water, sanitation, road repairs, etc., as was reported by elected leaders of the NC in the municipalities of Kathmandu, Janakpur, and Damouli. However, here too, personal and individual interests predominated.

The people sought the favour of NC politicians to fulfil a variety of their personal interests. Getting involved in dispute management has become a regular part of the business of many local Congress leaders. A tendency to seek political support to resolve family and social disputes increased after the restoration of party system in 1990. Politicians holding posts in party and elected bodies appear to have replaced the role of the traditional elite, known as *pancha bhalādami*, in managing local disputes and problems. To resolve the problems related to domestic violence, polygamy, the division of property among family members, quarrels among neighbours, and other small cases, the disputants usually preferred to knock on the door of politicians instead of filing complaints with the police, court, or bureaucracy. The number of people seeking such services from the party is so intense that an observation on 28 February 1995 in Dhanusha district is presented here as an example:

A poor-looking man was standing at the corner of the party office of the NC-Dhanusha district. When asked the purpose of his visit by a local Congress leader, he explained that he was bitten by a dog two months ago. He had gone to the hospital yesterday for treatment but the doctor did not care to examine him properly. He asked the leader to refer his case to the doctor. The leader promptly contacted the hospital by telephone and after his conversation with the doctor he told the visitor to go to the hospital tomorrow and mention his name to the doctor. Then the visitor left the office saying *jaya hos* (grateful appreciation).

The NC has been in power for most of the period since the restoration of democracy. To be a ruling party means to influence, manipulate, and control the state's power, resources, and the administration. Influential local leaders in the NC were always surrounded by people seeking jobs, promotion, political appointments, and other opportunities. They felt that the people's pressure for the party's political backing was suddenly and drastically reduced when it lost power at the centre after the 1994 mid-term elections. Nevertheless it still controlled the local government in many parts of the country, including the sample districts of Dhanusha, Kathmandu, Tanahu, and Bajhang. The crowd of people seeking the ruling party's favour turned towards the UML.

COMMUNIST PARTY OF NEPAL (UML)

During a month-long period of fieldwork in Dhanusha in February 1995, when the UML was in government at the centre, it was observed that its party office in Dhanusha district was often crowded with those seeking favours. This was a new experience, said the former office secretary of the UML-Dhanusha District Committee. Recalling his past experience when the UML was in opposition, he said that only a few persons, mostly the party's local leaders and workers, visited the party office for a short time. He said that the number of visitors, many of them unknown, suddenly increased after the formation of the UML government (interview with Durga Prasad Upadhyaya, 18 April 1995). Many visitors to the party office were job seekers. Some requested help from party leaders to get their relatives and friends released from police custody and prison. Others sought the support of the party to facilitate their work in government and semi-government offices. A similar scene was found in the UML's party office in Dhankuta and Tanahu districts in subsequent months of the fieldwork. Its leaders and workers of Dhankuta and Bardiya districts, where the UML controlled local government, were already familiar with such demands. But they also felt increasing pressure from the people after the UML formed its minority government at the centre. This was, however, short-lived. Soon the UML returned to opposition, and it was observed that only few post-holders of the party were to be found in the UML's party offices in Bajhang, Bardiya, and Kathmandu where fieldwork was done after the stepping down of the UML from power in September 1995. The experience of both parties makes it abundantly clear that people seek out relations with the ruling party to a far greater degree than with the opposition parties.

The UML's local units dealt with people's demands individually and organizationally. A number of its local leaders of the sample districts said that their party entertained the complaints and demands of those persons who had been recommended by the party unit or by party leaders. Besides, they helped in the personal and collective interests of the people of their own electoral constituency in their individual capacity. They correlated people's demands with votes. Though they were aware of the limitations of their individual and organizational capacity vis-à-vis the people's personal and collective interests, they said that they hardly ever responded negatively irrespective of the merit of the issues. They tried to satisfy all favour-seekers, mostly through words rather than deeds with a standard phrase: 'I will try my best'.

Part of the reason why people seek political support to resolve their personal problems is related to their perceptions of the state, the bureaucracy, and the political parties. The distinction between the state and party has become less meaningful, because political parties, especially the ruling party, are conceived of as a part of the state. The state has long been perceived as the provider of basic necessities to the people and the party is seen as the engine of social change and economic development. This thinking is encouraged by the NC's avowed ideology of 'democratic socialism' and the UML's main ideology of communism: both stand for an 'activist state'. However, the overall activities of these two parties, whether at central or at local levels, hardly follow their own prescribed ideology. Yet, time and again, and particularly during elections, they encourage the image of Nepal as an omnipotent state, the provider of basic necessities to the people, and of the political parties as dispensers of state resources.

Part of the reason for the increase in politicians' non-political roles can be found in the way the Nepali bureaucracy works. The bureaucracy in Nepal has long existed to satisfy the demands of the power elite rather than to serve the people. This has remained unchanged since the Rana period. The only distinct change that appeared after the restoration of democracy was the division of government employees along party lines, as pro-Congress or pro-Communist, each with their own formal organization. The other distinct feature of the Nepali bureaucracy is that it largely operates on the basis of personal connections, bribes, or recommendations from persons in power. Attaining justice through administrative channels is costly and time-consuming in Nepal. So it is standard behaviour to seek the help of an influential person in dealing with the state and government machinery. This is illustrated by the data of Table 4.7 which show that the quest of 'political favour for work related with the governmental offices' figured at the top of people's expectations in their relations to both the NC and the UML.

Individuals' problems and needs in aggregate form constitute the collective interest of the society. A number of opinion surveys, conducted separately by several institutions in different parts of the county in different timeframes, revealed a more or less common finding that 'poverty, price rises, and unemployment' are the most important national problems of Nepal, followed by other problems such as irrigation, drinking water, personal security, etc.(NOSC 1993; SEARCH 1994: CCD 1996). But these issues did not figure very prominently in the parties' agendas and priority lists. One critic observed the gap between the people's priorities and the parties' agendas and suggested:

For the political parties, issues like ideology, nationalism, democracy, Nepal's relations with India, the use of water resources, and foreign aid were more significant, but for the people, issues like skyrocketing prices, corruption, security of food and shelter, and comments about the main weakness of the dominant political parties were significant (Bhattachan 1993: 265).

Will the parties try to fill the gap between their agendas and the people's preferences in future? Will the NC and the UML's local organizations articulate and aggregate the people's demands and interests in an institutionalized manner? For affirmative answers to these questions, the parties' local units should have clear policies and ideas to solve the problems of unemployment, to reform the bureaucracy, and so on. But the party-society interface has largely been shaped by inter-personal and informal relations between local leaders and the people. Many influential NC and UML leaders of the sample districts perceived that they were expanding the party's support bases by their non-political work, i.e. by managing local disputes, assisting farmers to obtain credit, seeds, and fertilizer, helping businessmen, job-seekers, and others with their work in government and semi-government offices.

Responsive Functions

As public organizations, political parties have to hear and respond to the people's voices, needs, and interests. One of the ways parties keep close contact with society is by their involvement in development activities, mainly through their representatives on elected bodies. Development at the local level is primarily understood as infrastructure building. Communication between the leaders and the mass, the party workers and the people, the candidates and the voters during the election campaigns were overloaded with high promises of building physical infrastructures and providing social service and welfare, e.g. drinking water, schools, health posts/hospitals, roads/bridges, electricity, transportation, and communication. The local governments of the sample districts—whether controlled by the NC (in Dhanusha, Kathmandu, Tanahu, and Bajhang) or by the UML (in Dhankuta and Bardiya)—allocated approximately 80 per cent of the total budget for the development of drinking water, education, health posts, roads, etc. Both the NC and the UML's local leaders overwhelmingly specified achievements in the sector of infrastructure-building when asked under which heading there had been the most progress in their locality after the 1992 local elections (see Table 4.8).

TABLE 4.8: LOCAL DEVELOPMENT AFTER 1992 AS ESTIMATED BY
LOCAL PARTY LEADERS

Variables	NC	UML
Democratization	2	2
Agricultural development	2	2
Industrial development	1	1
Infrastructure-building	8	8
Privatization/liberalization	2	1
Social security and welfare	–	1
Welfare of minority/backward communities	–	–
Others	1	1

Maximum score 10 and minimum 1. N = 179. Data collected by structured interview.
Source: Hachhethu (2001)

NEPALI CONGRESS

The local leaders of both parties, NC and UML, took a non-partisan
line while giving their opinion about development which had taken
place in their own locality after the restoration of democracy. The
progress in infrastructure-building was perceived to be far higher
than in other areas of local development. The NC deserved more credit
for it, because it had been in power longer at the centre and also because
it controlled local government in many areas, including four of the
six sample districts. But a number of the local NC leaders interviewed
were of the view that whatever had been accomplished was less than
the promises that had been made and also less than it should have
been, given the resources allocated for it. In fact, development was a
neglected area for the NC's local organizations for two reasons. First,
the party was under less pressure to work for the collective interest
of the society than for the personal interest of the individual members
of society. Second, most of the Congress leaders and workers appeared
to others as persons promoting their own self-interest, i.e. their power,
position, and money, and not as workers for the general welfare of
the people.

The NC's collective and organizational ability to contribute to development was, therefore, offset by the personal interests of individual
leaders and workers of the party. Most of the long-term members of
the party had a tendency to seek power, position, and privilege as
recompense for their past struggles and sacrifices. The newcomers,
popularly known as *chaite* (because the ban on party membership

was lifted in the month of Chait), were generally perceived as opportunity-seekers. (As membership to the UML was opened in the month of Kartik, the equivalent term for opportunistic UML-members is *kārtike*.) The self-interest of party leaders and workers tempted them to manoeuvre resources allocated for development in order to promote their own interests. Development resources at the local level were commonly handled by User Groups. The User Groups were mostly constituted by allies of the politicians, the elected persons of District Development Committee. It was widely believed that many of these leaders often submitted fake bills of expenditure through the User Groups that they controlled. Food for Work was another scheme of development at the local level which elected persons could manipulate in their own interest. In Dhanusha, where the local government was controlled by the NC, a party investigation committee was formed in 1993: it found evidence of extensive leakage in Food for Work in many of the district's 101 Village Development Committees by village- and district-level elected leaders. But none of the guilty persons had to face legal action. The local government of Tanahu and Bajhang districts, controlled by the NC, also had a similar experience. The District Development Committee has its own Monitoring Committee to oversee development projects. The Chairmen of District Development Committees of Dhanusha, Tanahu, and Bajhang confessed that the Monitoring Committees in their districts found several cases of corruption in resources allocated for development by User Groups, but legal action was never taken because the culprits had political protection.

A number of the NC's influential leaders of the sample districts appeared to be developing a nexus with powerful lobbies, e.g. the business community, NGO directors, officers of line agencies, INGO staff, contractors, and so on. This resulted in political corruption at the local level. Corruption has in fact become the rule rather than the exception: it is highly visible and is reflected in the changing behaviour and life style of many of the NC's influential local leaders who hold strategic posts in the party and/or in elected bodies. It was, therefore, commonly felt by a number of the party's leaders and workers of the sample districts that their leaders were becoming increasingly unpopular among the people and that this would have an adverse impact on the credibility of the party as a whole.

The problem also lies in the NC local leaders' own narrow and short-sighted perceptions. They considered development to be one of the least important sources of party building. In their opinion many people who entered the NC after 1990 were motivated by their desire for money, a job, or other opportunities, rather than by commitment to the party's ideological goals or to development. Many Congress leaders of the sample districts thought that they could better contribute to an increase in the party's voters by producing loyalists through granting selective incentives. The NC's leaders and workers of Dhankuta and Bardiya felt that the decline of the Congress in their respective districts was mainly because the party had failed to distribute patronage. Many Congress respondents of other sample districts had a complaint that personal and factional interests of leaders prevailed over the collective interest of the party in the way the NC's patronage system operated. Party affiliation was considered only after other factors, i.e. self-interest, nepotism, kinship, and monetary incentives. In other words, they felt that patronage based on party affiliation had been neglected in favour of patronage on the basis of more personal factors.

The recruitment of teachers (the quota of school teachers increased to approximately 100 in all districts in 1993) was referred to by many Congress leaders of the sample districts to show the pattern of patronage distribution by the NC. A local leader of NC and Chairman of Bhir Gaun Village Development Committee (Dhankuta) was disappointed that not a single person among the 12 candidates with his recommendation had passed in the examination held for appointment of school teachers (interview with Bhakta Bahadur Bhandari, 20 May 1995). In Dhanusha, several Congress leaders were accused of taking bribes in the appointment of teachers. In Kathmandu, it was said that the party District Committee was completely bypassed in the appointment of 120 school teachers (interview with K.C. Rajan, 2 November 1995). The NC's organizational leaders of Tanahu district also had complaints that party influence was neglected in the recruitment of more than 100 teachers in this district. The Chairman of Bajhang District Development Committee, who dominated in the decision of recruitment of 90 school teachers for his district, was frank in saying that the merit factor was respected only after the consideration of personal connections and party affiliation (interview with Chet Raj Bajal, 6 November 1995). Other areas in which the elected leaders of the local government could provide patronage under their own jurisdiction were in constituting Management Committees of public schools and User Groups in development projects. Again, the members of such committees were selected by leaders on the basis of kinship, individual connections, and, to some extent, party affiliation too. By their patterns of patronage, NC local leaders were producing their own loyalists rather than followers of the party.

COMMUNIST PARTY OF NEPAL (UML)

The UML was in government twice but in both instances for a short period, so its ability to develop itself as an agent of national development has yet to be tested. In Dhankuta and Bardiya districts, where UML controlled the local government, the progress in infrastructure-building was notable. The party's local leaders and workers, however, admitted to a large gap between promise and performance. It gained in both the 1991 parliamentary elections and the 1992 local elections in these two districts, the party's populist slogans and propaganda helping it to achieve good results. But subsequently the elected leaders were not able to generate and mobilize optimum resources for development.

The BYVY programme, a lead programme of local development during the UML government (November 1994–September 1995), largely failed in many areas of the sample districts. Some of the UML local leaders of the sample districts identified several lapses in the programme. The NC controlled most of the local governments at the district and village levels. By making the Local Development Officer, an employee of the government, the channel for the money allocated to each Village Development Committee, the central government undermined the authority of District Development Committee, an elected body, which works as an intermediate institution between the central grant and village development. The authority of the people's elected representatives to the Village Development Committee was also overridden by a provision of the all-party committee at the village level. The all-party committee was made a focal point for project designing and implementation of the BYVY programme. But the reality was that the all-party committee could not be formed in many villages due to the NC's open call for non-cooperation in the BYVY programme. Non-cooperation from administrative and technical staff was another story. Abuse and misuse of funds were reported from several villages. Moreover the voluntary input of the people was also reduced drastically. The experience of the Chairman (UML) of Bhanumati Village Development Committee of Tanahu district, was representative. He said:

I was quite happy to know that my village would receive a grant of Rs 300,000 from the centre under the BYVY programme. This Village Development Committee had never got that much amount before. But my earlier enthusiasm now turns into frustration. Unlike my previous understanding that the whole amount would be sent immediately, I received Rs 100,000 as the first instalment two months after the budget was passed. Before I used this first instalment the NC members of this village resigned from the all-party committee. The comrades of my own party differed with me in designing the project. The Secretary of the Village Development Committee, a government employee, has not come to the office for the last one month without any notification which has impeded in bringing ahead the development projects designed under the BYVY scheme. I went to the district headquarters several times to find an overseer for technical support to the project but I could not find one yet. The sanctioning of the project by the overseer is required to get the second and the third instalments. So I am losing confidence that I can deal with such complex problems and procedures (interview with Dina Nath Sharma, 18 April 1995).

Thus many local leaders of the UML, like their Congress counter-parts, venture into other ways to build up their party. The case of Marekatare Village Development Committee, the birthplace of the Chairman of Dhankuta District Development Committee, was high-lighted as an example by the party leaders of Dhankuta district to justify their pessimistic view that contributing to development would not necessarily help in expanding the party's votes. A huge amount of District Development Commmittee funds flowed to the Marekatare Village Development Committee after the 1992 local elections, but the UML candidate in the 1994 general election still received far fewer votes from that village than the party candidate had got in 1991.

When the UML attained power after the 1994 mid-term elections, it tended to develop the party organization, at both the central and the local levels, as an active and powerful state organization rather than as an agent of development. The party controlled and manipu-lated state resources for the benefit of UML clients. It was found in the sample districts that the district level *sukumbāsi* Committee, formed by the government, distributed land to the landless on the basis of recommendations made by the party District Committee. Besides, the party District Committee influenced official decisions on the recruitment and transfer of government employees and school teach-ers. Since state resources were manipulated in this way in the interest of the party's leaders and clients, the party's potential to address the collective needs of the people and society declined considerably.

The use and abuse of state resources does make a difference to the credibility of the party and its leaders. The UML leaders and workers of Dhankuta and Bardiya were suspicious of the changing life style of their respective leaders, particularly the Chairmen of the District Development Committees of these two districts. But the Chairman of Dhankuta District Development Committee countered this by saying that the District Development Committee's Monitoring Committee found extensive leakage in Food for Work and development projects run by the User Groups. He confessed that action was not taken against any person because of political pressure from his own party leaders and workers (interview with Dharma Raj Poudel, 20 May 1995). The influential leaders of the UML, like their Congress counterparts, had directly and indirectly contributed to increased political corruption. The people's doubts regarding the moral and ethical standard of politicians therefore increased over time. They generally viewed the politicians, both central and local leaders, whether they belonged to the Congress or the Communist, as self-seeking and corrupt individuals.

CONCLUDING OBSERVATIONS

Nepali political parties have recently stepped into a new phase of party building. Of the several factors contributing to political parties in gaining public support, their image as 'an agent of change' is a vital one. Political parties in Nepal were founded in order to accomplish certain envisioned changes in social, economic, and political affairs of the country. Through their many struggles and sacrifices, both the NC and the UML have already established their separate credentials as 'democratic' and 'progressive' forces respectively. Their broad ideological identities, together with their catalytic roles in the 1990 mass movement and in making the present Constitution, further helped to establish their credentials as agents of change. But in the aftermath of 1990 political parties have suffered from several problems. The main weaknesses and shortcomings faced by the NC and the UML in the post-1990 period can be summed up in following points:

1. The support bases of the NC and the UML, built on the basis of their broad ideological identity in the early phase of democracy, are eroding over time. Since ideology and policy contents are missing in their efforts at party building, both are increasingly relying on other sources of vote maximization, i.e. money, power, and patronage.

2. The more a party depends on money, power, and patronage, the less is the party's capacity to mobilize the mass of the people. Since

political parties, by their patronage function, seek the loyalty of the affluent sections of society for the mobilization of public support, the ordinary people are excluded from benefits. This, in turn, leads to a narrowing down of the political space making it the exclusive domain of power holders and power brokers only.

3. Most rank-and-file leaders of both the NC and the UML are obsessed by their belief that they can maximize votes through the distribution of patronage rather than contributing to development activities.

4. Both NC and UML lack a clear vision, perspective, policy, plan, or programme for national development.

5. Parties are increasingly becoming an instrument for self-aggrandizement of the power elites and vested interest groups. This has a negative impact on the parties' advocacy of the collective interests of society. Nepali political parties have failed miserably in their basic duty of linking citizens' preferences with public policy.

Beset by these problems, the NC and the UML seem headed towards a reverse course as protectors of the status quo rather than as instruments of change. Their existence among the people and in the society at the grassroots level is mainly confined to physical presence not functional activity. So the mainstream parties themselves are creating a vacuum, ideologically and politically, in society.

The main political parties of Nepal remain the principal institutions that link the people and the government because of a lack of other effective intermediatory organizations between the state and society. One can anticipate healthy party-people relations if they take up appropriate reforms and adopt innovative measures. First, they have to assess the ground reality of the party in the changed context and situation. In modern competitive politics, the conduct of party affairs has become more and more an art of management directed towards addressing socio-economic and other problems of the society with special emphasis on the formulation and implementation of realistic policies and effective plans and programmes for development. The changing times and situation demand that each party should advance with new perspectives, new vision, new outlook, and setting new objectives. The formulation of realistic and effective policies and programmes rather than ideological rhetoric and leadership cults could be a new source of strength for the parties in competitive politics. Both the NC and the UML should therefore reorient themselves as policy-seeking and policy-implementing parties. The future of the NC and the UML depends upon their ability to formulate public policies and programmes that match the people's preferences. Their potential to rejuvenate themselves as the true representatives of the people has always been there. If they could expedite party-building processes in appropriate ways, balancing their interests in controlling state power with their responsibility to address the problems and needs of society, there would be no stopping their emergence as the long-awaited agents of change in Nepal.

REFERENCES

Baral, L.R. 1977. *Oppositional Politics in Nepal.* New Delhi: Abhinav Publications.
_____ 1983. *Nepal's Politics of Referendum: A Study of Groups, Personalities and Trends.* New Delhi: Vikas Publishing House.
_____ 1993. *Nepal: Problems of Governance.* New Delhi: Konark.
Bhattachan, K.B. 1993. 'Public Debate on Development: Sociological Perspectives on the Public Philosophy of the Development of Nepal'. Unpublished Ph.D. dissertation, Berkeley: University of California.
Borre, O., S.R. Panday, and C.K. Tiwari 1994. *Nepalese Political Behaviour.* New Delhi: Sterling.
Brown, T.L. 1996. *The Challenge to Democracy in Nepal: A Political History.* London: Routledge.
BS 1992. *Budget Speech of the Fiscal Year 1992/93.* Kathmandu: Ministry of Finance/HMG.
CCD 1996. *Nepal: People, Polity and Governance: A Survey Analysis of People's Response to the Democratic Experiment (1991–1995).* Kathmandu: Centre for Consolidation of Democracy.
Chalise, S.C. 1995. *Sociology of the Legislative Elite in a Developing Society: An Empirical Study based on the Members of the First Parliament of the Himalayan Kingdom of Nepal, after the 1990 People's Revolution.* Kathmandu: Nepal Foundation for Advanced Studies.
Chatterji, B. 1967. *A Study of Recent Nepalese Politics.* Calcutta: The World Press.
_____ 1977. *Nepal's Experiment with Democracy.* New Delhi: Ankur.
_____ 1980. *Palace, People and Politics: Nepal in Perspective.* New Delhi: Ankur.
_____ 1982. *Portrait of Revolutionary B.P. Koirala.* New Delhi: Ankur.
Chauhan, R.S. 1971. *The Political Development in Nepal 1950–70: Conflict Between Tradition and Modernity,* New Delhi: Associated Publishing House.
DW 1996. *Democracy Watch-1.* Kathmandu: Centre for Nepal and Asian Studies/ Tribhuvan University.
EC 1991, 1994, 1999. Election Commission, *House of Representative Members, 2048 (1991): Final Results, House of Representative Members, 2051 (1994): Election Results,* and *House of Representative Members, 2056 (1999): Election Results.*

ES 1995. *Economic Survey: Fiscal Year 1995–96*, Kathmandu: Ministry of Finance/HMG.

EMNC 1991, 1994, 1999. *Election Manifesto of the Nepali Congress, May 1991; 1994; 1999*. Kathmandu: NC Central Office.

EMUML 1991, 1994, 1999. *Election Manifesto of Communist Party of Nepal (UML) 1991; 1994; 1999*. Kathmandu: CPN-UML Central Committee.

Gupta, A. 1964. *Politics in Nepal: A Study of Post-Rana Political Developments and Party Politics*. Bombay: Allied Publishers.

Hachhethu, K. 2001. 'Party Building in Nepal: The Nepali Congress Party and Communist Party of Nepal (Unified Marxist-Leninist)'. PhD, Tribhuvan University.

———— 2002. *Party Building in Nepal: Organisation, Leadership and People: A Comparative of the Nepali Congress and the Communist Party of Nepal (United Marxist-Leninist)*. Kathmandu: Mandala Book Point.

———— n.d. 'Challenge for Democracy in Nepal'. Unpublished paper based on field survey in six districts (Ilam, Siraha, Chitwan, Palpa, Salyan, and Kailali) before the 1991 elections.

Hoftun, M., W. Raeper, and J. Whelpton 1999. *People, Politics and Ideology: Democracy and Social Change in Nepal*. Kathmandu: Mandala Book Point.

Hutt, M. (ed.) 1994. *Nepal in the Nineties*. Delhi: Oxford University Press.

IIDS 1993. *The Second Parliamentary Election: A Study of Emerging Democratic Process in Nepal*. Kathmandu: Institute for Integrated Development Studies.

Joshi, B.L. and L.E. Rose 1966. *Democratic Innovations in Nepal: A Case Study of Political Acculturation*. Berkeley: University of California Press.

Kohli, A. 1991. *Democracy and Discontent: India's Growing Crisis of Governability*. Cambridge: Cambridge University Press.

Koirala, B.P. 1979. *Democracy Indispensible for Development*. Varanasi: Tarun Publication.

Kumar, D. (ed.) 1995. *State, Leadership and Politics in Nepal*. Kathmandu: Centre for Nepal and Asian Studies (CNAS/TU).

Lawson, K. (ed.) 1980. *Political Parties and Linkages: A Comparative Perspective*. New Haven: Yale University Press.

ML 1991. *The Present Situation and the Party's Responsibility*. Kathmandu: Communist Party of Nepal, Marxist-Leninist. (In Nepali).

NPC 1992. *Approach to Eight Five Year Plan, 1992–1997*. Kathmandu: HMG National Planning Commission.

NC 1990. *What Nepali Congress Said*. Kathmandu: NC Publicity Committee. (In Nepali).

———— 1992. *Text of Economic Resolution, Passed by Eight National Convention of the Nepali Congress, 1992*.

———— n.d. *A Short Description of Elected Government's Notable Performance in Three Years*. Kathmandu: NC's Publicity Committee. (In Nepali).

NOSC 1993. *Political Opinion Survey of Kathmandu Valley, 1993*. Kathmandu: Nepal Opinion Survey Centre.

Panebianco, A. 1988. *Political Parties: Organization and Power*. Cambridge: Cambridge University Press.

Parmanand 1982. *The Nepali Congress since its Inception: A Critical Assessment*. Delhi: B.R. Publishing Company.

POLSAN 1991. *Nepalese Voters: A Survey Report*. Kathmandu: Political Science Association of Nepal.

_____ 1992. *Political Parties and Parliamentary Process in Nepal: A Study of the Transitional Phase*. Kathmandu: Political Science Association of Nepal.

SEARCH 1994. *The Three District Political Opinion Survey*, Kathmandu: SEARCH.

Shaha, R. 1978. *Nepali Politics, Retrospect and Prospect*. Delhi: Oxford University Press.

_____ 1992. *Essays in the Practices of Government in Nepal*. New Delhi: Manohar Publishing House.

Sharma, J. 1998. *Democracy without Roots*. Delhi: Book Faith India.

Sharma, S. and P.K. Sen 1999. *1999 General Election Opinion Poll: How Voters Assess Politics, Parties and Politicians*. Kathmandu: Himal Association.

The Constitution of the Kingdom of Nepal 2047. Kathmandu: Ministry of Law and Justice, 1990.

UML 1991. *Text of Communist Party of Nepal: Political Declaration, Approved by the Meeting of National Council, January 1991*.

_____ 1993. *People's Multi-Party Democracy: The Political Programme of Nepalese Revolution*. Kathmandu: CPN-UML Central Committee.

_____ 1996. *Text of Political Report Presented by General Secretary of the UML to the Party's National Council Meeting in Janakpur in February 1996*. (In Nepali).

Upreti, B.C. 1993. *The Nepali Congress: An Analysis of the Party's Performance in the General Elections and its Aftermath*. Jaipur: Nirala.

Weiner, M. 1967. *Party Building in a New Nation: The Indian National Congress*. Chicago: University of Chicago Press.

The State and Ethnic Activism

chapter five

How Representative is the Nepali State?

• *Karl-Heinz Krämer*

THE CONCEPTION OF THE STATE IN NEPAL

The Constitution of 1990 introduced important changes into the conception of the Nepali state.[1] It brought a new order of national power structure. There were many who called it a re-introduction of democracy. But since the 1950s had been more a time of experiments with democratic institutions than practised democracy, it seems more appropriate to apply the term 'introduction to democracy' to the year 1990.

As the 1950s had paved the way for the restoration of the monarch's traditional powers, the 1990s were thought to open the way to democracy and general participation. As a kind of symbol, the preamble of the new Constitution transferred sovereignty from the hands of the king into those of the people. But, as it had already been part of the cooperation provisions of those forces that had organized the movement for democracy in 1990, monarchy was not abolished. Moreover, it remained an integral part of the constitutional foundations of the state, but with different powers and terms of reference.

Nepal entered the stage of representative democracy. Universal adult suffrage, a two-chamber parliamentary system, constitutional monarchy, and multi-party democracy were emphasized as the cornerstones of the new Constitution. This was all intended to happen on the basis

---

[1]Special thanks to John Whelpton for his extremely valuable comments on my draft and for his help with English grammar.

of freedom and equality of all Nepali citizens safeguarded by an independent and competent judicial system. Especially laudable, in this context, are the fundamental rights mentioned in part 3 (articles 11–23) of the Constitution. Apart from several apparent contradictions in other articles, they correspond, as far as possible, to Western legal maxims.

But who is the Nepali people that has to feel sovereign since 1990? Article 2 of the Constitution defines the nation as follows: 'Having common aspirations and united by a bond of allegiance to national independence and integrity of Nepal, the Nepali people irrespective of religion, race, caste or tribe, collectively constitute the nation.' Traditionally, the relations between the Nepali state and society were based on state-centred orientations supported by patrimonialism, personalism, and state intervention (Kumar 1995: 4). This meant in practice that the central government had been dominated for centuries by a relatively small number of male members of frequently interrelated families. Social mobility of population groups other than the dominant Bahun, Chetri, and upper Newar castes was more or less non-existent.

The implementation of the ideals mentioned in the Constitution would have meant some kind of breaking down of the traditional structures. But the creators of the Constitution had already integrated some obstacles that set limits to such radical changes. Article 4 (1) of the constitution is particularly significant: 'Nepal is a multi-ethnic, multilingual, democratic, independent, indivisible, sovereign, Hindu and constitutional monarchical kingdom.' The former term 'monarchical' was changed into 'constitutional monarchical'. The terms 'multi-ethnic', 'multilingual', and 'democratic' were entirely new, all being ideas that had received special emphasis during the democracy movement of spring 1990 and the months of discussions that followed it. However, a turning away from the Hindu state that had, in a similar way, been vehemently demanded, was rejected by the party politicians and jurists responsible for the formulation of the new Constitution.

As a consequence, not only the religion but especially the Hindu social system, Hindu values, Hindu thinking and ways of living, as well as Hindu political thinking, were legally established by the state. In addition, there were a number of contradictions within the Constitution itself, which supported the traditional establishment and hindered social reforms. To be mentioned in this context against the

background of the communally defined multi-ethnic state are the right
of equality of all citizens irrespective of religion, race, gender, caste,
tribe, or ideology (Article 11), the right to property (Article 16), the
right of all communities to preserve and promote their languages,
scripts, and cultures, and to educate their children in their respective
mother tongues (Article 18), the right to profess and practise their
own religion (Article 19), but also the non-recognition of political
parties or organizations formed on the basis of religion, community,
caste, tribe, or region (Article 112).

PARTICIPATION IN HISTORICAL PERSPECTIVE

The Constitution of 1990 applied the term 'participation' to a very
broad spectrum of population in a way hitherto unknown in Nepal.
The power structure of Gorkha had been transferred to the new
state when Nepal was militarily and politically unified by the Gorkha
rulers between 1742 and 1816. Only very few Bahun and Chetri
families shared in state power at that time. It was the same families
which had earlier been in the Shah kings' good graces. For the
approximately 150 years that followed political struggles caused
occasional shifts of power within this circle. The Pande and Thapa,
and later the Rana, families were particularly prominent. The Rana
drive for power went so far as ousting all other leading families from
their positions of influence, including the royal Shah family. There
was no question of participation by anyone other than the Ranas.
    The events of 1950–1 could not be called a true revolution. The
Rana oligarchy was indeed overthrown, but the 1950s did not lead
to mass participation as might have been suggested by the slogan of
'democratization'. Rather, democracy, as it was practised in Nepal in
the 1950s, only served to hide the Shah monarchs' efforts to restore
their absolute power legitimated by tradition. As had already been
the practice in the unification era, only a small elitist circle became
participants in the post-Rana Nepali state. It was made up of the young
party politicians and their families who had started the anti-Rana
agitation from Indian territory and, thus, had laid the foundations for
the system changes of 1950–1. Many of these politicians were members
of Bahun families, especially from the eastern Tarai, as well as some
better-off Newar families from the Kathmandu Valley. Others belonged
to those families that had once been excluded from power participation
by the Ranas. Besides, 'Rana revivalists' organized themselves in the

Rastravadi Gorkha Parishad. Thus, even from the aspect of participation, the events of 1950–1 led to some kind of restoration rather than to revolutionary changes.

However, there was considerable dissension and rivalry even within this new political elite, and the kings, Tribhuvan and Mahendra, played their cards well in using it for their own interests. A broader participation of the people was, for the first time, implemented through the parliamentary elections of 1959. But even this participation was limited to the people's right to vote. The nomination of candidates who were to have the chance to be elected as 'representatives' of the people remained within the closed circles of the traditional elites dominating the political parties.

The introduction of the Partyless Panchayat system brought this cautious democratization to an end. The elite that had dominated the political parties before split into two groups. The old core of party politicians either was in prison or tried to organize party activities from underground or from Indian soil. Another group of mainly young party politicians changed over to King Mahendra's side enthusiastically. Compared to the traditional party camp, there were more Chetri than Bahun among them. Apart from a few Newar families, the rest of the population was hardly represented in either group.

INSTITUTIONALIZATION AND EXERCISE OF STATE POWER AFTER 1990

Compared to the 1950–1 events, the 1990 movement for democracy and human rights established itself as a mass movement that formally abolished the Panchayat system. Greater awareness, based on better education and foreign influences, led the traditionally disadvantaged groups and the poor masses to pin their hopes on the new Constitution. But they were quickly disappointed. One of the main symbols of Nepali traditionalism, the linking of the state and the Hindu religion, remained a fundamental feature of the new Constitution. The supporters of the traditional system rejected demands for secularism and special rights for cultural minorities as marginal issues for a democratic Nepali state,[2] while critics on the other side even went as far as talking about

[2]Bishwanath Upadhyaya, for example, the chairman of the Constitution Recommendation Commission, stated that 95 per cent of the suggestions brought before the commission had been related to marginal issues such as culture, language, and religion.

a failure of the democracy movement. As everybody knows, the former were successful in the end.

Varying explanations may be offered for the success of the traditionalists. The party political elites responsible for drafting the new Constitution either saw their personal advantage best served by the preservation of traditional structures, or the old forces were in fact so strong that compromise was forced on the fathers of the Constitution against their own inclinations. In any case, the 1990s have proved time and again that even the younger party politicians are deeply rooted in traditional thinking. A special reason for this must be seen in the Nepali education system that, for decades, had successfully propagated the idea of a Nepali mono-culture. Did the disadvantaged groups have any place at all in Nepali history books? Had the party leaders, who overwhelmingly come from the high Hindu castes, ever had a critical look at the Bahuns' conception of Nepali historiography? Did they know anything at all about Nepal's different ethnic groups, their languages and their cultures?

Party politicians found themselves caught in a dilemma on this issue. Because of their own traditionally oriented education they just could not understand the concerns and reservations of the disadvantaged groups. And this has been reflected in the programmes of the different parties until today. Social inequalities and problems may be recognized to some extent, but most politicians do not try to get to the bottom of the historical and cultural reasons. This applies even to the numerous leftist parties which, according to their political approach, should have a greater interest in the disadvantaged sections of society. They take Western communists' critiques of their own societies in terms of class consciousness and transfer it to Nepal, where the numerous political, social, and economic inequalities are not based on an existing class system but on the hierarchical conceptions of history and society developed by members of some high Hindu castes and embodied in the law code formulated in the middle of the nineteenth century.[3]

The Constitution of 1990, tries to transplant a Western democratic system to Nepal. But sticking to the principle of the Hindu state is regarded as a necessity to safeguard Nepali identity. This means that it is taken as a matter of course that the Nepali identity is identical with the conception of historiography and the culture of the high-

[3] I disagree with those commentators who see class divisions as a factor in Nepalese society, partly cutting across and partly reinforcing caste/ethnic divisions.

caste elite. Every kind of critique along these lines is met with a total lack of understanding and it is seen as an attack against the traditional, cultural foundations of the Nepali state. An example would be those occasions when MPs wear their respective ethnic costumes or use their ethnic or regional languages in parliament or other government institutions. The use of the Nepali language may make sense, at least in parliament, since the MPs need a common language, and there is no other language than Nepali to fulfil this task. But it is hard to understand why the few MPs not belonging to high Hindu castes must deny their traditional costumes. Are not the latter traditional Nepali clothes too?

Part of the meaning of democracy is participation and equal opportunities for all sections of society. However, very little has changed in the socio-political sector in the 1990s. The Constitution has laid the key to such changes in the hands of the political parties. It is their job to implement and strengthen democracy in the country. But, to a great extent, the political parties lack democratic structures themselves. They continue to be dominated by those elite sections of society that have ruled the country for centuries. In part they may behave in a modern Western way, but at the same time many of them are still deeply rooted in hierarchical and traditional thinking, which is diametrically opposed to the equal participation of all population groups.

One classic example may be the Nepali Congress, the grand old lady among Nepal's parties. The delegates of the party congress only elect the president, the vice-president, and the general secretary of the party. The Central Working Committee (CWC), which is so important for the party's political line, is nominated by the party president giving the latter an extremely powerful position.[4] At its central level the Nepali Congress has been dominated by Bahuns since its inception, and this tradition, far from being changed in the 1990s, has, instead, been reinforced.[5]

[4]Until recently, only five members of the CWC were elected. This ruling was changed before the party convention of January 2001, where 18 CWC members, i.e. half the total, were elected.
[5]On 1 July 1999, i.e. immediately after the general elections, the Central Working Committee (CWC) of the Nepali Congress comprised 30 persons, 16 of whom were Bahuns, alongside 5 Chetris, 3 Newars, and 6 others. Furthermore, the position within the list of members is of highest importance. There was only 1 non-Bahun among the first 10 positions (Sher Bahadur Deuba, no. 8). Similarly, there were only three women among the 30 members of the CWC, all of them

The dominance of Bahuns is to be found in almost all the political parties. Within the main opposition party, the Communist Party of Nepal (Unified Marxist-Leninist) or CPN (UML), it is even stronger than in Nepali Congress, even though there is slightly more democracy in electing the central organs and top officials of the party. There is a striking lack of grassroots democracy in all the Nepali parties. The local party cadres are in a very strong way subject to the directives of the central party leadership. It is especially deleterious that the local level does not participate in the selection of representatives for the national level, i.e. the candidates for the parliamentary elections. Within all parties, the latter are nominated by the central party elites.[6] Consequently, the power and influence of the Bahun families dominating the central party organs are preserved while, at the same time, the participation of other population groups, who may play an important role at the local level, is hindered at the centre.

This can be illustrated by an example from the 1999 parliamentary elections (Krämer 2000). Almost 40 per cent of the MPs elected in 1999 were Bahuns (whose share in the total population was only 12.6 per cent according to the 1991 census). The remaining 60 per cent was dominated by Chetris and some elite Newar castes. The ethnic groups were clearly under-represented compared to their share (more than 40 per cent) in the overall population (Krämer 2000: 386–7). There were almost no Dalits at all in the lower House of Parliament. They were not even nominated as candidates by the party leaders, even though the number of Dalits in Nepal is almost equal to that of Bahuns.[7]

The well-known weekly magazine *Spotlight* wrote, as a first assessment of the election results: 'Even political leaders are betraying their own classes and championing the cause of other classes. "Nepal is

---

coming from Bahun families: two Koiralas and one relative of the Koiralas (Shailaja Acharya). (All data taken from the web site of the Nepali Congress: *http://www.south-asia.com/nepalicongress/*).

[6]On the basis of Krishna Hachhethu's work (2002), John Whelpton points out that the local units, on paper, have quite substantial powers. However, they often don't insist on making use of them, preferring to let the centre identify a 'consensus' candidate. If the local units asserted themselves fully, it would often result in one faction over-riding another with the danger of subsequent splits.

[7]The avowed policies of the parties are totally different. For example, the Nepali Congress wrote in its 1999 election manifesto: 'The downtrodden and deprived section of society must represent fairly in the process of nation's political decision and their participation is a must in the Parliament and other institutions .... A provision will be made for the fair representation of these people in the different hierarchy of the Nepali Congress' (NC 1999).

the only country in the world where leaders of Hindu religion have won from Muslim-dominated constituency. Likewise a Nepali speaking person was also elected from non-Nepali speaking areas," said a political analyst. It again proves the capability of leadership. They are able to win elections from constituencies of different ethnic and linguistic group.'[8] This deplorable state of affairs will hardly change as long as the party rank-and-file has no say in the selection of candidates.[9]

Another typical example in this context is the position and participation of women. Three parliamentary elections have taken place since 1990. But none of the parties finally made up its mind to nominate more than the 5 per cent female candidates prescribed by the constitution. The percentage of female MPs is even lower; only 12 women elected in 1999, five more than in 1994.[10] It is hardly surprising that this male body of mainly traditionally oriented MPs blocked a bill granting female inheritance rights for years. There are many male MPs who even openly reject the legal, social, and economic equality of women, as very recent discussions in parliament have proved.

SELF-PERCEPTION OF MINORITIES (MSI OPINION SURVEY)

The aspect of representation and participation from a bottom-up perspective is the special concern of this book. The groups who call themselves *janajāti* (nationalities) and who have joined together under the umbrella organization of the Janajati Mahasangh have been the focus of my research for the last decade. In January 2000, the Kathmandu-based Media Services International (MSI 2000) conducted

[8]*Spotlight*, 21 May 1999. Apart from the fact that there are no Muslim majorities in Nepal, this statement simply withholds the fact that the major parties nominated Bahuns (or Chetris) as candidates even in constituencies with predominantly ethnic populations. Thus the electorate had no choice but to give their votes to Bahun or Chetri candidates.

[9]It is devastating that the Nepali press often identifies itself with the corresponding political outlook of the high-caste party leaders. This may be due to the fact that most of the chief editors of the dailies and weeklies are Bahuns too, and so find themselves in a similar position as the party politicians. Thus many papers may be politically independent but not socio-politically.

[10]Of the 2238 candidates taking part in the 1999 elections 138 were women. In the 60-seat National Assembly (the Upper House) the number of female MPs rose from 5 to 9 in 1999, which is still less than 10 per cent. Of the 12 female MPs in the parliament, 6 are Bahun. Surprisingly, there are two Yadav among the women MPs; Chitra Lekha Yadav even became Deputy Speaker.

an opinion poll survey with a sample size of 1068 in 15 districts encompassing the mountain, hill, and Tarai areas. The interviewees were selected from among the members of 14 Janajati groups.[11]

Fifty-three per cent of the Janajatis interviewed by MSI did not think that there had been any improvement in their lifestyle despite the introduction of a democratic system in 1990. Of the 36 per cent who felt some improvement had been made, 44 per cent said that improvement was visible in the social sector, 38 per cent mentioned the political sector, and 19 per cent the economic sector.

Political Sector

Surprisingly, 44 per cent of those polled said that the Janajatis had a fair representation in politics, while only 43 per cent denied this. When the latter were asked to mention specific political areas where they saw no fair representation of the Janajatis, 33 per cent mentioned parliament, 31 per cent the cabinet, 16 per cent political appointments, 11 per cent the local development committees, and 9 per cent the political parties. There are greater differences between the Janajati groups: 88 per cent of the Rai, 68 per cent of the Tharu, 64 per cent of the Gurung, 51 per cent of the Thakali and Danuwar and 42 per cent of the Limbu thought that their nationalities had a fair representation in politics, while groups like Yolmo, Lepcha, and Satar totally denied this.

One of the sectors most criticized by the ethnic elites is the representation of the Janajatis in the administration. Fifty-nine per

[11]The opinion poll was conducted between 5 and 15 January 2000, with a grant from the London-based Westminster Foundation for Democracy (WFD). My special thanks goes to Ram Pradhan of MSI for his kind cooperation and for providing the evaluation data. The 15 districts were as follows (number of respondents in brackets): Bhojpur (121), Chitwan (51), Dang (122), Ilam (40), Jhapa (61), Kaski (79), 3 districts of Kathmandu Valley (139), Lamjung (140), Makwanpur (52), Palpa (80), Panchthar (78), Sindhu-Palchok (80), and Sunsari (25). The 1,068 respondents came from the following groups: Chepang (52), Danuwar (51), Dhimal (31), Gurung (140), Jhangad (25), Jyapu-Newar (140), Lepcha (40), Limbu (78), Magar (80), Rai (121), Satar (30), Thakali (79), Tharu (121), Yolmo (80). 187 of them were from urban areas, 881 from villages. 496 of the respondents were women against 572 men. 699 (65.4 per cent) called themselves Hindus, 325 (30.4 per cent) Buddhists, 15 (1.4 per cent) Christians and 5 (2.2 per cent) others; 24 persons did not respond to this question. Almost half of the respondents (503) were illiterate; only 80 were educated up to university level. Most of the respondents came from the age group 21–50 years.

cent of the respondents were of the view that they did not have a fair representation in the administrative sector.[12] When asked if it could be improved in case a certain number of seats were reserved for members of their community, 79 per cent of them answered 'yes', especially those from rural areas.[13] This outlook increased with growing education level.[14] There were also greater differences in the attitude of specific ethnic groups. While among the Dhimal (97 per cent), Lepcha (85 per cent), Yolmo and Satar (83 per cent), Thakali (78 per cent), Rai (72 per cent), and Magar (71 per cent), the number of those who thought that there was no fair representation in the administration was very high, only 23 per cent of the Limbu and 27 per cent of the Gurung shared this opinion. With the exception of the Jyapu (26 per cent) and the Yolmo (50 per cent), all groups overwhelmingly thought that there should be reservation of seats for the Janajatis.

Social Sector

Sixty-five per cent of the respondents, with a greater proportion in urban (83 per cent) than in rural areas (61 per cent), said that caste-based discriminations still exist in Nepal, while 29 per cent denied this. Participation in social ceremonies, weddings, and funerals (56 per cent),[15] decision-making vis-à-vis social and community activities (20 per cent), the domain of justice dispensation (13 per cent) and the lack of appropriate reward despite notable achievements (4 per cent) were mentioned as specific areas of caste-based discrimination. There were clear regional differences. Among all the lowland communities surveyed, the proportion believing that caste discrimination existed was always less than 50 per cent,[16] while the hill groups, with exception of the Lepcha, overwhelmingly answered in the affirmative, with the Rai (98 per cent) in lead position. There were also opinion differences based on gender: 69 per cent of the men and 60 per cent of the women interviewed were aware of caste-based discrimination. This may be a consequence of the lower level of school enrolment among women, since the awareness grows

[12]Twenty-one per cent believed that the representation was fair while 20 per cent volunteered no opinion on the matter.
[13]Rural areas 85 per cent of the respondents, urban areas 56 per cent.
[14]Illiterate 56 per cent, school level 60 per cent, university level 73 per cent.
[15]This aspect was mentioned more often in urban (69 per cent) than in rural areas (53 per cent).
[16]Satar 47 per cent, Tharu 39 per cent, Dhimal 35 per cent, Danuwar 27 per cent, Jhangad 8 per cent.

with the level of education.[17] Sixty-seven per cent of the respondents said that the level of caste-based discrimination has decreased after the democratic reforms in the early 1990s; only 2 per cent saw an increase. There were some groups among which less than 50 per cent saw any significant changes after 1990 like Dhimal (42 per cent), Yolmo (38 per cent), Lepcha and Satar (30 per cent), Danuwar (29 per cent), Magar (28 per cent), and Tharu (26 per cent). The greatest confirmation of changes came from Rai (94 per cent), Jyapu (86 per cent), Jhangad (84 per cent), Chepang (77 per cent), Thakali (76 per cent), Gurung (68 per cent), and Limbu (67 per cent).

For ethnic elites the rating of the ethnic languages has been of great importance, since language is one of the basic features of culture. The 1990 Constitution is ambiguous in its treatment of language. On the one hand, Nepal is defined as a multilingual state (Article 4), but the 122 living languages of the country, on the other hand, are treated differently (Tamang 2000). Nepali, the mother tongue of about 50 per cent of the population, is called 'language of the nation' (*rāstra bhāsā*) and 'language of official business' (*sarkārī kāmkājko bhāsā*). The other languages are defined as 'national languages' (*Nepālkā rāstriya bhāsā*) (Article 6), with no mention of what this means in practice. On 1 June 1999, the Supreme Court finally ruled that the use of ethnic languages like Nepal Bhasa (Newari) and Maithili in government offices is unconstitutional and illegal.[18] This decision caused great resentment among ethnic activists. In March 2000, the Nepal Janajati Mahasangh organized a National Conference on Linguistic Rights, in which 75 organizations participated. Four resolutions were adopted:

Adoption of a 'National Declaration on Linguistic Rights'.

Rejection of the Supreme Court verdict as undemocratic and against the universal norms and values of human rights.

Immediate realization of a language survey.

Formation of a Language Co-ordinating and Monitoring Committee under the convenorship of Padma Ratna Tuladhar.

Against this background, it is interesting to compare the

[17]Illiterate 57 per cent, school level 69 per cent, university level 89 per cent.
[18]In response to the demand of local language speakers, Kathmandu Metropolitan City had decided on 25 August 1997 to use Nepal Bhasa, and Dhanusha DDC on 18 November 1997 and Rajbiraj Municipality on 25 November 1997 to use Maithili, as their official languages in addition to Nepali. These decisions were legally challenged and cases were filed at the Supreme Court. A Single Bench of the Court by an interim order prohibited the use of local or regional languages in March 1998 (Tamang 2000).

corresponding results of the MSI opinion poll. Fifty-five per cent of the respondents thought that the government does not do enough to preserve and develop the cultures, customs, languages, and costumes of the nationalities; only 28 per cent believed that it does. Men (60 per cent) were more aware than women (50 per cent). Awareness is greater in urban areas (72 per cent) than in villages (52 per cent). Forty-one per cent of the respondents mentioned special programmes to preserve the tradition and culture of the Janajatis as most important areas where improvements can be initiated by the government, followed by study and research designed to highlight the cultures, languages, and customs of nationalities (34 per cent), and the preservation of traditional costumes and practices of nationalities (20 per cent).

Asked which language they preferred for their children's education, 42 per cent mentioned Nepali, followed by English (29 per cent). Only 28 per cent voted for education in their mother tongue. Since none of the groups involved in the poll traditionally speak Nepali as their mother tongue, this may raise some doubts in the language politics of the ethnic elites.[19] Nevertheless, there may be several reasons for the preference for Nepali. The most important is the language policy of the Nepali state, which offers no openings for speakers of national languages. Here again, we find great differences between the various communities. The highest vote for Nepali as the language of education came from the Tharu (65 per cent), followed by Chepang (62 per cent), Danuwar (60 per cent), Gurung (54 per cent), Jhangad (50 per cent), and Magar (47 per cent). Remarkable support for education in the mother tongue came from the Rai (91 per cent) and the Limbu (57 per cent). There was significant support for English by the Yolmo (50 per cent). In general, the higher the level of education, the greater the support for education in the mother tongue or English.

Economic Sector

Fifty-nine per cent of the respondents knew about instances of nationalities being denied economic opportunities; only 21 per cent denied this. The awareness was higher among persons with university education. As specific areas of denial of economic opportunities the

[19]One explanation may be the language shift that has affected many of the ethnic groups. Today the majority of the Magars (67.9 per cent) and half of the Gurungs (49.3 per cent) have become native speakers of Nepali (Whelpton 1997: 59).

following were mentioned: recruitment for employment (mentioned by 43 per cent),[20] facilities given to the landless (21 per cent), obtaining loans from financial institutions (17 per cent), special programmes meant for nationalities (14 per cent), and scholarship opportunities (5 per cent).[21] There were few differences between rural and urban areas on this issue. But there were great differences between the various ethnic groups. Jhangad (80 per cent), Yolmo (79 per cent), Rai (75 per cent), Jyapu (73 per cent), and Lepcha (70 per cent) are strongly aware of economic discrimination, while a great proportion of Dhimal (65 per cent), Tharu (38 per cent), Chepang and Danuwar (33 per cent), and Magar (31 per cent) denied this. The list of jobs preferred by the Janajatis for their family members was topped by the civil service (34 per cent), followed by the Royal Nepal Army (17 per cent), the police service (12 per cent), foreign military service (10 per cent), public organizations (9 per cent), and foreign employment (8 per cent).

THE MSI OPINION POLL AND THE DEMANDS OF ETHNIC ELITES

In many aspects, the poll results support the demands of the ethnic elites as they have been brought to public notice in the papers of the Nepal Janajati Mahasangh.[22] The poll confirms that a majority of the members of the ethnic groups share the opinion of the ethnic elites that the Janajatis still face disadvantages in modern democratic Nepal, that they feel especially discriminated against in the social sphere, and that they are aware of the economic disadvantages they face.

On the other hand, it is clear that there are some differences in the priorities set by the elites, on one side, and the ethnic people in the districts, on the other. Among the latter, those with university education come closest to the argumentation of the elites. It seems that the degree of awareness depends very strongly upon the level of education. But education fulfils a double function in modern Nepal. It is not only the vehicle for ethnic awareness but is also the means by which traditional state elites preserve the status quo and their own political, social, and economic positions within it.

Döhne, who examined the situation at three high schools in

---

[20]This feeling is higher among better educated persons. It is probably the case that illiterate people will find less well paid jobs more easily.

[21]Among those with university education, 9 per cent see problems in getting scholarship opportunities.

[22]Their demands are best summarized in the document of the Lapsiphedi conference of 1994: NAHC (1994). See also NJM (1996).

Okhaldhunga district, found that the dominance of the traditional state elite left its traces in the founding history of all three schools and that it is even present in the daily school routine: 'Special groups of population, the Tibeto-Mongolian ethnic groups, and, to an even greater extent, the occupational castes thought to be untouchables, are still hindered in the Nepali school system in respect of participation and prospects of success. Furthermore, the chances for the students to integrate knowledge imparted by school into their everyday life tasks and circumstances seem to be closely dependent on their socio-cultural background' (Döhne 2000: 279).

The poll respondents from ethnic groups may have been considering primarily the realities of their current situation when 42 per cent of them expressed a preference for Nepali as the medium of education for their children. The ethnic elites go further when they lay so much stress on aspects such as language, culture, history, and religion. They have become aware that language is the most important pillar of every civilization, culture, or nationality. As Kamal Prakash Malla put it: 'Language is not only a symbol of identity, of ethnicity or nation but also the essential identifying element of its existence .... If a language is lost, the identity of the concerned ethnic group will certainly be lost, and there are very rare examples of revival of lost languages' (Tamang 2000: 8). Thus the ethnic elites have taken the initiative to fight for their linguistic rights as a precondition for the survival of their ethnic identities.

The Nepali state introduced some minor reforms in the 1990s, but they have not been enough to guarantee the survival of ethnic cultures.[23] The ethnic elites want their ethnic languages to be taught at school and to be used in government documents, public affairs, and everyday life, alongside the Nepali language. This has become very clear from the national declaration on linguistic rights signed by the participants of the National Conference on Linguistic Rights, which took place in Kathmandu in March 2000 (Tamang 2000: 18–24). The

[23]For example, radio news in quite a number of ethnic languages is broadcast by Radio Nepal and the Royal Nepal Academy has included the research of ethnic languages into its programmes in the 1990s. But the state policy is still double-edged using differences among the ethnic groups for its own interests. One example may be the Tamangs, whose principal activist organization, the Tamang Ghedung, recently decided to use the Tibetan script for writing their language. The government, instead, was more interested in the use of Devanagari and took the wishes of a smaller group of Tamangs, who supported the use of Devanagari, as a binding rule (Stella Tamang, personal communication).

ethnic elites see the fulfilment of these demands as a condition for participation and equality of their groups in the modern Nepali state.[24] They want sustainable improvements for their groups as a whole and thus differ from many poll respondents who seem to be satisfied with better chances for their own children within the existing system.

There are similar reasons for the differences between the political opinions of ethnic elites and ethnic grassroots. On the one hand the highly educated ethnic elites have broader political ambitions than the rural population. The former are closer to state-level politics and have greater awareness of the discrimination faced by members of their ethnic groups there. In addition, the ethnic elites have a broader perspective in mind. They want to improve their groups' situation and chances and they know this will only be possible if they get access and rights at the central political level. That the ordinary members of ethnic groups are equally aware of discrimination in the political sector becomes obvious in matters which directly affect the local situation, such as the question of participation in the administration. A very high percentage believes that only some kind of reservation politics can help to improve the over-representation of elite groups.

Comparisons with India are always a tricky affair and disliked by many Nepalis. But they can, nevertheless, be helpful to assess the chances of ethnic demands for participation in Nepal. In contrast to Nepal, India has declared herself a secular state and has introduced a reservation system for backward castes and tribes. But this did not prevent the dominance of upper and dominant castes according to region. In northern India this dominance has been specially strong, because electoral politics were oriented along the Hindu-Muslim cleavage. In southern India, politics were organized around caste lines, and this led to the empowerment of lower castes who constitute a majority there.

In north India the scheduled castes and tribes had primarily supported the dominant national party, the Indian National Congress. Though its leaders typically came from the upper castes, the party managed to get the support of the scheduled castes and tribes because it established itself as a party with a non-communal orientation, and partly also because the traditional patron-client relationship in the

---

[24]I still wonder why they don't go a step further and demand education in ethnic languages, cultures, and history as a compulsory subject for all Nepali students. This would be the only way to open the minds of those traditional elites who still think of Nepal as a state of one language, one culture, and one religion.

villages was still alive (Varshney 2000). This situation in north India has slowly changed in recent years with the decline of the Congress Party which was closely connected to the rise of national and regional parties with caste or ethnic orientations.[25]

This development in India suggests that the reservation of seats alone will not provide greater chances for participation. The Nepali Constitution, on the one hand, has defined the state in a communal way by making it a Hindu state. On the other hand, it has denied the recognition of parties oriented along communal—say ethnic, caste, or regional—lines.[26] Thus, Nepal's multi-party system is dominated by national parties which find themselves in similar contradictions to the Indian National Congress. In their party programmes, they may call for participation and political, social, and economic equality, but in practice they uphold the traditional cleavages based on caste, language, religion, and culture.

ETHNIC RESISTANCE AND THE MAOIST MOVEMENT

The politics of Nepal's national parties has left niches that cannot be filled by parties and organizations oriented along ethnic or regional lines because of the constitutional limitations mentioned above. This situation has helped the CPN (Maoist) to establish itself as a strong political force in the most backward rural areas of the country within the last few years. Recently, the Nepali Congress government has declared its willingness to enter into talks with the Maoists. But it still claims not to know the Maoist agenda even though everybody knows what the Maoists' demands are since they presented them to the Deuba government in late 1995.[27] The programmes of the leading national parties hardly contain any concrete steps to eliminate the basic roots of backwardness, poverty, and discrimination,[28] while the Maoists' demands specify quite a number, including:

[25]For recent situational studies see Chandra (2000), Corbridge (2000), and Jaffrelot (2000).

[26]Only a few parties which espouse such ethnic or regional interests (such as the Nepal Sadbhavana Party or the Rastriya Jana Mukti Party) have been recognized by the Election Commission.

[27]Paradoxically, the government has nominated Sher Bahadur Deuba as negotiator for talks with the Maoists. The latter started their so-called People's War in February 1996 because the then Prime Minister Deuba was totally deaf to their demands. Thus the government's chief negotiator has to bear a great responsibility for the escalation of the conflict during his prime ministership.

[28]The ruling Nepali Congress, for example, hardly touches basic ethnic demands

Nepal should be declared a secular state.

Girls should be given equal property rights to those of their brothers.

All kinds of exploitation and prejudice based on caste should be ended.

In areas having a majority of one ethnic group, that group should have autonomy over that area.

The status of Dalits as untouchables should be ended and the system of untouchability should be ended once and for all.

All languages should be given equal status.

Up until middle-high school level arrangements should be made for education to be given in the children's mother tongue.

In both the Tarai and hilly regions there is prejudice and misunderstanding in backward areas; this should be ended and the backward areas should be assisted.

Decentralization in real terms should be applied to local areas which should have local rights, autonomy and control over their own resources.

Those who cultivate the land should own it.

The land of rich landlords should be confiscated and distributed to the homeless and others who have no land.

The homeless should be given suitable accommodation; until HMG can provide such accommodation they should not be removed from the land on which they are squatting.

Poor farmers should be completely freed from debt.[29]

The ethnic organizations have often been accused of being close to the Maoists, even of co-operating with the CPN (Maoist). But the argumentation should be the other way around. It is the Maoists who have come close to ethnic and Dalit demands. As a matter of fact, the organizations of the Nepal Janajati Mahasangh had publicized their

---

concerning ethnic languages, culture and religion when it writes: 'The party will avow itself to preserve and promote the language, art, culture and religion that reflect the national identity of Nepal and its people. The Royal Academy, which looks after the promotion of literature, arts and culture and its activities, will be made more effective. People dedicating their lives to the promotion and preservation of arts, culture and literature will be honoured with public felicitations. The religious freedom of minorities will be preserved' (NC 1999, web site of the Nepali Congress). This is more an avowal to the language and culture of the central elite than a concession to ethnic demands. The official 1999 election manifesto of the party has more extensive coverage on the theme but it too is deaf to ethnic demands (NC 1999: 38).

[29]*The People's Review*, 7 May 1998.

demands and strategy long before the CPN (Maoist) was formed in February 1995. It has been part of the basic strategy of Maoist politics in Nepal to win the downtrodden sections of Nepali society as infantry for their political ambitions. In terms of ethnic composition, the leadership of the CPN (Maoist), so far, hardly differs from that of the leading national parties.

The CPN (Maoist) still has to prove that it offers more than hope for the disadvantaged sections of society. As long as its means are terror and brutal force, ordinary people will suffer even more than before, especially since the government reacts in the same way. It is a matter of fact that the Nepal Janajati Mahasangh is not as united as it may seem. There are some sections within this ethnic movement that are indeed very sympathetic to the Maoist movement. They deviate from the moderate leadership of the Janajati Mahasangh and try to extend their influence whenever they can.[30] Thus the Janajati Mahasangh will also have to prove that it can hold to its non-violent path.

One important question is: How representative are the ethnic organizations? The opinion poll analysed above may prove that the ethnic rank-and-file more or less identifies with the demands and intentions of the ethnic elites. But there are sections of society that do not find representation and participation in Janajati politics and demands. The most prominent group are women. Ethnic leaders may argue that, contrary to Hindu society, women have equal rights in ethnic society. But women are not in fact equal to men in Nepal's ethnic societies nor do they play any significant role in the ethnic organizations. The women's share in the ethnic leadership is as poor as in the leadership of the political parties.

Another question that has to be clarified is the position of the Dalits. The latter are excluded from Janajati circles according to the Janajati self-definition (NAHC 1994: 15). They thus fail to find a place in the dialogue between the Janajati Mahasangh and the Nepali state. The Dalit groups are discriminated against by the traditional state elites in the same or partly even in a harsher way than the ethnic communities. In the interest of its own credibility the Nepal Janajati Mahasangh must make it clear that the Nepali state is not only constituted of Hindu castes that dominate the state and have all rights on their side and ethnic groups that are all disadvantaged on the other. There are

---

[30]The recent event when Gore Bahadur Khapangi tried to topple general secretary Parshuram Tamang may illustrate this (Stella Tamang, personal communication).

sections of Hindu society that are strongly discriminated against even though they share the language and culture of the ruling elite, and there are sections of ethnic societies that already have better representation and participation in modern Nepal than others, as the responses to the MSI opinion poll have in part shown.

REFERENCES

Chandra, K. 2000. 'The Transformation of Ethnic Politics in India: The Decline of Congress and the Rise of the Bahujan Samaj Party in Hoshiarpur' *The Journal of Asian Studies* 59(1): 26–61.

Corbridge, S. 2000. 'Competing Inequalities: The Scheduled Tribes and the Reservations System in India's Jharkhand' *The Journal of Asian Studies* 59(1): 62–85.

Des Chene, M. 1998. '"Black Laws" and the "Limited Rights" of the People in Post-janandolan Nepal: The Campaign against the Proposed Anti-terrorist Act of 2054 VS' *Himalayan Research Bulletin* 18(2): 41–67.

Döhne, T. 2000. *Zwischen Bildungsgewinn und Erfahrungsverlust: Schulerziehung in einem Bergdistrikt Nepals.* Frankfurt: Brandes & Apsel.

Gellner, D.N., J. Pfaff-Czarnecka, and J. Whelpton (eds) 1997. *Nationalism and Ethnicity in a Hindu Kingdom: The Politics of Culture in Contemporary Nepal.* Amsterdam: Harwood.

Hachhethu, K. 2002. *Party Building in Nepal: Organisation, Leadership and People: A Comparative of the Nepali Congress and the Communist Party of Nepal (United Marxist-Leninist).* Kathmandu: Mandala Book Point.

Jaffrelot, C. 2000. 'The Rise of the Other Backward Classes in the Hindi Belt' *The Journal of Asian Studies* 59(1): 86–108.

Khanal, K. and K. Hachhethu 1999 (2056 VS). *Amnirvācan 2056: sansad ra sarkārkā cunautiharu* [The general election of 2056: challenges for parliament and government]. Kathmandu: Centre for Nepal and Asian Studies.

Krämer, K.-H. 1996. *Ethnizitä und nationale Integration in Nepal: Eine Untersuchung zur Politisierung der ethnischen Gruppen im modernen Nepal* (Beiträge zur Südasienforschung, Südasien-Institut, Universität Heidelberg, Band 174). Stuttgart: Franz Steiner.

—— 1999. 'Democracy and Civil Society in the Himalayas: Problems of Implementation and Participation in Multiethnic Societies'. Unpublished paper presented at the POLSAN conference on 'Civil Society and Democratization: The Contemporary World Scenario', 17–18 February 1999.

—— 2000. 'Elections in Nepal: 1999 and Before' in Informal Sector Service Centre (publ.), *Human Rights Yearbook 2000.* Kathmandu: INSEC, pp. 29–47.

—— 2000. 'Requiring a Social History: Must Nepali history be Re-written?'

198   Resistance and the State: Nepalese Experiences

in R.P. Thapa and J. Baaden (eds) *Nepal: Myth and Realities*. Delhi: Book Faith India, pp. 499–521.
——— 2001. 'Nepal' in D. Nohlen *et al.* (eds) *Elections in Asia and the Pacific: A Data Handbook*. Oxford: University Press.
Kumar, D. 1995. 'State, Leadership and Politics: A Preliminary Note on Transition' in D. Kumar (ed.) *State, Leadership and Politics in Nepal*. Kathmandu: CNAS, pp. 1–15.
MSI (Media Services International) 2000. *Opinion Survey Regarding Perceptions and Feelings of the Janajatis* (provisional report).
NAHC 1994. (National Ad Hoc Committee for International Decade for the World's Indigenous Peoples, Nepal.) *Nepālkā ādivāsiharubāre rāstriya paramārsha-gosthi (2050 caitra 10–13 gatesamma: lapsiphedi, kāthmādaun): prativedan* [Proceedings of the National Consultation on Indigenous Peoples of Nepal (23–26 March 1994), Lapsiphedi, Kathmandu: Report]. Kathmandu.
NC 1999. *Nepāli kāngresko ghosanapatra—āmnirvācan, 2056* [Manifesto of the Nepali Congress—General Elections 2056]. See also 'The Nepali Congress Manifesto: Highlights' at *http://www.south-asia.com/Nepalicongress/*).
NJM (Nepal Janajati Mahasangh) 1996 (VS 2053). *Nepāl janajāti mahāsangh tesro mahādhiveshan (2053 jeth 25–27 gate: lalitpur)* [Third General Assembly of the Nepal Janajati Mahasangh (Jeth, 25–27, 2053, Lalitpur)]. Kathmandu: Nepal Janajati Mahasangh.
Shrestha, P. (ed.) 2000. *Governance in the Doldrums: Who really Governs Nepal?* Kathmandu: South Asia Partnership-Nepal.
Shaha, R. 1982. *Essays in the Practice of Government in Nepal*. New Delhi: Manohar.
Tamang, P. 1997 [2054 VS]. *Janajāti ra rāstravād (kehi lekhaharusangālo)* [Nationalities and Nationalism (a collection of works)]. Kathmandu: Jana Sahitya Prakashan Kendra.
——— (ed.) 2000. *Proceedings of National Conference on Linguistic Rights, 16–17 March 2000, Kathmandu, Nepal*. Kathmandu: Nepal Federation of Nationalities.
Thapa, G.B. and K.-H. Krämer (forthcoming). 'The CPN (UML)' in S.K. Mitra and M. Enskat (eds) *Political Parties in South Asia*. Westport, CT: Praeger.
Uprety, P.R. and C.B. Budhathoki 1999. *Political Instability in Nepal: Impact on Nepali Democracy*. Kirtipur: Central Department of History, Tribhuvan University, and Friedrich-Ebert-Stiftung.
Varshney, A. 2000. 'Is India becoming more Democratic?' *Journal of Asian Studies* 59(1): 3–25.
Whelpton, J. 1997. 'Political Identity in Nepal: State, Nation, and Community' in Gellner *et al.* (eds).
——— 1999. 'Nine Years On: The 1999 Election and Nepalese Politics since the 1990 Janandolan' *European Bulletin of Himalayan Research* 17: 1–39.

chapter six

An 'Indigenous Minority' in a Border Area: Tharu Ethnic Associations, NGOs, and the Nepalese State

• *Gisèle Krauskopff*

INTRODUCTION

How has a self-conscious ethnic movement taken shape among the Tharu groups inhabiting the Nepalese Tarai? What are its characteristics, its means of action, its relationships with political action and with the central state authority?

I have collected information about this topic quite haphazardly in recent years mainly because of the events which followed the political changes of 1990 in Nepal and because of my long involvement with the Tharus of Dang valley who have since 1981 invited me to participate in several 'Tharu conferences'. But the great political upheaval of 1990 must not be allowed to obliterate the past: what happened before in terms of ethnic formation and ethnicity has to be borne in mind in order to understand the present situation.

Thus this chapter will describe the genesis of the different Tharu ethnic associations and compare them in historical perspective. The chapter is constructed around the divergent strategies vis-à-vis the state of the two main movements: the Tharu Welfare Society, a cultural and social association established in 1949, the (Tharu) Backward

This paper is dedicated to Sigrun Eide Ødegaard from Norway who devoted a Master's thesis to ethnic politics among the Tharu and worked specifically on the development of the Tharu NGO, BASE, before her untimely tragic death in a car crash in Africa at the age of 30 in July 1999. She carried out several months of field work mainly in Kailali district in a Rana Tharu village. She had published an article on the subject (1999) but most of her work remains at present unpublished.

Society Education or BASE, a recent grassroots organization turned NGO. These two organizations were created in very different political and social contexts. The impact of the encompassing political order in shaping ethnic groups and their boundaries has always been central but it is leading today to a specific 'democratic ethnicity' that I shall try to define and analyse.

The underlying question will be to measure the political dimension of such an ethnic movement in the specific context of the Tarai as a border area and more precisely the potential link between Tharu ethnicity and political activism. Since my most recent field visit was in 1998 I do not have sufficient information on the influence of the Maoist insurrection (specifically in the western valley of Dang) or on the concrete consequences of the recent political decision (July 2000) to 'free' the Kamaiya (*kamaiyā*), that is the poorest class of Tharu landless farmers in the western Tarai, mainly servants whether bonded or unbonded.

In dealing with the present topic, I wish to put the recent changes and so-called ethnic processes in continuity with what in the past made 'the Tharu' exist as distinct cultural communities all over the Tarai. The central role played during the nineteenth century and earlier by the local Tharu gentry, especially their control of land, led to a changed definition of their socio-cultural boundaries (Krauskopff 1989, Krauskopff and Deuel 2000). I believe that the role of elite competition is still central in the modern process of 'ethnicity'. I agree with Paul Brass that one key point is to study 'the relationships established between elites and the state, particularly the role of collaborators and opponents of state authority and state intrusion into regions inhabited by distinctive ethnic groups' (Brass 1991: 14).

FROM CASTE ASSOCIATION TO CULTURAL ETHNIC ASSOCIATION

Birth of a Caste Reform Association[1]

The Tharu Welfare Society (Thāru Kalyānkārini Sabhā) was founded in 1949, an early date for an ethnic association in Nepal. It is today the representative body of the Tharu in the Nepal Federation of Nationalities (Nepāl Janajāti Mahāsangh). However, in an article pub-

---

[1]Tharu ethnicity and modernization. See Guneratne (1998); he devoted the last chapter of his thesis to the Tharu Welfare Society (1994: 321–80). There is much new material on the Society and on the language issue in Guneratne (2002), which reached me too late for inclusion here.

lished in Nepali in a Tharu journal, one of its founding members, Keval Chaudhary (2049 VS), mentions as an ancestral figure Amar Bahadur Faujdar of Bara district who in 1922 settled 'the rules to develop the Tharu caste (*jāt*)'. This interesting remark in a paper devoted to the history of the Tharu Welfare Society, as seen by one of its founding members, helps us to measure the influence played by the caste reform movements in India in the genesis of the association and to understand its relatively early formation. At the time of its creation, the Tharu Welfare Society could best be defined as a caste association.

This is not the place for an extensive discussion of the role of caste associations in ethnicizing groups in India, whether castes or tribes. These movements were closely linked to the impact of the census operations from the last quarter of the nineteenth century onwards. They were particularly active during the first part of the twentieth century in India. A reading of the British censuses of this period offers numerous examples of their growing influence. Hence in the Census of the United Provinces of Agra and Oudh (1933) Turner summarized the process in the following way:

By tradition the census has come to be regarded as great opportunity for persons low in the caste scale to press their claims to higher social status. In 1901 and 1911 the claims came mainly from individuals but in 1921 caste sabhas had begun to spring up who pressed such claims with great persistence. Since 1921 the sabha movement has developed to such an extent that all save the most backward castes and tribes now have more or less well-organised societies, who bombarded me until long after the tables were printed with requests for new caste names (Turner 1933: 528).

For the low castes the goal was to raise their community in the social scale; this meant making a claim to Brahman, Rajput, or Vaisya descent and adopting a new caste name to fit the claim. Proselytism and re-conversion, the spread of education, the abolition of the seclusion of women, of widow remarriage, the reduction of expenditures, of dowries, the abolition of dancing and drinking—these were the main means of action (Turner 1933: 552). As we shall see the early goals set up by the Tharu Welfare Society were similar.

The census-compilers linked the burgeoning of the caste associations to the declining influence of the village panchayats and to the development of communications which enlarged panchayat assemblies to the district level. As early as 1911, the census stressed the role of the more educated younger generation 'who pursue a constant policy of opposition to their elders' and influence of Congress activists who undermined the previous authority of the local chaudhary or panchayat leader unless he shared their political views. Turner cited an opposition between the panchayat, 'an ancient and indigenous institution of Hindu society', on the one hand, and the *sabha*, 'a modern product, the result of the Western concept of association', on the other. The sabha associations advocated the uplift of their group by means of practices which expressed modern welfare goals in Sanskritized discourse. Significantly, the census of 1911 noted that 'the representative assembly (of the sabha) ... is far removed from even the members of the sabhas and still more so from those of *the castes who are not members and probably know nothing of its existence*' (Turner 1933: 551; emphasis added). In other words, caste associations expressed the wishes and goals of the elite.

The early date of 1922 given by Keval Chaudhary for the Tharu Welfare movement is significant in this regard. I do not know anything about Amar Bahadur Faujdar but his name tellingly reveals his status as the main central government representative of the district.[2] The role of the local *border elite* is evident here and it would be worthwhile to research the relationships between this early reform movement in Bara District and similar ones in the neighbouring area of Champaran in Indian Bihar at the beginning of the twentieth century (both areas being inhabited by related Tharu). For in the 1940s a relationship did exist, as the case of the Tharu of Champaran illustrates. In the Indian census of 1941 the Tharu of Champaran were classified as a Scheduled Tribe and in 1946 they organized a large conference to contest this classification. They were successful and in the Census of 1951 they were classified as a Backward Class. The caste association held its first session in May 1946 and defined the Champaran Tharu language 'as the common Bhojpuri dialect of the Hindustani language as spoken by the other people of the area' and not as 'a different aboriginal dialect', adding that in Nepal the Tharu speak Nepali (Roy Choudhuri 1952: 247). To support their claim, the Tharu of Champaran declared that all their marriage and funeral ceremonies were exactly as observed by others caste Hindus and moreover that 'his majesty *the Maharaja of Nepal and the Nepal government have recognised the Tharu as caste Hindus*'! (Turner 1933: 248; emphasis added). According to the same document, the influence of the Arya Samaj was then spreading, and the Tharu of Champaran

[2]*Faujdar* were the highest administrative authority at the district level.

'were taking the sacred thread and alcohol consumption had been highly reduced' (Turner 1933: 250).

It seems that the Nepalese Hindu legal classification was here used as proof of the Tharu being a caste and not a tribe, an opposition which was not pertinent in Nepal at this time, unlike in British India. Considering the relatively low status of the Tharu in the Ranas' legal code (a clean caste, *pāni calne*, but drinking alcohol, *matwāli*, and subject to enslavement, *māsinyā*), it is somewhat surprising that the Champaran Tharus made use of it in this way.

Champaran, like the neighbouring Bara district of Nepal, shelters a solid Tharu elite of landowners who had established early connections with Hindu little kingdoms since at least the seventeenth century (Krauskopff and Deuel 2000). This is reflected in their early struggle for recognition as Kshatriyas, a process at work much before the census operation. However the strategy employed to climb the social scale changed according to the political, administrative, and legal system. In 1952 Roy Choudhuri concluded his paper with the following comment: 'It will not be strange if in another few decades they become a separate caste or become merged in the Rajput caste of Bihar' (Roy Choudhuri 1952: 250). But, in fact, times have changed and the Tharu of Champaran, for evident political reasons, are now trying to be re-listed as Scheduled Tribe, a status which brings far more benefits in today's India.

It seems evident that the actions of the founders of the Tharu Welfare Society in Nepal were influenced by what was happening in India, under the census 'objectification' (Cohn 1990) and the official classification of Scheduled and Backward tribes and castes. Their motivations were evidently those of a landed Tharu elite aspiring to a higher status. Their actions were also influenced by the political changes which were taking place in India but directed towards Nepal, including the development of the Nepali Congress opposition against the Rana oligarchy.

State Classifications and the Elite

The movement at the base of the Tharu ethnicity in Nepal was paradoxically built on rules which opposed the village traditions of ordinary Tharu farmers. It was an elite movement in continuity with a much earlier trend of 'Kshatriya-ization' of the elite, as excellently analysed for the Bhumij in central India by Sinha (1962) or, to quote another example closer to the Tharu, as it developed at an early date among the Kooch and the Rajbamsi of the eastern Tarai in Bengal (Mukhopadhyaya 1999).

Similarly Srivastava, who did his fieldwork in 1948–50 among the Rana Tharu of Nainital district in India (Uttar Pradesh) and far western Nepal, described how a section of the Rana Tharu of Nainital sought recognition as Kshatriyas in order to escape the status of Scheduled Tribe (as in Champaran). To reach this goal a social reform movement (*jāti sudhār*) was initiated in 1930 by a handful of educated Tharu. As a first stage they tried to suppress some local customs: for instance, raising poultry incurred a fine of 25 rupees and sharing a waterpipe with the lower section or eating pork was punished by excommunication! These regulations were not at all popular among the villagers. Therefore, at the time of Indian independence, when a similar movement redeveloped, more stress was put on welfare activities but the dominant trend remained the same: to promote the use of Brahman priests for ceremonies, to adjust some festivals to the Hindu ceremonial calendar, to put an end to alcohol consumption, and to reduce the free movement of women, by means of very heavy fines (Srivastava 1958, 1999).

During its first conference in 1951 the Tharu Welfare Society also stressed the need to reform marriage rules, to cut the cost of marriage ceremonies, and to oppose 'blind superstitions'. As noted above, the uplift of the Tharu involved translating welfare goals (more exactly the struggle against backwardness) into traditional discourse.

Since it made regulations and imposed punishments, the Tharu Welfare Association was not only a welfare organization but a juridical body. It worked within the framework of the Rana legal code (which remained in force until 1963). This legal code had some of the same effects in Nepal as the Census of India did in India: in both cases hierarchical classification by the state generated attempts to climb the social scale and it was characteristic of caste organizations in both contexts to use fines and punishments to modify local customs. But such measures, it should be noted, were advocated by elites who had already changed their own way of life.

On a general socio-historical level, therefore, a comparison with other reform movements which emerged in Nepal in the 1950s among minorities would be fruitful to understand the present Janajati movement. Hence the Thakali Social Reform Organization (Thakāli Samāj Sudhār) was founded at an early date in Pokhara, in 1954, by an urban elite to reform customs by stressing the need to reduce the cost of some ceremonies (Manzardo and Sharma 1975). The cultural context was totally different, since the Thakali are a Buddhist group of successful traders and dwellers of the high valley of the Kali Gandaki, but the general aspirations of the elite and the rules enacted by the Thakali reform movement echo the practices of the Tharu Sabha and Indian caste associations.[3] The representative body of the Tamang, the Nepal Tamang Council (Nepāl Tāmāng Ghedung), was also founded in 1956 as were similar associations among the Gurung, the Magar, and the Kiranti. These associations were often founded by ex-Gurkha officers, returning from India, or by Nepalis from Darjeeling. In most cases these movements were generated by an elite from outside Nepal. Taking into account the different cultural and religious backgrounds, the strategies adopted by these different organizations should be studied comparatively, as should the role of this elite in the new political context and the spread and influence of the ideology of the Nepali Congress Party.

A Political Platform for the Elite

In the Indian context Rudolph and Rudolph (1960) have argued that caste associations have been a way of initiating the participation of the traditional electorate in democratic politics. It is evident that in Nepal, at least in the case of the Tharu, they supported the elite aspirations in the new national political landscape of the so-called 'first democratic period of Nepal'.

During the period preceding the collapse of the Rana regime in 1950, the Tharu elite of Tarai was in close contact with India, some of the leaders living in India where the anti-Rana movement was based. But after the political change, the strategy of the Nepal Tharu evolved differently from those in India. The political, historical, and social situation of the Tharu in Nepal is different in that they form a majority and the Tharu elite owns land in the richest parts of the Tarai, which borders the powerful Indian state.

One of the main manifestations and means of action of the Tharu Welfare Society has been the regular organization of conventions and conferences, which can tell us a great deal about the strategy and sociology of the movement. My only source for the early conferences is the historical text published by Keval Chaudhary and referred to

---

[3]Interestingly enough, where the Tharu stress the need to reduce marriage expenditures, the Thakali insist on the cutting the costs of funeral ceremonies. On the Thakali reform movements, see Fisher (2001).

above (Chaudhary 2049 VS). It gives a good idea of the association's early goals, its members' ideology, and its relationship to the central state and political parties.

The first meeting of the Tharu Welfare Society was held at Kakari in 1951, in Bara district. This part of the Tarai appears as a kind of stronghold of the movement in its early stages. In Keval Chaudhary's own words (himself from Sunsari district), the main goals at that time were development in the social, economic, and educational spheres. For such a development, they wished to suppress several forms of marriage (child marriage, marriage with too great an age difference, polygamy), alcohol consumption (*madyapān*), blind superstitions, and unnecessary expenditures (*phajulakharci*). Such demands are typical of reform movements directed by an educated elite, as we have seen for the numerous caste associations in India at an earlier period.

The second conference in 1952 moved to the nearby Rautahat district and the third one was again held in Bara in 1953. Several leading political figures of the Nepali Congress Party were invited to the third conference: M.P. Koirala and B.P. Koirala, the two competing brothers of the leading family of the Nepali Congress Party, Naradamuni Thulung, another founding member of the Nepali Congress Party, who was at that time a Minister, and four central district officers or *barā hakim*. Keval Chaudhary adds that 2100 Company Rupees (as the Indian currency was still known colloquially) were collected.

The fourth Tharu Welfare Society conference was held in 1954 in Deokhuri, a remote and backward area of western Nepal, in the home village of Parsu Narayan Chaudhary, a Dang-Deokhuri landlord and early member of the Nepali Congress Party, who was close to the Koirala family. He held important positions in the new Advisory Assembly of the post-Rana government. He is still one of the main leaders of the association.

The fifth conference was held in the eastern Tarai district of Saptari, home of a solid elite of Tharu (Krauskopff and Deuel 2000), but the sixth was held in two geographically very distant places, at Kancanvadi (Morang) and Basauti (Mahakali), that is, in the two most extreme Tarai districts of Nepal. As early as 1955, the wish to build relationships between all the Tharu groups of Tarai was expressed. At Kanchavadi, the Chief District Officer Niranjan Samser, Parsu Narayan Chaudhary (of Dang-Deokhuri), Nar Bahadur Gurung (Chitrakar), Ramadin Chaudhary, Tej Narayan Jimdar, Khutan Tavdar, Tilak Can Biswas, Ramananda Prasad Singh (a Tharu leading figure of Saptari), and 'other distinguished persons' attended the conference. The resolutions taken were similar to those listed above. At the seventh conference in 1957, held in Keutaliya (Rupandehi), M. Hu (China), Nar Bahadur Gurung, and some Indian representatives from Gorakhpur were invited.

Then the conferences stopped until 1979 with an exception in 1963–4, at dates noticeably linked to political and legal changes in Nepal. The relationship of the Tharu Welfare Society with the overall political situation, and more precisely with Nepali Congress activities and party politics, is evident. The first conference was held after the collapse of the Rana regime and important (non-Tharu) representatives of the Nepali Congress party were present. More research would be necessary to substantiate the tight link between the Nepali Congress party and the elite of the Tharu Welfare Society but the connections of some Tharu leaders with the Koirala family and the Congress Party, as well as their links to central governmental bodies during the transitional period, are well known.

In 1959 the first general elections in Nepal led to the nomination of B.P. Koirala, leader of the Nepali Congress, as Prime Minister of Nepal, but for only one year. The political situation then deteriorated; B.P. Koirala was imprisoned, and the ban on political parties was introduced by King Mahendra in 1960. A leading Tharu figure, Parsu Narayan Chaudhary, went into exile in India. The suspension of the conferences between 1956–7 and 1979 (with an exception in 1964) is undoubtedly linked to the ban imposed on political parties and associations in 1960 and the political retreat of some of its leading members. The early Panchayat era was not a time for any kind of association, even purely cultural. The next meeting had to wait for the period after the referendum of 1980, when it became somewhat easier to hold political meetings.

However it appears somewhat paradoxical that conferences stop as early as 1956–7, in a period otherwise favourable to meetings and associations. Could it be that having succeeded in being recognized by the new government, the Tharu elite ceased to emphasize their ethnic base? If so, it would reinforce the essential link between the emergence of an ethnic- or caste-based movement like the Tharu Welfare Society and elite competition to reach the core of authority.

The 1964 conference was held in Sarlahi at a time of crucial change with the formal implementation of the Panchayat system, the new land rights (Land Reform), and the introduction of the new legal code. I do not have precise information on the topic of the conference except that Rishikesh Shaha, a well-known figure of the opposition was present. It seems probable that the Land Act of 1963, as well as the new regulations about marriages, were the main concerns.

A new period, more favourable to such meetings, started with the referendum on whether to introduce a multi-party system in 1980. Later that year political dissension became part of the Tharu Welfare Society's conferences. Internal competition inside the elite along political lines was sufficiently significant to be noted as the main event in the historical article written by Keval Chaudhary (he refers to 'the opposition between the Yellows, pro-Panchayat, and the Blacks, pro-multi-party'). This realignment of the Tharu Welfare Society leaders along new conflicting political and ideological tendencies confirms the political nature of the association. One of the founding leaders of the Tharu Welfare Society, Parsu Narayan Chaudhary, shortly afterwards entered the national government.

The Tharu Welfare Society, created initially as a caste association by an elite to support the promotion of their group by reforming the customs of the ordinary people, became clearly a political platform in the 1950s for the same elite to reach the central sphere of authority. The early creation of the Tharu Welfare Society was stimulated by its historical links with India and reinforced by the Congress Party activities with which the Tharu elite was linked. But the Tharu Welfare Society never acted as a political party. During the time of its close association with the dominant oppositional force of the Nepali Congress, it emphasized the modern discourse of social reform and education, the struggle against backwardness which could be removed through education, and the suppression of some 'bad habits' like drinking or feasting. It did not seem to be concerned with the economic situation of the majority of Tharu farmers. It must however be remembered that during the 1950s, the great changes which were to push many hillmen to settle in the Tarai had not yet occurred. Big estates belonging to a non-resident aristocracy and some very few local Tharu landlords controlled most of the land and were still in need of the local labour force.

Towards a Cultural Umbrella Association

Opposition to the Panchayat system following the 1980 referendum opened a new period for the Society which culminated with the return of democracy in 1990. An important cultural performance—an event which was to become an essential part of all such meetings—marks the eleventh conference, held in 1984 in Kailali district. During the twelth conference in Rupandehi in 1986 the (new) rules 'to promote the development of the association and of the Tharus' were established. The conference held in 1991 adopted a new and more ambitious strategy by which the association would seek to extend its scope to all 22 Tarai districts 'from the Mechi to the Mahakhali', trying to expand its audience as far as possible. In Keval Chaudhary's own words, it was necessary 'to reinforce social relations between the Tharu in every district'.

The stress was now put on publications, especially by students. It was also considered a priority to conduct development programmes. As in earlier meetings, links with the central authorities were maintained through the recurrent invitation of important political figures. In 1993 G.P. Koirala, the Congress leader and Prime Minister of Nepal, inaugurated the conference; in 1995 it was the Communist Prime Minister, Man Mohan Adhikari. The Tharu Welfare Society is offically apolitical. But the quest for recognition from prominent central political figures is recurrent as is the strategy of accommodation and collaboration with the centre.

Beginning in the 1990s the importance of the ethnic question became more apparent. The Tharu Welfare Society was still a reform movement but it ceased to be inspired by the 'caste association' ideology. Its participation in the Federation of Nationalities from 1992 confirms a realignment in line with the aspirations of tribal groups and minorities. It must be remembered that as early as 1956 a Backward Classes Organization was established in Nepal which included the Tharu Welfare Society, Gurung and Kiranti organizations, and, most noticeably, a Dalit organization (Gurung 1997: 526). By contrast the Nepal Federation of Nationalities of today has rejected the integration of the Untouchables. The political discourse has shifted from 'backwardness' to 'indigenousness' and therefore, as we shall see in the last part of this chapter, the Tharu Welfare Society has changed its cultural emblems. As inhabitants of the lowland, *madesh,* and as speakers of Indo-Aryan languages related to those spoken in north India, the Tharu have to put up with an atypical position in an organization where the majority of member-organizations represent Tibeto-Burmese-speaking minorities of the hills. The Tharu are also one of the largest minorities in Nepal.

The 1990 conference is briefly described in the Tharu journal *Hanli* (see also Guneratne 1994: 336–9). This conference was held in the City Hall (Sabha Griha) of Biratnagar and was inaugurated by Krishna Prasad Bhattarai, then Prime Minister of the interim government and President of the Nepali Congress. In his inaugural speech, when paying homage to his 'Tharu brothers and sisters', he insisted on the issue of communalism, stressing the danger of the 'false words that bring destruction like in India' and he emphasized the necessity of development of all 'the backward *jāt*' which had been impeded by the 30 years of the Panchayat system, the necessity of good programmes, of social fraternity and openness and the values of democracy. 'All of us are backwards,' he said: 'Hatred between *jāt*, between *anyajāti* and *janajāti*, will weaken the country.' During the same programme, however, Parsu Narayan Chaudhary asked for the government to institute reservations in order to raise the Tharus' condition. Another important personality, Ramananda Prasad Singh, presented his theory of the Tharu being descendants of the Buddha, and Keval Chaudhary submitted his paper on the history of the Tharu Welfare Society quoted above.

From 1990 onwards the competition between the old leaders and the younger generation re-emerges, as seems to have been the rule at each new phase.[4] According to Guneratne (1994: 338–9), who attended this conference, a conflict arose when the new composition of the central committee was announced. The youthful representatives asked for an election to be held; Ramananda Prasad Singh answered that they must propose their candidates, but the proposal remained unanswered. Then Parsu Narayan Chaudhary highlighted the non-political nature of the organization, stating therefore, that elections were not necessary. He thereby pacified the conflict—mainly instigated by the local younger generation—saying 'We cannot fight with our hosts'. To maintain a consensus seems essential and for that the traditional role of the elders remains respected.

The internal organization of the Tharu Welfare Society reveals a government-like body, with a President, a Vice-President, a General Secretary, a Treasurer, and several Ministers, one for culture, one for organization, one for youth (including recently a Minister of Communication, and last but not least, a co-ordinator for NGOs). Each of the 22 districts has its own committee, including Kathmandu. The members of the Central Committee are 'chosen' (it is not clear how) from among the district representatives and changed every two years.

[4]According to Ramananda Prasad Singh, the Tharu Welfare Association was created partly as a reaction by young educated Tharu to the political and social conservatism of their elders (Guneratne 1994: 322). Cf. the comments above of the Census of India of 1911 and 1933 about the genesis of the caste associations.

Each member has to pay 25 rupees and donations are essential, including donations made by NGOs, and even from some public funds.

According to an interview I had in 1996 with a Kathmandu-based young leader from Deokhuri district, it is clear that a new generation hopes to gain higher positions in the old association. But interestingly enough this young leader has established his own association, the Tharu Cultural Society (Thāru Sanskriti Samāj) in 1992, with several young Kathmandu-based Tharu (mainly from the eastern Tarai, a pattern echoing the creation of the Tharu Welfare Society nearly 50 years ago). This middle class of young urban Tharu is a new sociological group linked to a more general rise in the level of education. Some of them are akin to the old Tharu landed gentry but most have studied at university in Kathmandu and are civil servants or work in banks. This new Cultural Society works in close contact with the Tharu Welfare Society. The label stresses the purely 'cultural' goal of this group who regularly organize prestigious cultural exhibitions in Kathmandu. If the Tharu Welfare Society has been a political platform to reach the central core of authority, new associations like the Tharu Cultural Society are a kind of 'sub-platform' for a new modern, urban, middle-class elite who compete with their elders to assume some control in the central Tharu movement. It is also a way to counteract the aristocratic functioning of the Tharu Welfare Association.

Besides cultural programmes the Tharu Cultural Society supports the project of a Tharu museum. Its first cultural show was held in Chitwan in 1992, noticeably the closest Tarai district to Kathmandu. Another important programme was organized in 1994 in Bardiya district, focused on a dancing and singing contest with troupes coming from all over Tarai addressed to a mainly local audience. As is customary, the Prime Minister and the Minister of Tourism were invited to inaugurate the show. BASE, the biggest Tharu NGO from the nearby Dang valley, was also deeply involved in the management of this event. The same year the Tharu Cultural Society was one of the main organizers of 'the First International Tharu Cultural Conference' held in Saptari district in which all the Tharu organizations participated. The last programme I saw in 1996 was an ambitious cultural show trying to reach a Western audience and sponsored by the Tharu Welfare Society with the support of the Ministry of Tourism. It was held in two places, a central Kathmandu theatre for the Nepali audience and in a five-star hotel in Kathmandu, with ticket reservations at $25, for the Western audience; it included a dance show, a handicraft exhibition, and a Tharu buffet. This association is a kind of post-1990 democratic offshoot of the Tharu Welfare Society. Its members are Nepalized, Kathmandu-based, and educated: they constitute a new Tharu middle-class elite.

The Mushrooming of Satellite Associations

It is not possible to draw up a complete list of the mushrooming cultural and welfare associations which have emerged during the last decade. But this efflorescence of new activities and ideas is worth noting as a crucial part of the development of Tharu ethnicity in the new post-1990 context. All these associations may be thought of as satellites of the Tharu Welfare Society, drawing a web all over the Tarai and at the local level. Each has its own chosen field of action. Some of them publish journals or booklets to spread their view or to document different aspects of the Tharu customs and languages. Most of them are, in fact, youth or student associations dealing with literary activities and the promotion of the Tharu languages and of new emblems of Tharu ethnicity.

For example, the Progressive Tharu Youth Organization (Pragatishil Thāru Yuba Sangathan) fights for the spread of Theravada Buddhism through the idea of the Tharu origin of the Buddha or the Buddhist origin of the Tharus, a new myth, which is in fact the slogan of an old leading personality of the Tharu Welfare Society, Ramananda Prasad Singh, who has more or less retired and converted to Buddhism. The movement is based in eastern Saptari district and in Kathmandu. They publish books dealing with Buddhist subjects and a journal, *Chirakha*, mainly in the Tharu language of the eastern Tarai.

The language question, to which we will come back to later is supported by the Council for Tharu Literature (Thāru Bhāsā Sāhitya Parishad), established in 1990. This is also based in Saptari and is neither a student nor youth association; its leader is a well-known person of Saptari and of the Tharu Welfare Society. A journal, *Tharu Patra* (dated VS 2050 Baisakh), gave an interesting description of its first meeting in 1991 (in the language spoken in the eastern Tarai), showing that most of the leading personalities of the Tharu Welfare Society were present: its 'Prime Minister', the President of the Saptari Committee, the 'Minister for Culture' in the Central Committee, the founder of the original movement, Ramananda Prasad Singh, Tej Narayan Panjiar,[5] as well as some political officials such as the mayor of Saptari

---

[5]See Krauskopff and Deuel (2000) in which Tej Narayan Panjiar participated and articulated his historical discourse on the Tharu.

city. Other local organizations, like the Progressive Tharu Youth Organization, the Centre for the United Tharu Nationalities (Tharu Janajāti Milan Kendra, based in Janakpur: it published a Who's Who of the Tharu in 1990), and the Indian Tharu Welfare Federation (Bharatiya Tharu Kalyankarini Mahasangh), the association of the Champaran Tharu of Indian Bihar, were also represented. The goal of this linguistic association is to promote 'The Tharu Language' (i.e., the language spoken in the eastern Tarai), with the publication of grammars and lexicons. It, too, is clearly a satellite organization of the Tharu Welfare Society.

Numerous associations have their roots in eastern Tarai, a focal place for the Tharu ethnic movement and where the Tharu elite has historically, a solid base. Other small associations are burgeoning in central and western Tarai but are less well publicized. For example, the United Centre of Tharu Youth (Tharu Yuba Milan Kendra) based in Kapilavastu, or the Tharu Ekatā Kendra, or the Tharu Yuba Chattra Sangh—all these labels clearly indicate that these local associations are mainly organized by young people (*yuba*), as has been described for Chitwan by Guneratne (1994: 357). These youth and student groups bear witness to the rising level of education of the new generation at the local level.

Some of these associations support the publication of journals, an activity which should be stressed as an important channel for the building of ethnicity in a modern state with higher levels of literacy. The most important journal in this regard at the national level is 'Tharu Culture' (*Thāru Samskriti*) which was also edited by the Tharu Welfare Society during the 1970s and contains for the issues I have seen (1976–1977–1978), poems, descriptions of customs, and historical documents concerning the Tharu.

A few examples of these irregular journals can be given as follows. The Hauli Family (Hauli Pariwār) of Sunsari district and the Council for Tharu Culture and Literature (Thāru Sāhityak tathā Sānskritik Sankalan) have published a journal called *Hauli* since 1985 which appears four times a year. *Lab Purnimā* (The New Full Moon) is a monthly paper by and for young people, also published in Saptari district. Another example is *Upahār* diffused in Dang-Deokhuri, first published on the occasion of the First International Tharu Conference of 1994 (described below), and sponsored by Parsu Narayan Chaudhari. The Tharu Youth Family (Thāru Yuba Pariwār), based in Kathmandu, has published a journal called 'Morning' (*Bihān*) since Dasain 1994 in collaboration with the United Council of the Tharu Languages (Thāru Bhāsāk Sāmājik Sankalan). They carry on with an older publication of 1991 which failed to appear regularly. They advocate the promotion of the Tharu language, in their case the Dangaura Tharu language, but clearly manifest their affiliation with the Nepali Congress at the local level. The Dasain 1994 issue gives the Dang Congress MP's political proposals for 1991 and a paper on the history of the Nepali Congress in Dang. This association has also published a book on Dangaura marriage traditions, called *Māngar*, in 1993. If this journal is an open platform for a dominant political party, it keeps to the common line, with the publication of songs, poems, and other original texts, an activity which actually never stopped even during the Panchayat years.[6]

Whatever their political opinions, most of the small journals and associations stick to cultural goals, mainly promoting languages and protecting customs, besides advocating new ideas to support Tharu ethnicity. They also offer to some young educated Tharu the opportunity to publish essays, poems, and songs in their mother tongue. Poems and songs are vehicles for new ideas, an aspect I have not enough room to develop here. The same can be said of the dances and comic performances which are a recurrent feature of the pan-Tharu ethnic conferences. Hence the leader of a dancing group of Kailali district told me: 'If we talk, people would prefer to go fishing. They listen and understand much better when it is sung.'

This brief overview of the mushrooming youth associations indicates their close ideological and practical connections with the Tharu Welfare Society. They appeared in the years after 1990 as democratic offshoots generated by a new middle-class 'elite', to promote reformist ideas and compete (through collaboration) with the older generation. They are platforms to voice their claims to the central authority and some may even have links with political parties. They favour the reformist stance of the elitist and conservative Tharu Welfare Association in the new context, particularly at the local level. The Tharu Welfare Society, however, stands as an encompassing structure reinforced by its membership in the Nepal Federation of Nationalities. This evolution confirms the collaborationist attitude of all these associations towards the national government and the Nepali state.

The political nature of the Tharu Welfare Society lies in being a pressure group. From the beginning it has been an elite association, created by the descendants of the delegate chieftains of the previous Hindu little kings, a landed gentry who first aspired to institutionalize

[6]On the Tharu cultural and editorial activities of this period see McDonaugh (1997) and Krauskopff (1996).

a Kshatriya status but later on, in a new political context, changed its means of action. As analysed by Brass (1990), the competition between the central authority and the local elite is the dominant force at work. During the first democratic phase of Nepal, it sustained the political rise of some of the Tharu leaders through a historical link with the Nepali Congress opposition. The emphasis on education and on backwardness, rather than on ethnically based demands, illustrated the impact of the Congress Party's anti-communalist ideology at this period. In the second phase, after 1990 and the return of party politics, the association adopted a more ethnic discourse emphasizing the cultural dimension of 'Tharu' identity. Its influence spread through the development of local satellite organizations which softened the potential conflict between generations and diverse political opinions.

The consensual trend which can be observed is worth noting. It may be a feature rooted in socio-cultural traditions which favour solidarity and has been noted by anthropologists and other observers of the Tharu since the nineteenth century. Based on the strong and centralized organization of villages and households, the existence of councils of elders to take decisions and organize community life, combined with the respect for the headman, who is often also a village priest, and the specific agrarian structures in the Tarai, may have impeded fission. The same pattern may be at work in the present structure of the Tharu ethnic movement.

However, I do not have precise information on the impact of the movement during the early period and, more importantly, on the Welfare Society's influence at the local level, which was certainly limited if not strongly resented. In an area like Dang valley the influence of social reform was to my knowledge very superficial and may have concerned only one or two wealthy Tharu landlord families who are still to day 'Vaishnav', that is, vegetarian (they neither eat pork nor drink alcohol). In the case I know the best, the family was the local representative of the Tharu Welfare Society. In such families, women do not move freely even if they are more educated and the Brahman priest is called for name-giving, marriage, and other purification ceremonies. It is difficult to date the spread of the Vaishnavite trend but, as in the eastern Tarai, it predates the existence of the Tharu Welfare Society and is related to the administrative position of Tharu landlords and their connections with the Hindu 'little kingdoms' of the earlier period.

To be active in an association like the Tharu Welfare Society was by its very nature reserved to a very small elite of the rich and educated who were not tied to their fields as the vast majority of Tharu farmers were. Significantly, membership even today is open only to Tharu 'who hold a minimum college degree and are actively engaged in social as well as professionally related activities'. The earlier trend to reform custom and to 'invent tradition' must be analysed in this class context. The resentment of the poor against decisions of the Welfare Society confirms that these movements were and are not only directed by the elite but that participation is also the privilege of an elite.[7]

FROM REBELLION TO A GLOBAL HUMAN RIGHTS DISCOURSE

Political Opposition and Ethnic Awareness during the Panchayat Era

As noted above, the Tharu Welfare Society has promoted reformist ideas in line with the Nepali Congress ideology and, after 1990, a politically neutral discourse of culture and ethnicity. It has avoided raising the specific agrarian problems of the Tarai. The question therefore arises whether there also existed oppositional trend which may have taken the agrarian situation of the majority of the Tharu into account. My information on this topic during the Panchayat period is, alas, very limited and informal. One educated Tharu of my field research village, who became a UML nominee to the Upper House after 1990, had devoted much effort in the 1980s to publishing traditional Tharu songs and myths. His excellent texts were based on careful fieldwork, which he valued as a way to make connections with village people. At that time he supported the idea of writing a Tharu dictionary to promote the Tharu language. When I reminded him of his cultural goals and activities during a private informal chat we had more than ten years later in the 1990s, he smiled ....

His cultural activities during the Panchayat period had been the visible tip of an iceberg, that is, of a much more radical movement based on economic and political goals. I once had the opportunity to see a page of a journal called *Gotchāli* ('Comrade') and was exposed several times to my friend's jokes on the double meaning of the word.[8]

---

[7]Thus Guneratne (1994: 366) mentions the case of the payment of a very heavy fine in 1992 in Chitwan for a case of elopement, which generated considerable resentment among the landless farmers since no real breach of the rules had occurred. The fine was paid solely for appealing to the Society for a decision.

[8]*Gotchāli* is the Tharu term used by young men to address each other. The feminine form is *gohi* and is very widely used. In the village, whatever my classificatory relationships with the women, I was their *gohi*, 'friend'. This is an

But as a female and a novice ethnographer more involved with the elders and the specialists who preserved tradition, I failed to take the opportunity to carry out research on this point.

According to McDonaugh (1989: 200) 'the association for the improvement of Tharu language and literature in the west of Nepal', of which this friend was a founding member, was established in the early 1970s. It 'seems to have had mixed aims': reform of cultural practices like drinking, promotion of Tharu unity, but also 'calling on Tharu peasants to stand together in the struggle for their rights against exploitative landlords' (McDonaugh 1997: 277). The journal *Gotchāli* was immediately banned and some members jailed, which explains their later reliance on purely cultural publications.

What struck me when these books were presented to me is that they were well known and highly valued. This association and its activities were successful in term of winning a local audience (McDonaugh 1989, 1997). The period following Land Reform seems to have generated considerable political awareness as well as action on agrarian grounds. According to McDonaugh (1997), during the same period the Tharu (at least in the village where his research was done) manifested strong opposition and solidarity against landlords when the villagers were dispossessed of their previous, more advantageous sharecropping and tenancy contracts. The village under study was strongly anti-Panchayat at the time of the referendum of 1980, then communist. The case of the tenants of the Kanphata Yogi monastery lands of Jalhaura is another example. From 1961 to 1964 they struggled, and even went to court, to protect their new land rights and oppose the heavy system of corvées which was then practised (Krauskopff 1999: 60). My own experience in the field, at least after 1990, has been of strong verbal support for the communists on the part of ordinary farmers.

The Land Reform programme of 1961–63 generated a very tense situation in Dang which may have been the basis for the movement referred to above and for the later development of a more politicized ethnic identity at the beginning of the 1970s. Land Reform, as is well known, had an unfavourable effect on Tharu sharecroppers in Dang. A combination of official regulations (based on what was current in the hills, a half share or *adhiyā*) and cheating by most landlords (mostly

___

interesting aspect of Tharu culture, at least in Dang, which stresses the importance of gender solidarity (of women on one side, and of men on the other) independently of any kinship or elder/younger relationships.

hill people) led to the erosion and eventual suppression of the tenant farmer's former shares (*potet*, usufructuary rights); traditionally the sharecropper had been entitled to four-fifths (*pānckur*) or three-quarters (*caukur*) of the crop; now he had to accept half, or sometimes two-thirds (*tinkur*), which some Tharu farmers were still able to claim (Krauskopff 1989, McDonaugh 1997). But the heavy system of free work was maintained under the same terms, explaining the opposition of the villagers of Jhalaura against the monastery of Dang. At the same time, immigration from the hills intensified (after the eradication of malaria), creating a very unsettled situation.

Thus in Dang a strong opposition seems to have been at work which was not solely based on cultural grounds but also on economic ones. To be able to bring their case to court, it is evident that the ordinary Tharu farmers of Dang received help, probably from politically involved groups. In the 1970s, however, some Tharu resorted to emigration, sometimes of entire villages, to Buran (Bardiya district) where they could obtain better sharecropping conditions and maybe escape Panchayat repression. Clearly under the Panchayat regime there were strict limits to the expression of opposition, as illustrated by the small 'literary association' referred to above which was banned even though it expressed itself in cultural phraseology.

The Tharu Workers' Liberation Organization becomes an NGO

A similar opposition with an economic basis re-emerged in 1985 around the issue of Kamaiya or bonded farmers; once again it had to express itself differently, this time as an NGO called BASE. Compared to the Tharu Welfare Society, the most important Tharu NGO, BASE or Backward Society Education, exemplified a very different trend of action.[9] Its relationships and position toward the central government differ from the Tharu Welfare Society described above. Its social base is different and its channel of action has been to secure the support of international donors, not of the Nepali state. In a way they have turned their eyes to another centre of power in the global context of international funding. This very successful and efficient NGO emerged at the congruence of two socio-political phenomena: the work of a

---

[9]There are of course many small NGOs all over the Tarai often working with women or heath development, for instance the Tharu Mahila Bikas Sansthan based in Saptari, which received funds from UNICEF to organize literacy classes in 35 villages.

charismatic young leader from a landless family, and the intervention of international donors (a characteristic feature of Nepalese economy since the 1960s) and of the global human rights discourse in the context of the democratization of Nepal after 1990. Last but not least, the Tharu Welfare Society is linked to the landlord elite of the eastern Tarai whereas BASE is an emanation of the western Tarai, specifically of Dang valley where Sanskritization never really succeeded and where the economic and historical background is very different.

In 1985, during the transitional period which led to the upheaval of 1990, five young boys of Dang valley formed a small group in order to develop a literacy programme for uneducated Tharu villagers. Their leader was from a family which had lost its land to a high-caste landlord. As is often recounted in Dang, it was not only due to the Brahman's cunning but to the Tharu inability to read and their dependency on high-caste officials or landlords to deal with the administration. As usual, literacy appears to these young men as the main means to raise the consciousness of the poorest and specifically of the Kamaiya or agricultural servants. Their slogan was 'education is necessary' and their club was called 'the Club of Four Edges', one edge being a village and a club a square of four villages. Their leader was quite young at this time, a rebellious and energetic personality. From his very early youth, he remembers having fought incessantly against Brahmans and other high-caste people, suffering from the discrimination at school, and feeling very bad about the low status of his people and family. He was a rebel.

Initially the group sought funding from a locally involved NGO (No Frills NGO) and was able to run a vegetable garden to support their literacy night classes in the villages. They immediately succeeded in attracting the local people, each house paying only one rupee for the provision of kerosene for the lights. The organization expanded rapidly in Dang, managing ten clubs and involving forty villages. Then its leader had the opportunity to be trained in Thailand and India. He received money from the No Frills NGO to participate in a tribal rights conference in 1988 in Thailand, which broadened his perspectives.

From this time the movement was called the (Tharu) Workers' Liberation Organization (Tharu Shramik Mukti Sangathan). As a Tharu organization, it could not be registered and hence it could not receive money from development agencies. Until 1990 the group faced many troubles in Dang. Its leader was jailed on several occasions and it lost the support of No Frills NGO because of its political involvements. In 1991 the Workers' Liberation Organization succeeded in being registered with the help of the well-known Tharu lawyer (and leading member of the Tharu Welfare Society), Ramananda Prasad Singh, but they changed their name to 'Backward Society Education' or BASE and were then able to receive foreign funding. The name of the association did not include an ethnic label for pragmatic reasons, i.e. in order to enable official registration.[10]

Besides literacy, the main goal of this Workers' Liberation Movement-turned-NGO, was in fact to fight against the Kamaiya system in Dang, hence its first label. BASE's second-year report states:

On the surface the kamaiya system is a contractual agreement between an agricultural labourer and a landowner, where labour is exchanged for payment in cash or kind. Contracts last for one year and are negotiated in the month of Magh (January/February). Often the contract is made only orally. If a kamaiya is not satisfied with terms and condition, he can in principle choose a new master. However in reality most of the kamaiyas do not have this freedom of choice and are forced by social and economic compulsions to accept the terms imposed by their masters. The kamaiyas live on a breadline and are often obliged to take loans from the landlords, mortgaging their muscle power. The landlord dictates solely the terms and conditions on which loans (in cash or kind) are given .... The illiterate kamaiya signs the pawn paper with a thumbprint, unaware, that it can keep him and his family in endless debt for generations. For the landlord it is more important to secure a permanent source of cheap labour, than to recover the original debt itself. If another landlord pays off the debt the kamaiya family must move to the new master's farm and work there. The end result is equivalent to a form of slavery (BASE 1993: 25).

Slavery and bonded labour are the two forceful emblematic words used to attract Western funds from international donors. The Kamaiya problem become known as a Tharu ethnic problem, more specifically a problem of the Tharu of the western Tarai, when in fact it occurs all over Nepal and in the eastern Tarai as well under another name.

After its successful registration as an NGO, the extraordinary development of BASE led to its becoming the biggest grassroots NGO in Nepal (Ødegaard 1999). With the help of a foreign adviser involved in the area, the association applied for a very important grant from DANIDA, the Danish aid agency. Then from Dang the

---

[10]The use of the term 'backward' surprised me the first time I saw it on a signboard in Tulsipur bazaar, because of its associations with British colonial classifications. When I confessed my feeling to the leader of the group he insisted on the pragmatic reason for the choice.

movement spread all over the five western districts of Tarai, mobilizing most of the young people, the more educated teaching the uneducated peasant and Kamaiya. The DANIDA support programme started in 1991 under the title 'Tharu Education for Transformation'.

Although the name of the NGO does not contain any reference to an ethnic label, for evident political reasons, it is in fact an ethnically based NGO, as the programme title confirms. In 1992, nine of the eleven central committee members were Tharu, the other two being high caste and strongly involved social workers; all the advisers were foreign development workers. In practice low-caste people like the Badi (dancers and prostitutes) were also targeted by the programme. In its second-year report, BASE is defined as 'an independent social grassroots association, committed to the development of the poor Tharu, and other disadvantaged communities in Western Nepal' (BASE 1993). It insists on the lack of education as an essential cause of the Tharus' deprivation of land and political and human rights.

Over the years BASE has developed different domains of activity. The main sectors remain education (through informal night classes and formal education) and the raising of Kamaiya consciousness of rights ('to free them from slavery'). But BASE has also developed health programmes with the usual concern for child and maternal care, AIDS awareness (specifically directed towards the Badi) through traditional midwives, the building of local clinics, and family planning. Another programme focuses on income-generating activities, specifically for women and Kamaiya. Infrastructure and savings and credit projects are also carried out. In brief, BASE supports the usual range of activities of most internationally funded NGOs in Nepal.

Bonded Labour and Global Discourse

What stands apart is the Kamaiya question: it is politically controversial and provokes intra-ethnic tensions. Compared to its very dynamic and successful literacy programme, BASE's programme of 'consciousness-raising' appears quite inconsistent. The literacy programme has spread all over the western Tarai with nearly 800 night classes taught in 325 villages in 1994–5. Ordinary houses serve as informal classrooms and the local language is used to prepare students to reintegrate in the national system when possible.

The Kamaiya problem is actually a complex one. There are different sorts of Kamaiya. The same word is used for an ordinary peasant-worker as well as for bondage. I have actually met Kamaiya working in relatively poor Tharu families, being fed and more or less paid, because of a need for manpower, for instance when the householder was too busy to till his land (the typical case being that of a local healer or priest). I have seen a non-indebted family of Tharu share-croppers (*mohi*) sending one son to a wealthy family to increase their revenue. I have heard young people (at the beginning of the 1980s) who preferred to split from the joint family (which lived from share-cropping) for independence and the benefit of their own Kamaiya revenue. I have known a family of Kamaiya attached to a Tharu small landlord who paid them an annual fixed amount and gave them a piece of land to build their house on, a situation which can easily lead to bondage.[11] BASE itself worked with three categories of Kamaiya, including the bonded labourers: those in debt who live in a house provided by the landlord; those in debt who live in their own house, including other family members working under sharecropping; those who are not in debt and live in their own house.

In her interesting comparative study Rankin (1999) argues that local Tharu practices linked to a specific economic system have to be opposed to the system generated by big feudal estates and the en-croachment of the central Nepalese state.[12] In her opinion the uniform discourse of human rights and the 'freedom of work' does not suit this complexity.[13] The study by Guneratne (1996) on the status of *baharya* landless workers in Chitwan in the early twentieth century provides an interesting historical perpective: this floating population of labourers adjusted, quite to their own benefit, to variations in the demand for labour, which was generally high before the complete settlement of the Tarai. The untied position of the *baharya* was in some respects a favourable one because he did not pay taxes. A farmer could easily move from being a *baharya* to becoming a sharecropper, and vice versa.

[11]I did my field work in a Tharu village where both landlord and *jimidār* were Tharu, which could explain why I never heard of complaints about bondage even if some people had debts. Strangely this village became the centre of attention after 1990 for its very backward practice of corvée (Krauskopff 1999).

[12]Besides the study by Rankin (1999), two reports, one by a Nepalese NGO (INSEC), which works in the same field as BASE (INSEC 1992), and one which describes similar practices in other areas of Nepal, by Anti-Slavery International and INSEC (Robertson and Mishra 1997), are worth consulting.

[13]The official 'liberation of the Kamaiya' in July 2000 and its appalling consequences illustrate only too well such simplistic thinking.

In fact the 'itinerant system' of the Tharu which is often vaguely referred to as their dominant means of subsistance in the past, is rooted in this practice. This reveals the early existence of different classes of Tharu farmers, based on different relationships to the land they tilled. The evolution of this agrarian situation was tightly linked to the nature of local leadership in relation with the central authority.

These examples and their historical background show the complexity of the situation which has led to terrible hardship for some Tharu agricultural workers. The economic context has profoundly changed with the over-exploitation of Tarai which accelerated after the eradication of malaria. I must add that the situation of the tenants, *mohi* (those who succeeded in registering their tenancy rights during the Land Reform programme of the 1960s) is not really better: sharing a fixed sharecrop between brothers can easily lead to landlessness. It is what has happened to a few families I have known since the 1980s. Some farmers have tried to buy a small piece of land to secure their position, but still need extra revenue.

The role of bonded labour in the Tharu ethnic movement and its influence on its political or non-political dimension is central. It is particularly sensitive in the western Tarai among the Tharu and has therefore become one of the important hobby-horses of numerous international NGOs working in the field of human rights whose goal is to suppress the so-called slavery. It is where the ambiguous position of the BASE movement takes its root: reinforcing the lobbying power of BASE, it has also channelled its discourse from an ethnically and politically oriented one to one that is apparently non-political, and which also focuses on development and human rights.

Two facts must be emphasized: the role of the Kamaiya system in Tharu society itself and the intervention of international donors and of the human rights policy in shaping the future of the small grassroots rebellious group in relation to ethnicity and more specifically political ethnicity.

The economic situation of Tharu farmers encompasse the problem of bonded labour and would be the only viable basis for a strong political platform of resistance. But I do not think it can support the formation of a political and ethnic movement for the single reason that it raises unavoidable tensions within the Tharu community itself, at least in Dang, the area I know best.

The BASE movement clearly confronted this problem when they supported and organized strikes in two important villages. One has been my main field site and is known as the home of wealthy Tharu landlords who hire Kamaiya and who still use the illegal facilities of free work, *begāri*, from all their tenants.[14] The corvées have more or less disappeared in other villages, specifically in villages with Pahari landlords (Krauskopff 1999). This does not mean that the Paharis are more generous but they offered a less favourable sharecropping arrangement (*adhiyā*) which then excluded free work since many of them settled in Dang after the 1960s. There is a real land distribution problem in the Tarai where big feudal estates still exist and which has not been solved by Land Reform (on the contrary); but until the total settlement of the Tarai, which dates from the 1950s and 1960s, the rarity of labour created a specific situation from which the paternalist position of some present landlords derives.

The actions of the Workers' Liberation Organization raised strong opposition from the Tharu landlords and the tension created in the villages led to the abandonment of this strategy. In the village where I did my field work, the main landlord built a wall in the middle of the well which was on the limit of his garden and used by all the village community: the relationship with the village tenants was broken. This landlord was also the chief, in charge of the welfare of the village, himself a famous priest.[15] The village community—a very

[14]I had the opportunity to attend one meeting in December 1990. All the villagers were called but it was mostly young non-farmers who were present. Farmers were working on their landlords' fields. The meeting was very open, anybody could give his opinion under the leadership of Dilli Bahadur Chaudhary. The topics were the following: how to suppress the corvée system; how to revitalize Tharu culture. The leader, Chaudhary himself, gave a virulent talk on corvées and other exploitation of agricultural workers but softened it with an appeal to maintain Tharu unity: 'We can solve the class problem without becoming the enemies of the landlords ...' The resolutions were written down: limiting corvée regulations; promotion of boys' and girls' education; activities of the members of the association; supporting the poor by paying their primary and high school fees; building schools in every village; helping the farmers with their tenancy registration (*mohi*); pacifying the relationships between landlords and tenants; on the day of the first of Magh, organizing a cultural programme; and enquiring why some people are pro-Congress or pro-Communist.
[15]On the 'affective' nature of the bond between Tharu landlords and their tenants see also Rankin (1999). On the evolution of landownership in the last twenty years, see the study by McDonaugh (1997) which shows that the Tharu did succeed in making some gains. But the situation in the village where I did my study is different since the landlords there have always been Tharu and their tenants had *tinkur mohi* (i.e. two thirds sharecrop, however progressively diminished when new contracts were fixed) which implies the additional obligation to give free work. It is not the case for halves sharecropping arrangements practised by

basic social unit in Tharu society—'was destroyed' was a comment commonly heard. It was not the first time that the village had experienced being split into two halves, but previously it had succeeded in maintaining ritual solidarity (Krauskopff 1989). Today, however, many Tharu tenants have had to settle outside the protective boundaries of the village, living in small multi-ethnic hamlets.

BASE finally opted for the path of consensus with the local Tharu landlords, often kin or very respected elders. Highly politicized intra-ethnic tension would have led not only to ethnic divisions but would have risked the loss of international funding. I have not been in Dang since 1998, but the news I have heard of the situation after the official ban on the Kamaiya system has illustrated what BASE had been trying to prevent: the Kamaiya were kicked out of their shelters with some poultry and agricultural implements.[16] 'Some of the people have stayed hungry for a couple of days. Some of the political organizations look the other way and blame that the Kamaiyas belongs to rival political parties. The government talks of package for Kamaiyas in the capital, but no such package has reached the far flung districts where the displaced Kamaiyas are continuing to suffer' (Dilli Bahadur Chaudhary of BASE, quoted in *Spotlight* 18–25 August 2000).

In 1994–95, in repeated informal conversations I had with him, BASE founder and chairman Dilli Bahadur Chaudhary defended himself against the charges of being a communalist or politically involved. He had refused the higher positions offered to him in influential social and governmental institutions in Nepal. He wanted to maintain his local contacts. Using an ethnic base in order to advance in politics was apparently not his goal.

This apparent lack of political ambition on Chaudhury's part may be the reason why BASE shares a platform with the Tharu Welfare Society during the social and cultural programme that is today the key national event of the pan-Tharu ethnic movement. Cultural activities are a less important sector of BASE activities, but it is a field in which they cooperate, at least by giving financial help. BASE

---

those (mostly Pahari) who bought the land after the land reform. Besides good land is extremely expensive, which explains why the Tharu who succeeded in buying a few acres have had to move out of the village on to second-grade land.

[16]The news came mostly from Far Western Kailali and Kanchanpur district, in August 2000, describing thousands of men, women, children, pigs, dogs and poultry out in the open without a shelter over their head and nothing to eat. The Nepali press reported extensively on the Kamaiya issue.

organized its own yearly cultural programme on the date of the Tharu festival of Maghi in mid-January (the date of renewal of Kamaiya contract) which is traditionally a time of rejoicing, feasting, drinking, and dancing.[17]

It is evident that this positive emphasis has reinforced Dangaura Tharu self-identity and self-appreciation at the local level. The most striking change is that the younger generation, those who are even uneducated, now move with ease and pride in the bazaar of Dang. With its high-profile funding, the Tharu NGO has disturbed the local ethno-political order. High-caste persons often comment on the supposed incapacity of BASE's Tharu leader for such high responsibility ... but it was common to see important local people wandering or waiting in front of the central office of BASE, or to meet its young leader hosting high officials in the best restaurants of the area. The enthusiastic young opponent had become a 'big man', and as such was approached in the usual way.[18] This rapid improvement in his status culminated when he received the Reebok Human Rights Award in 1994 (recommended by Anti-Slavery International who support BASE's anti-bonded labour programme) and went to the USA for the ceremony. His return to Dang was an impressive one: he was received with garlands of flowers by the highest officials of the district (Ødegaard 1999: 75).

What seems to me most noticeable is that the oppositional trend of the early movement, its focus on economic problems, has been channelled by the intervention of international donors, which transformed the grassroots association into a heavy administrative machine. In 1996–7, after which time I stopped collecting direct information in Dang, it appeared that this NGO had also become a platform for gaining social position. Such motivation may have been at the root of the movement itself; it may have been a way for a charismatic and well born young man to reach a higher position. If this status-raising process is central, it would reinforce the idea that

[17]According to Sigrun Ødegaard, the 1995 programme in Kailali was a very big event, held in an area where BASE was not yet well established (1999: 69). The invitation of important political persons, as usual, served to impress local high castes who were not very happy with the emphasis put on Tharu culture.

[18]The growth of the NGO and specifically of its administration have raised many problems which have led to criticisms from the main international donors that BASE is 'not democratic enough', to a reduction of its grant, and to advice to re-focus its activities on the main topic, the Kamaiya problem (Ødegaard 1999: 75).

DECEMBER 7, 1994
Wednesday
9:30 am - 12:00 noon
Matthews Arena
Northeastern University
238 St. Botolph Street
Boston, MA

Keynote Speaker: Trudie Styler

All seating is reserved.
To request a ticket for you and a guest
please call immediately
Tina Santana (617) 341-7411

Parking is limited.
MBTA:
Orange Line "Mass. Ave."
Green "E" Line "Symphony Hall"

AWARD RECIPIENTS
Adauto Belarmino Alves, Brazil
Rose-Anne Auguste, Haiti
Dilli Chaudhary, Nepal
Samuel Kofi Woods, Liberia

BOARD OF ADVISORS

Jimmy Carter	Ui Lu
Kerry Kennedy Cuomo	Angel Martinez
John Duerden	Michael Posner
Paul Freeman	Sting
Peter Gabriel	Rose Styron
Rafer Johnson	Marilyn Tam
C. Joseph LaBonte	Leonard Zakim

Plate 6.1. Announcement of, and invitation to, the Seventh Annual Reebok Human Rights Award 1994, shared by Dilli Bahadur Chaudhary from Nepal.

ethnic movements arise out of competition within the elite, the landed gentry, the educated class, or the entrepreneurial class in the new democratic world. None the less, the strategy of this local, lower-middle-class leader of peasant background and his attitude to the central authority of the Nepalese state is deeply different from the elitist conceptions and strategies of the Tharu Welfare Society.

The achievements of BASE were partly constructed in opposition to the central government and its elite. By searching for international funding and support, the group adopted a 'non-national strategy'. The founders were not at all landed gentry but a class of teachers or young, more or less educated villagers who championed the cause of the underprivileged. They are in a way the rural echo of the class of urban youths who have created numerous cultural associations.

By contrast, as discussed above, the Tharu Welfare Society was born in a totally different period, supported an apparently non-political ethnic movement, and followed an elitist strategy within national institutions. It originated in the formation of a landed elite who collaborated with the central state, whether Hindu little king or kings and prime ministers of greater Nepal over several centuries. The biggest Tharu ethnic organization is the prolongation in modern Nepal of the aspirations of this elite which never put the agrarian problem on its agenda.

A DEMOCRATIC ETHNICITY

It is noteworthy that these two forces never oppose each other. Does the combination of these two very different movements, which regularly unite for major cultural programmes—the elite mobilized by the Tharu Welfare Society and the low-class and ordinary Tharu people involved by BASE, one from the eastern Tarai, the other from the western Tarai—does this combination presage a strong basis for a more powerful ethnic movement?

A pan-Tharu movement had supporters as early as 1956 but it had to wait until 1979–80 and specifically the democratic 1990s to really emerge. The consensual situation which prevails in all the Tharu ethnic associations supports the emergence of a strong unified pan-Tharu movement. But this movement cannot deal directly with the economic situation of the poor that is the peculiar agrarian situation of the Tarai. This surely impedes the rise of a strongly political and oppositional ethnic movement among the Tharu. Rather, the complex economic problems of bonded labour and landlessness, class differences and agrarian status, may lead to intra-ethnic divisions. This is not say, of course, that political opposition based purely on economic grievances could not arise in future.

A Pan-Tharu Consensus

Backward Society Education shares with the Tharu Welfare Society and other satellite groups the same consensual goals based on cultural programmes and conferences which recently manifested as a concrete unification of the Tharu from eastern and western Tarai. This process exemplifies how a new ethnic category with new boundaries and symbols is constructed in the context of the present situation of Nepalese minorities.

In the past the deeply Sanskritized elite of the eastern Tarai, which already had considerable connections with Kathmandu and the central authorities, would never have considered travelling regularly to the very backward Tharu area of the Dang valley where the Tharus still eat pork and drink copious amounts of alcohol. But in 1994, during a conference in Bardiya, members of this elite participated in the big cultural programme managed by BASE, the Tharu Welfare Society, and its satellite associations. The same year the 'First International Tharu Conference' was held in Saptari. I shall describe this conference which helps us to understand the construction of the Tharu ethnic movement, based on a cultural and development programme and on a consensus between all the associations we have described.

Between 18 and 22 February 1994, the First International Tharu Cultural (Song and Dance) Conference (*pratham antarāstriya thāru nritya tathā sangiti mahāsammelan*) was held in Bakdhuwa-Jandaul (Saptari), a wealthy village inhabited by Kochila Tharu. It was very well organized by the Tharu Cultural Society, BASE, and the Tharu Welfare Society.

The spatial organization of the conference gave a good idea of its implications: a central stage was established for the inaugural talks and the cultural performances. Behind the stage, a huge tent was reserved for the forums of the different associations and the most important guests. The public, several thousands of people, were seated in front of the stage, on one side the women, on the other side the men. Encircling the stage except on the audience side, bamboo huts sheltered the dance groups and their attendants, who had come from far away by trucks or rented buses (Kailali-Saptari is 800 km). Interestingly enough, each group was devoted, not to the ethnic divisions of the Tharu as revealed by anthropological studies, but to each district of the Tarai (in other words they corresponded to the divisions of the Nepalese state and to the internal organization of the Tharu Welfare Society). Thus, in order, clockwise, were groups from: Jhapa, Morang and Sunsari, Udayapur, Saptari, Sarlahi, Dhanusha, Mahotari, Rautahat, Bara and Parsa, Chitwan, Nawalparasi, Rupandehi, Kapilvastu, Dang, Surkhet, Bardiya, Banke, Kailali, and Kanchanpur.

Behind the audience ground several stalls offered Tharu books and journals for sale; one was even selling photographs of the event, developed each day in Rajbiraj. All around were the characteristic stalls of any fair (*melā*) serving tea and sweets, grilled meats and grilled fishes, cigarettes and *pān*, as well as a barber shop and a police post; the policemen had nothing to do during the four days (it was a noticeably peaceful meeting) except to enjoy the atmosphere and the show. The place was enclosed by bamboo fences outside which others sold fruits or sweets brought from the neighbouring villages.

The first day of the conference was dedicated to inauguration speeches. A young girl from Dang let a pigeon fly off; then a lamp was lit in front of a photo of the King and the Queen of Nepal and the national anthem sung. The Nepalese flag was hoisted as well as the conference blue flag. The important guests paraded through the audience followed by most of the dance troupes to the accompaniment of music. The main guest also lit a lamp in front of the photograph of the royal couple, which was decorated with flower garlands. There followed lengthy welcome speeches, as in any official inauguration: by the Saptari Central District Officer in Nepali and by the leaders of the main associations mentioned above and other guests. The President of the Tharu Language Association said: 'Culture is the identity of a particular ethnic group. Without culture, no existence of the Tharu is possible.' Most of the speakers stressed the need for unity of all Tharu groups from 'Mechi to Mahakali'. A man gave a speech on the origin of the Tharus who are not from Rajasthan, but descendants of Buddha.[19] Stress was put on the equal development of each group of Nepal and the protection of their languages. A speaker claimed that the Tharus were the indigenous (*ādivāsi*) people of Nepal (and not from Rajasthan). A more virulent Tamang speaker spoke of ethnic rights. Parsu Narayan Chaudhary simply presented a new journal called *Upahār* and added: 'Tharu history has been written by the dominant

[19]During one of my strolls, I was asked by an educated Tharu why anthropologists and other academics have spread the false idea that Tharu originated from Rajasthan: 'Academics tell lies', he said.

groups but we should write it ourselves.' At the end of the day the president of the inauguration committee concluded on the necessity to unite and announced that he himself, coming from the western Tarai, had taken a wife from the eastern Tarai. To sum up, within a classic national Nepalese inauguration frame, most of the speeches were about the need for the Tharus to have one language, the necessity of development, and of unity; there were the recurrent references to the Buddhist origins of the Tharu and their indigenousness.

Then the dance contest could start. Tharu culture is a 'song and dance culture' (McDonaugh, 1989). This may be why most Tharu conferences are organized around a song and dance contest and why the term culture is equated with songs and dances in the conference title. But it is an old tradition in Nepal and South Asia to use songs or poems to promote ideas. It was an amazingly varied performance; some shows were sharply criticized because they showed the influence of Hindi movies or 'disco' (specifically of troupes from Biratnagar and Janakpur, two cities of the eastern Tarai). The most acclaimed were those who had adapted and changed well-known local traditions. The creative process was prized and awarded. Girls were now performing dances usually reserved for men. A very professional troupe from Deokhuri (supported by the Tharu Cultural Society) has inverted the traditional sex roles with girls playing drums and dancing a usually male dance. Some dances and songs clearly aimed to stimulate changes in society. An interesting aspect was the high quality of the comic performances (*swāng*) which are a traditional part of any Tharu dances performance. They parody some Tharu stereotypes, like drunkenness, stupidity, exploitation, submission, etc. One remarkable troupe from Siraha, which received an award long ago from King Mahendra, danced for hours but outside the stage, for they were really exceptional, raising cries and deep pleasure from their audience. The show lasted three nights.

The final day of the conference was devoted to a seminar on the development of the Tharu. Small working groups were formed. The presidency was offered to the chairman of BASE and the conclusions which emerged can be summarized as the following:

Socio-economic development: development of cottage industries with governmental support, of irrigation, fertilisers and mechanical agricultural tools. The most important problem is deforestation: tree nurseries and protection of the forest are necessary.
Youth role: development of linguistic exchanges between the young

in order to promote language uniformity. They must publish poems and stories in Tharu and create journals. Marriage proposals between east and west must be advertised in these journals. Seminars must be held twice a year in every district for young people and women and a national conference once a year.

Preservation of Tharu culture: Everybody must learn from the old people. Specific Tharu dances must be preserved. Schoolbooks must be published in Tharu and discussions on the subject promoted at the primary and secondary level.

Women's role: equality in all spheres; technical education must be developed. Dowry[20] must be abolished. Alcohol and gambling must be suppressed.

Relationships between all the associations: the Tharu Welfare Society must co-ordinate all the associations but BASE should also have a preponderant voice .... *All must fight for human rights.*

To sum up, this pan-Tharu conference was dominated by development rhetoric, human rights discourse, and the maintenance of consensus. The younger generation, including women, was very active and involved.

BEING INDIGENOUS IN A BORDER AREA

The Language Question in a Border Area

The language question provoked much discussion during the conference. The Tharu do not speak the same language, but the situation of each language varies in each area. Hence in the census of 1971, there were very few speakers of the Tharu language registered in the eastern districts of Tarai. In the census of 1991, the number jumped from five to more than 80,000 in Saptari district. The eastern Tarai elite no longer accepts, as they did at the time of the census of 1971, that their language should be labelled Maithili or Bhojpuri. It is a problem specific to the eastern Tarai for in Dang or Chitwan, the Tharu speak a language undoubtedly different from Nepali and have always been counted as 'Tharu-speakers' or as 'Tharu'. According to Guneratne (1998: 765–76), the elite of the eastern Tarai has urged the people to append the term Tharu after their name in the census returns and was determined

---

[20]The dowry is a typically elitist practice of the most Sanskritized Tharu. In Dang brideprice is still common but is also criticized by the younger generation.

to prove that Tharu is distinct from Maithili, and even that Maithili originated from the Tharu language.

I had lengthy conversations on this subject with Tej Narayan Panjiar, a Tharu historian of this area with whom I worked for the publication of a book on the history of the Tharu (Krauskopff and Deuel 2000). In his view, some of the documents we translated and which were written in the so-called Maithili-Bhojpuri language, as was common in the pre-unification period in the Sen and the Kathmandu Malla kingdoms, were actually a proof of the long-standing existence of Tharu as a dominant language in the court, substantiating his idea that the Tharu once lived (and ruled) in the Kathmandu Valley (Panjiar 1993: 21)

This Maithili-Bhojpuri Tharu language question is an ethnic emblem for a newly constructed identity; but it is a sociological and political problem rather than a purely linguistic one. Only the Brahman and Kayastha high castes are supposed to speak 'pure' Maithili.[21] On the Bhojpuri side, the parallel existence of the Bhojpuri language association in Birganj with no connection to the Tharu is another illustration of the sociological (class, caste, or minority) cleavages in this part of Nepalese Tarai.[22] Moreover, in the present political context, language is intimately connected with the question of being a *madheshi*, i.e. whether one is identified as of Indian origin or not.

Tharu activists want the Tharus to be considered indigenous people of Nepal, as implied by their participation in the Nepal Federation of Nationalities. Thus they have no interest in supporting the Sadbhavana Party of the Tarai, nor does it seek their support.[23] A new barrier is constructed through the manipulation of a linguistic label.

Quite apart from the specific language problem facing the Tharus of the eastern Tarai, there is the question of the multiplicity of languages spoken by the Tharu. Nowadays it is conventional to distinguish 'eastern' and 'western' Tharu and to ignore the many other distinctions

[21]On the question of the Maithili language, see Burghart (1996).

[22]For instance the Nepal Bhojpuri Pratisthan, based in Birganj, works in close contact with other Bhojpuri associations in India. In India, research on Bhojpuri oral literature includes Tharu folklore.

[23]The Sadbhavana party is then not a representative of all the Tarai people. Its demand that Hindi should be recognized as a national language of Nepal does not concern the Tharu and other minorities. One can therefore wonder why a party supporting a group of people living in Tarai has been registered as a political party.

which could be made on strictly linguistic grounds. This bi-partition reflects the dominance of the eastern Koshila on one side and the Dangaura on the other within the pan-Tharu ethnic movement, which is also reflected by the two biggest associations, a distinction which is fundamentally more sociological than linguistic.[24]

Interestingly enough, the language question does not play a similar role among the Tharu in India where they are a very small minority in two different states, Bihar and Uttar Pradesh (differently classified in the two states: as a Scheduled Tribe in Uttar Pradesh and as a Backward Class in Bihar). The emergent trend among ethnic demands by Tharu in India concerns access to forest resources, an issue which is not— or not yet—to be found in Tharu ethnic discourse in Nepal.[25]

I do not think that language diversity is in fact an acute problem for the people themselves. The linguistic question which specifically and significantly concerns mainly the eastern Tharu is linked to that of indigenousness. The linguistic association working on the language problem was created in Saptari, the 'Maithili-Tharu'-speaking area. The language problem is the problem of the symbolic relationship between Maithili- and Bhojpuri-speaking high castes (who are identified as ethnically Indian) and the forceful and politically powerful idea that the Tharu are indigenous to Nepal. It was necessary for the highly Sanskritized elite of the eastern Tarai, who dominate the Tharu Welfare Society, to reinforce their Nepaliness.

Significantly, the Progressive Tharu Youth Association, which champions the idea of the Tharu as descendants of Buddha, is deeply involved with the Maithili-Tharu question, as expressed in a leaflet quoted and translated in Guneratne (1998: 766). During another conference in 1996, the leader of this association displayed books and journals dealing with Buddhist subjects and on a panel had listed the

[24]Since 14 August 1994 the news on Radio Nepal has been read in two Tharu languages: *paschimi* Tharu (*deshauri thāru bhāsā*), in fact the Dangaura language, and *purbi bhāsā*, from the eastern Tarai. Henceforth all national languages with over one million speakers would have five minutes of radio news in the relevant zone of the country.

[25]According to one informant from Champaran in Bihar, the Indian Tharu Welfare Organization, founded in 1971, has the following goals: raising the socioeconomic status of the Tharus; abolishing child marriage and dowry system; fighting for the access to forest resources; gaining registration as Scheduled Tribe. They also show interest in the new legend of the Buddhist origin of the Tharu. In Uttar Pradesh, a new movement, the Tharu Shakti Sangathan, has recently started among the Tharu of Bareich district mobilizing the people around the impact of the new forest regulations and the extension of the Dudwa national forest reserve.

name of the Buddha's jewels and clothes with their Tharu equivalents. The Maithili-Tharu language question and the new legend of the Tharu origin of the Buddha are voiced by the same people, the most Sanskritized Tharu elite of the eastern Tarai, which was strongly involved in the genesis of the Tharu Welfare Society.

The Buddha is a Tharu

In 1988, a well known Tharu leader of the Tharu Welfare Society, Ramananda Prasad Singh, published a small pamphlet in English entitled 'The Real History of the "Tharus"'. It was originally released at a press conference in Patna, in Indian Bihar. This text, which supports the idea of the Buddha being Tharu and therefore the Tharus the descendants of the Sakya clan, was widely publicized after the return of democracy in Nepal.

The text starts with a strong rejection of the once-favoured myth of the Rajput origin of the Tharu: 'Some so-called writers who came forward as social anthropologists have lent support to this theory.... Now, I categorically reject these theories about the Tharu origin. What I have found in history is altogether different. I do not say this on mere conjecture but on the basis of solid facts of ancient Indian history' (Singh 1988: 1).

The demonstration rests first on Majumdar's 1940 study of blood groups, which purports to show that the Tharu are of Mongoloid origin. The question of the racial origin of the Tharu has been much debated among anthropologists in India and Majumdar's theory is probably the most-quoted study on the Tharu: 'The sociologists of India agree ... that theories of their being Australoids is nothing else but fiction', a remark immediately followed by this statement: 'They originated in Nepal and are the remnant of the Sakyas and Kolyas' (ibid.: 2).

What Ramananda Prasad Singh is emphasizing here is on the one hand the indigenousness of the Tharu (that they are from Nepal as it exists today!) and on the other the 'revolutionary' work of the Buddha, who opposed the caste system, that is the Brahmans. This fits rather neatly with the dominant anti-Brahman and anti-caste discourse of the minorities and of the Nepal Federation of Nationalities in contemporary Nepal.[26]

[26]The international boundaries are specifically meaningful for the Tharu who live on both sides of the Indo-Nepalese border, but mostly in Nepal, a country unified by its anti-Indian feeling. If the Rana Tharu of the far western Tarai are

To demonstrate his theory, Singh calls mainly on linguistic and sociological facts: for example, that the *sakhuwā* (Shorea Robusta) was the national tree of the Sakyas or that the Buddha's father's name, Suddhodana, 'pure rice', derives from the Tharu *odhana*. The Buddha's marriage to his own maternal cousin would, he claims, have been impossible for a Kshatriya. The followers of Theravada Buddhism were called Sthavira: 'Tharu' derives from this word. The Tharus were forcibly converted to Hinduism by priests. Finally he asserts that the Tharu practise rites similar to those of the Buddha's time. Singh insists on the physical similarity of the Buddha's features (as represented in statues) and those of the Tharu. Furthermore, the area of Kapilvastu is today heavily populated by the Tharu and the Tharu immunity to malaria proves (according to Hodgson's studies!) that the Tharu inhabited the Tarai since at least 3000 years. Singh also quotes Sylvain Lévi's well-known commentary on Taranatha's history of Buddhism about the 'Tharu of Champaran' and their link to Ashoka and even refers to Padmasambhava's biography which mentions his visit to Tharu territory in the eighth century.

Ramananda Prasad Singh has himself converted to Buddhism. A *stupa* has been established at Prasabani in Saptari and is under the care of a Tharu with the help of a Kathmandu-based Yuba Baudha Samuha which proselytizes Buddhism and has converted one Gurung, one Magar, one Tamang, and one Tharu to Theravada Buddhism. The *stupa* was constructed with Thai financial help. The ordained Tharu monk is now living in a monastery in Kirtipur. This Buddhist proselytism is very superficial in the field of religious practice and concerns once more an elite of the eastern Tarai and specifically of Saptari district. A Kathmandu-based association publishes Buddhist literature translated into Tharu and Nepali, for example the Dhammapada (1992) translated by Ramananda Prasad Singh himself. Tej Narayan Panjiar, the historian, is another advocate of this idea.

One cannot avoid raising the question of the influence of Dr. Ambedkar's ideas. His analysis of the caste system and his conversion to Buddhism had a very strong influence in India, initially among

---

still turned towards their Indian kinsmen of Nainital, it seems that the Tharu of Champaran, keep closer contact with the Tharu national elite of the central and eastern Nepalese Tarai. The Bharatiya Tharu Mahasangh of Champaran is often presented at the conferences organized by the Tharu Welfare Society. Interestingly enough it was a Tharu of Champaran who championed the idea of the Buddhist origin of the Tharus during the first international conference of 1994.

his own Maharashtrian caste, the Mahars, but subsequently among Untouchables (Dalits) everywhere in India. I have no proof of any contact of the Tharu intelligentsia with Ambedkar's movement but it does not seem impossible. The movement may have spread from Bihar where the Tharu also support this idea and where R.P. Singh gave his first conference on the subject.[27] This Buddhist proselytism is for the time being a very elitist and intellectual trend peculiar to an area where the elite earlier had to fight to be recognized as Kshatriyas speaking Maithili. It stands at the crossroads of two strong ideas: the indigenousness of the Tharu and, following Dr Ambedkar's influence in India, opposition to the dominant Brahman elite and more specifically the Maithili Brahman elite. Only time will tell if such a movement has a future.[28]

Another interesting aspect of this discourse is the influence of the naturalistic Western mode of thought of the nineteenth century in which indigenousness, language, and racial features were central in classifying people and when ethnic substance was assumed to be inherited. Thus, the Tharu tribe, as defined by the first British civil servants, who were inspired by this naturalistic vision, is taking shape. The favourite authors of this new Tharu intelligentsia are not anthropologists but the British census-compilers of the nineteenth century.

New Ethnic Boundaries, Hierarchical Status, and Fission

The building of this new ethnic category militates against the previous tendency towards fission and separation along status lines. Visiting the different district houses during the First International Tharu Cultural Conference, I noted the absence of the Rana Tharu (mainly inhabiting Kanchanpur). The district house of Jhapa had no representative, which could easily be explained by the fact that no Tharu live in Jhapa: Jhapa is the territory of the Rajbamsi, who are not at all involved with the Tharu ethnic movement and whose majority live in Bengal.[29] By contrast, the Danuwar of Sarlahi and Mahotari districts,

[27]Ambedkar's main idea was that the Untouchables or Dalits were early Buddhists who had suffered oppression and discrimination from the Brahmans and that present-day Untouchables should convert to Buddhism.

[28]The influence of Theravada Buddhism is well documented among the Newar, but as shown by Bechert (1996) a similar movement has developed among the Gurung of Rupandehi Tarai district, mainly supported by Gurungs of the lower-status '16 clans'.

[29]They are however called the 'Bengali Tharu' by most of the eastern Tharu.

who have their own ethnic representation in the Federation of Nationalities, attended the conference and some initially introduced themselves as Tharu.[30]

Two facts must be stressed: the Rana and the Rajbamsi mostly live in India and both have undergone a strong and earlier transformation which leads to internal fission, from status difference to ethnic difference. Both groups have opted for a royal ethnic label. Because of their remote situation in Nepal, the Rana Tharu have been historically and culturally linked to India and influenced by what was happening there in term of tribal rights (Srivastava 1958, 1999). Even with the rise of democracy in Nepal and the influence of BASE in the far western Tarai they remain aloof. According to my friend, the late Sigrun Ødegaard, the Rana Tharu had formed their own organization the Rana Reform Society (Rana Sudhar Samaj) which failed to register in 1995, whose label sounds like an echo of earlier caste associations. It can be seen that the Rana do not claim the Tharu ethnic label and stick to their royal pedigree. They totally refuse to accept the idea of the Buddhist origin of the Tharus, which does not suit their own feelings and beliefs (Ødegaard 1999), being attached to the well-known history of their original flight from Rajasthan which has left deep marks on every aspect of their culture.

I should like here to insist on the recurrent trend to internal fission along status lines among the Rajbamsi and the Rana, which in my opinion plays a role in impeding relations with the rest of the Tharu, especially in the case of the Rana. It goes against the consensual trend which supports Tharu ethnicity in Nepal and may be rooted in sociopolitical features. In the case of the Rana, the fissile tendencies along status lines have been 'successful'. According to Srivastava (1958, 1999) and older British reports, the Tharu of Naini Tal are divided into two hierarchical sections which do not intermarry and do not exchange the water pipe. The higher section has been working hard to prove that they are Rajput of the Sisodya clan and that is why, at the beginning of the twentieth century (maybe earlier?), they tried to gain recognition as Kshatriyas in the census and adopted the label Rana Thakur of the Sisodya clan.[31] They have even recently made a trip to Rajasthan to prove their claim.

[30]The ethnic label Kochila-Danuwar is heard even in Dang valley where it is a Dangaura clan.

[31]Another interesting fact is the case of the Buxa of Naini Tal and Derhadun district who share a similar way of life and culture as the Rana Tharu but bear a

The case of the Rajbamsi may sound very different but they also live mainly in India, and have undergone a much earlier and successful Kshatriya-ization, which is usually described in two steps (Mukhopadhyaya 1999): a very early one, in the sixteenth century, had transformed one strata of the Kooch into the Rajbamsi under the influence of the Cooch Bihar kingdom; a second posterior step led to the division between the Kshatriya-Rajbamsi and the others under the influence of a caste association social reform movement which started at the beginning of the twentieth century, as for the Rana and other groups in India.

This bi-partition leading to new marriage regulations does not appear to have developed along the same lines in Nepal.[32] A good illustration is the society of the Dangaura Tharu[33] which remained a very open one, a configuration rooted in the local history and cultural context. What was the role of the overall political context in precipitating this trend? How far have these hierarchical sub-divisions interfered with the rise of a pan-ethnic movement? In the case described here the existence of an internal caste-like hierarchy prevented these groups participating in the development of the Tharu ethnicity which, as we have seen earlier, was facilitated by the ideological stress put on consensus.[34] In short, pre-modern processes of 'ethnic' formation still have an important influence on the ethnic movement of today.

---

different ethnic label, as noted as early as 1866: 'It is remarkable how two so similar tribes have maintained such a separation, in spite of living in such close proximity' (Colvin 1865).

[32] Since at least the nineteenth century, and specifically since the enforcement of the Rana legal code, the tendency has been to a strengthening of the barrier between the different Tharu groups through marital and commensal prohibitions. The orthodox way of life was stronger in the deeply Vaishnavite eastern Tarai whose elite was already in close contact with Kathmandu (Krauskopff and Deuel 2000). But the regulations which were enforced in Dang show that in the middle of the nineteenth century the Dangaura Tharu were easygoing in terms of marriage regulations and food exchange even with the so-called Untouchables (Regmi 1969).

[33] A sociological bi-partition does exist between, on the one hand, the priestly clans, holding priestly privileges and a magical right to a specific territory, and, on the other hand, their client lineages, groups with neither a prestigious genealogy, nor a link to the land. The priestly section has formed a kind of aristocracy whose rights were based in the nineteenth century on ritual privileges combined with administrative and land-control privileges. But the sub-division led neither to endogamy nor to a closed hierarchy of status groups. The existence of the 'client' group may even illustrate the process of integration of new families into the territory controlled by a local Tharu god (Krauskopff 1989).

[34] In this regard it would be instructive to compare these bi-partitions to

CONCLUSION: ETHNICITY AGAINST POLITICAL OPPOSITION?

My main concern has been to attempt to estimate whether the Tharu ethnic movement can or cannot lead to ethnic politicization in a more radical and oppositional sense than so far seen.

As the description of the cultural conference showed, the Tharu movement is characterized by a strong emphasis on consensus and, through the dominance of an elite, by collaboration with the central authority. Its main goal is to turn the Tharu into a powerful and effective pressure group. For that purpose, the elite has remodelled the Tharu ethnic category under the influence of two essential ideas: the Nepaliness of the Tharu and their alignment with other minorities of Nepal and opposition towards the Brahman elite. Conversion to Buddhism, collaboration with the other so called *ādivāsi* of Nepal, creation of a clear language barrier with the *madheshi*—all serve these ends. The very first Tharu ethnic association has consolidated its influence through collaboration with all other movements, even with BASE which started out from totally different premises.

Certainly Nepali political regulations forbade the formation of an ethnically based political party. But it seems to me that the existence of a strong ethnic movement among the Tharu, in which consensus is prevalent, impedes the development of oppositional trends. The transformation of the Tharu Workers' Liberation Organization into a powerful non-political NGO or a powerful pressure group is the most significant illustration of the quasi-impossibility of Tharu ethnicity being built into a powerful oppositional force addressing economic grievances and class dichotomies. The rebellious group voicing the claims of underprivileged Tharu adjusted to the international features of human rights activism. Globalization and elitism, development and culture, seem to direct Tharu ethnicity. This consensual ethnicity may only be 'cultural', a form of ethnicity I have labelled 'democratic ethnicity'.

A more political oppositional trend raising the agrarian question of the Tarai seems first to have led to a pro-communist tendency among the underprivileged Tharu, at least in Dang (McDonaugh 1997). This is why the question of the relationship of the ethnic struggle to the

---

similar intra-ethnic processes frequently found in Nepal, such as the sub-division, now controversial, between the higher 'Four Clans' and supposedly lower 'Sixteen Clans' among the Gurung, or the non-hierarchical opposition between the 'Twelve Clans' and the 'Eighteen Clans' among the Tamang, etc.

Maoist insurgency seems to me meaningful. For if the Kamaiya raise their voices would it be as Tharu or as a disadvantaged class? Does their ethnic affiliation cause them to restrain their actions as happened in the case of BASE?[35] The Maoist insurgency must be understood in the context of a paradoxical situation where ethnicity keeps economic reforms off the political agenda or leaves responsibility for them to internationally funded NGOs.

The apolitical position of the two organizations is not rooted in the same body of concepts. Both lead however to an emphasis on the Tharu community conceived as a group of individuals, a species, and not as inhabitants of a shared territory. Both the Tharu Welfare Society's ideology and its strategies of collaboration and respect towards the central authority are rooted in the past, a time when the state was the king's body and Nepal a sacred territory (*desh*). The mode of action adopted by BASE, which depends on support coming from outside Nepalese territory, reveals a new attitude to the state, if not a negation of it: a dissolution of the sacred substance of Nepalese territory. The difference between the two main Tharu ethnic movements thus exemplifies a radical change in the state's role and representation.

REFERENCES

BASE 1993. *Second Year Report (1992–1993) Tharu Education For Transformation*, submitted to DANIDA (manuscript).
Bechert, H. 1996. 'The Original Buddha and the Recent Buddha: A Preliminary Report on Buddhism in a Gurung Community' in S. Lienhard (ed.) *Change and Continuity: Studies in the Nepalese Culture of the Kathmandu Valley*. Alessandria/Turin: Edizioni dell'Orso/CESMEO, pp. 367–74.
Brass, P. 1991. *Ethnicity and Nationalism: Theory and Comparison*. New Delhi: Sage.
Burghart, R. 1996. 'A Quarrel in the Language Family: Agency and Representation of Speech in Mithila' in R. Burghart *The Conditions of Listening: Essays on Religion, History and Politics in South Asia*. Delhi: Oxford University Press, pp. 362–408.

[35]Here again the action of human rights-based NGOs in Nepal are noteworthy. In 1996 the Kamaiya Liberation Forum, *Kamaiyā Mukti Manch*, co-ordinated the actions of all the agencies working on behalf of the Kamaiyas. They aimed to create awareness and to win collaboration from the landlords. However their actions spread the discourse of 'Liberation of the Kamaiya' globally. In July 2000 the Nepalese Government officially 'freed' the Kamaiyas; they were then expelled from their homes and reduced to the status of itinerants.

242   *Resistance and the State: Nepalese Experiences*

Chaudhary, Keval 2049 VS (1992). 'Thāru kalyānkārini sabhāko a itihāsik-pratibedan' *Hauli* 7(2): 37–8.

Cohn, B.S. 1990. 'The Census, Social Structure and Objectification in South Asia' in B.S. Cohn *An Anthropologist among the Historians and Other Essays.* Delhi: Oxford University Press, pp. 224–54.

Colvin, E. 1865. *Census Report, North West Provinces,* I, Appendix 60.

Fisher, W.F. 2001. *Fluid Boundaries: Forming and Transforming Identity in Nepal.* New York: Columbia University Press.

Guneratne, A. 1994. 'The Tharus of Chitwan: Ethnicity, Class and the State in Nepal'. PhD diss., University of Chicago.

_____ 1996. '"The Tax-Man Cometh": The Impact of Revenue Collection on Subsistance Strategies in Chitwan Tharu Society' *Studies in Nepali History and Society* 1(1): 5–35.

_____ 1998. 'Modernization, the State, and the Construction of a Tharu Identity in Nepal' *The Journal of Asian Studies* 57(3): 749–73.

_____ 2002. *Many Tongnes, One People: The Making of Tharu Identity in Nepal.* Ithaca & London: Cornell University Press.

Gurung, H. 1997. 'State and Society in Nepal' in D.N. Gellner, J. Pfaff-Czarnecka, and J. Whelpton (eds) *Nationalism and Ethnicity in a Hindu Kingdom, The Politics of Culture in Contemporary Nepal.* Amsterdam: Harwood.

INSEC 1992. *Bonded Labour in Nepal under Kamaiya System,* INSEC, Kathmandu: Sahayogi Press.

Krauskopff, G. 1989. *Maîtres et possé: Les rites et l'ordre social chez les Tharu (Népal).* Paris: Editions du CNRS.

_____ 1996. 'Emotions, mélodies saisonnières et rythmes de la nature: La littérature orale des Tharu de Dang' in C. Champion (ed.) *Traditions Orales dans le Monde Indien.* Paris: EHESS, pp. 383–402.

_____ 1999. 'Corvées (Begari) in Dang: Ethnohistorical Notes' in H.O. Skar (ed.).

_____ and P. Deuel 2000. *The Kings of Nepal and the Tharus of the Tarai.* Kathmandu and Los Angeles: CNAS-Rusca Press.

McDonaugh, C. 1989. 'The Mythology of the Tharu: Aspects of Cultural Identity in Dang, West Nepal' *Kailash* 15(3–4): 191–206.

_____ 1997. 'Losing Ground, Gaining Ground: Land and Change in a Tharu Community in Dang, West Nepal' in D.N. Gellner, J. Pfaff-Czarnecka, and J. Whelpton (eds). *Nationalism and Ethnicity in a Hindu Kingdom: The Politics of Culture in Contemporary Nepal.* Amsterdam: Harwood.

_____ 1999. 'Aspects of Social and Cultural Change in a Tharu Village Community in Dang, West Nepal, 1980–93', in Skar (ed.).

Manzardo, A. and K.P. Sharma 1975. 'Cost-cutting, Caste and Community: A Look at Thakali Social Reform in Pokhara' *Contributions to Nepalese Studies* 2: 25–44.

Mukhopadhyaya, R. 1999. 'Kshatriyaization among the Rajbamsi' *Man in India* 79(3–4): 347–58.

Ødegaard, S.E. 1997. 'From Castes to Ethnic Groups?' Unpublished Master's thesis in Social Anthropology, Oslo University.

_____ 1999. 'BASE and the Role of NGOs in the Process of Local and Regional Change' in Skar (ed.).

Panjiar, T.N. 1993. 'Faceless in History' *Himal* 6(4): 20–1.

Rankin, K.N. 1999. 'The Predicament of Labor: Kamaiya Practices and the Ideology of "Freedom"' in Skar (ed.).

Regmi, M.C. 1969. 'Law on Dangeris Tharus' *Regmi Research Series* 1(2): 46–8.

Robertson, A. and S. Mishra 1997. *Forced to Plough: Bonded Labour in Nepal's Agricultural Economy*. London and Kathmandu: Anti-Slavery International and INSEC.

Roy Choudhuri, P.C. 1952. 'The Tharus' *Man in India* 32(4): 246–50.

Rudolph, S.H. and L.H. Rudolph 1960. 'The Political Role of India's Caste Associations' *Pacific Affairs* 33: 1–22.

Singh, Ramananda P. 1988. *The Real History of the 'Tharu'*, Patna, 17 May, (pamphlet).

Sinha, S. 1962. 'State Formation and Rajput Myth in Tribal Central India' *Man in India* 42: 35–80.

Skar, H.O. (ed.) 1999. *Nepal: Tharu and Tarai Neighbours* (Bibliotheca Himalayica III.16). Kathmandu: EMR.

Srivastava, S.K. 1958. *The Tharus: A Study in Culture Dynamics*. Agra: Agra University Press.

_____ 1999. 'Culture Dynamics among the Rana Tharus: The Past in the Present' in H.O. Skar (ed.).

Turner, A.C. 1933. *Census of India, 1931*, Report of United Provinces of Agra and Oudh, Vol XVIII, Part I. Allahabad: The Superintendant, Printing and Stationery, United Provinces.

chapter seven

The History of the Messianic and Rebel King Lakhan Thapa: Utopia and Ideology among the Magars

• *Marie Lecomte-Tilouine*

INTRODUCTION

The Magars form the largest minority in Nepal, with one and a half million individuals recorded in the 1991 census.[1] They are scattered throughout the country, but are more concentrated in their original territory, the Magarant, located in west-central Nepal. The majority of Magars are peasants, but Magar men are numerous in the Indian and the Nepalese armies and often emigrate temporarily to India to earn money. Since the 1990s the Magars have been closely linked with Maobadi activism, both as victims and actors, especially in the districts of Rolpa, Rukum, and Pyuthan.[2] Despite the great number of articles that have been published in newspapers, information on this secret war is scarce and difficult to analyse, because it often originates from biased sources such as the police, journalists who have not done fieldwork, leaders of the movement, or villagers talking from hearsay. According to the latter, who are perhaps the best source for an understanding of the sociological origin of the guerrillas, the majority of the Maobadis are young men, relatively

---

[1]This is a revised and expanded version of an article published in the *European Bulletin of Himalayan Research* (Vol. 19, 2000). It was complemented by field data gathered in Lakhan Thapa's village and I wish to express my gratitude to the villagers of Kahule village in Bungkot VDC, Gorkha district, for their warm welcome and their cooperation.

[2]On this subject, see de Sales (ch. 10 below), and on the Nepalese Maoist ideology in general, see Ramirez (1997).

educated, who have no hope of finding salaried work and are unwilling to work as farmers like their fathers. They live in groups in the forests, where they hide during the day. Villagers often say, 'During the day the policemen walk, during the night the Maobadis walk.' Maobadi armed groups mainly attack police stations and their aim, according to the people, is to get rid of the police as well as the wealthy men.[3] Many wealthy families in the hills owned lands both in the Tarai and around their houses, but they usually preferred to spend most of the year in the hills where the climate is more temperate. Many have already been forced to quit the hills to settle in the Tarai, in order to flee from the Maobadis. However, the simple peasants also fear the Maobadis, because burglars take the opportunity of the guerrilla war to rob the common man. The villagers say that they cannot distinguish the Maobadis from the *dāubādīs*, a name for these opportunist thieves. Playing on this powerful name, many also say that they prefer the Maobadis to the Khaubadis, 'the eaters' or corrupted politicians from the capital. The ideology of the Nepalese Maoist movement is strongly egalitarian and communistic: these two features are attractive to the Magars because they have always stressed the sense of equality and mutual help which prevails among their group.

The question of status is also largely debated within the framework of the other major ideological movement which has emerged in the last decade in the Magar community: ethnic revivalism. Indeed, parallel to the secret war, ethnic associations, ethnic meetings, and ethnic publications have flourished. These two streams developed at the same time. Though they are not tightly connected, there are some intersections between them[4] and some striking examples of

---

[3]Their target, as formulated in the text entitled 'Strategy and Tactics of Armed Struggle in Nepal' which was adopted by the central committee of the Maoist party of Nepal in March 1995, is as follows: '... the target of armed struggle will be the confiscation of the lands of feudals and landlords and their distribution amongst the landless and poor peasants on the basis of the land-to-the-tiller principle, and in order to cut the roots of imperialist exploitation to attack projects such as industries, banks, etc. which are in the hands of comprador and bureaucratic capitalists, and also projects run by government and non-government organizations' (CPN-Maoist 1997). The Maobadis' main allies tend to be farm workers, bonded labourers, landless peasants, porters and poor peasants, cart pullers, rickshaw pullers, and drivers of tempos and taxis. Their strategy is to take peasant revolution as the backbone, and to rely on and unite with the peasants to surround the cities from the countryside.

[4]On the links between Magar ethnic activism and Maoism, see Marie Lecomte-Tilouine (2003, 2004).

individuals who are activists in both movements, such as the Magar poet, Jit Bahadur Sinjali, who is (or was) both an ethnic activist and a Maoist militant, and the more recent case of Suresh Ale Magar.

In many respects these two movements appear as two distinct paths: one advocates peaceful changes within the law, the other advocates the use of violence and revolution.[5] Both advocate something approaching a utopian ideology, i.e. they aim to build an ideal society where there will no longer be rich or poor, low or high, alcoholism, etc.

In this paper I shall discuss and analyse the case of a Magar rebel of the nineteenth century whose story shares many features with that of the Maoist guerrillas. Interestingly, this rebel is a major figure in Magar ethnic activism and is also recognized as a revolutionary by the Maoists.[6] This rebellion may shed light on current events by placing them in a historical continuity of revolutionary movements; in return, the current situation will help to articulate the recent reinterpretation and instrumentalization of this old rebellion within the framework of ethnic and/or political Magar movements.

Lakhan Thapa was probably born in 1834. He joined the Magar battalion originally established Prithvi Narayan Shah, but after he had attained the rank of captain he quit the army in 1869 and settled in the village of Bungkot, in Gorkha district. There he organized a rebellion against the government of Jang Bahadur, creating a real utopian kingdom. He built a palace with an exercise ground for his 'soldiers' and in 1871 he was consecrated as a local king by the population. He used to say:

> Jagadamba Kalimata offered me this prediction (*bardān*): 'Jang Bahadur has sold Nepal to the barbarians (*mleccha*), the people call for help. Displace Jang, relieve Mother Nepal of the burden of sin, re-establish the *satya yug* in Nepal!' Let's go, my brothers, be ready! (Rana Magar 1997)

[5]These two paths are also specifically related to each of the two major subgroups constituting the so-called Magar ethnic group. While ethnic activism is apparently more prevalent among the 'southern' Magars, Maoism is strongly connected with the 'northern' Magars. However, this occidental taxinomy is not used by the Magars themselves, who distinguish between the eastern and the western Magars, on the basis of more accurate geographical observations.

[6]In 'Strategy and Tactics of Armed Struggle in Nepal', one reads, 'Here, even after the development of the centralized Nepalese state, the Nepalese people have been fighting and opposing in their own way the atrocities let loose by the ruling classes, especially the Ranas and the Shahas. Notable among these are many clashes within the different ruling classes and the rebellion of Lakhan Thapa against the Ranas' (CPN-Maoist 1997).

Although Lakhan Thapa was hung to death in front of his house in 1876, he is believed to have used his tantric powers to bring about the death of Jang Bahadur seven days after his own.

In his well-known history of Nepal, Balchandra Sharma describes Lakhan Thapa as 'ridiculous'; the *Ajanta Standard Dictionary* (n.d.: 490) goes further: the entry under his name reads, 'a worthless person; a good for nothing fellow'. Who was this 'ridiculous' and 'worthless' man in whom the Magar ethnic activists have found a potent symbol of their movement? An official acknowledgement of the ill treatment meted out to this Lakhan Thapa was the first of the ten claims the Nepal Magar Sangh set before the Nepalese government in the 1990s.

In February 2000 the anniversary of Lakhan Thapa's death was the occasion for a great meeting organized jointly by various Magar associations: the Magar Samāj Sevā Kendra (Lalitpur), the Nepal Magar Sangh (Kathmandu), the Sorathī Kalā Kendra, and the Central Magar Students' Union.[7] The *Rising Nepal* of 24 February 2000 announced that His Majesty's Government had decided to declare the late Lakhan Thapa as a 'first martyr' and to provide Rs 500,000 to install his statue in the village of Bungkot, in Gorkha district, where he led his action and died. An article in the same newspaper, dated 6 March 2000, reported that the Magar association had expressed its appreciation to the Government for this decision, but its members had gone further, asking the Government to establish a statue of Lakhan Thapa in Thapathali, to rename it 'Place of the Martyr Lakhan Thapa', to issue a stamp bearing his portrait, and to rename the Mankamana cable car 'Lakhan Thapa Cable Car'.

Numerous articles and even some books have recently been devoted to the life and deeds of Lakhan Thapa. All are written by Magar authors. Some older texts also mention him, but only in passing. I shall first

---

[7] From the *Kathmandu Post*, 15 February 2000. 'Lalitpur, Feb 14. People from different walks of life gathered here today to mark the 124th death anniversary of Lakhan Thapa, the first martyr of Nepal. Lakhan Thapa was born in 1834 in a remote village of Bungkot, Kahule VDC in Gorkha. He retired as army captain after 14 years of service and later became a religious preacher. He started revolting [sic] the general public against the rule of Jang Bahadur. As a result, he was hanged to death in his own residence at the age of forty-two. The programme was jointly organized by Magar Samaj Sewa Kendra (Lalitpur), Nepal Magar Sangh (Kathmandu), Sorathi Kala Kendra and Central Magar Students' Union. On the occasion, Minister for Local Development Chiranjivi Wagle assured any kind of support to the task or plan related with martyr Lakhan Thapa. He said, "We will soon include Lakhan Thapa in the school curriculum." At the function, various other speakers highlighted the role played by martyr Thapa. The programme was chaired by Nepal Magar Sangh district chairman Dharma Raj Thapa.'

sketch out his biography using these older documents, whose biases are obviously different from those of the more recent ones. I shall then examine his new image as moulded by Magar scholars, and I shall examine the differences between these two views as well as relating them to the oral tradition still prevalent in Lakhan Thapa's former 'kingdom', Bungkot.[8]

Only the more recent writings debate the birthplace of Lakhan Thapa. According to Shivalal Thapa Magar, one of his chief biographers,[9] he was born in Arghau, a village located in Kaski district, central Nepal. When he was 4 or 5 years old, he was taken away from there to Lucknow by his father, who was a soldier in the British Indian Army. According to this author, he was educated there. Other Magar writers have rejected this hypothesis. According to Rana Magar (1997: 73), Lakhan Thapa was probably born at Mankamana,[10] as he bears the name of the famous saint who founded the sanctuary of the goddess Mankamana. Why, argues this author, would he have gone from India to Bungkot, a village close to this sanctuary, and why would he have enrolled in the Nepalese army if his parents were in Lucknow and his father was in the Indian army? Similarly, Rana Magar finds it whimsical to believe that Lakhan Thapa's name derives from the city of Lucknow rather than from the name of the saint Lakhan Thapa, as S. Thapa Magar stated. According to Harsa Bahadur Bura Magar (1997), it is ascertained that Lakhan Thapa was born in VS 1891 (1834) to a Magar family residing in Kahule, a hamlet located in Bungkot, in the neighbourhood of Mankamana. This author also rejects S. Thapa Magar's version of Lakhan Thapa's birth and childhood. Why, he asks, would Lakhan's father have risked taking his family along the dangerous path, 'infested by tigers, bears and brigands' leading to India? Bura Magar also notes that the line of the saint Lakhan Thapa's younger brother inherited the priesthood at the Mankamana temple and still maintained the custom of adding the name of the

---

[8]The documents consulted for this article are as follows: military reports published in the Regmi Research Series; an undated chronicle published in Nepali by Gyanamani Nepal; and the biography of Jang Bahadur Rana written by his son. With this corpus I contrast recent Magar writings, which claim to be based on local oral traditions and the oral traditions I could collect in the village of Bungkot.

[9]The most often quoted references about Lakhan Thapa are H.B. Bura Magar 1997 (2054 VS) and Shivalal Thapa's book *Ojhelmā Parekā Magarharu*, which contains one chapter on Lakhan Thapa and one on his friend Jaya Simha Cumi Rana. The chapter on Lakhan Thapa is reproduced in Shivalal Thapa (2052 VS b).

[10]The Mankamana temple is located in Gorkha district.

founder to their own, that is Lakhan Thapa (the first). On the basis of his name, Bura Magar argues that Lakhan Thapa the second was from this same lineage.

In VS 1911 (1854), aged 20, Lakhan Thapa joined the Nepalese army and was attached to a Magar battalion, the Purāno Gorkhā Gana, which had been created by Prithvi Narayan Shah. The history of this Magar battalion sheds some light on the participation of this ethnic group in the great geo-political changes which occurred in Nepal during the eighteenth and nineteenth centuries. The Purāno Gorkhā Gana had taken part in the 'unification' of Nepal, playing an important role in the successive annexations of the eastern Chaubisia kingdoms, the Kathmandu Valley, the western Chaubisia and Baisia kingdoms, and Kumaon and Garwhal.

This battalion of Magar tribal recruits was first attached to the Shah Thakuris' cause and helped them in their conquests. Soon after that blitzkrieg, the battalion distinguished itself in 1815 during the Anglo-Nepalese war. When Lakhan Thapa joined it, these deeds were still quite fresh and they certainly contributed to the fame of the Purāno Gorkhā Gana. Soon after he was recruited, however, the Purāno Gorkhā Gana, which was then under the command of Jang Bahadur, the usurper Prime Minister, was sent to rescue their previous enemies, the British, during the Sepoy Mutiny. Lakhan's battalion was sent to Lucknow in 1857. Indeed the Purāno Gorkhā Gana was one of the 25 Nepalese battalions which were sent to help crush the Sepoy Mutiny. This event certainly upset the Nepalese order and should be placed in its proper context if it is to be understood.

Obviously, the position of the Nepalese soldiers was difficult under these circumstances. In fact, more generally, it should be noted that Magar soldiers have often served causes which have not directly concerned them or the defence of their territories. Leaving aside the feelings of the soldiers who 'unified' Nepal, it seems that during the reign of Jang Bahadur rebellions emerged among the tribal recruits of the Nepalese army.[11]

[11]According to an undated chronicle of the kingdom of Garh (Dabaral Charan 1973), 'Ram (sic) Bahadur Shah gave orders for the conquest of the hill principalities. This order set off a wave of jubilation in [...] the army. Soldiers were paid full salaries during a campaign, and also expected to profit from plunder.' Interestingly, the main thesis of the Maoist text 'Strategy ...' is that the Nepalese people are by nature violent, and that '[t]he reactionary propaganda that the Nepalese people are peace-loving and that they don't like violence is absolutely false.' The text is an apologia for the use of violence. It remarks that, 'Until today,

The Ramsay narration reports a rebellion which is surprisingly similar to the Lakhan Thapa case but took place 20 years earlier, in June 1857—just before Jang's decision, in July of the same year, to send 14,000 men to India to reinforce the British army:

> On the 2nd of June a serious event was expected at Kathmandu, owing to the state of feeling which was supposed to exist in the *sipahis* of Gurung class, and the measures which the Darbar intended to adopt should they hesitate in pronouncing sentence of death upon a Gurung Jamadar, who had confessed being engaged in a conspiracy to assassinate Maharaja Jung Bahadur. It had been decided to attempt to annihilate 1700–1800 men, (52 guns had been placed in position for the purpose) should they not promptly pass the sentence of death that was required of them. Happily, the Resident succeeded in inducing the Minister to change his plans and a bloody struggle was averted, which, had it taken place, might have led to a revolution and a total change in the Nepalese policy towards the British Government. (Hasrat 1971: 334)

Although we do not know exactly if this rebellion was linked to the decision to send the Nepalese army against the sepoys, this affair is a precedent for the Lakhan Thapa rebellion. In addition, it shows one aspect of the then Nepalese government's policy toward ethnic problems. As this case illustrates, this policy consistently induced the members of an ethnic group (here organized in a single battalion) to punish their defecting member or otherwise receive collectively the same punishment.[12] This perverse and efficient totalitarian policy seems also to have been adopted in the case of Lakhan Thapa, whose denunciation and arrest was led by a group of soldiers among whom historical documents attest the notable presence of Magars.[13]

The British Resident also mentions another agitator whose politico-

---

whatever general reforms have been achieved by the Nepalese people have had behind them the force of the violent and illegal struggle of the people,' but it severely criticizes the engagement of Nepalis in other people's struggles: 'Foreign imperialism and its running dog, the domestic reactionary ruling class, have conspiratorially turned the brave Nepalese into mercenary soldiers.' (CPN-Maoist 1977) Long before 'foreign imperialism', Nepalis, and especially Magars, were engaged as mercenaries. Thus B. Acharya (1975: 169) writes of the Malla kings of the Kathmandu Valley: 'They also used to invite Khas and Magars from Gorkha and Tanahu for military assistance.'

[12]While the Ramsay account appears to indicate that the Gurung rebel was not killed, a letter written by the same resident, quoted by Whelpton (1991: 211), reports that he was put to death by his own regiment at the Tundikhel.

[13]He was perhaps executed by Magar soldiers as well, but no document mentions who hanged him.

religious discourse may be brought together with the allegations against Lakhan Thapa. A man, whose identity is unknown, is said to have wandered through Nepalese villages in the year 1852, claiming that Jang Bahadur was planning to sacrifice 150 children to the gods and that he was himself in charge of collecting them. The terrified mothers, it is said, offered him huge amounts of money in exchange for their children. This man was arrested and taken to the Tundikhel in Kathmandu, where he was forced to confess his crimes in front of the army.

Although detail is lacking, the similarity with Lakhan Thapa's case is striking. Indeed, Pudma Jung Bahadur Rana (1974: 302–4) states that before his rebellion Lakhan Thapa had already been arrested and judged by Jang Bahadur for having extorted money from villagers, disguised as a 'holy man':

He had for some time been in the habit of masquerading as a saint about the streets of Gorkha, and of extorting money from the simple-minded rustics who gave credence to his pretensions. He had been sent over for trial to the Maharaja, before whom he confessed that he was assuming that disguise merely for bread, and then he was let off as a silly fellow from whom no danger could be expected. He then used this pardon for the purpose of further cheating the people to whom he represented that he had won forgiveness from the Maharaja by virtue of his saintly qualities. The pardon had encouraged him in his malpractice, till he was arraigned of the charge of fomenting a rebellion and hanged ...

This account does not allow us to know exactly what the 'malprac-tice' of Lakhan Thapa was at this early stage, for numerous holy men wander and beg in the Nepalese villages without being prosecuted. This first arrest of Lakhan Thapa may indicate that his speech already had a subversive tone against the government, before he decided to instigate an organized rebellion.

As for the man mentioned by the resident, his tongue was cut out in front of the troops after he had confessed his crime. Why were this confession and this torture organized in front of the army? Was this man a soldier? Or was the scene intended to edify the army?

Other historical details tend to indicate that under Jang Bahadur the army was viewed as a reduced and idealized image of the whole society. Thus, it was in front of the army, for instance, that the king announced to his 'people' the nomination of Jang Bahadur as Raja of Kaski and Lamjung in 1856 (Hasrat 1971: 332). In fact, since its creation by Prithvi Narayan, the composition of the Nepalese army had always reflected the social structure of the kingdom. It had been divided by this king into four ethnic battalions, reflecting the division of society into four classes to which he often alluded in his memoirs: Bahun, Khas, Magar, Thakuri (Naraharinath 1953: 7). This initial ethnic organization of the army was retained (or recreated) under the Rana regime. But in each battalion there were both artisanal castes and high castes, presenting an image parallel to the caste system: the head of the army was the king (or the prime minister), the highest positions were given to his family and high-caste individuals, the bulk of the troops were mid-ranking groups (including all the tribal groups), and this ensemble was served by low castes, such as musicians or blacksmiths. This organization in a way mirrors the codification of the groups as it appeared in the code of Jang Bahadur,[14] dated 1854. As dreamed of by any dictator, the army plays the role of an ideal society which is made real, organized and modelled at will, where control and command are not obstructed by individuals.

Under Jang Bahadur, the *mise en scène* of the execution of the rebels is particularly symbolic and sets a striking example. It explicitly connects an individual with the group to which he belongs, as a reminder that from the king's bird's-eye view only communities can be seen, rewarded or punished when they, or any of their members, commit a misdeed.[15] Such was the case of the Gurung soldier mentioned by Ramsay, whom Jang Bahadur planned to see executed by the 1700 men of his own battalion, who were themselves surrounded by 52 guns which were ready to fire. The case of the man who was forced to confess his crimes on the Tundikhel in front of the army before having his tongue cut out and being paraded in this state in all the villages he had visited was also symbolic; as was the case of the five

[14]Whelpton (1991: 210) writes that Jang Bahadur 'decided to segregate the different group [sic] in their own regiments. The intention ... was to minimise the danger of mutiny ...'.

[15]Whether mono-ethnic or not, the company was a single body. Thus, when Bakhtwar Singh Thapa was dismissed and imprisoned by Bhimsen Thapa, the Samar Jung Company he had commanded was equally punished: 'Men of all other companies were given a weekly holiday on Saturdays, but the Samar Jung Company was denied this privilege. Even its flag, known as "Devata" was not spared, and was treated in an undignified manner. The flag-bearers ... used to raise the flag above their shoulders, and install it on the ground when necessary. Bhimsen Thapa enforced rules requiring the flag of this company to be carried on the shoulders in a low position, instead of being raised, and to be thrown on the ground as occasion demands .... These rules were strictly followed even by the Rana rulers and remained in force till democracy was proclaimed in Nepal' (Acharya 1972: 66–7).

people who were beheaded at the five gates of Kathmandu for having plotted to assassinate Jang Bahadur. Lakhan Thapa's execution was symbolic as well, as we shall see.

As a leitmotif, the Magars tell of the military bravery of their ancestors, claiming that it has not been recognized by the state, whatever high-caste leadership they helped to create. For example, in the history of the unification of Nepal, they picture themselves as heroes who built the country, without considering the possibility that they themselves cut the branch on which they sat by annihilating the power they had in petty kingdoms such as Palpa where they were numerically dominant and closely linked to the royal family. This situation is perhaps due to the fact that the petty kingdom which grew into a nation by swallowing its numerous neighbours was precisely a former Magar territory, where members of this group were numerous and closely related to the royal family through their cults. In a way, the Magars undoubtedly have the feeling that Gorkha's victory is also their own. In current historical reconstruction, the Magars present themselves as the champions of the Thakuri, welcoming them in their territories, protecting them against the Muslims, consecrating them as kings in many places, offering them their princesses, and serving them faithfully in their temples and their armies.[16] In many regards, Lakhan Thapa's action, as recounted by Magar scholars, is fully in continuity with this relationship between the Magars and those who hold power.

LAKHAN THAPA'S REBELLION AND THE 'KINGDOM' OF BUNGKOT

In 1869 or 1870 Lakhan Thapa and his faithful friend, Jaya Simha Chumi Rana, received three months' leave. They went together to Bungkot, where his friend's family—and maybe also his own—lived. There they decided not to return to the army and started to build a utopian and rebel kingdom. It is said that they constructed a palace and an exercise ground to train their 'soldiers' in Bungkot. His army amounted 1500 men (Rana 1974), described as Bhote (Regmi 1980). S. Thapa Magar presents it (2052 VS a: 22–3) as a huge army led by two heroic generals: Supati Gurung and Sukadeva Gurung who were shot to death by Jang Bahadur's soldiers after Lakhan Thapa's arrest. A report on Lakhan Thapa's arrest dated March 1876 provides a precise

---

[16]On this subject, see Lecomte-Tilouine (1997).

description of this palace (Regmi 1980). Written by soldiers sent to Bungkot by Jang Bahadur, it reads, 'The house in which Lakhan Thapa lives is surrounded on all sides by a wall 8 cubits wide and 16 cubits high, like that of a fort.' The building boasted five floors, as is indicated in an extract from a chronicle published by Joshi and Rose (1966: 43–4). Lakhan went still further and was consecrated as king by the local population, according to some sources (S. Thapa Magar, V.K. Rana Magar). The biography of Jang Bahadur written by his son Pudma Jung Bahadur Rana reports this fact, but in a more ambiguous way: '... a rebellion of a somewhat curious nature disturbed the peace of the country. A certain Gorkha, formerly a soldier in the army, set himself up as a king ...' (Rana 1974: 302).

This point seems to trouble some Magar scholars, such as Harsa Bahadur Bura Magar (1997: 23). Without providing any historical reason, but simply because it seemed unthinkable for him that such a 'devotee of the king and the country' (*rājabhakta, deshabhakta*) could proclaim himself king, this author denies the reality of this consecration. Bringing Lakhan Thapa to a more suitable position in his view, he states that he merely declared himself Prime Minister. V.K. Rana Magar (1997: 77) does not deny the reality of the royal consecration, but tries to find an excuse for Lakhan Thapa's pretension, attributing it to the influence of the royal blood which flowed in the veins of the Magars of Gorkha:

When he said, 'Having killed Jang Bahadur, I must reign', Lakhan Thapa Magar was perhaps more motivated by his 'blue blood' [in English in the Nepali text] than by anything else. Indeed, there was a time when the Magars were the kings of Gorkha. They were kings and their descendants acted in this way from the effect (*prabhāva*) of their blood. There is nothing ridiculous in this.

However, the royal consecration is not mentioned in all sources and remains unconfirmed. Whether it happened or not, it fits well in the political context of the time, when the seizure of power was usually marked by the accession to the title of Raja.[17] Jang Bahadur himself

[17]'Human Rights Movement in Nepal' quotes other cases of self-proclaimed tribal kings among the Gurungs: 'No sooner had Lakhan Thapa's revolt been suppressed than another rebellion by Gurungs in Lamjung broke out against the Rana regime. Shukdev Gurung, who proclaimed himself as the government and Baudh king and opposed the Ranaism, was immediately taken into custody. He ... died in the prison [in] March/April 1876 because of inhuman torture. In the same connection, Supati Gurung of Gorkha also proclaimed himself the Baudh king .... These movements started spontaneously as a reaction against depriving the tribals from their tribal rights.'

felt the necessity to be consecrated as the king of two provinces of Nepal (Kaski and Lamjung) by the king of the country or the 'king of kings', in order to legitimate and make permanent his ambiguous and fragile position as omnipotent Prime Minister. In the same way, numerous rebel leaders of the Sepoy Mutiny proclaimed themselves kings. These leaders are even said to have offered Jang Bahadur the kingship of Lucknow if he would join their side, as reported by a British resident in Nepal:

From the moment he reached Gorakhpur, on his march towards Lucknow, Maharaja Jung Bahadur, by his own account, was in communication with the rebel leaders, who offered to make him the king of Lucknow if he would join their cause and turn upon the British army. This had an ill-effect upon the Gorkha soldiery, many of whom openly gave out that they would return to the plains during the next cold season to annex certain of our districts (Hasrat 1971: 336).

Lakhan Thapa was among those Nepalese troops who were in contact with these rebels and perhaps found in them a model for his own political programme.

Whatever the historical veracity of Lakhan Thapa's consecration, he had built a fort or palace and gathered weapons and men, thus building a veritable utopian kingdom within the kingdom, and indeed at its most symbolic point, in the vicinity of Mankamana's temple. Obviously, Lakhan Thapa did not merely provoke an unorganized and spontaneous revolt. He seems, on the contrary, to have worked methodically, following a well-established programme, to build an alternative government, as his fort, his army, and his accumulated wealth attest. His proposition to the emissaries of Jang Bahadur is another clue showing further evidence of the institution of a government within his 'kingdom'. In their report dated March 1876 (Regmi 1980), these emissaries noted:

Lakhan Thapa has promised to appoint some of us as generals, and others as colonels and captains. He designated Jahare Chumi as a general, and Biraj Thapa Magar, Juthya Thapa and Jitman Gurung as colonels.

This short extract is particularly interesting. Taken from a report written by Major-Captain Shumshere Jung Thapa Chetri, who led the expedition, it shows Lakhan Thapa trying to engage these men in his own army, and offering them very prestigious positions. As a matter of fact the proposition was made to Magars and Gurungs. With regard to the reported attitude of Lakhan Thapa, one wonders under what circumstances this first expedition to arrest him was conducted. We may legitimately suppose that these soldiers were strategically chosen from among the Tibeto-Burmese populations and that they acted as spies, pretending to adhere to Lakhan Thapa's cause to show him up more easily.

The utopian kingdom of Lakhan Thapa was centred around his palace, which combined a royal with a military aspect, as it was not only a palace but also a fort, surrounded by a thick, high wall, as well as an arms depot. In addition to these two aspects, and on the model of every Nepalese fortress, Lakhan Thapa's palace also had a highly religious dimension. It is said repeatedly that Lakhan Thapa claimed to be the reincarnation of the saint Lakhan Thapa, the latter being called the first, and the former the second. We will never know for certain whether Lakhan Thapa the Second was a descendant of Lakhan Thapa the First, a fact which would have facilitated his pretensions. If his adoption of the name suggests that he was from the lineage of priests attached to the Mankamana temple, as noted by H.B. Bura Magar, other facts suggest the opposite. First, he was recruited as 'Lakshman Thapa' (Bura Magar 1997: 13), which shows that he adopted the name 'Lakhan' later, in keeping with his new pretensions. A second and more revealing fact is his establishment of a temple dedicated to Mankamana inside his own fort. An extract from a chronicle (Nepal 1983) relates clearly how Lakhan established a new cult of Mankamana:

Again under the reign of this king, in the area of Gorkha, a plotter (*luca*) of Magri caste declared: 'I am the avatar of Lakhan Thapa, it is not necessary to go to Sri Mankamana to offer the *pujā*, I will do it here; I worship her by making the *sandhyā pujā*, having myself built a house with several floors and having placed a sacrificial post in it.' In this way he gained the confidence of the people, who flocked from many villages to offer *pañabali* and other sacrificial ceremonies. By doing this, the villagers ceased going to worship in Sri Mankamana's temple, causing the goddess to be angry.

This account shows that Lakhan Thapa made a point of separating the worship of the goddess from her famous temple, and consequently from her traditional priests. This fact still reinforces the assumption that he was not the legitimate priest of the goddess, and that he was even opposed to the latter by diverting the devotees from the path leading to the Mankamana temple and inducing them to come to him instead.

As can be seen, this chronicle reproaches Lakhan Thapa most strongly for having founded a new cult to the goddess in an illegitimate place, thus usurping a significant aspect of power. The diversion of worship from an instituted temple to a private residence seems to have constituted a serious offence and an act of political bravado. A chronicle relating the history of the Newar kingdoms reports a similar case, which was severely punished (Wright 1970: 250–1). During the reign of Jaya Prakash Malla, a certain Sodhan, the head of the monastery of Bu Bahal in Patan, acquired a particular authority over his disciples through the tantric powers he deployed when he sat on the body of a man sacrificed by a yogi. He then settled with them in a house where he gathered the emblems of the gods and made each of his disciples the incarnation of a divinity. He diverted the devotees from the temples to make them come to his place, where, he said, all the gods were. It was sufficiently serious as an offence for him to be sacrificed on the command of the king of Patan, along with his disciples, who were each offered in sacrifice to the sanctuary of the divinity they were supposed to incarnate. The chronicle does not report any other crime apart from this diversion from the legitimate place of worship.

To understand the significance of the diversion operated by Lakhan Thapa (the second), it is necessary to emphasize the role of Mankamana and her priest Lakhan Thapa (the first) in the history of the kingdom of Gorkha, and by extension that of the country (Nepal) which was unified by the sovereigns of Gorkha. According to many legends, whether oral or contained in the chronicles of Gorkha (*Gorkhāvamsāvalī*), Mankamana is the form taken by the wife of Ram Shah, who reigned over Gorkha during the first half of the sixteenth century. According to the chronicle of Gorkha, this queen was venerated during her lifetime. She exhorted the men of Gorkha to fight against the powerful army of Lamjung, telling them that they would be protected by their *dharma*. The Goddess and Gorakhnath are said to have marched in front of the men of Gorkha, who were not wounded by the enemy's weapons, even when they were hit. After the victorious outcome of the battle, the chronicle says, offerings were brought to the queen (Naraharinath 1964: 42).

The queen maintained close relations with Lakhan Thapa, a Magar ascetic who was her servant and advisor. The eminence of the political role he played in the kingdom may be measured by a brief mention of him in the Gorkha chronicle. The chronicle records that it was Lakhan Thapa who took over the reins of government during the prolonged absence of King Ram Shah, who went away for several months in order to practise austerities (Hasrat 1971: 109). Gorakhnath himself, in an audience he gave to the king and Lakhan Thapa at the top of a wooded slope, entrusted the protection of the royalty of Gorkha to Lakhan Thapa. Many episodes in this text refer to this ascetic, of whom numerous feats are reported, such as the ability to be in two places at the same time. One day the king asked him whether he could obtain for him the favour of reigning over the territory of Nepal, and Lakhan Thapa answered, 'It is not for you, but for your descendants (*santān*); but why do you ask me this? Ask it of your wife who is an incarnation of Devi.' The text relates that one day the Magar ascetic saw the latter in the court of the palace, accompanied by her divine troop. He then followed the divine queen, who was mounted on a lion, up to Beni, where Gorakhnath and other gods were having a meeting. That day, the queen revealed to Lakhan that she was the goddess Mankamana and told him of her wish that he and his descendants should offer her worship. One day Lakhan Thapa suggested that the king should touch his wife's body in the middle of the night on certain dates. He would then realize that she was cold. He also advised him to remain awake during the night of *Bhaumāstamī*, which is the day of the *pūjā* addressed to the goddess-queen. The king did as suggested and saw the queen in her divine form, accompanied by Lakhan Thapa and Gorakhnath. On this occasion he obtained from her the promise that one of their descendants would rule Nepal (Naraharinath 1964: 33–9). Finally, when Ram Shah died, according to the chronicle, as soon as the queen threw herself onto her husband's burning pyre, their two bodies disappeared, to the astonishment of the crowd. At the very same time, Lakhan Thapa also disappeared (Naraharinath 1964: 54). Lakhan Thapa's role and his relations with the queen are therefore exceptional and enigmatic.

Another version of the origin myth of goddess Mankamana relates that the king was surprised one night when he found that the queen was not in her room. He then discovered her in the form of the Goddess, accompanied by Lakhan Thapa who had assumed the form of the lion upon which she was mounted.[18] The prosaic reader of the chronicle will be astonished by the queen's nocturnal escapades with this Magar, and will perhaps suspect a more ordinary adventure, rendered strange by this deification. Was the infidelity of the queen unthinkable, was it a precaution against a possible rise of the Magar community, was the king weak, or must one quite simply believe in

[18]These oral myths are reported by Unbescheid (1985) and Shrestha (forthcoming).

wonders? Whatever the case may be, other queens of the Shah line of Gorkha, such as the wife of Krishna Shah, Ram Shah's grandson, were thereafter regarded as incarnations of Mankamana. More generally, this goddess provided the kingdom with her protection throughout its history. These stories show how the relation of the Thakuri kings with the goddess was mediated by this Magar ascetic and his descendants. This configuration is not unique, but corresponds with a widespread model in the old confederation of the 24 kingdoms of central Nepal.[19]

By presenting himself as an incarnation of this famous mediator, did Lakhan Thapa aim to restore the power of the Shah kings, which had been usurped by Jang Bahadur, or was this an act of self-promotion? Without doubt, he intended to get rid of Jang Bahadur. According to Pudma Jung Bahadur Rana (1974: 302–3):

His graceful manners and persuasive tone soon procured him an armed following of 1,500 men, at the head of whom he threatened to march to the capital, and after assassinating Jung Bahadur, to seize the reins of government, and inaugurate the golden age of Nepalese history. On receiving news of this insurrection, the Maharaja at once despatched a few companies of the Devi Dutt Regiment to put down the fanatic, instructing them not to use force unless they were met with force. Happily the rebels surrendered their arms after a brief resistance, and were soon caught and sent over to Kathmandu in chains. The ringleader 'Lakhan' and twelve of his firmest supporters, whom he probably called his 'apostles', were brought in bamboo cages, and the rest on foot. Subsequent investigation brought to light the details of the whole plot. They were then to march to the capital, where Lakhan was to be proclaimed king amidst the shouts of the whole population.[20]

[19]A comparison with Lecomte-Tilouine (1997) shows that the same mythic motifs are present both in the Lasargha shrine dedicated to Alam Devi and in the Mankamana temple. In both cases the goddess is most important for the royal Thakuris and is served by a Magar priest. In both places the *Buddleia asiatica* tree is venerated: as the tree on which the palanquin of the goddess was placed in the middle of the Lasargha shrine, and as the walking stick of Lakhan Thapa, which grew as a tree after his disappearance, in Mankamana. In both places, a hole is considered holy: this is a hole into which the goddess disappeared in Lasarga, and into which Lakhan Thapa disappeared in Mankamana. These two shrines appear as variations on the themes of the Goddess, the Thakuri king, the Magar priest, the Buddleia tree, and the hole. This suggests a common underlying structure which should be investigated in other similar places.

[20]This is the same text as the one quoted by Joshi and Rose (1966: 44): 'According to a semi-official account, the leaders of the agitation had planned to kill Jang Bahadur at Deorali on his return from a hunting expedition with the Prince of Wales in the Terai and to "march to the capital, where Lakhan was to be proclaimed king amidst the shouts of the whole population"'.

The chronicle quoted by Gyanamani Nepal does not report any endeavour to launch an assault on the part of Lakhan Thapa and his troops, but only one arrest for an illegal gathering of weapons.[21] However, the report of Major-Captain Shumshere Jung Thapa Chetri specifically devotes a passage to the action:

On Falgun 26, 1932 (approx. 9 March 1876), Lakhan Thapa, accompanied by a large number of Bhotes armed with muskets and swords, proceeded toward the west pretending to join (Prime Minister Jung Bahadur's) entourage, but actually with the intention of making an attempt on his life (Regmi 1980).

This report then discloses Lakhan Thapa's project as follows:

He has announced that Prime Minister Jung will be assassinated, that the Second Prince (Upendra Bikram) will become king, and that he himself will succeed (Prince Upendra Bikram). He said he would assassinate (Prime Minister Jung Bahadur) at an opportune moment either at Tarku or Manang-Besi (in Lamjung district). If this was not possible, he would go to Tibet, secure the help of the Tibetans, accomplish his mission, and then become king (ibid.).

As reported here, Lakhan Thapa's project fits perfectly within the context of the time, as it exploits the conflict between Nepal and Tibet and the eternal competition between brothers for the throne. In this document, it looks more like a realistic political programme, using the various forces which were involved, than a simple utopia born of the imagination of an isolated villager. Interestingly, his plan consisted not only of killing Jang Bahadur, but also installing King Surendra's younger brother Upendra on the throne, and in the longer term, of sitting on the royal throne himself. This ambition does not fit well with the status of a martyr, that is, with the supposedly disinterested sacrifice of oneself for one's country, but we should emphasize that the report quoted here may have blackened Lakhan Thapa's reputation intentionally.

Lakhan was arrested by the army, apparently while he was still in his fort. This detail either contradicts the claim that he was marching towards the west in order to lay an ambush, or else it should be

[21]'At this time, in the year 33, this cunning Magar having said, "I am going to take my revenge against Shri 3 Maharaj", held a counsel with bad men who were obeying him. They gathered swords, rifles, bows and arrows. The people of Gorkha learned about that and having spied on them and verified the facts, went to Nepal to bring the news to Shri 3 Maharaja who sent soldiers and officers to bring him back' (Nepal 1983: 45, n.9).

presumed that this attempt failed before he was arrested. The chronicle published by Nepal states precisely:

Having encircled the house of this conspiring Magar, nearby Gorkha, they put under iron all his henchmen and seized all the weapons they had gathered, then led them to Thapathali. The examination of the facts took place during a lawsuit and [Lakhan Thapa] was put in jail as well as his principal accomplices, while all the others were let free. Later, in the month of Paus of the year 33, this plotter Lakhan Thapa was hung in front of his house as well as alongside his principal accomplices. His house and his temple were destroyed and razed to the ground (Nepal 1983: 45-6).

M.C. Regmi adds some interesting details:

The Prime Minister ordered Colonel Tek Bahadur Rana to reinforce the troops under his command with those in Palpa, if necessary, and capture Lakhan Thapa and his accomplices. Major-Captain Shumshere Jung Bahadur Thapa Chetri was ordered to render necessary help to Colonel Tek Bahadur Rana, capture Lakhan Thapa and his accomplices if they passed through Palpa, and send them to Kathmandu, and report the matter to Prime Minister Jung Bahadur through the Indrachok Police Station. In addition, he was ordered to take necessary security measures to protect Prime Minister Jung Bahadur from assassination in case he visited Palpa in the course of his tour (Regmi 1980).

Pudma Jung indicates the sentence which was passed on Lakhan and his close relations:

Lakhan and six of his followers, who had taken an active part in the conspiracy, were sentenced to death; the others whose offence was merely that of passive participation were pardoned, and allowed to go back to their homes. Lakhan was hanged on a tree in front of the shrine of the goddess Manokamna who, as he alleged, had inspired him to the deed of blood (Rana 1974: 303).

These 'historical' texts, produced rather soon after the event, dwell only briefly upon the end of Lakhan Thapa, but note that he was hung on the site where he had conducted his action—beside his house or the temple of Mankamana—after he had been judged in Kathmandu. It is significant that the execution took place there, as if to show to his former partisans the particularly striking symbol of his defeat and his imposture. The goddess herself was made a witness to the death of her alleged elected devotee, in accordance with an extremely humiliating and cruel idea of Jang Bahadur.

Before comparing the above with the contents of Magar publications on Lakhan Thapa, it should be noted that in his book on the

Josmani sect Janak Lal Sharma (1963) offers another interpretation of Lakhan's political action. According to this author, Lakhan Thapa was a *siddha* of the powerful Josmani sect, which developed under its sixth *santa*, Shashidhar, during the reign of Prithvi Narayan. These ascetics initiated many influential people at the court of this king and later received several land grants from Jang Bahadur to establish monasteries in the Gulmi area. Shashidhar is known to have had eleven gurus and the Josmani sect, which developed in Nepal, seems to have been a mixture of different streams, such as Nathism and Hatha Yoga. This sect was not restricted to the twice-born castes and recruited many adepts from among the Nepalese tribal groups. Shashidhar had four famous disciples, whom he sent in the four directions to preach: one was a Magar, one was a Gurung, and one was a Sunuwar. Lakhan Thapa is said to have been initiated by Mokshamandal, the Magar disciple of Shashidhar. The most famous of Lakhan Thapa's Josmani *santa* contemporaries was Gyanadil Das. He was born in Ilam and initiated in Okhaldhunga and he founded a new monastery in the Gurung village of Rumjatar. Janak Lal Sharma (1963: 87–8) reports that there were numerous Matwali in his monastery and that this provoked the anger of the local Brahmans. This author describes Lakhan's fort as a Josmani monastery and writes that Jang Bahadur arrested him because he felt that this sect represented a threat. As a matter of fact, Gyanadil was arrested and led to Kathmandu at the same time as Lakhan. If the latter was sentenced to death because of the army and the weapons he had gathered, no such charge could be found against Gyanadil, who spent six months in jail and soon became very influential in Jang's entourage. He initiated many prominent people, such as Ranaudip, Jang's younger brother. He finally left the Kathmandu Valley carrying a white flag and a *nagara* drum offered to him by Jang Bahadur, which he installed in his monastery. In this account, Lakhan's political action seems to be inserted into a wider religious organization which took the revolutionary step of treating the twice-born and the alcohol-drinkers as equals. Lakhan's membership in the Josmani sect explains why he was 'parading disguised as a holy man', as recounted by Pudma Jung Rana.

We shall now compare this tentative reconstruction of Lakhan Thapa's life, which has been based on contemporary and ancient sources, with recent presentations by Magar scholars, which are apparently based on oral traditions.

I shall base my discussion mainly on an article by Shivalal Thapa Magar, whose writings on Lakhan Thapa (e.g., 1996a and b) are particularly significant, because they are often reproduced, summarized, or discussed by other Magar authors. Furthermore, this author is the secretary of the central committee of the Magar Association of Nepal (Nepal Magar Sangh), a fact which gives some official weight to his writings. The psychological portrait of Lakhan Thapa is developed in greater detail than it is in the preceding writings, and it goes without saying that it is of a radically different tone. He is described as 'small of size, but having much wisdom', 'solving problems quickly', 'skilful in combat, the handling of weapons, and horsemanship', 'going everywhere himself during the combat', and 'disciplined and friendly'. As a loyal son, says Shivalal Thapa, his project was to found a family on his return to Nepal and to bring his parents there with him. Moreover, this author insists on his faithful friendliness, and repeatedly mentions the close friendship between Lakhan and Cyami (i.e. Chumi), which led them both to the same death.

In this posthumous psychological portrait and biography, Lakhan Thapa is presented as the very archetype of the Magar: a modest villager who emigrated to India, a valiant soldier and faithful friend, moved by the suffering of his people, and, finally, a martyr. All of these aspects link him with the self-portrait the Magars make for themselves: with their supposed 'rightness',[22] and to their shedding of their blood for the motherland which they have established as a symbol of their identity, as their insoluble print on the country. Lakhan Thapa is described as an enterprising and very generous man. He not only took the initiative to build his palace, but, according to Shivalal Thapa Magar, he also built himself a temple equipped with four gates. There he placed a round stone icon and other stone statues, and installed various divinities in them through his tantric powers, including those of Gorakhnath and Gorakhkali. His palace contained great richness, which he also produced through his supernatural powers. This extraordinary man, says M.S. Thapa (1992), used each day to assume the form of a child in the morning, an adult in the afternoon, and an old man in the evening. He displayed his powers spectacularly on an occasion reported by Shivalal Thapa Magar:

When Jaya Simha Chumi decided to follow the example of his friend Lakhan Thapa and did not return to the army after their three months of leave, he was reprimanded by his grandmother who told him, 'Whence came this Lakhan

---

[22]The adjective *sojho* is often applied to the Magars. It means 'uncrooked, straightforward, open, frank, honest', but has also a negative connotation of 'simple-minded'.

Thapa to die here? He perverted our Jaya Simha. Our grandson, who was very well employed, is to become a good for nothing like him.' Having heard that, Lakhan Thapa addressed her. 'What do you need grandmother? Rice?' And he touched an empty basket and filled it with rice. Then he added, 'Do you need vegetables?' and he filled the house with the vegetables she desired. Having thrown sacrificial rice, he even made the stones and the wood move, and these arrived of themselves by walking. This is how he gathered richness. After having filled up his great reserves of rice he distributed some. When they saw these acts, all were surprised (S. Thapa Magar 1996b: 6–7).

In this account by S. Thapa Magar, the intervention of the supernatural allows Lakhan Thapa to be described in a completely royal role of rich benefactor and spendthrift, concerned to ensure, like Ram Shah or Henri IV, that no one should suffer hunger in his 'kingdom'. As for the incredulous reader, he may wonder how Lakhan gathered the money to finance his rebellion. The speech credited to the grandmother is revealing. It offers a view which is the opposite of the author's general presentation of the events. This embedded counterpoint suggests from the very start the fate of Lakhan's rebellion.

According to Thapa Magar, the reaction against Lakhan's revolutionary kingdom did not emerge from the government but from the local high castes.[23] Very symptomatically, in the present context of ethnic revivalism, he ascribes this reaction to a conflict of caste:

All these acts [of Lakhan Thapa] displeased the local Bahun-Kshetri. They were jealous to see that those who were their herders and ploughmen had become kings and ministers (Thapa Magar 1996b: 5).

To show the reader the extent to which the local Bahun-Kshetri had subjected the Magars within their own territories, Thapa Magar notes, 'They were so deeply established in Gorkha that even the place names consisted of their clan names (Devakota Gaun, Thapa Gaun, Vagle Gaun).' Interestingly, Lakhan Thapa's arrest, and even his death, is now attributed by Magar authors to the high castes and not directly to Jang Bahadur. Thapa Magar recounts how the Thapa Kshetri of Simudipani stole a box containing documents from the palace of Lakhan Thapa: 'On one of these documents was written "I am a devotee of Gorakhkali. The goddess sent me here to become the king. Jang Bahadur governs the country tyrannously, I must raise my weapons

[23]The chronicle quoted by Nepal attests that Lakhan Thapa was denounced by the 'people of Gorkha' (see note 21).

against him. My faithful minister is Jaya Simha Chumi. We must prepare a good army."' (ibid.)

The Kshetri of Gorkha, he continues, went to Jang Bahadur with these documents. As a result, the latter sent his soldiers to Gorkha with orders to hang Lakhan Thapa. But just after that, reports Thapa Magar, Jang Bahadur's wife had a dream. She saw a man with white moustaches and a beard, who told her, 'If Lakhan Thapa is killed, your husband Jang Bahadur will die exactly seven days after. If you want to spare your husband, tell him not to kill Lakhan Thapa.' The queen, so the story goes, woke up and told her dream to Jang, who did not even listen to it. Then she wrote eight letters to her husband, but he did not read them. While she was bringing him the ninth letter, she fell unconscious at the feet of Jang Bahadur, who finally asked one of his guards to read it. When he had heard its contents, he declared, 'I have made a serious mistake' and immediately sent soldiers with new orders: 'Go and tell them that Lakhan Thapa should not be hung.' The soldiers rushed to Gorkha but when they reached the Budi Gandaki river they were prevented by the felon Thapa Kshetri from crossing it. Indeed, when they learned that soldiers were approaching with the order to spare Lakhan's life, the Thapa Kshetri ran to the river and for three days prevented the Bote and Majhi ferrymen from taking them across. Meanwhile, the army of Jang Bahadur surrounded the rebel army and seized Lakhan Thapa as well as Jaya Simha Chumi. 'They could have escaped, but they were not fleeing death, and as heroes they were ready to die.' The soldiers read out the death sentence which had been pronounced by Jang Bahadur and took the two men to hang them from nearby trees.

These events are reported in a similar way by M.S. Thapa (1992), who states, however, that it was the Bhusal Jaisi of Bungkot who prevented the soldiers from crossing the river, and adds that when the Magars of Bungkot came to know what they had done, they expelled them from their village.

The most striking part of Lakhan's life in the Magar writings is certainly his death. Most of them report the same facts, but here I will again quote from Thapa Magar's account. Before his execution, Lakhan Thapa addressed the crowd thus: 'If my body rots and falls to the ground after my hanging, know that Lakhan Thapa is dead. But if my body dries and shrinks, know that Lakhan Thapa is alive. Keep preciously the cord with which I was hung, I will come back one day' (Thapa Magar 1996b: 6).

Even now, local people tell of how Jaya Simha Chumi's body rotted and fell to pieces whereas Lakhan Thapa's body dried up and remained tied to the tree, as he had predicted. In a similar account, written by Samjog Lapha Magar (1997), Lakhan Thapa is also supposed to have said before his execution, 'Jang Bahadur will be my *sati'*, thus predicting the supernatural deed which is nowadays attributed to him: the death of Jang Bahadur. Indeed, Lakhan died on the second day of the month of Phagun, and seven days later, as had been predicted, Jang himself died in strange suspicious circumstances. It is sometimes said that he was killed by a tiger, but for Shivalal Thapa Magar (1996b: 6), 'It is probably because it was difficult to write that Jang Bahadur was killed by the tantric powers of a Magar, that some historians say that he was killed by a tiger.' M.S. Thapa (1992) reports that some people believe that Lakhan Thapa assumed the shape of another man after his death and killed Jang Bahadur. He mentions a story according to which Jang was killed by a young Magar whose wife had been seduced by the Prime Minister.

Through his own death, followed by Jang's death, Lakhan becomes a prophet and a messiah. He announces the signs of his immortality which are to be read on his own corpse, which he intends to prevent from rotting, as a manifestation of his perenniality. He confers the status of a relic on the instrument of his death when he asks that it should be carefully preserved. And, finally, he presents his death as his victory over Jang, who is described as his *sati*. The fate of Jang is thus closely attached to that of Lakhan through this apotheosis, this grandiose victory of a victim transformed through his death into a divinity.

In a way, the current Magar presentation of Lakhan's life tends to exonerate Jang Bahadur, who is presented merely as a Pontius Pilate. He is shown to be frightened by his own decision, and to recognize that he has made a mistake. In fact, he is even said to have gone himself to Bungkot to beg Lakhan's corpse for a pardon: 'When Jang learned [from his soldiers] the news [of Lakhan Thapa's execution], he had no more peace of mind. He jumped on a horse and, followed by his army, reached the spot where Lakhan Thapa had been hung. He then asked for pardon from the hanged corpse of Lakhan Thapa' (Thapa Magar 1996b: 6).

Lakhan was deified through his death. Several Magar authors note that the villagers of Bungkot worship him every year during the month of Paus, offering him animal sacrifices. He is worshipped as a Bhayāri Devatā, a divinity related to the earth; people who have suffered violent death are commonly worshipped as this god. If the nineteenth-century texts specify that the palace of Lakhan was destroyed by the army, the local tradition, as reported by S. Thapa Magar (1996b: 6), states that it remained uninhabited for a long time because people thought that 'one day Lakhan Thapa will come back alive'.

I went to Bungkot's Kahule hamlet in April 2001. A primary school named Lakhan Thapa was built on the spot of his palace and a memorial is under construction. During their construction the villagers dug up two inscribed pillars and three carved stones: one looks like a Shiva *linga*, the other like a stone window, and the last one is a flat stone engraved with geometrical drawings. They are said to be the remains of Lakhan's palace. There I was able to speak with Jaya Simha Chumi Rana's great-grandson who is now in charge of the rituals of Lakhan Thapa. He told me the story of his ancestor. It is in fact close to what is reported by the recent Magar writings but with a very different orientation:

Lakhan Thapa and Jaya Simha Rana were soldiers in the army. When Jang Bahadur was ruling, both of them were in the same company. They asked together for leave and went to Jaya Simha Rana's place. After two months they did not feel like going to Kathmandu. Jaya Simha's mother reprimanded them both: 'Here there is no good food, there are no vegetables; you must go quickly to join your army.'

The two men told her: 'Mother, what do you need?' [Jaya Simha's] mother said: 'We have no unhusked rice, no husked rice, nor any vegetables.'

They answered: 'Don't worry, this will be ready today evening.' And one of them sowed rice in the ricefield while the other planted vegetables. Then they both went to their occupations. After half an hour the rice was germinating in the rice field, as well as the vegetables. Around twelve the rice had flowered and so had the vegetables. Around one, the rice was ripe. They cut it to cook it the same evening, dried it and beat it so that it was ready. They also prepared the vegetables in this manner.

[Jaya Simha's] mother was astonished. Seeing that they had prepared rice and vegetables in one day, she told them: 'Oho, what a wonder has been done by you, my sons.' 'This is not so extraordinary, we can do many other things,' they answered. [Jaya Simha's] mother added: 'If it is thus, you can become kings.' The two of them answered: 'Yes, we can be the kings of this village: see!' and so saying, they built a palace, a pond to raise fish, a temple for the gods. They also built a stone fountain. After having done all that they wrote on a piece of paper: Lakhan Thapa, the king, and Jaya Simha Rana, the minister, and put it in their pocket. They lost the written paper, which was found by Siracan Thapa Ksetri who had come to their place of worship to make offerings.

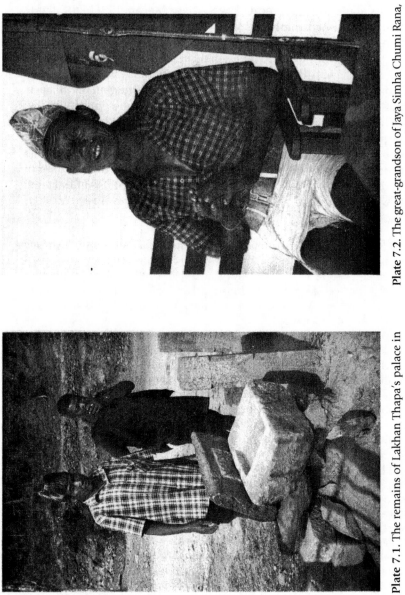

Plate 7.1. The remains of Lakhan Thapa's palace in Kahule, Bungkot, Gorkha district.

Plate 7.2. The great-grandson of Jaya Simha Chumi Rana, the current pujari or priest in Kahule, who carries on the cult established by Lakhan Thapa.

Having found the paper he went to King Jang Bahadur and made a report. He gave the paper to Jang Bahadur who said: 'Eh, someone has established a kingdom inside my kingdom' and ordered his soldiers to go and arrest them. From Bungkot they took them to Kathmandu. During the inquiry, they confessed that what was written on the paper was true. Jang said: 'We have conquered all the villages and possessions of the Bhure Raja and until now we are reigning. Now you are trying to push me out of the throne.' They answered: 'No, we are not trying to push you out, we are only displaying the improvement of our condition (*pargati dekhāune*), we won't take the royal throne.' King Jang Bahadur said: 'Take them to the place whence you have fetched them and kill them there.' The soldiers took them to the palace of Kahule in Bungkot, Gorkha. To its right side they hanged Lakhan Thapa in a Khirra tree, to its left side they hanged Jaya Simha Rana in a peach tree. As soon as Jang Bahadur had given this order his queen started to have bad dreams: she saw an old man who told her that her husband would die soon after their death. She went several times to warn him, saying that they were like gods and should not be killed, but until her ninth attempt the king did not agree. When she came for the ninth time, he thought that one should listen even to the speech of women and sent to Bungkot the order to spare their lives, an order which he gave to some soldiers. But when they reached the Budhi Gandaki, they met Lakhan Thapa and Jaya Simha's enemy: Siracan Thapa Ksetri. He gave the order to the Majhis to not lead anyone across the river before the execution of Lakhan Thapa and Jaya Simha Rana and not to even bring the news that someone was willing to cross. For three days, they refused to lead across the soldiers sent from Kathmandu by Jang Bahadur. When they finally reached Bungkot, Lakhan Thapa and Jaya Simha Rana had already been executed. Seven days after their death, Jang Bahadur was killed by a tiger while he was hunting in a forest. Hence the Magars use to have this saying: Lakhan Thapa the corpse, Jang Bahadur Rana the *sati*.

Lakhan Thapa dried on his rope, he flew up in the sky but the body of Jaya Simha rotted, people say. The soldiers searched for Jaya Simha's son, but he had been hidden and was spared. Because the blood of Lakhan Thapa was mixed with the blood of Jaya Simha, we did his death rituals, took his belongings and his gods. Because their blood was mixed, we had to do his death ritual in the same way as if somebody's blood touches me, I must perform his death ritual. Every year, the first *pancami* (fifth lunar day) of Pus (February-March), be it in the bright or the dark fortnight, we perform the worship of five gods. I have been the priest since VS 2014 (1957). The five gods are Kāli Nāg, Bhuyār, Bāhra Barāha, Caunta Bairāhi, and Bhairavi.

Question: Is this cult addressed to Lakhan Thapa? Is Bhuyar a form of Lakhan Thapa?

No, these five gods were worshipped by Lakhan Thapa. I carry on the cult he used to perform. We offer rice to Kāli Nāg and Bhumi first. For these two I must choose a virgin boy, a grandson or someone else, since only a virgin boy can worship them. Then a sheep is offered to Bāhra Barāha. Chicken, roosters, goats, whatever people bring is offered to Bairāhi and finally a rooster is cut for Bhairavi.

Question: And what is the relation between Lakhan Thapa and Mankamana's Lakhan Thapa ?

There's no relation, they are different. Mankamana is also an important goddess, we worship her.

Jaya Simha's great-grandson's version of the events shows some pecularities. He insists on the magical deeds of Lakhan and makes no mention of a political aim or will, apart from a desire for 'improvement'. This narrative may suggest that Jang Bahadur was killed soon after he had killed holy men. The priest even seems to view Jang as the legitimate king, when not dissociating him from the dynasty which unified Nepal. Similarly, he does not link Lakhan Thapa the first with Lakhan Thapa the rebel. The priest also refers to a personal animosity between Siracan Thapa Ksetri and Lakhan without references to any group antagonism. This Ksetri is even presented as a devotee of Lakhan's shrine, a point which complicates the 'ethnic' scenario. The priest also clearly denies the traditional existence of a cult addressed to Lakhan, but added that 'the Sangh [i.e., the Magar Association] had recently established a ceremony, a worship of his statue'. However, the fact that some Magar writers do make an association between the god Bhayari and Lakhan who had suffered a violent death is not surprising since the earth-god is often related to violent death among this group, though it is not a general rule. What has remained in the locality is the tradition of worshipping Lakhan's gods, and his method of worshipping them. But we must note that this set of gods is very commonly worshipped in this region and thus does not reveal any specific custom which would have been founded by Lakhan Thapa but rather his deep integration into local Magar traditions. His possible opposition to the Hindu order was nevertheless expressed to me by an old Newar from a neighbouring hamlet who told me that he had not heard much about Lakhan Thapa from his elders except that he used to say: 'One must eat everything, be it chili, be it beef ...'

Lakhan Thapa's rebellion was obviously a messianic movement. It is significant that the local tradition remembers the leader's charisma and supernatural powers much more than his strategic or political programme. Jhum Bahadur Roka Magar (1999: 8) goes as far as attributing a pre-natal will to the messiah, described as a kind of avatar: 'Great men such as the hero (*vir*) Lakhan Thapa Magar are obliged to take birth on this earth because tyranny, oppression, and despair prevail in this country.' As common in messianic movements, the deeds of the messiah have a strong emotional power over the minds and bodies of his followers, as expressed by Jivan Ale Magar:[24] 'Our bodies shiver when we hear or read about the first martyr Lakhan Thapa Magar, about the terrible sufferings he endured without bending down and keeping the head high, about his courage, his deep love and loyalty towards his motherland.'

Numerous parallels can be drawn between this rebellion and revolts organized during the same period among the tribal groups of India. The leaders of these revolts were ascetics, holy men, reincarnations. They were endowed with magical powers, notably the ability to transform bullets into water. They promised their followers the return of a Golden Age when the tribes were not dispossessed of their lands.[25] All of these attempts ended in blood.

These messianic and utopian rebellions took no account of the reality of the structures they would have to fight, or the gap between the two sides' weapons and organization. As Fuchs underlines (1992: 22), the tribal groups 'had no material and political resources to defend themselves, and thus were forced to take refuge in religious and magical means to find redress.' This is Mannheim's famous thesis according to which the non-consideration of reality is characteristic of utopia and typical of the dominated classes. Should we then take it that a utopian movement is a still-born form of rebellion, the desperate and final reflex of an oppressed group, which has no effect? I shall answer in the negative, because if utopia does not take reality into account it is then by nature revolutionary.[26] Now, as Bloch (1977) has shown, utopia is also an anticipation of the future.[27] That which is a utopia in the nineteenth century may well become a realistic ideology in the following centuries, because utopia shakes up reality.

[24]This is an excerpt of a beautiful Nepali text on Lakhan Thapa that was written discretely for me by Jivan Ale Magar and put as discretely in my notebook, while I was discussing with Ratna Chumi Rana, priest of Kahule, Bungkot. I wish to thank him now.

[25]On this subject, see Fuchs (1992).

[26]It would be more exact to say that utopia does take reality into account but in a different, shifted register. Thus the leaders of Indian tribal messianic rebellions used to say that they would transform British bullets into water. Reality was known but understood in a different register: a religious or magical one versus a technical one.

[27]On the history of utopia, see Tower Sargent and Schaer (2000).

Thus, messianic utopian revolts annihilated in blood are not mere checks, but models. They are in fact sacrificial models, and of the same nature as those which, in the Hindu world, are the foundation of the universe and royalty. As such, they confer power, they are generative.

Several recent Magar writings express this dimension, such as Sagar Thapa Magar's poem:

> Go ahead Magar people (*jāti*),
> Looking to the pages of history!
> Let's make Lakhan Thapa's dream come true
> Working all together! (S. Thapa Magar 2000)

Or the role attributed to Lakhan's rebellion by Balkrishna Kaucha Magar (1998: 9): 'Even if the kingdom [of Bungkot] did not last long, it was followed by opposition all over the country and it is Lakhan Thapa who brought new ideas and a new kind of kingdom to the people.'

It is said that through his 'sacrifice' Lakhan was thus able to get rid of Jang Bahadur. The initial sacrificial model also confers another type of power. It becomes for future generations the founding myth and model upon which new types of political action, more realistic or less idealistic this time, can stand.

In his story as presented by S. Thapa Magar or M.S. Thapa, Lakhan Thapa appears more as a martyr of caste conflict than of the Rana regime, which is his official 'title'. J.B. Roka Magar's article on Lakhan Thapa (1999) reinforces this link: for this author Lakhan was executed because the Ranas could not tolerate tribal claims for justice and autonomy. The demand that the government should nominate Lakhan Thapa as the 'first martyr' was thus not a neutral claim from the Magar Association's point of view. Rather than being just another condemnation of the already much-blackened Rana regime, it was a political act aiming at competing with the high castes on their own ground and outside the traditional political game for, as stated by Balkrishna Kaucha Magar (1998: 10): 'Lakhan Thapa is a partyless martyr.' Indeed, martyrdom became a new form of political legitimacy after the fall of the Rana regime in Nepal, just as the 'résistants' took all the political positions in France after World War II. The martyrs and the individuals associated with them have acquired, so to say, a symbolic right as compensation for what they have endured. Interestingly, each party has its own martyrs and is also seen by opposed groups as creating new martyrs when it is in power. Thus the communist parties, which were martyred under the Panchayat regime, are now creating martyrs for the Maoist groups.[28] Even when they do not suffer a violent death, political leaders transform their natural deaths into the gift of their selves, by offering their corpses to the country, in the political act which consists of offering one's eyes. This act is highly visible: for instance, the removal of Man Mohan Adhikari's eyes featured in large colour photographs on the front pages of Nepalese newspapers. Although political parties founded on ethnic or caste grounds are denied a legal existence, ethnic activists have noticed that most of the martyrs come from high castes. M.S. Thapa (1992) thus writes in the prelude to his article on Lakhan Thapa: 'Whereas Tanka Acharya, who was not executed because he was a Bahun, was called a "living martyr" and paraded on a cart, the Nepalese make fun of Lakhan Thapa Magar, Thiravam Malla, Bhimadatta Pant, Laldhvag Gurung, Chokabahadur Gurung, Ramprasad Rai, Ratna Bahadur Bantava (Rai) ...' And for J.B. Roka Magar (1999), had Lakhan Thapa been a high caste he would have received the highest honours.

In their different versions of Lakhan Thapa's life, the Magar ethnic activists reveal their political positions. The Magar associations include both individuals acting to promote the dignity of the Magar group, such as Harsa Bahadur Bura Magar who plays down Lakhan Thapa's personal ambition in order to raise him to the level of a defender of the country, and individuals of a more revolutionary bent who aim to fuel communal conflict on an ethnic basis by interpreting their history as a simple and unidirectional subjection. This may lead to the identification of one group as the oppressive ruling class and of the others as the oppressed proletariat.[29] As if to illustrate Mao's writing

[28]On martyrdom in Nepalese communist ideologies, see Ramirez (1997).

[29]An article published in the *Kathmandu Post*, 12 January 1999, suggests a close link between ethnic and political activism among the Magars: 'Kathmandu, Jan 11. Nepal Magar Association (NMA), member of the Nepal Nationalities Federation, today announced that they have no affiliation with the underground Nepal Communist Party (Maoist). The association announced this at a press conference organized today. Addressing the press conference, Gore Bahadur Khapangi Magar, chairperson of the association, said though the association has no affiliation with the Maoists, the Magars are being victimized. He said most of the victims of the Maoist Movement have been Magars. "If you look at the number of those who've died in the police-Maoist clash you'll see that most of them were Magars", he said. In a press release distributed today, the association has condemned the government for arresting its members on false charges. The association has demanded that the government release those who were arrested on charges of being Maoists, resettle those who were displaced by the conflict and compensate those who have lost their family members. Khapangi said the

as quoted by the Nepalese Maoist party,[30] Magar scholars aim to change their current status by revising history as written by the dominant castes. This idea is expressed by numerous authors, such as Samjog Lapha Magar (1997): 'That which is called the history of Nepal is a partisan and illusory history, which we reject. History is the writing down of that which is dead, but history itself never dies. This is why it is time now for all the Magars to write down their history.' However, the history they have chosen to dig up is the story of a popular (and ethnic) rebellion, as if they are speaking of the present situation through the past. The parallel is obvious in some recent writings about Lakhan Thapa, such as Balkrishna Kaucha Magar (1998: 9): 'At that time it was not possible to resist Jang Bahadur's power after having established a new kingdom, just as the present government look for those who oppose its politics, like the Maobadis, and kill them.' And the recent declaration of an independent government, the 'people's local government',[31] in the tiny village of Bhawang, Rolpa, led by Santosh Buda and Khim Bahadur Thapa, may be viewed as a re-enactment of Lakhan's dream, although it is now supported by a much wider organization.

I would like to end with a poem written by Lakshman Ale Magar[32] in which the suffering of a group deprived of its own history is beautifully rendered. When nothing else is left, an attachment to the land is the major link to an identity, through the striking image of the soil imbued by the blood of the ancestors, which combines the two basic forms of identity which are distinguished in Europe (blood and territory). This image comes back as a leitmotif in Magar writings and

---

association had submitted a memorandum to this effect to the government three months back. He added that none of the successive governments have been serious about the nationalities movement. Citing one such example, he said, "When the association apprised the then Home Minister Khum Bahadur Khadka about the high incidence of Magar killing he said in a place where Magars are the majority who do you expect to die? Certainly not the Brahmins."' In the same way the *Kathmandu Post*, 10 January, reports a similar suspicion addressed to the chairman of the All Nepal Nationalities Association: 'Newly elected chairman Ale Magar, when asked if his group was associated with communist parties, denied any such link. But he admitted that "though the association shares beliefs with leftist parties, we have no affiliation with any political party."'

[30]'... The only intention of the proletariat to know the world is to change it' (sic). See CPN-Maoist 1997.

[31]*Kathmandu Post*, 20 May 2001.

[32]This poem, entitled, *Lekhnu cha itihās hāmīle*, is published in *Gyāvat*, Baisakh 2050, p. 69.

sheds new light on the importance of martyrdom and violent action: on the dire necessity which perhaps compels them to 'write history with warm blood'.

WE ARE WRITING HISTORY OURSELVES

We are the priests of this country,
It is we who were the kings here,
History was given to be ours,
Why is it now out of our reach?

If we look and search in history
Our name is in the first place.
We are the protectors of this country,
Nobody should think that we are weak.

We are the original inhabitants of this land.
We know everything over there,
We take care of them all.
History brings us its help.

Our power is boundless,
Equal to the heroes and valiant warriors.
History, we write it with warm blood,
As did our immortal ancestors.
(...)
Look, all these hills, all these fields,
All are imbued with our ancestors' blood,
Saying: 'Where is the karma of our descendants here?'
Today they are worrying.
(...)

REFERENCES

Acharya, B. 1972. 'General Bhimsen Thapa and the Samar Jung Company' *Regmi Research Series* 4(9): 161–7.
_____ 1975. 'Social Changes During the Early Shah Period' *Regmi Research Series* 7(9): 163–72.
Ajanta Standard Dictionary Nepali-English, edited by 'three authors'. Delhi: Ajanta Prakashan, no date.
Bloch, E. 1977. *L'esprit de l'utopie*. Paris: Gallimard.
Bura Magar, H.B. 1997 [2054 VS]. *Rāstrakā gaurav tathā Nepālkā pratham sahīd Lakhan Thāpā Magar (dvitīya)* [The nation's pride and Nepal's first martyr Lakhan Thapa Magar (the second)]. Kathmandu: P. Bura Magar.

Cavenagh, Captain O. 1851. *Rough Notes on the State of Nepal, its Government, Army, and Resources.* Calcutta: W. Palmer, Military Orphan Press.

CPN-Maoist 1997. 'Strategy and Tactics of Armed Struggle in Nepal (document adopted by the Third Plenum of the CC of the CPN (Maoist) in March 1995)' *The Worker* 3 (Feb 1997). Also available at <http://www.maoism.org/misc/nepal/nepal.htm>.

Dabaral 'Charan', S.P. 1973. 'From the Yamuna to the Sutlej' *Regmi Research Series* 4: 43–54.

Fuchs, S. 1992. *Godmen on the Warpath: A Study of Messianic Movements in India.* New Delhi: Munshiram Manoharlal.

Hasrat, B.J. 1971. *History of Nepal.* Hoshiarpur: V.V. Research Institute Book Agency.

'Human Rights Movement in Nepal', anonymous text published by Human Rights Internet. See http://www.hri.ca/partners/insec/Yb1993/Ch1.shtml

Joshi, B.L. and L. Rose 1966. *Democratic Innovations in Nepal.* Berkeley: University of California Press.

Kaucha Magar, Balkrishna 1998 [2055 VS]. 'Pratham sahid Lakhan Thāpā Magarprati apamān ki irsyā' [Disobedience or rivalry towards the first martyr Lakhan Thapa Magar], *Janajāti Manc* 4(1).

Lapha Magar, Samjog 1997 [2054 VS]. 'Nepālko pratham sahīd kaptan Lakhan Thāpā Magar [Nepal's first martyr Captain Lakhan Thapa Magar] *Raha* 4(3) (Baisākh/Jestha): 14–15.

Lecomte-Tilouine, Marie 1997. 'Entre orthodoxie hindoue et cultes tribaux' *Archives de Sciences Sociales des Religions*, 1997, 99. Revised and translated into English as 'The Enigmatic Pig' in *Studies in Nepalese History and Society* (2000) 5(1): 3–41.

———. 2003. 'La désanskritisation des Magar. Ethnohistoire d'un groupe sans histoire' *Purushartha* 23: 297–327 (eds M. Carrin & C. Jaffrelot, *Tribus et basses castes: Résistance et autonomie dans la société indienne*).

———. 2004. 'Ethnic Demands within Maoism: Questions of Magar Territorial Autonomy, Nationality and Class' in M. Hutt (ed.) *Himalayan 'People's War': Nepal's Maoist Rebellion*, pp. 112-35. London: Hurst & Co. in September 2001.

Naraharinath, Yogi (ed.) 1953 [2010 VS]. *Divya Upadesh.* Kathmandu: Shri Bagishvara Chapakhana.

——— (ed.) 1964 [2021 VS]. *Gorkhā Vamsāvalī.* Kasi: Aryabirsangh.

Nepal, Gyanamani 1983 [2040 VS]. 'Siddha autariko rajāin garne utkantha' [The human reincarnation's desire to reign] *Prajñā* 12(2, 44): 40–6.

Rana, Pudma Jung Bahadur, 1974 (reprint). *Life of Maharaja Sir Jung Bahadur of Nepal.* Kathmandu: Ratna Pustak Bhandar.

Ramirez, P. 1997. 'Pour une anthropologie religieuse du maoïsme népalais' *Archives de Sciences Sociales des Religions* 99: 47–68.

Rana Magar, V.K. 1997 [2054 VS]. *Gorkhā Magarharu* [The Magars of Gorkha]. Kathmandu: R. Ranamagar.

Regmi, M.C. 1980. 'The Lakhan Thapa Affair' *Regmi Research Series* 12(5): 72–5.

Ricoeur, P. 1997. *L'idéologie et l'utopie* . Paris: Seuil.

Roka Magar, Jhum Bahadur 1999 [2056VS]. 'Pratham sahid Lakhan Thāpā magarko mulyānkan ojhelmā' [The evaluation of the first martyr Lakhan Thapa kept under shade] *Sāng* 1(1).

Sharma, Janak Lal 1963 [2020 VS]. *Josmani santa paramparā ra sāhitya* [The Josmani Santa tradition and its literature]. Kathmandu: Royal Nepal Academy.

Shrestha, Kesar Lall, forthcoming. *Speaking Stones*.

Thapa, M.S. 1992. 'Pratham Sahīd Lakhan Thāpā Magar' [The first martyr, Lakhan Thapa Magar]. *Kairan* Jan.-Feb.

Thapa 'Guruchan' Magar, Shivalal 1996a [2052 VS]. *Ojhelmā parekā magarharu* [The Magars kept in the shade] (eds) Indira Thapa Guruchan Magar & Sharmila Thapa Guruchan Magar. Tanahun.

———— 1996b [2052 VS]. 'Pratham Sahīd Lakhan Thāpāmagar (dvitīya)' [The first martyr Lakhan Thapa Magar the Second] *Soni* 4(4): 3–7.

Thapamagar, Sagar, 2000 (2057 VS), 'Āhvān [The awakening]' *Kanung lām* 6(2): 18.

Tower Sargent, L. and R. Schaer (eds) 2000. *Utopie: La quête de la société idéale en occident*. Paris: Bibliothèque Nationale de France/Fayard.

Unbescheid, G. 1985. 'Blood and Milk or the Manifestation of the Goddess Manakamana' *Journal of the Nepal Research Centre* 8: 95–130

Whelpton, J. 1991. *Kings, Soldiers and Priests: Nepalese Politics 1830–1857*. New Delhi: Manohar.

Wright, D. (ed.) 1970 [1877]. *History of Nepal*. Delhi: Cosmo Publications.

The State and Maoist Insurgency

chapter eight

Democracy and Dissent in Nepal: An Overview With Some Perceptions from the Valley of Dhorpatan

• *Colin Millard*

INTRODUCTION

Between October 1996 and August 1998 I lived in a Tibetan medical school situated in the Norzinling Tibetan refugee settlement, in the valley of Dhorpatan in the Baglung district of north-west Nepal. Living alongside the Tibetan refugees there are six Nepalese ethnic groups present in the valley. Before coming to Dhorpatan I heard conflicting views about the safety of being there. In February 1996 the Communist Party of Nepal (Maoist), which had been involved in constitutional politics through its political wing, the United People's Front, went underground and declared a 'People's War' with the aim of bringing down the government and establishing a republic. From the beginning of the 'People's War' up to the present day, the epicentre of Maoist activity has been the Rukum and Rolpa districts, immediately to the west of Dhorpatan. The popularity of the Maoists in the remoter rural areas can be accounted for by the fact the 'People's Movement' that brought down the Panchayat regime and ushered in party political democracy in 1990 has brought no benefits to the vast majority of Nepal's rural poor.

Undoubtedly the major events of the democracy movement occurred in Kathmandu Valley. All the accounts that have been written about the movement outline events as they unfolded in this location. What is striking is the lack of information about what was occurring in rural areas where the largest proportion of the population live. Hoftun (1993) who was present in Kathmandu at the time of the movement remarks that in the period of political instability immediately after the downfall of the Panchayat system, violence and unrest continued for some time in Kathmandu. After the authorities managed to calm the situation down, repeated reports were heard of violence continuing outside the Valley. As a result, as Hoftun points out, for many villagers the word for 'democracy', *prajātantra*, became associated with crime. A major source of inspiration for the democracy movement was the break up of the Soviet Union and the fall of eastern European communist regimes, particularly Ceaucescu, in 1989. It seems ironic then that Nepal is now heralded by the international Maoist community as the vanguard of their movement. Whilst I was in Dhorpatan, I spoke with members of all caste and ethnic groups about what they thought about the changes that have been wrought since democracy. In what follows I will present those views and suggest some factors that have caused large numbers of Nepalese to turn to Maoism as the panacea for their problems.

COMMUNISM AND MAOISM IN NEPAL: A BRIEF HISTORY

Communist Factions and the Establishment of the Communist Party of Nepal (United Marxist-Leninist)

State tolerance of groups expressing forms of political awareness is a relatively recent phenomenon in Nepal. During the Rana period, from 1846 to 1951, Nepal was kept relatively isolated from the rest of the world. But the Ranas could not stop the influence of the independence movement in India, and it was within this context that the two oldest Nepalese political parties were formed by Nepalese dissidents living in exile in India: the Nepali National Congress Party by B.P. Koirala and others in 1947; and the Communist Party of Nepal (CPN), founded by Pushpa Lal Shrestha in 1949. Since then communism in Nepal has grown and developed, flowing with international trends and the idiosyncrasies of local personalities. Differing attitudes, such as those towards the monarchy, to Nepal's relationship with India and China, the Sino-Soviet rift, parliamentary democracy, and armed struggle, have led to splinter groups (Khadka 1994). There are presently around 20 communist groups in Nepal, representing a variegated range of communist shades. In Nepal's first election in 1959, divisions within the party over attitudes towards the monarchy led to it achieving only four seats. The Nepali Congress party won a landslide victory taking 74 of the total 109 seats.

The first major split in the NCP occurred after King Mahendra's 'bloodless coup' in 1960. Claiming that the recently elected Congress Party had not succeeded in maintaining law and order, he resorted to his emergency powers and disbanded the government, imprisoning the Prime Minister B.P. Koirala and several of the other main political leaders. Afterwards, the secretary general of the NCP, Keshar Jung Rayamajhi, in keeping with his former attitude, took a conciliatory approach to the monarchy and agreed to work with the Panchayat system. Due to widespread disapproval at this amongst party members, at the third Party Congress in 1962, he was thrown out of the party and Tulsi Lal Amatya became the general secretary. The next major split occurred as a consequence of the Sino-Soviet rift in the mid-1960s: this cleaved the NCP into several contending groups (Nickson 1992).

By 1965 the party had gone into decline. In the late 1960s Pushpa Lal, his brother-in-law, Man Mohan Adhikari, and Mohan Bikram Singh, all made separate attempts to revitalize the movement (Whelpton 1994). Man Mohan's group was initially influential, but in time its Eastern Koshi Provincial Committee, headed by Mohan Chandra Adhikari, Chandra Prakash Mainali, and Radha Krishna Mainali, broke away and in 1971 instituted what can be looked upon as Nepal's first Maoist revolution. Inspired by the cultural revolution in China, and the Naxalites in Naxalbari just across the border in West Bengal, they started a guerrilla movement to 'eliminate class enemies', known as the Jhapa movement after the district in which it was centred.[1] The movement was brutally suppressed by the army under the orders of the then Panchayat government, but not before the insurgents had succeeded in chopping off the heads of seven local landowners (Shrestha 1997).

After the failure of the Jhapa movement, the group, whilst maintaining its adherence to Maoist principles, gave up terrorist activity and in 1978 formed the basis of the Communist Party for Nepal (Marxist-Leninist). During the party's Fourth Convention in 1989 it dropped its adherence to Maoism and agreed to work with the Congress in opposing the Panchayat regime. Pushpa Lal's groups, which had been founded in 1968 as the Nepali Communist Party (PL), was taken over by his wife Sahana Pradhan after he died in 1978 and eventually merged with Man Mohan Adhikari's group in 1987 to become

[1] For an account of the Naxalite movement see Ray (1988).

284   *Resistance and the State: Nepalese Experiences*

the NCP (Marxist). In the months immediately preceding the May 1991 election marking the restoration of democracy in Nepal after 30 years, the NCP (M) and the NCP (ML) merged and became the NCP (United Marxist-Leninist). It fared well in the election, acquiring enough votes to act as a powerful opposition. Although the Nepali Congress won 110 of the total 205 seats to the 69 seats of the NCP (UML), the share of the poll gives a clearer indication of the electoral strength of the two parties with the NCP (UML) at 29.3 per cent, compared to the Nepal Congress at 39.5 per cent (Nickson 1992). In the 1994 general election disillusionment with the Congress party led to Man Mohan Adhikari to be voted in as what Sharma rightly refers to as 'the first Communist Prime Minister in the post-Cold war period' (1998: 241), albeit for only nine months. The NCP (UML) is divided by internal contrary forces: on one side there is a moderately left-wing socialist group which has a flexible attitude towards the monarchy; and on other there is a contingent who are strongly against the monarchy and believe in armed struggle.

MAOISM IN NEPAL

The Sino-Soviet split in 1965 led to a proliferation of Maoist factions in Nepal. During the rift a group headed by Mohan Bikram Singh and Nirmal Lama broke away from the pro-Soviet NCP(M) and held what was referred to as a fourth Party Congress; the group thus adopted the name NCP (Fourth Convention). After the downfall of the 'Gang of Four' in 1976 the group splintered. Nirmal Lama remained as head of the NCP (Fourth Convention), which aligned itself with the new Chinese leadership. Another group, headed by Mohan Bikram Singh, was avowedly Maoist and looked upon Deng Hsiao Ping as counterrevolutionary; this group adopted the name NCP (Masal). In keeping with the general attitude adopted by Maoist-leaning parties, both of these groups boycotted the 1980 referendum.

NCP (Masal) took the same attitude to the 1991 election, but in March 1991 a group led by Baburam Bhattarai broke away, declaring that they would take part in the election, under the banner of the United People's Front (UPF, *Samyukta Jan Morchā* in Nepali). Their aim was to expose the inadequacies of the system by fielding candidates, who if elected would not take up their seat in the parliament. In any case, the constitution that was drawn up in 1990 was not valid in the eyes of any of the Maoist factions, because it went against one of the main demands of the democracy movement, which stated that an elected Constituent Assembly should draw up the new constitution; the Constitutional Reform Commission which had drawn up the constitution had not been formed in this way. In the election, the UPF, which comprised an amalgamation of several Maoist groups, came out as the third largest party winning 9 of the 205 seats. Though the UPF took part in the elections, this was only as an act of protest against the system; in principal it is against multi-party democracy, it is anti-monarchical, and believes that 'new people's democracy' (*naulo janbād*) can only be achieved by working outside the constitution (Whelpton 1994: 58–9). Both the UPF and CPN (UML) look to Mao's essay 'On the Doctrine of New Democracy' written in 1940, as providing an outline of what they are trying to achieve, but differ in their ideas about the means by which it should be implemented (Whelpton 1994: 55).

Prior to the 1994 elections divisions between Baburam Bhattarai and Niranjan Govinda Vaidya led to a split in the UPF. The faction led by Vaidya stood for election but did not win any seats. Baburam Bhattarai's faction boycotted the 1994 election. At that time little was known of Pushpa Kamal Dahal (normally known by his *nom de guerre*, Comrade Prachanda), who had become the leader of the Unity Centre in 1993, which then became the CPN (Maoist) in 1995; it is against the monarchy and parliamentary democracy, and aims to establish the 'dictatorship of the proletariat' by bringing down the state through violent means. The UPF, headed by Baburam Bhattarai, functioned initially as the political wing of the CPN (Maoist). On 4 February 1996 it submitted to the Prime Minister Sher Bahadur Deuba, a memorandum listing 40 demands. As the government did not make any response to these demands, on 13 February 1996 the CPN (Maoist) formally declared the beginning of the 'People's War'.

On the same day there were reports of eight attacks in three districts on police stations and local government offices. In the ensuing weeks the attacks continued, many of them occurring in Rukum and Rolpa districts. The main targets were police, politicians, banks, landowners, Village Development Committee offices, and offices of international non-governmental organizations. Initially landowners and politicians received serious injuries to their hands and legs, but from March 1996 onwards killings started to occur (Amnesty International 1997).

THE NEPALESE STATE

Before proceeding to consider political dissent in Nepal in more detail, I would first like to briefly consider the object of that dissent: the Nepalese state. Since the establishment of the kingdom of Nepal in

1769, the state has taken broadly four main forms: the Shah period from 1769 to 1846, the Rana period from 1846 to 1951, the Panchayat period from 1960 to 1990, and the period of parliamentary democracy since 1991. After the fall the Rana regime in 1951, Nepal made its first attempt at democratic government, but this was abruptly brought to an end in 1960 when King Mahendra assumed emergency powers and banned all political parties.

During the reign of the Shah kings, the administration of the kingdom was based on three indigenous territorial concepts: *muluk* as 'possessions', *desha* as 'realm', and *desh* as 'country' (Burghart 1996: 231–6). The word *desh* refers both to a 'country' and the people who inhabit it. A *desh* was seen to have a changeless nature or *dharma*, which derived 'by virtue of its being remembered in the present by "men of good character" as the way of life of the country since time immemorial' (Burghart 1996: 234). These three concepts had associated systems of authority. The king exercised proprietary authority over his possessions (*muluk*), which was enshrined in tenurial relationships; he exercised ritual authority in his realm (*desha*), which centred on the king's tutelary deity; and ancestral authority was invoked with regard to the countries (*desh*) within the king's domain.

In administering his realm and the 'countries' within it, the king had to uphold the *dharma* of the realm and the *dharma* of the country; if they were in disagreement, the Brahmanical codes endorsed the local customs (ibid.). Burghart points out that this attitude did not derive from altruism, but was most likely due to political expediency. As long as activities in the 'country' did not interfere with the state, they were left as they were. Ernest Gellner's comments about agrarian society are appropriate here: 'the state is interested in extracting taxes, maintaining the peace, and not much else, and has no interest in promoting lateral communication between its subjects' (1983: 10 quoted in Pfaff-Czarnecka 1997). Burghart notes that the boundary of the king's possessions was not coterminous with that of his realm; the boundaries of his possessions were not fixed: they could expand or contract according to the acquisitive power of the king. People residing at the border could be in the unfortunate position of being part of two polities and having to pay taxes to both. There is a resonance here with Nissan and Stirrat's (1990) ideas of pre-modern state formations. They claim that such states are politically and culturally heterogeneous, they are defined by the centre rather than the boundary, power is expressed in ritual idioms, and boundaries are porous and weak.

A major shift in the categorization and administration of the state of Nepal occurred under Rana rule in 1854. This year saw the institution of Jang Bahadur's Muluki Ain or legal code. The aim of this code was to embrace the whole of the population of the state within the Hindu caste system. Various administrations had introduced the caste system in Nepal before, but never to the extent it was now to take (Gurung 1997). For non-Hindu groups their status changed dramatically under this code. Before it they had been recognized as territorial groups (*jāti*), now they had become social groups (*jāt*) in a hierarchical system. All groups were slotted into a five-tier hierarchy of pure and impure castes (Höfer 1979).

During the period of Rana rule, attempts were also made to homogenize the population under the aegis of the dominant Parbatiya culture. In 1814 the Nepalese notion of flexible borders led to conflict with the East India Company. The consequence of this was the Treaty of Sagauli in 1815 in which the territorial boundaries of Nepal were fixed. By the time of the Muluki Ain in 1854, Nepal was beginning to assume some of the characteristics which Nissan and Stirrat identify as typical of the modern state: a territory defined through ritualized boundaries, and a homogeneous population. Nissan and Stirrat's third category—power coming from the people—had to wait another hundred years. In an article on post-oriental identities, which holds that rigid categories are formed in a society by the documenting procedures of colonial authorities, Rogers (1994) qualifies his argument by saying that this form of discourse is not uniquely colonial. Such documentation processes are concomitant with the expansion of state power. In this way, the classification of social groups found in the Muluki Ain law code has had far-reaching consequences to the present day.

A similar process of homogenization under the domination of Parbatiya culture occurred during the Panchayat system from 1960 to 1990. In this period the political rhetoric revolved around the three notions of the nation, democracy, and development. There was no place for political parties or interest groups. In the king's political speeches the rhetoric of nation-building and national development was mixed with Vaishnavite devotional religion. National service was likened to service to one's redeeming deity; such an attitude should be without self-interest, hence political interest groups were against Nepal's national interests (Burghart 1996). The new legal code that was implemented in 1962 makes it no longer legally possible for someone to claim superiority over another through caste, race, or culture, but, as Dahal (1995) notes, this did not transform ingrained social practice.

REASONS FOR DISSENT

Despite forty years of development and nine development plans, Nepal remains one of the world's poorest countries. A large proportion of Nepal's mainly rural population live in poverty and there is a high prevalence of diseases associated with nutritional deficiency (Shrestha & Mulmi 1997). There is a glaring disparity between the few who have wealth and the vast majority who do not. The false image that the Panchayat system was the true system to represent the best interests of the Nepalese people became increasingly evident during the 1980s with general awareness of corruption within the system. Over the last few decades, Nepal has received a large amount of international aid (Seddon 1987), much of which is said to have contributed to the personal fortunes of corrupt politicians.

Nor have the hopes of the democracy movement, after ten years of democracy, been fulfilled. After the Panchayat system had been replaced with multi-party democracy, many of the Panchas, the politicians who had served in the Panchayat government, entered the Congress Party and were soon back in power (Hoftun 1993). Corruption is still widely perceived to exist, the standard of living conditions for most rural people remains low, and none of the numerous governments that have been in power since democracy have done much to change the exploitative land relationships in rural areas (Shrestha 1997). Just as during the Panchayat period, rural and urban elites worked the system to their advantage. In this way the political dominance of the Parbatiya high castes has remained intact.

Another major source of tension in Nepal is burgeoning unemployment resulting from the combination of a continuously expanding population and a sluggish economy. The difficulty has been exacerbated in rural areas by the Indian and British armies, traditionally important sources of employment, significantly decreasing their recruitment numbers. The problem of an increasing population and slow growth in the economy has been compounded by a trend in rising levels of education. In 1965 primary school enrolment was at only 20 per cent; by 1987 it had risen to 82 per cent. In 1965 the numbers of students enrolled at secondary schools was 21,000; in 1986 it had risen to 497,000 (Nickson 1992). By 1990 successive development programmes had led to increasing numbers of educated people, with political and economic aspirations. The government had dealt with this situation by providing graduate and secondary school leavers with employment in the civil service. Education was not the only requirement in acquiring a position; employment has been largely controlled by the higher castes of the Bahun and Chetri. International aid was used to create new posts, but this could only be sustained for so long. In 1960 there were 27,000 staff employed in the public administration, by 1990 the number had risen to 100,000 and was stretched to the limit (Nickson 1992). Discontent among the increasing numbers of educated people who could not find work contributed to the groundswell of opposition to the Panchayat government (Hoftun 1993). Ten years later the same problem persists.

THE POLITICIZATION OF IDENTITY

The first census in Nepal occurred in 1911. Since then there have been nine further censuses, all of which used different criteria to categorize the population. The most recent census was in 1991. At that time the population was 18.5 million and on a 2.05 per cent annual growth rate (Gurung 1998). The 1991 Census lists 27 ethnic (previously 'tribal') groups and 30 caste groups. Gurung (1998: 41) notes the absence from this list of several castes and gives the total of at least 35 ethnic and 36 caste groups; the missing groups were presumably subsumed in the category of 'other'. This issue of missing groups from the census data has also been noted by Dahal (1995), who pointed out that the census did not clearly identify separate cultural groups. (This is also borne out by my own findings, which will be discussed later.) A recent survey of languages spoken in Nepal gives a total of 52: 36 Tibeto-Burman, 14 Indo-Aryan, one Munda, and one Dravidian (Gurung 1998: 60). The on-the-ground reality is that Nepal is home to an abundance of divergent social and cultural forms.

We have seen how the relationship between the population and the state has changed historically from territorial groups (*jāti*) to social groups (*jāt*). Increasingly over the last few decades, discourse has centred on the new relationship of the citizen within the nation-state. The task for the nation-state is to instill in its citizens a feeling of belonging to one national polity. Since the 'People's Movement' and the establishing of democracy in 1990, pluralism has become very much a part of the modern day political agenda. The new form of pluralism involves constitutional recognition of ethnic diversity, and minority groups are in principle free to articulate their interests.

This new inclusive character of the state was enshrined in the 1990 Constitution, which defines Nepal as 'a multi-ethnic, multilingual, democratic, independent, indivisible, sovereign, Hindu and Constitutional Monarchical Kingdom' (quoted in Gellner 1997: 6).

Recently I took a taxi journey in Kathmandu. I asked the taxi driver where he was from. My aim was to elicit his exact origins in Nepal. He replied in unequivocal English, 'I am a citizen of Nepal.' Certainly the state discourse has power in areas where the media and state institutions have a strong presence, but this is confined mainly to urban areas. Most of Nepal's population live in rural areas and here the homogenizing power of the state is much less pervasive. In rural areas it is still possible to find people who refer to the Kathmandu Valley as Nepal, and think of where they live as somewhere else. Ethnic identity exists but national identity is an altogether more opaque phenomenon. Dahal (1995) identifies three main broad ethnic divides in Nepal: that between the Pahāde (hill people) and the Madhesiya (*madise*, people of the plains); that between the high-caste Hindus and the Janajati (*janajāti* refers to a range of ethnic groups found in both the hill regions and the Tarai; previously they were referred to as 'tribal groups'); and that between the high-caste Hindus and the Dalit or untouchable groups.

Sentiments for change had been growing for some time before the 'People's Movement' which led to democracy, but the power structures of the Panchayat regime had been sufficiently strong to keep them at bay. With democracy reinstalled the growing upsurge for cultural freedom found unimpeded expression. Whelpton (1994) records that in 1991 74 political parties in Nepal were preparing for the upcoming election; 47 of these applied for recognition by the Election Commission, and 44 were accepted. Since the beginning of democracy in 1990 and the new possibility of freedom of expression, as one of Holmberg's (1996: xii) Nepali friends pointed out, 'everyone is a politician now.' Expressions of identity in ethnic terms have increased since democracy was established in 1991, and there has been a trend for ethnic groups to substantialize themselves and put forward claims to be indigenous people.

In fact politicized forms of ethnic identity had existed long before democracy. In 1991 movements which were underground or restricted came to the surface and began to flourish. Gurung (1997) points out that in the ten years of political freedom from 1950, during Nepal's first experiment with democracy, a number of ethnic organizations had been established, only to be stamped out by the succeeding

Panchayat regime. From the 1950s on a growing number of associations have developed to represent the interests of ethnic or caste groups. Dahal (1995: 162) claims that by 1963 there were 44 such organizations. One of the most prominent ethnic organizations to have been established in recent times is the Nepal Janajati Mahasangh (Nepal Federation of Nationalities or NEFEN), founded in 1990. At present it has member associations representing 33 ethnic groups from both the hill region and the Tarai. The Mahasangh redefines the word *janajāti* to mean not 'tribal' but 'nationality' (Fisher 1993). In doing this, the word has come to convey the sense of 'ethnic movement'. The Mahasangh wants to redefine the previously underprivileged position of the Janajati. Rather than being seen as 'tribals' in opposition to the state, they are in fact nationalities within the state. The Mahasangh defines Janajati groups in negative terms: they are 'fundamenatally non-Hindu' (Fisher 1993: 12). In saying this, the aim is to reject the hierarchical Hindu caste structure of the dominant Parbatiya group. The Mahasangh leaders point to the constitutional ambiguity of non-Hindu ethnic groups in Nepal. A number of articles within the Constitution unequivocally acknowledge the plural nature of Nepalese society, yet other articles concerning the Hindu state contradict this. Another prominent organization is the Utpidit Jātiya Utthān Manch (Forum for the Uplift of the Oppressed Castes), formed in 1987 to represent the interest of untouchable castes in the hill region and the Tarai. It is well represented with organizations in 50 districts out of a total of 75; it is opposed to Hinduism and would like to see the introduction of a secular state.

PERCEPTIONS OF DEMOCRACY AND DISSENT IN THE VALLEY
OF DHORPATAN

Dhorpatan: The Place

Dhorpatan is the name given to a valley in northwest Nepal lying south of the Dhaulagiri mountain range. The bottom of the valley is some 3000 metres above sea level, the surrounding hills reaching up to 4500 metres. Despite the altitude, for most of the year the region is green and luscious. This is due to the high levels of precipitation in the area; the northern limit of the monsoon rains being the Dhaulagiri Mountains. The valley itself marks the southern extremity of the Dhorpatan Royal Hunting Reserve, one of Nepal's nine national parks. The valley runs east-west along the Uttarganga River. The large flat

fertile plains along the valley floor make it highly suitable for agriculture and grazing animals. There are two main routes to the valley: a
three- or four-day walk either from Baglung to the east or from Tansen
to the south. The plain is broadest at the western end of the valley and
up until the 1980s, an airstrip situated here was in frequent use; now
it is overgrown and hardly noticeable. There is a National Park office
located at this end of the valley, which in 1996–7 always seemed to
have a core of between five and ten staff. During my time in Dhorpatan
trekkers occasionally passed through on their way to Dolpo, but
considering the great natural beauty of the region, surprisingly few
tourists come there. Also during the same period on a few occasions
helicopters arrived bringing tourists with a predilection for hunting,
but this stopped after Maoists looted a group in the summer of 1998.
Even before the Maoist insurgency, there was certainly nothing in
Dhorpatan like the tourist industry that exists in some of Nepal's
other national parks.

Dhorpatan: *The Maobadi*

People were certainly aware of the presence of Maoists in the area,
who are generally referred to as *Maobādi*. This is especially so as the
Tibetans and some of the Nepalis trade with people in the Maoist
stronghold districts of Rukum and Rolpa, and this had continued
unabated as far as I could see since the Maoist insurgency. I never
encountered or heard of any problems associated with Maoist activity
in Dhorpatan itself, but in May 1997 news came of the killing of a
Congress politician in a location just to the west of the valley. Killings
connected with the Maoist insurgency had been going on for some
time before I arrived in Dhorpatan. I was told that about six months
prior to my arrival, a conflict had occurred in the villages of Hukum
and Maikot just to the west of Dhorpatan, and the Maoists had killed
seven people.

The July 1998 edition of *Asiaweek* ran an article detailing how a
Western tourist who was hunting in the Dhorpatan Hunting Reserve
had his high calibre rifle stolen by Maoists and was told to leave and
tell the government not to send any more hunters. An article in the
Kathmandu Post for 14 April 2000 states there had been 35 hunters
in the party who had been 'attacked and looted' by the Maoists. In
response to this the warden hired four new guards. After this he received threatening letters from the Maoists and consequently left. The
same *Asiaweek* article also gave an account of four trekkers having to

be airlifted from the game park as they entered an area where the police were firing at rebels from helicopters. One young Tibetan told me that there is a high prevalence of communism in the area around Dhorpatan. He said people hear that communism is about the redistribution of wealth, and as most people in the area are extremely poor, this notion is very appealing, especially to disillusioned youth who turn to Maoism because it promises to better their living conditions.

On my last visit to the valley in August 1998, due to the escalating problems with Maoists in Rukum and Rolpa districts, the area had been closed for tourists. Just before my arrival in Dhorpatan I was told that the Nepali police had set up a large camp at the western end of the valley and a curfew had been imposed on the area. As a consequence many Nepalese came up to the valley later than normal. I was also told, though I never managed to confirm the story, that the Maoists had threatened to destroy the National Park Office, and they had told local people that if anyone from the authorities caused problems with them, they should let them know and they would deal with it.

Dhorpatan: The People and Perspectives

The valley is host to six Nepali ethnic groups and a Tibetan refugee camp with a population of about 250 Tibetans. There are five Tibetan settlements spread out along the valley. It takes approximately one hour to walk from the first to the last. There are very few Nepalis who stay permanently in the valley. Most come at the beginning of spring and leave after the potato harvest in October, their permanent homes being in the lower valleys to the south. In the summer months the valley is vibrant with activity as in addition to the 250 Tibetans, about 1000 Nepalis arrive to work their smallholdings.

Dhorpatan is situated in the western reaches of the Baglung district. The 1991 census lists the Magar ethnic group as the numerically dominant group in the district constituting 28.2 per cent of the population (Gurung 1998: 58). The largest group in Dhorpatan are the low-caste Bishwakarma, then in roughly equal proportions there is the Magar group and the Nauthar group; there are also a few members of the Parbatiya, Chantyal, and Thakali groups. Here there is evidence of the inadequacies of the 1991 census: two of these groups, the Nautar and the Chantyal, although exhibiting social and cultural features marking them as distinct groups, were not recognized as such in the census data. It seems that either they were included in the category of

'Other', or more likely they were subsumed into another ethnic category. In addition there is hardly any mention of these groups in the anthropological literature of the region.

Up to now relationships between the various groups in the valley have been basically amicable; some are clearly disadvantaged compared to others, but there has been no conflict organized along caste or ethnic lines. Since democracy and the lifting of the ban on political parties in 1990 a new form of consciousness has developed in the region; this consciousness has more to do with political ideologies than motivations according to caste or ethnic affinities. Nowadays conflict does exist in the region, not between ethnic or caste groups, but between political groups, and between militant political groups and the state. Many people associate these developments with democracy and consequently have an entirely negative image of what it means.

From conversations I had with people in Dhorpatan, what the state means to them is a range of institutions, which deal with: education, healthcare, taxation, law and order, and the economy. But in reality there are very few schools in the area, health provision is negligible, and crime is widely thought to be on the increase. With the advent of democracy in 1990 there was great hope that the state would be better able to improve the living conditions of people in rural areas. But the general perception has been that this has not happened. Almost everyone I asked in Dhorpatan about how things had changed in the area since democracy replied that the situation had become worse. One Chetri friend told me: 'The situation was better before democracy. During the time of the king everything was unified and if people committed a crime then they were punished. At this time there was less crime. Now there are many different groups and leaders, and crimes have increased and go unpunished.' One Bahun I asked told me: 'The situation became worse after democracy. Before there was one rule and people abided by it, now crimes occur more often and go unpunished. The aim of many politicians is to pocket as much money as they can.' This was the opinion not only of members of high castes. One low-caste person from Dhorpatan told me: 'The situation was better before democracy, now there are too many political parties and everyone is fighting.' Nor are these sentiments confined to Dhorpatan; a Bahun friend in Kathmandu told me: 'The situation was better before democracy, now the poor are worse off than before, inflation is continuously becoming higher, and people now have expectations that go unfulfilled.' Whilst I was in Dhorpatan I spoke with members of all the caste and ethnic groups about what they thought about the changes that have been wrought since democracy. In what follows I will present some of these opinions.

The Bishwakarma

The untouchable Bishwakarma group is the most abundant in the valley. They can be found throughout the valley. About 30 Bishwakarma lived in a small settlement a short distance from the medical school. At first when I arrived in Dhorpatan, I thought of the Bishwakarma as a Parbatiya occupational caste. I came to this conclusion because, in a manner of speaking, they are the odd-job men of the valley. When the possibility of some sort of wage labour arises, such as building a wall, a new house, or collecting timber, it is usually the Bishwakarma who provide the labour. For instance, throughout the time that I was in Dhorpatan, many people were replacing the old wooden roofs of their houses with slate, and it was a group of Bishwakarma labourers that was doing the arduous quarry work to provide this slate.

When I broached the subject of their untouchable status with the Bishwakarma staying near the medical school, they were keen to dissociate themselves from the Parbatiya occupational castes such as the Kami (blacksmiths), Sarki (leatherworkers), and Damai (tailors); these, they were quick to assert, are below them in the caste hierarchy. In an area towards the middle of the valley there is a cluster of houses where a few blacksmiths work. The Bishwakarma who lived near the medical school claimed to be of a higher social status than these, and this was also thought to be the case by Tibetans I asked. Whatever the case may be, in practice they are treated as an untouchable group just like all the other Kami living in the valley.

Most of the Bishwakarma are poor; I heard that a few had become wealthy, though there was certainly no sign any of these in Dhorpatan. They have a high level of illiteracy. Many of the young can now read and write, but the vast majority of the older generations cannot. In some areas of Nepal the government has implemented programmes aimed at increasing adult literacy. One Bishwakarma man I spoke to about this said that he had never had the opportunity to follow such a programme; his life consisted solely of working in the quarry all day and then not being able to sleep at night because his body ached so much.

All the Bishwakarma whom I asked about how things had changed since democracy had a negative view of the situation. One person said to me that the situation was better before democracy, now there are too many parties and everyone is fighting. Another speaking in a similar vein said nowadays the situation is worse, people from the same family can be members of different parties, and a son can end up killing his father over politics. I was told that there is now a Bishwakarma Member of Parliament in Kathmandu. None of the Bishwakarma I spoke to knew his name or his party. The closest I heard from them was, that he was 'some kind of communist'. One Bishwakarma told me that money coming from the government in Kathmandu filters through a stream of officials and before it arrives at its destination most of it has been siphoned away; this he claimed was the reason for the rise of communism and the Maobadi.

THE NAUTHAR

After the Bishwakarma, it is difficult to say whether the Nauthar or the Magar is the next largest group in the valley; some people say one, some the other. Like the Bishwakarma, the Nauthar are not listed in the 1991 census, nor in the 1854 Muluki Ain legal code. De Sales makes a passing comment about them (1993: 92) in her article on the origins of the Chantyal group. Fortunately a young Nauthar who has done a degree in social studies at Butwal University helped me. Realizing the lack of information about his group, for some time now he has been gathering information about Nauthar customs and history.

The Nauthar have their permanent homes in the cluster of villages of the Bowang and Adhikarichaur Village Development Committees in the valleys just south of Dhorpatan. The total population of the Nauthar is around 2500. 'Nauthar' means 'nine clans' and refers to the original number of clans that constituted the group. Two of these clans have now ceased to exist. The young Nauthar who gave me information about the group was one of the only people that I spoke to in the valley who had a positive opinion of the changes since democracy. This is hardly surprising considering that he is part of the Village Development Committee. He told me that the Panchayat system was no good. Now, with democracy, people have the power to vote for people who they think will represent their interests. He added that under the present system even poor people are becoming politicians.

THE MAGAR

The Magar are found distributed throughout Nepal, but their highest concentration is in the western hills. Like many other Nepali caste and ethnic groups, in the changing political climate in Nepal over the last few decades the Magar are becoming increasingly self-conscious and politicized. In 1986 an association called Nepal Langhali Sangh was formed in Kathmandu. In 1993 it became the Nepal Magar Association, which has the prime aim of representing the interests of the Magar as a united group.

As I have mentioned, the main focus of the Maoist insurgency which began in 1996 is the Magar-dominated Rukum and Rolpa districts to the west of Dhorpatan. In these districts there has been very little provision by the state and grievances had been building up amongst young Magar for some time before the outbreak of the 'People's War' in 1996 (Whelpton 1999: 20). This is not to say that it is only the Magar who are involved in the 'People's War', but they certainly make up a large part of the activists. Not all Magar approve of this situation. One Magar I met in Dhorpatan said that the situation was better before democracy, now there are too many parties all fighting each other. At one point I was interested in spending some time in some Magar villages to learn about their social organization and culture. I asked an old Magar man in Dhorpatan, which, in his opinion, would be a suitable village for me to visit. He replied that political problems were present in all Magar villages and presently none of them could be guaranteed as safe.

THE PARBATIYA, CHANTYAL, AND THAKALI GROUPS

The Parbatiya, Chantyal, and Thakali groups are present in only small numbers in the valley. With the exception of one Chantyal man to whom I spoke, the feeling seemed unanimous that since democracy life had become worse in Dhorpatan. The Chantyal man thought that things were now better because people were free to choose their own government. While he was explaining this to me his wife interrupted him explaining that she liked the king.

THE PEOPLE'S WAR

Since the first parliamentary election after the re-establishment of multi-party democracy in Nepal the numerous governments that have been in power have not improved the living conditions of Nepal's majority rural population; poverty remains rife, unemployment is high, and economic growth continues to be slow. Part of the problem has been the vitiation of the power of the state since the mid-term elections of 1994, which resulted in no single party in the ensuing period having a clear electoral mandate. In the four-year period leading up to the victory of the present Nepal Congress government in the May 1999 election, six coalition governments had governed Nepal. The failure of parliamentary democracy to show any signs of resolving Nepal's social and economic problems led the Communist Party of Nepal (Maoist), on the 13 February 1996, to formally announce the beginning of the 'People's War'.

Rukum and Rolpa districts remain the main focus of Maoist activity, but they also have a strong presence in the surrounding districts of Jajarkot, Pyuthan, and Arghakhanchi, and in the central districts of Sindhu-Palchok, Ramechhap, and Sindhuli. Though these are the main areas of their control, they have grassroots support throughout Nepal. According to the assessment of Gopal Siwakoti, a Kathmandu human rights lawyer, they are politically active in 30 to 40 of Nepal's total 75 districts (*Christian Science Monitor* 3 May 1999).

The main objective of the armed insurgency is to overthrow the state and replace it with the 'new people's democracy' (*naulo janbād*), which will take the form of the 'dictatorship of the proletariat'. The Maoist leadership has employed various strategies to achieve this. They target those whom they consider to be 'class enemies' such as politicians, police, businessmen, landlords, and moneylenders. The June 1996 edition of *The Worker*, the journal of the CPN (Maoist), documents various incidents that occurred on the day of the declaration of the 'People's War' on 13 February 1996. One incident occurred at Chyangli in the Gorkha district, in central Nepal. This involved a group of people taking over the office of the Agricultural Development Bank and burning the loan papers of the local peasants. We are also told that in the evening of the same day, armed youths seized three police outposts, one in each of the districts of Rukum, Rolpa, and Sindhuli. So began a pattern which continues to this day of the Maoists capturing police outposts and taking weapons and ammunition, taking money by force from local landlords and moneylenders, and taking over local banks and burning the evidence of loans given to peasants (Sharma 1998: 24). Sometimes such activity pays well. The 19 May 2000 edition of the *Kathmandu Post* reported that 200 Maoists had taken over a bank in a mid-western hill village, and seized Rs 1.5 million (US $22,500) in cash, Rs 5.5 million (US $82,500) in gold and silver, and two twelve-bore rifles.

In October 1998 the CPN (Maoist) announced that the 'People's War' was moving into its fourth phase which involves the consolidation of 'base zones'. In keeping with Mao's revolutionary strategy their approach is to surround cities with 'liberated' villages and then to move the offensive into urban areas. The Maoists have completed their objectives of previous phases of establishing areas for the development of insurgency and mobilizing the people for guerrilla war (Sharma 1998).

The Maoists are armed with knives and rifles stolen from the police; they also have home-made bombs made from pressure cookers and pipes. The police stationed in remote outposts are poorly armed and have little chance against the explosive charges thrown by Maoists. The Maoists may have a stash of up to four tons of gelatine, which they stole four years ago from a construction project in Charikot (*Nepali Times* 14 July 2000). The following description of the attack on the Panchakati Police station in Jajarkot district on 7 June 2000 gives an idea of what is involved. It was reported that the police station was destroyed by a group of about 1,000 Maoists. At the time of the attack there were 51 police inside the station. The police reported that the Maoists lit up the station with flare-tipped arrows and then bombarded them with home-made explosives.

Their campaign is also directed at the wider Nepalese economy as the recent fire bombings of the Surya Tobacco company plant in Simara and the Colgate-Palmolive plant in Timara clearly demonstrate. Although most Maoist activity occurs in rural areas, sporadic events also occur in the cities. In June a bomb exploded at a branch of the Agricultural Development Bank in Pokhara, which caused extensive damage to the building, but fortunately no human causalities (*Rising Nepal* 18 June 2000). Up to now tourists have not been a major target, but this may change. In April there were reports of trekking groups being robbed and an attack on a Pokhara tourist resort (*Nepali Times* 14 July 2000).

Another ploy used in their campaign is the boycotting of elections. Due to the boycott of the 1997 election in the districts of Rukum, Rolpa, and Jajarkot by the Maoists, who threatened to kill anyone who won, in 42 village centres no nominations were filed, and elections could not be held in over 70 village centres (Shreshta 1997). The CPN (Maoist) announcement early in 1999 that they were to boycott the election in May forced the Election Commission to hold the election on two days, 3 and 17 May, to prevent the situation getting out of hand. This did not prevent the Maoists on 5 March from beheading Yadunath Gautam, a CPN (UML) candidate who was to stand for the Rukum Constituency No. 2.

Both the government and the Maoists have been criticized by Amnesty International for human rights abuses. On the Maoist side these include the injuring and killing of civilians and opposition politicians. Amnesty International received numerous reports of people receiving death threats by letter or by a message pinned on their door (1997). Since the 'People's War' began in 1996, Maoists have killed 200 people and many more have been attacked and injured. Such 'class enemies' are usually either shot or killed with *khukuri* knives. There are also reports of the CPN (Maoist) organizing 'people's courts' in west Nepal, which mete out cruel punishments to those who are found guilty (Amnesty International 2000). The October 1999 edition of *The Worker* includes a photograph of one such 'people's court' with the caption, 'punishment meted to a tyrant'.

Throughout the 'People's War', the authorities have also been continuously criticized by human rights groups for the heavy-handed way in which they have attempted to deal with the insurgency. Official sources in November 1999 reported that 5,000 people have been arrested since the beginning of the conflict and the police have killed 760 people. Many of these deaths have been reported by the police as legal killings occurring in so-called 'encounters' with armed Maoist groups. But contrary evidence shows that police have resorted to lethal force in situations which in no way demanded such extreme measures (Amnesty International 1997). The police claim that the people killed by them were Maoists, but other reports state that this was not always true.

It has also been alleged that many people were killed by the police in extra-judicial executions. Although it is difficult to ascertain the veracity of the circumstances of killings in remote regions, Amnesty International have received numerous reports of such occurrences. Their 1997 report includes cases of: suspected Maoists being shot by police whilst running away; a Maoist being executed in the forest; and another pushed off a cliff by the police; and so on. There have also been allegations of suspected female Maoists being raped by police officers.

Many people who have been held in custody in connection with the 'People's War' have given accounts of being subjected to severe police brutality. The two main forms of torture are *falanga*, where the soles of the feet are beaten with a bamboo stick, and *belana*, which involves the potentially crippling effects of rolling a weighted bamboo stick down the prisoner's thighs. Other forms of torture, including electric shocks, have been reported. There are also reports of prisoners dying whilst in custody (Amnesty International 2000).

THE 'PEOPLE'S WAR' IN THE CONTEXT OF THE REVOLUTIONARY INTERNATIONAL MOVEMENT

The Revolutionary International Movement (RIM) was founded in 1984 as an attempt to bring together Maoist groups internationally. In 1984 representatives from Maoists groups around the world met in London and formed the Revolutionary International Movement. Mohan Bikram Singh's group, CPN (Masal), was represented at the meeting and was one of the nineteen groups to sign the declaration of the movement. The CPN (Maoist) continues to be a part of RIM. The October 1999 edition of *The Worker* contains a statement by RIM applauding the achievements of the 'People's War'. Another group that was represented at the meeting was *Partido Communista Peruano-Sendero Luminoso* (Peruvian Communist Party-Shining Path). Since that time CPN (Maoist) has remained firmly supportive of the activities of the Shining Path in Peru.

After President Fujimori's coup in Peru in April 1992 and the capture of Shining Path's charismatic leader Abimael Guzmán (otherwise known as Comrade Gonzalo) in September, the movement quickly declined in strength (Stern 1998). Mikesell (1993) tells us that following Guzman's imprisonment, the London staff of the International Emergency Committee to Defend the Life of Abimael Guzmán received a large amount of mail from Nepal declaring support for him. Both Nepal and Peru share many characteristic features that make them fertile ground for insurrection. Both countries have been marred by corruption, little economic growth, exploitative land relationships, backward mountain regions, rural debt, inflation, labour migration, and so on.[2] Thus it is hardly surprising that in staging its 'People's War', the CPN (Maoist) should look to Peru's Shining Path as a major source of inspiration.

CONCLUSION

There are two main possible approaches the government can take to solve the problem of the Maoist insurgency: it can try to extirpate Maoist activity through force; or it can take a more low-key approach

[2]The similarities between the socio-economic conditions in Peru and Nepal, and between Maoism in Nepal and Peru's Shining Path have been documented by Nickson (1992) and Mikesell (1993). Both articles predated the beginning of the 'People's War'. For further discussion of these articles, see David Gellner's introduction above pp. 18–21.

which involves the gradual attrition of Maoist forces by intelligence-based special-force activity combined with social development programmes in the affected areas (Whelpton 1999: 34). The latter approach would require time and a long-term vision on the part of the government. The political instability of the last six years in Nepal has been antipathetic to this; governments, as a matter of political expediency, have tended to be reactive rather than taking an adaptive long-term approach.

The first real attempt by the government to address the problem occurred before the 'People's War'. In November 1995 the police implemented 'Operation Romeo' in Rolpa district. Extra police were sent to the area and new police posts were established. The police aimed to undermine local support for the Maoist by encouraging local officials to start development programmes (Amnesty International 1997). Since the start of the 'People's War', the police have taken a much more hardline approach. I have mentioned that prior to my last visit to Dhorpatan in August 1998, there had been a large police presence in the area. This was most likely connected with the government's counter-insurgency operation code named 'Kilo Sierra', which ran from 26 May to 7 November. During this time government sources state that 1,659 people were arrested (Amnesty International 1999). This only served to increase the negative opinion of the government held by local people.

So far the army has not been employed in counter-insurgency operations; up to now (Sept. 2000), it has been exclusively the task of the police to control Maoist activity. Due to the political sensitivity of the issue this policy is unlikely to change. An article in the *Nepali Times* on 14 July 2000 reports one senior policeman to have said: 'When Sri Lanka has a civil war, it is the army which is made to fight. But when there is a similar war brewing in Nepal, the political parties field a police force with its hands tied. Either the police has to be empowered to fight like an army, or the army has to be brought out of the barracks.' The present Prime Minister, Girija Prasad Koirala, initially toyed with the idea of using the army, but instead it seems that a paramilitary police force is to be trained and supplied with sophisticated weapons, to the cost of around Rs 2 billion.

It is certainly true that the government in Sri Lanka has made use of extensive military force to try and bring an end to the activities of Tamil separatists; yet after twenty years of fighting, and considerable loss of life, the war still continues. Even the considerable military intervention of the Indian army in 1987 did not bring an end to the conflict. There is no reason to assume that military force, whether the police or the army carries it out, is going to be any more successful in Nepal. The only real solution must be an initiative which combines social and economic development with dialogue with the insurgents. Recently a committee has been set up headed by the former Prime Minister Sher Bahadur Deuba with the aim of attempting such a dialogue; it remains to be seen what will come of it.

REFERENCES

Amnesty International 1997. *Nepal: Human Rights Violations in the Context of a Maoist 'People's War'*. See *http://web.amnesty.org/ai.nsf/indexc/ ASA310011 97?OpenDocument2of-countries/nepal*
_____ 1999. *Nepal: Human Rights at a Turning Point?*
_____ 2000. *Nepal: Human Rights and Security.*
Burghart, R. 1996. 'The Formation of the Concept of the Nation-State in Nepal' in R. Burghart *The Conditions of Listening: Essays on Religion, History and Politics in South Asia*. Delhi: Oxford University Press.
Dahal, D.R. 1995. 'Ethnic Cauldron, Demography and Minority Politics: The Case of Nepal' in D. Kumar (ed.) *State Leadership and the Politics in Nepal*. Kathmandu: CNAS.
De Sales, A. 1993. 'When the Miners Came to Light: The Chantel of Dhaulagiri' in G. Toffin (ed.) *Nepal, Past and Present*. Paris: CNRS.
Fisher, W.F. 1993. 'Nationalism and the Janajati: Diversity in Ethnic Identity Strengthens Nepali Nationalism' *Himal* 6: 11–14.
Gellner, D.N. 1997. 'Ethnicity and Nationalism in the World's only Hindu State' in Gellner *et al.* (eds).
_____, J. Pfaff-Czarnecka, and J. Whelpton (eds) 1997. *Nationalism and Ethnicity in a Hindu Kingdom: The Politics of Culture in Contemporary Nepal*. Amsterdam: Harwood.
Gellner, E. 1983. *Nations and Nationalism*. Oxford: Blackwell.
Gurung, H. 1997. 'State and Society in Nepal' in Gellner *et al.* (eds).
_____ 1998. *Nepal: Social Demography and Expressions*. Kathmandu: New Era.
Höfer, A. 1979. *The Caste Hierarchy and the State in Nepal: A Study of the Muluki Ain of 1854*. Innsbruck: Universitätsverlag Wagner.
Hoftun, M. 1993. 'The Dynamics and Chronology of the 1990 Revolution' in M. Hutt (ed.) *Nepal in the Nineties*. Delhi: Oxford University Press.
Holmberg, D. 1996. *Order in Paradox: Myth, Ritual, and Exchange Among Nepal's Tamang* (2nd ed.). Delhi: Motilal Banarsidas.
Khadka, N. 1994. 'Factionalism in the Communist Party in Nepal' *Pacific Affairs* 68: 55–76.
Mikesell, S.L. 1993. 'The Paradoxical Support of Nepal's Left for Comrade Gonzalo' *Himal* (April/May): 31–3.
Nickson, R.A. 1992. 'Democratisation and the Growth of Communism in

Nepal: A Peruvian Scenario in the Making?' *Journal of Commonwealth and Comparative Politics* **30**: 358–86.

Nissan, E. and R.L. Stirrat 1990. 'The Generation of Communal Identities' in J. Spencer (ed.) *Sri Lanka: History and the Roots of Conflict*. London: Routledge.

Pfaff-Czarnecka, J. 1997. 'Vestiges and Visions: Cultural Change in the Process of the Nation-Building in Nepal' in Gellner *et al.* (eds).

Ray, R. 1988. *The Naxalites and their Ideology*. Delhi: Oxford University Press.

Rogers, J.D. 1994. 'Post-Oriental and the Interpretation of Premodern and Modern Political Identities: The Case of Sri Lanka' *The Journal of Asian Studies* **53**: 10–23.

Seddon, D. 1987. *Nepal: A State of Poverty*. Delhi: Vikas.

Sharma, J. 1998. *Democracy Without Roots*. Delhi: Book Faith India.

Shrestha, M.P. and S.L. Mulmi (eds) 1997. *Health in Nepal: Realities and Challenges*. Kathmandu: Resource Centre for Primary Health Care.

Shrestha, S. 1997. 'Nepali Cart Before Horse' *Himal: South Asia* **10**: 14–16.

Stern, S.J. 1998. 'Beyond Enigma: An Agenda for Interpreting Shining Path and Peru, 1980–1995' in S.J. Stern (ed.) *Shining and Other Paths: War and Society in Peru, 1980–1995*. Durham and London: Duke University Press.

Whelpton, J. 1994. 'The General Elections of May 1991' in M. Hutt (ed.) *Nepal in the Nineties*. Delhi: Oxford University Press.

_____ 1999. 'Nine Years On: The 1999 Election and Nepalese Politics since the 1990 *Janandolan*' *European Bulletin of Himalayan Research* **17**: 1–39.

chapter nine

Guns, Kinship, and Fear: Maoists among the Tamu-mai (Gurungs)

• *Judith Pettigrew*

APRIL 2000

It is my second day in the village after an absence of two years.
Nani (my 'sister') and I have only managed to snatch a few brief
moments over the last 24 hours to catch up on each other's news.[1]
I am in Nepal with a combined British and Nepali interdisciplinary
ethno-history and archaeology research team en route to excavate a
Tamu[2] (Gurung) ancestral village. The team consists of Nepali and
foreign archaeologists, Tamu shamans, local porters, my research
assistant and me. After the morning meal the archaeologists leave for
a village tour and Nani and I are about to have a chat. As she is busy
in the house I walk around the courtyard. Standing at the fence looking
out over the familiar village landscape I hear what I think is the sound
of a gunshot. When Nani comes out I tell her what I think I have
heard. As she walks to the edge of the courtyard to look out across the
village she asks me a series of detailed questions: 'Where did the shot

[1]This chapter was drafted in 2000. Final corrections and the postscript date
from February 2002. For helpful comments I would like to thank: Paloma
Gay y Blasco, Mark Turin, Sandra Rouse, Louise de la Gorgendière, Sharon Hepburn,
Don Messerschmidt, David Gellner, and Ernestine McHugh.

[2]'Tamu' is the singular of 'Tamu-mai', the term that the people who are better
known as 'Gurungs' apply to themselves when they speak their own language
Tamu Kyui. As this paper is based on research carried out primarily in Tamu
villages and conducted through Tamu Kyui I use the terms 'Tamu' and 'Tamu-
mai' throughout.

come from?' 'How many shots did you hear?' 'Are you sure it was a gun?' I am not, but it is some time before she is satisfied that I have made a mistake. In the past a comment like this would have provoked minimal curiosity and would have been dismissed as 'Just someone hunting in the forest'. But this time is different and Nani appears to be frightened. 'What are you frightened of?' I ask. She is quiet for a while and then answers, 'I am frightened of the Maobādi'.[3]

An unmarried middle-aged woman, Nani lives with a young female relative and two small children in her large family home in a Tamu village a day's walk away from Pokhara in Kaski district.[4] Her mother died in the early 1990s and her father, a highly respected ex-Gurkha officer, died some years ago. The death of both her parents combined with the out-migration of several young male relatives who lived in the house have left her feeling particularly vulnerable. Nani has always been scared at night. The thick wooden doors of the large house, which were perceived to be able to keep out unwanted visitors, no longer provide adequate security. 'With just two of us here and the children anyone could get in', she comments. Nani is reluctant to say more but confirms what I have heard from other people: the Maoists are in the forests and sometimes they come into the village looking for guns and money. The following day she tells me in hushed tones that not only are the Maobadi in the forest but they also come into certain hamlets of the village during the day to give speeches. I ask her if Tamus are involved, she is non-committal 'I don't know, maybe, mostly they are other *jāt.*' Other villagers express similar opinions.

Until relatively recently most Tamu villagers, when asked who the Maobadi were, answered that they were 'Brahmans, Chetris, Magars, other people from other districts'. While the Maobadi were an abstraction it was possible to think of them as 'outsiders'—remote, distant, unconnected people who posed a threat but not a local one. Maoists, however, can no longer be thought of in these terms as they

---

[3]The Communist Party of Nepal (Maoist) declared a 'People's War' in February 1996. While the epicentre of the movement is the western hill districts of Rukum, Jajarkot, Salyan, and Rolpa, the Maoists are active throughout Nepal. Maoists have been a presence in Gorkha district—in which Tamus are in a majority—since relatively early in their campaign. Maoist activity in Kaski district—the focus of this paper—is more recent. Most conversations in this chapter took place in Tamu Kyui. I am responsible for translating them into English.

[4]While the village consists of a majority of Tamus it also includes Damai and Kami occupational caste groups.

are now present in the local landscape and while they are mostly strangers they are not exclusively so.

This paper draws on a series of conversations with Tamus concerning Maoist activity in the districts of Kaski and Lamjung. These conversations reveal two recurring themes: older people's reluctance to accept that Tamu youth are involved in the Maobadi and their surprise when they discover women's involvement. The key to these responses I suggest are to be found in village-based relations of power, gender, and kinship which favour men and older people. By joining the Maoists young Tamu women are exploring different possibilities of being a woman and together with young men are experiencing themselves and are experienced by others as people with power. Participation in the Maoists, I suggest, also enables village youth to realign themselves in relation to the discourse of modernity, which up until now has entirely focused on the town. Like the town the Maoists provide paths out of the village into a world where the older structures and alliances are re-configured. Participation in town life is limited to those with resources such as money and education but participation in the Maoists is available to all.

While the presence of the Maobadi in the local landscape is real and my middle-aged Tamu informants perceive them as a threat, the Maoists have also become a focus around which pre-existing unexpressed concerns are surfacing. Talking about the Maobadi provides an indirect way of talking about conflict between neighbours and kin and the fears associated with these conflicts.

TALKING ABOUT THE MAOBADI

Three weeks after the discussions with Nani I am travelling through the uplands en route back from the excavations. It is raining heavily and we decide to stay overnight in a shepherd's hut. We are a small 'advance party' escorting an ill colleague back to the village. We sit around the fire joking and chatting through the long evening. As the night is cold we block off the hut's second entrance to increase the temperature. There is some banter about blocking off the door so that the Maobadi cannot come in. Aachyō, a farmer who is presently employed by the Project to porter and assist with the excavations, comments 'Don't worry the Maobadi are not in the *hye* (uplands) around here. I am often up in these parts and I have never met them.'

A few days later I am in a different village visiting a middle-aged friend I have known for many years. In the early morning as we sit beside the fire drinking tea. Didi comments: 'The Maobadi are in the forest just outside the village.' 'Who are they?' I ask. 'Outsiders', she comments but adds: 'Young Tamu people meet up with them in the forest but they are not Maobādi, they just meet them.' While Didi is frightened she is not as fearful as Nani. She is neither as well off nor alone and she insists that although the Maoists are in the vicinity, they do not come into her village.

The Maobadi are in the forests: the ecological zone between the villages and the uplands. Those I spoke to see them as a threat, which escalates in relation to relative wealth. People with large houses, guns, money, and gold are more at risk than poorer less well-resourced people. That the threat comes from the forest is congruent with Tamu ideas about the forest as a potentially frightening place. People have an ambivalent relationship with the forest. While they are dependent on it for firewood, bamboo, medicinal, and edible plants, it contains many dangers. People working in or walking through the forest are vulnerable to attack by ghosts, angered gods, and other spirit forms. Illness and even death can be attributed to an encounter with a forest spirit. The demise of several villagers known to me on return from the forest was attributed to their having been 'eaten' by a forest spirit. Despite widely employed strategies to cope with the uncertainties of the forest including collective calendrical rituals and individual offerings to local gods, the dangers are never fully mitigated.

Human danger in the forest is not new—the lower trails that lead to the town are perceived to contain thieves and other various categories of 'bad people' (*akyhuraba mhi-mai*). Villagers believe themselves to be powerless in the face of such people but they can minimize their risk by travelling in large groups, avoiding carrying large sums of money, and not wearing expensive jewellery. Maoists are just the latest edition to the pantheon of intimidating human and spirit forest-based beings. 'Maoists' are a shifting ever-expanding category, which includes the guerrillas and a bewildering mixture of others who masquerade as Maoists and lacking ideological commitment to anything other than themselves are perceived to wreck havoc of a much worse kind. I frequently heard it said, 'While Maoists want money and guns they speak nicely and explain their ideas whereas the others just want money.' 'Fear of Maoists' is also a fear of what can be done in the name of Maoism. As an informant explained:

Anyone could kill you these days and say it was the Maobadi and nothing would be done about it. You could be killed by your enemies or by people who are angry with you for some reason and want revenge. You could even be killed for no reason at all by people who just don't like you or are jealous of you. It's frightening.

The spatial landscape is being re-drawn and the boundaries between the 'safety' of the village and the 'danger' of the forest are becoming more diffuse. The forests which have always been potentially fearful places, have become frightening in a new way and the dangers that lurk in them transgress the existing boundaries between 'safety'/ 'danger', 'self'/'other'. For Nani, who rarely leaves the village and has always made strong distinctions between the 'safety' that lies within and the 'danger' that lurks outside, it is un-nerving. The fears of the night are simultaneously more pronounced and more diffuse. It is probable that someone will come for money and/or her father's gun, a gun to which she is particularly attached. Who will come, however, is less certain.

The changing spatial landscape brings into question the possibility of changes in the social landscape. While it is undeniable that there are new forest-based dangers, which extend into the village it is less clear what role Tamu people play in this re-alignment. The middle-aged and elderly villagers I spoke to are reluctant to acknowledge that local youth are involved with the Maoists. This may be partly to do with definitions. When Maoists move into an area those in leadership positions are usually from other districts while a significant proportion of the 'rank and file' are recruited locally. If villagers like Didi and Nani define 'Maoists' as those in authority then it is possible for them maintain that Tamu youth are either 'not Maoists' or 'meeting Maoists but not joining them'. Alternatively it may simply be true that young people in the Tamu villages do not join the Maoists. I suggest, however, that the picture is more complex and that people join the Maobadi for diverse and complicated ideological, personal, social, economic, and cultural reasons. People also join because of intimidation or because they have become personally entangled in complex situations in which joining is the best or only option. In many cases excessive police violence has prompted involvement.[5] A major factor in recruitment is disenchantment with the present political and socio-economic climate. It is well known that democracy has not fulfilled its promises, that corruption is widespread, and the most

[5]This reason does not presently apply to the area I work in as there are almost no police posts and police presence in the villages is rare.

marginalized remain on the margins. Maoist activity is particularly extensive in the most impoverished areas of the country.

On the basis of socio-economic status it could be argued that the Tamu-mai are in a relatively better position than many other people and because of this do not choose to join the Maoists. The picture of a relatively wealthy people highly recruited into the British and Indian armies is, however, incomplete. Although significant numbers do serve in these armies, they do so in lower numbers than previously, and most young men who seek to enter the more highly sought after British army do not succeed because of intense competition and limited places. While many young people obtain work overseas, there remain significant numbers of youth who do not wish to farm but find it difficult to get other employment. Over the course of the last ten years I have watched many young men leave the village to seek outside employment. Some succeed but there are others who don't and return to the village disappointed. Although significant numbers of young Tamu people have received an education, most face limited job opportunities, particularly within the government bureaucracy.

During the elections in the early and mid 1990s I was based in the village and had an opportunity to observe political activity affiliated with electioneering. While there was a strong base of support for the Congress Party in the area, there was also considerable support for various communist parties. Large numbers of young people in particular supported the communists. On one occasion I was present when several older women warned their young male relatives against becoming involved in communist political activity in the village and urged them to vote for the Congress Party. The women perceived communism to be dangerous in part because of the experiences of family members who served in the British army during the communist insurrection in Malaysia. Despite the resonance of the experience of fighting communists and high-profile Congress electioneering in the area, support for the communist parties during the early election campaigns remained high. While this may represent an ideological receptivity among some young Tamus to left-wing ideas which may well find expression in support for the Maobadi, it is necessary to be cautious. 'Communism' in 1990 meant a great many things and was often more about alternatives and increased opportunities than left-wing policies. For example, among the Kathmandu-based thangka painters that Sharon Hepburn (personal communication) studied, communism meant 'not Congress, and not Panchayat ... and the government will give us facilities'.

The Maobadi include people from diverse ethnic backgrounds. As their presence expands in Kaski district it could be expected that they would recruit Tamus. Although people I interviewed stated that Tamus in Kaski (and some said Lamjung also) are not Maobadi, evidence from Lamjung suggests otherwise.

POKHARA—MAY 2000

'Bir Maya'—a married woman in her thirties who works outside the home—is originally from a Lamjung village. We are in her sitting room. I ask her about the political situation. She shakes her head and comments: 'Things have really changed in Nepal, you don't know what might happen at any time. It is not a peaceful country anymore. It is very worrying.' 'Are Tamus involved?' I ask. She replies:

I used to think they weren't, but now I know that they are. Recently they came into my village looking for guns. The most shocking thing for my relatives was that they knew some of the members of the group—they were from the local area and they were Tamu. The thing that astonished them most of all was that there were teenage Tamu girls in the group who performed gymnastics.[6] They could hardly believe their eyes. Before they left the Maobadi told the villagers that if they ever identified any members of the group they would be killed.

Shortly afterwards 'Yam Bahadur', a retired Gurkha in his forties who lives in Pokhara, tells me what he calls an 'amazing story' about how a development office has been bombed in a village close to the town:

One day a pregnant woman arrived at the office saying that she was tired and as she couldn't reach her destination that night she asked if she could stay the night in the office. Everyone loves a pregnant woman and so the staff let her stay. But she wasn't pregnant with a baby she was pregnant with bomb-making equipment. During the night when everyone was sleeping she got out her explosives and put them round the office and then she blew it up. In the morning when the staff arrived the office had been bombed and the woman had gone.

Much of what people know about the Maobadi has been passed to them through the telling and re-telling of stories, which may or

[6]This is likely to refer to the 'dance' sections of Maoist 'cultural' performances which often accompany Maoist-convened mass meetings and are aimed at maintaining the populist facade.

may not be 'true'. I am less concerned here with the precise details and 'truth' of Maobadi stories than I am with examining people's reactions to these stories and in doing so to explore the cultural meanings of these images. I am also interested in examining ways in which the Maoists have become a focus for the expression of previously unstated concerns about village conflict.

In order to explore older Tamus fears about the involvement of their youth, and the attractions that the Maobadi might hold for them, I consider dominant constructions of kinship, gender, and hierarchy in village Tamu society. This examination emphasizes the 'greyness' inherent in these constructions, as prescriptiveness co-exists with fluidity. The behaviour of young Tamu Maoists that shocks older villagers is in fact based on pre-existing understandings. What is different is their particular combination and the threatening associations.

KINSHIP AND HIERARCHY

Tamu people place enormous emphasis on people's relatedness to others. The first step to knowing a person is to work out their relationship to you and in the absence of one to create one. Kinship in a Tamu world places people in known categories that guide social interaction. Kinship, however, is not the only basis for relationship: people are also linked through friendships forged by membership in co-operative work and age-grade groups. In a world that is far from the projected ideal of harmony, cohesion, and mutual assistance, work and age-grade colleagues, along with kin, provide the most consistent source of support, security, and certainty.

Idioms which emphasize solidarity co-exist with idioms of divisiveness. Relationships with kin are just as often fraught with problems. The reasons are complex and multiple and are often to do with long-standing arguments, differences of opinion, and sibling rivalry. Such problems are expressed in shifting alliances and sometimes the violation of expected norms of behaviour. For example, I know of a case when a male householder would not give the required 'wife-giver's cloth' (*asyõkoi*) to enable a funeral to take place because of long-standing animosity with the lineage of the deceased. I also know of a family where the usual norm of patrilineal inheritance has been ignored in favour of inheritance on the mother's side of the family.

Reciprocity and hospitality are highly valued by the Tamu-mai. Visitors frequently appear unannounced and depending on their status must be treated lavishly. The notion of abundance often outweighs reality and requires careful negotiation so that giving is balanced with retaining while still maintaining honour. Importance is placed on presenting an image of solidarity in front of outsiders. This desire particularly marks villagers' dealings with high-caste Hindus with whom Tamus often experience an ambiguous relationship that combines derision with admiration and resentment. During my recent visit I was informed about a feud between two youth groups but told 'not to tell the visitors' (three foreign and two Nepali archaeologists). Most importantly, I was under no circumstances to tell the Nepalis: a Brahman and a Chetri.

In the face of adversity Tamus stick together.[7] When confronted with difficult or painful situations they rely on each other for assistance and support. As McHugh writes:

... the usual response to perceived suffering or spiritual danger is to immerse the person in human company and to offer gifts. People come to sit all night with the bereaved after a death, and friends and neighbours will also fill the house of someone who has suffered lesser misfortune like a robbery or the elopement of a child .... A woman in childbirth may also be surrounded by companions while she labours. The presence of others and gifts that acknowledge relationship bring comfort to those in distress (McHugh 1993: 209).

The other side of this enveloping and supportive ethos is that people make constant demands on each other for various forms of assistance that—as noted above—cannot always be met. As McHugh (1989: 78) explains, it is rude to refuse and so people make excuses saying that they have prior commitments or that there is no more of a certain requested item. Outward harmony is maintained and resources are protected but at a deeper level this behaviour—which everyone participates in—creates a widespread sense of mistrust. The separation between ideal and actual behaviour causes suspicion and, as McHugh (ibid.) notes, Tamus often doubt 'the truth of others' words and question others' commitment to relationships'. Others' actions are watched closely and people are especially sensitive to personal snubs and to lapses in gift-giving and hospitality. Suspicion of other people's behaviour is paralleled by a concern about one's own behaviour. Tamus worry that they have not measured up and have made mistakes or omissions, which could lead to retribution. Just as they worry about possible slights and insults to deities and

---

[7] As Macfarlane (2001), supported by McHugh (2001), notes, this ethos remains central even in urban centres like Pokhara.

ancestors which will lead the aggrieved to take revenge on themselves or their loved ones, people worry about slights to fellow humans and wonder about their effects.

An egalitarian ethos co-exists with marked status differences that occur along lines of gender, age, and wealth. Clan-based relations of hierarchy among the Tamu-mai are contentious. The writing of seventeenth- and nineteenth-century Hindu-authored genealogies (*vamsāvalī*) portrayed one group of lineages, the *Sǭi* (Np. *Cārjāt*), as being 'superior' to the other, the *Kugi* (Np. *Sorājāt*). This is highly contested by the *Kugi* (see Pettigrew 1995). *Sǭi* s, because of historical alliances, have had greater opportunities to create status and consider themselves to be of higher status. *Kugis*, on the other hand, do not recognize them as such and look to domains such as the army and ritual practice to acquire status. In the village that I know best, more *Sǭi* men are prominent members of the influential Village Committee, but the wealthiest family is a *Kugi* 'army family'.

Relationships are conceived of in hierarchical terms with young people showing respect and deference to older people. Older men who form the majority of the Village Development Committee hold formal positions of power within villages. Middle-aged or older women also participate but in much lower numbers. Young people are excluded from these positions unless they have a specified professional role such as Annapurna Conservation Area Project development worker. While the 'traditional' forms of youth collectives such as the *rodhi*[8] no longer exist, contemporary youth collective activities centre on 'youth groups'. These groups do not have the formal institutionalized organizational structure of the *rodhi* and play a mainly social role such as dancing to raise funds for activities and outings. While a structural position suggests that young people have few scripts for power, an emphasis on agency illustrates that it is not so clear-cut. Despite normative comments by both old and young about the lack of power of the latter there are many ways in which young people do not conform. A friend commented on her youth:

Officially young people are meant to do what older people say but actually they don't. When I was a teenager my male friends in particular used to spend much of their time going back and forwards between the village and Pokhara. They were either meant to be at school or collecting grass for the buffalo but

8'Youth associations' in which young people participated in social activities, undertook co-operative agricultural work, and learnt craft and other related skills.

they weren't. They were wandering round the bazaar and most of the time their parents didn't know what they were up to.

It is often more about maintaining the appearance of respect and obedience than actually ensuring it. As McHugh (personal communication) comments, there is

often surface agreement to parental directives although the actions of teenagers were not in keeping with those ... [P]arents often knew (the lack of conformity being obvious and sometimes even involving parental cooperation) about this yet as long as all the surface respect-and-obedience behaviours were in place, they were willing to accept their children's actions ... [I]t seemed like preserving the structure of status and power and their outward appearances was more important than preventing deviations in behavior by the children.

Young people's lives are especially complex. Many no longer wish to farm and struggle to get 'ahead' by 'going to foreign' or re-locating to the town. This is an option, however, that is more readily available to young men. Out-migration for young women is more difficult and usually depends on having a pre-existing network in a foreign country and must be fitted in with the constraints of parents' marriage plans. The roads that lead out of the village and towards the consumer images and goods of a wider world are notoriously convoluted. Youth underemployment is widespread and 'going to foreign' requires monetary resources and a particular type of knowledge that village youth often do not have. Many fall prey to unscrupulous agents who take their deposits but don't provide visas or jobs. While some remain in the village by choice, there are others who remain from lack of choice.[9] A common answer to enquiries about residence and livelihood is 'I am not educated, I am poor, I didn't get a chance, and so I stay in the village, what to do? I am not lucky.' A young man I have known for many years recently re-located to the outskirts of Pokhara where he has bought some land. He explains that while he wishes to farm he doesn't wish to do so in the village:

It's just too hard there. Every year hail comes and, if you are unlucky, you lose some of your crop. When this happens, you have to buy rice from the town and carry it up to the village and that's really hard. If I lose some of my crop down here, I just go into town, buy the rice and transport it back on the bus.

[9]While it is generally agreed that most young people prefer to live what is perceived as an easier life in the town there are some who choose to remain in the village.

The education in the village isn't very good. I want my children to have more choices than I did and by moving to the town they have choices.

Lack of choice is matched by the consumer images of abundant choice that emulate from the town and increasingly through the recently acquired battery-operated televisions in the village. The rapidly expanding consumerist world of the town is one where new supermarkets and new specialist stores constantly open and where people increasingly communicate by email. The usual choice for young Tamu urban school-leavers waiting to go to college is computer training. This creates a stark contrast with a village-based world that is largely unchanging and technologically unsophisticated. In the ten years of my research, while a few people have bought televisions, no new shops have opened in the village and the only expansion of available consumer goods is the availability of soft drinks. The continuous movement of people between village and town ensures that village youth encounter the urban consumerist world on a regular basis. These youth who are identified as villagers, with the attendant negative connotations of this designation, do not observe from a neutral stance. Financially unable to participate, they are relegated to the position of outsider-observer. Frequent encounters with the town are more the privilege of young men whose movements are less constrained than women's. Young women have fewer opportunities for deviating from 'traditional' gender roles and thereby are somewhat less exposed to the urban/village contrast and its associated conflicts than their male counterparts.

GENDER CONSTRAINTS AND CONTRADICTIONS

Tamu women are often described by their Hindu neighbours as being strong-willed, outspoken, and autonomous. As Des Chene (1998: 42) notes, this may be said in criticism (strong-headed, wilful) or in admiration (resilient, courageous). Anthropologists have also portrayed them in a similar fashion:

What will strike the visitor to this and other highland Tibeto-Burman areas is the confidence and openness of the women. Although they may eat after men, though they do not act as priests, or engage very actively in public life, or plough, they do most of the other things that men do and are considered to be their equals .... Talking with both Gurung men and women, they regard the sexes as equal, and if anything, argue that women, who hold the purse-strings and guide the family and village society, are the most powerful ... They run shops and businesses; in their husband's absence they often run the farm, hire labour, sell crops and arrange everything to do with planting and harvesting (Macfarlane & Gurung 1993: 26–7).

British officers who recruit and work with Tamu men have expressed similar opinions: 'Gurkha women ... enjoy a freedom unusual in the East and are well able to stand up for themselves ... and are very outspoken' (Leonard 1965: 48 quoted in Des Chene 1998).

My fieldwork and the work of others have built on this earlier work and have added other levels of complexity. Although there are few ritual or purity restrictions and a relatively loose division of labour, there are, as Des Chene points out,

many quiet forms of constraints on the 'freedom' of Gurung women woven so finely into the texture of daily life that they can be difficult to discern ... structural constraints of the marriage system, inheritance, and domestic authority, and ... cultural constraints of public opinion, family honor, and definitions of possible female comportment (Des Chene 1998: 42).

Young women in particular emphasize the constraints on their movements, the scrutiny of their behaviour, and the pain of leaving home on marriage to move to the lowest-ranking position in their in-laws' home. The restrictions on women's behaviour, which are often very subtle, are differently negotiated by women. Some years ago my then research assistant decided to buy a pair of trainers to wear while walking between villages. She wore them for several weeks and then abruptly stopped wearing them. When I asked her why, she replied that villagers had told her that such shoes were not appropriate footwear for a woman. As the young wife of an absent soldier she felt obliged to conform. In contrast, my present research assistant, an unmarried woman in her thirties, always wears trainers when walking between villages. As she is unmarried and not expecting to marry, she is in a position to make decisions with less concern for the opinion of others.

Ideas about deference, respect, and moral female behaviour are closely linked to ideas about how to use the body. Women are expected to act with decorum, to dress modestly, and to move graciously with minimal exposure of flesh even when carrying large loads of buffalo feed or firewood. Women's bodies are much more circumscribed than men's and while men frequently dress in Western clothes and

318 Resistance and the State: Nepalese Experiences

take part in sports, women do not.[10] A friend outlines some of the ideals of female behaviour in relation to the body: 'Women have to control their bodies. They shouldn't make big movements, they should walk slowly, they shouldn't run and they shouldn't walk around too much on their own.' While notions of bodily decorum apply to women of all ages, the restrictions on travel are directed in particular towards young unmarried women. Older women, whether they be married, single, or divorced, often travel widely between town and village and to other districts.

TAMU YOUTH AMONG THE MAOISTS

Membership in the Maoists directly addresses the structural inequalities, which constrain young people, as Maoism emphasizes the equality of all regardless of age or gender. Positions of leadership are awarded on merit rather than on the basis of age, gender, or clan/caste affiliation. Without adequate data it is impossible to describe accurately relations of hierarchy within the Maobadi. Guerrilla organizations usually impose many constraints on their members and subtle (or not so subtle) hierarchies evolve. From what is known, however, it is clear that young people, both female and male, are in positions of authority within the Maobadi, leading squads of combatants and organizing and directing propaganda campaigns. According to Maoist literature, women

are leaders, commanders of guerrilla squads constituting of men and women .... In each guerrilla squad it has made the policy of recruiting at least two women guerrillas (in each guerrilla squad there are about 9–11 members). Women guerrillas work as combatants at night and do propaganda and production work during day time. Where circumstances demand, exclusive women's guerrilla squads have been constituted, but this is more of an exception than the rule .... Where women are not directly involved in fighting guerrilla warfare they are working as support force for the People's War. They function as organisers, as propagandists, as cultural activists, as logistics suppliers, as nurses for the wounded fighters and cadres, as espionage workers ... They are also trained to prepare locally made gun-powder (Parvati 1999: 7).[11]

[10]While some young townswomen wear Western clothes and take part in sports, older and married women usually do not.

[11]Research undertaken in 2002 suggests that gender relations within the Maobadi are complex. Ex-Maoist women whom I interviewed complained that, although they spent a lot of time educating village women about the need for

When I ask people why they are frightened of the Maoists, they tell me that it is because 'people have died'. Maoists threaten death and this is shocking but expected. What is shocking and unexpected is that Tamus, including young women, are involved. When Maoists entered my friend's village, the enduring images that they and she emphasized were those concerning the membership of the group and their behaviour. They were Tamus, people they knew, young women with guns who threatened them with death. My friend explained to me that while her relatives felt that the loss of a gun and some money was very disturbing and the threat of death even more so, the social and kinship implications of the encounter were deeply shocking. In this brief encounter accepted notions of social relationships, based on an orderly progression of age overlaid with ideas of gender-appropriate behaviour, were completely subverted.

It is difficult for older Tamus to accept the involvement of village youth in the Maobadi. It is widely believed that many of the town-dwelling youth have 'gone off' (*nhoyai*) and are behind much of the socially disruptive behaviour in Pokhara. Despite frequent evidence to the contrary it is still believed that village youth are 'well behaved'. 'Well behaved' means more or less accepting a version of the world in which both young men and women respect and obey their elders, accepting that the elders will make important life decisions on their behalf, accepting the orderly progression of age which confers status and power in a protracted and drawn-out manner, and, in the case of young women, accepting additional gender-imposed constraints. While many young Tamus do not accept certain aspects of this vision— for example, elopement is quite common and young people negotiate and interpret constraints differently—most continue to accept the over-riding principles of this worldview.

By joining the Maoists young people forge new relationships to the existing power relations in the villages. They acquire a previously denied public voice, albeit often at the end of a gun. From the per-spective of villagers, if Tamus are Maoists the division of people into recognizable and predictable categories on the basis of kinship,

gender equality, they themselves did not enjoy equal relationships with their male colleagues. One informant stated that she '... wished to join a women's party as that is the only place where I can fight for women's rights'. In April 2002 I interviewed members of a family who were forced to leave their village, as they were supporters of the Congress Party. Male Maoists had sexually abused several of the female members of this family.

gender, and hierarchy is brought into question. While villagers' knowledge of Maoist ideology—and therefore the full implications of the dogma—may be limited, they are aware that those who join the Maobadi have new allegiances. The usual manner of relating in which the young acquiesce to their elders and where tasks are allocated along lines of hierarchy and gender no longer hold any potency. At any time the son or daughter of a friend or relative may walk into your courtyard and reveal the changed nature of their relationship to you and, knowing your resources, will know what to demand. When I asked a friend to what extent he thought the wealthier villagers are under threat he said:

It depends on how much people know about what they have in their houses. If it is known that they keep a lot of money or gold then they are definitely more vulnerable. Of course the people close to you know what you have and so do their children as throughout their lives they have helped out in your house.

Even more frightening is the thought that someone who holds a grudge against you will turn up. People are aware that landlords and moneylenders who are deemed to have exploited others are targets, but they do not know how people are selected for retribution or threat. Nor do they know how relations between wealthy villagers and poorer employees are evaluated. Will people be judged on the basis of what are considered 'normal' hierarchical relations along the lines of caste? People talk about how their neighbours treat others—particularly those considered to be of lower status—but they do so from their own particular situated position and in the context of the history of past relationships. Villagers also worry about being accused of being Maoist sympathizers. What would happen if the police entered the area and accused them of being involved with the Maobadi? Concerns about Maoists, those who pose as Maoists, and the police are juxtaposed to pre-existing ones discussed earlier concerning the trustworthiness and behaviour of others. Just as talk about angry and vengeful aggrieved deities is analogous to talking about angry and aggrieved people, talk about 'fear of Maoists' is also talk about fear of neighbours. Village conflicts and fears are projected onto the Maobadi when Tamu youth become guerrillas. As Maoists they provide the link, bringing local knowledge and local conflicts into the realm of the wider political arena.

While men can shoot and many own guns, women do not. There is a long tradition among Tamu men of joining armies and going to war and there is a related tradition of women staying at home. Women

are not expected to travel widely unless in the company of male relatives. Women involved in Maoist activity, however, travel extensively
and in the company of unrelated men. Young gymnastic-performing
female Maoists challenge ideas of moral embodied behaviour. The
exaggerated free-flowing movements of gymnastics, which involve the
total body, are in direct contrast to the usual controlled embodied
way of being a woman. The performance of 'cart-wheels' and other
similar movements construct a different female spatiality, one that
is more aligned to a male way of using the body. Likewise the images
of women with guns subvert usual notions of martiality and gender.

Maoist women construct a different notion of the female body
alongside a different notion of movement and relatedness, which
combine to challenge received ideas about female personhood. These
images, however, despite their ability to shock older villagers build on
pre-existing understandings. In spite of widely expressed prescriptive
ideas of correct female behaviour there are many ways to be a woman.
My friend who talked about her youth earlier in the paper and who
is presently concerned about the behaviour of her own teenage
daughters admits that her own behaviour was far from the ideal:

I was one of the few girls who stayed on at school and because of this I became
very friendly with my male classmates. I used to go everywhere with them. I
didn't stay at home and only walk around with other girls or my relatives.
Your Nani [my 'sister'] used to tell me off and tell me to stop walking round
with the boys and behave like a girl but I didn't! Off I went! As you can see
it didn't affect me. I married well [to a British Gurkha] and to this day I am
still friendly with some of those 'boys'.

CONCLUSION: MODERNITY AND THE MAOBADI

I suggest that participation in the Maoists enables village youth to
participate in a new type of modernity. Young villagers see themselves
and are seen as marginal to the 'good and proper life' (McHugh 2001:
114) offered by town living and enjoyed by those with the money to
re-locate. By taking up the Maoist option, they no longer have to look
to the town and 'foreign' to be 'at the heart of the action'. Membership
in the Maoists re-configures perceptions of a consumerist world
that excludes them. The rhetoric of Maoism constructs an alternative
version of modernity, one in which the consumerist version is
rejected on ideological premises. Village youth reject that which they
were previously excluded from and in doing so re-position themselves
as centre-stage. Images of rural youth which were previously unseen
or were presented as 'backward' in media terms are now literally 'front-

page' as the covers of popular magazines are now as likely to feature gun-toting young women as they are to feature the ubiquitous beauty queens of recent years.

Images of young Tamu Maoists subvert dominant constructions of interaction based on kinship, hierarchy, and gender. This paper illustrates, however, that there has always been more than one way to relate to kin, be a young person, or to be a woman. While the images of young armed gymnastic-performing women include some behaviours which fall loosely within the accepted parameters of female behaviour, they shock because they are unexpected, extreme, public, and threatening. They shock also because they illustrate that the concept of a 'safe' Tamu village world and an 'unsafe' forest are indistinguishable. Propaganda- and gun-carrying Maoists transgress various village spatial boundaries from the public ones of street and resting-place to the private ones of courtyard and veranda.

Paralleling the violation of spatial boundaries is the violation of boundaries between people. With the arrival of the Maoists, affiliations are becoming less clear and previous understandings based on kinship, age, and gender can no longer be relied on to guide social interaction. New alliances have formed and along with them is the ever-present possibility that local knowledge and conflicts will be brought into the realm of the wider political arena. The fear and uncertainty associated with the Maobadi is also a fear about what can be done by others on the pretext of Maoism. Maoists reflect pre-existing worries that people have concerning the behaviour of others. While vengeful neighbours have always been present it was perceived that they were kept largely in check by the old allegiances and the customary village-based manner of maintaining order backed-up when necessary by the police. The spread of guerrilla activity, however, has brought a feeling of lawlessness. New alliances combined with fear of what can be done in the name of Maoism are exacerbated by the widespread belief that the police can no longer provide even the nominal security of the past and may in fact perpetrate violence. As the spatial and social boundaries are re-configured, the village is in danger of becoming as much a 'jungle' as the forest and frightened villagers are left to wonder what they can do to deal with such unprecedented threats.

POSTSCRIPT

Since this chapter was first written in 2000 the 'People's War' has escalated significantly. In November 2001 the Maoists broke a four-month-long ceasefire and launched attacks on army and police posts. In response, the government of Nepal imposed a State of Emergency, which effectively suspended most civil rights and for the first time deployed the army to fight the Maoists. After a year of continued conflict and a rising death toll among Maoists, state forces, and civilians alike, as well as a political crisis in Parliament, the king sacked the Prime Minister and put the democratic process on hold on 4th October, 2002. January 2003 saw a second ceasefire called between the Maoists and the government, and the establishment of a schedule for peace talks. The talks collapsed in August of that year, and were followed by an escalation of violence: over 1,000 people died in the following four months alone. On 1st February 2005 King Gyanendra seized power and arrested democratic party leaders. The aftermath of the royal coup saw a deterioration of security and no government peace plan. In September 2005 the Maoists announced a unilateral ceasefire in order to facilitate building an alliance with the political parties. The government did not reciprocate the ceasefire and the Maoists withdrew it in early January 2006, which prompted an escalation of violence. Human rights groups, such as Amnesty International and Human Rights Watch, have extensively documented the human rights violations committed by both the Maoists and state forces (www.amnesty.org.uk, www.hrw.org), and the conflict has cost over 13,000 lives since 1996, with hundreds of thousands displaced. In 2004 Amnesty International reported that Nepal had the highest number of 'disappearances' in the world in 2003 and 2004. At the end of 2005 the media watchdog, Journalists without Borders, noted that more than half of its 1,006 cases of censorship came from Nepal (www.Worldpress.org).

The Maoists claim the districts of Lamjung and Kaski as part of their Tamu Autonomous Region: Tamuwan. Tamu-mai are in leadership positions in Tamuwan and the villagers quoted in this article, who, in 2000 were reluctant to accept that Tamu-mai could be Maoists, no longer dispute this, nor do they dispute the involvement of women. They are now aware that some Tamu women have achieved seniority in the party, since a well-known Maoist leader in Lamjung, Kausila Tamu (now deceased), was a young Tamu woman. Despite the involvement of some Tamu-mai in the movement, the vast majority of people in these villages are non-aligned civilians. Daily life is severely disrupted as villagers try to survive in the 'crossfire' between the warring sides (see Pettigrew 2004, in press). Forced to feed and shelter Maoist combatants, and to participate in

Maoist-led activities, they are frequently suspected by the security forces of being insurgents, sometimes with tragic consequences. Vulnerable to accusations and counter-accusations, and in fear of their lives, and the possible abduction of their children, significant numbers of Tamu-mai have relocated to urban centres.

Recent ethnographic research on motivations for joining the Maoists supports and amplifies the arguments made in this article. For some youth the choices are clearly considered, for others circumstances are serendipitous, and still others join due to unavoidable contingencies. Some fight because they believe in the cause or to address structural inequalities of gender, caste, poverty, and marginalization, while some join to avenge the death of family members and friends. For still others the Maoists provide opportunities, skills, and subsistence. Some join because they were under suspicion by the security forces and had few options but to participate; others join in reaction to arrest and torture or because their friends joined. Some found the dancing and rhetoric at propaganda events appealing or were attracted by the power acquired when carrying a gun. Some are conscripted, while others join voluntarily. By whatever route they join, once in the movement, should they change their minds, all will encounter difficulties leaving (as well as encountering problems and stigma when returning home).

Since this piece was written, the literature on the 'People's War' has burgeoned (for overviews, see references given on p. 357). Considerable attention has been paid to gender issues (for example, Gautam 2001; Gautam, Banskota, & Manchanda 2001; Leve 2005; Mainali 2004; Manchanda 2001; Thapa 2003; Parvati 2003a, 2003b; Pettigrew & Shneiderman 2004; Shakya 2003; Sharma & Prasain 2004). The relationship between ethnicity and the Maoist movement has also received attention (see de Sales this volume; Lecomte-Tilouine 2004, this volume; S. Sharma 2004; Shrestha 2004), as has the role of youth in the movement (Shneiderman & Turin 2004). Despite this extensive literature, there has been relatively limited ethnographic research on the insurgency. This is primarily due to security concerns, access problems, and ethical issues, as well as the fact that the study of violence is a relatively new field of anthropological enquiry. The work that has been undertaken focuses on the relationship between development and the insurgency, ethnicity, the ethics of fieldwork, the impact of the insurgency on rural civilians, women in the Maoist movement, and children and mental health. This work needs to be expanded upon to ensure that the predominantly macro-orientated analysis of the insurgency is balanced with locally focused ethnographic insights.

ORTHOGRAPHY

Most non-English words in this chapter are Tamu Kyui, which is an unwritten Tibeto-Burman language with no standard orthography. I have chosen to use a phonetic approach and render words in their simplest possible spelling.

REFERENCES

Des Chene, M. 1998. 'Fate, Domestic Authority, and Women's Wills' in D. Skinner, A. Pach, and D. Holland (eds) *Selves in Time and Place: Identities, Experience, and History in Nepal.* Lanham: Rowman & Littlewood, pp. 19–50.

Gautam, S. 2001. *Women and Children in the Periphery of the People's War.* Kathmandu: Institute of Human Rights Communications Nepal.

Gautam, S., A. Banskota, & R. Manchanda 2001. 'Where there are no Men: Women in the Maoist Insurgency in Nepal' in R. Manchanda (ed.), pp. 215–51.

Lecomte-Tilouine, M. 2004. 'Ethnic Demands Within Maoism: Questions of Magar Territorial Autonomy, Nationality and Class' in M. Hutt (ed.) *Himalayan 'People's War,'* pp. 112–35. London: Hurst.

Leve, L. 2005. '"Failed Development" and Rural Revolution in Nepal: Rethinking Subaltern Consciousness and Women's Empowerment' (www.yale.edu/agrarianstudies/papers, consulted 31/1/06).

Leonard, R.G. 1965. *Nepal and the Gurkhas.* London: HMSO.

Macfarlane, A. 2001. 'Sliding Down Hill: Some Reflections on Thirty Years of Change in a Himalayan Village' *European Bulletin of Himalayan Research* 20–1: 105–10.

Macfarlane, A. & I.B. Gurung 1993 [1990]. *Gurungs of Nepal: A Guide to the Gurungs.* Kathmandu: Ratna Pustak Bhandar.

McHugh, E. 1989. 'Concepts of the Person among the Gurungs of Nepal' *American Ethnologist* 16: 75–86.

McHugh, E. 1993. 'Culture and the Transformation of Suffering among the Gurungs of Nepal' in C. Ramble and M. Brauen (eds) *Anthropology of Tibet and the Himalaya*, pp. 208–14. Zurich: Volkerkundemuseum der Universitat Zurich.

McHugh, E. 1998. 'Situating Persons: Honor and Identity in Nepal' in D. Skinner, A. Pach, and D. Holland (eds) *Selves in Time and Place: Identities, Experience and History in Nepal*, pp.155–73. Lanham: Rowman & Littlewood.

McHugh, E. 2001. 'Sliding, Shifting, and Re-drawing Boundaries' *European Bulletin of Himalayan Research* 20–1: 113–17.

(continued on page 357)

chapter ten

The Kham Magar Country: Between Ethnic Claims and Maoism

• *Anne de Sales*

INTRODUCTION

I dentity politics were unheard of in the early 1980s, when I carried out my first fieldwork among the Kham Magar, a Tibeto-Burman population of west Nepal. If people felt like comparing or defining themselves, they focused on very local differences: on the dialects of different villages, their specific festival calendars, their different ways of covering haystacks (by means of a cover made of goatskin or with a straw roof), the different itineraries they followed with their flocks, or the boundaries of their communal territories. Subjects like these were discussed again and again. Such conversations presupposed a common shared identity, of course, but there was no context in which Kham Magars needed to articulate it. For example, relations with their cousins, the Magar, the largest minority in Nepal, were undefined and the exploration of differences between Kham Magars and Magars did not appear to be important, at least to the Kham Magar themselves. In sum, Kham Magar villagers preferred to see themselves and to be seen as the inhabitants of one 'country', *desh* in Nepali (the term has been adopted into the Kham Magars' Tibeto-Burman language). A 'country' is a given natural environment in which one is born and where one lives alongside others similar to oneself. It is the Kham Magars' 'country' that has turned out to be the stronghold of the 'People's War' launched four years ago by the revolutionary Maoist

This paper was originally written in French in 1999 and appeared in *Puruṣārtha* 22 (2001). The translation is by David Gellner, whom I wish to thank here.

movement. The life of the Kham Magar has been turned upside-down by this, and many of them have died.

The present essay seeks to answer several questions: Why was this region chosen by the Maoists? How have rural people reacted to the campaigns of politicization originating in the towns? How is that they have found themselves involved in, and how have they allowed themselves to be dragged into, fatal combat? And, finally, how do processes of identity formation develop in the face of these new pressures? I begin by presenting the necessary historical background, in particular the democratic revolution of 1990, which was a turning point for identity politics in Nepal. I will then attempt to explain (i) why the Maoists based themselves in the Kham Magar country, (ii) what techniques the Maoists have used, and (iii) what the motivations of the Kham Magar may be. There is a certain paradox in revolutionaries basing themselves on a tribal heritage from which in principle they distance themselves. Whereas the ethnic ideologues who are concerned with the problems of defining the cultures which they claim to defend often find themselves without any means of political action, the Maoists have skilfully appropriated certain traditional techniques in their strategy for conquering the Kham Magars' territory.[1]

THE HISTORICAL AND POLITICAL CONTEXT

The Revolution of 1990: The Beginnings of Mass Politics

The 'People's Movement' (*jan āndolan*) was officially declared on 18 February 1990 by the Movement for the Restoration of Democracy (MRD) which brought together liberal parties and communists, both of which were banned under the Panchayat regime. After numerous demonstrations, with an official death toll of forty-one, King Birendra lifted the ban on political parties on 8 April. In mid-November he promulgated a new constitution which established parliamentary democracy. The revolution of 1990 marked the beginning of mass politics, for which forty years of profound social change had prepared the country.[2]

---

[1] I will not attempt here to give a complete account of the Maoist movement, which has spread well beyond the region and the population that I analyse here. For early reflections on the Maoist movement, see Ramirez (1997). On Magar ethnic activists, see also Lecomte-Tilovine (ch. 7).

[2] In this first section on the history of Nepal I follow Hoftun, Raeper, and Whelpton (1999), who describe the two democratic revolutions Nepal has experienced in the last half century.

The first democratic revolution in 1950 had put an end to a century of dictatorship by the Rana Prime Ministers. Ultimately, the revolution lasted for a very brief period and only served to restore the Shah dynasty, which had been kept away from the centre of power since 1846. The revolution was the work of a small elite of intellectuals and politicians who had been educated in India and had participated in the nationalist movement for independence there. None the less, the 1950–51 revolution served to open up to the world outside a country that had been turned in on itself since its formation under Prithvi Narayan Shah and his descendants in the second half of the eighteenth century.[3] During the years of his short reign (1951–55), King Tribhuvan, in alliance with the Congress Party and under the close control of India, developed a series of policies which already revealed the priorities that would change the face of the country: economic development financed from abroad (especially India and the USA), and education.

Tribhuvan's son Mahendra took over the reins of power in 1960 after seventeen months of a Congress Party government elected by universal suffrage, and in 1962 he installed the Panchayat system. This regime, described as 'guided democracy', in reality allowed the king to reserve all powers to himself. The ideology on which it was based was inscribed in the Constitution of 1962 and had a profound influence on the country.[4] The project was to build the unity of the nation and to develop national sentiment. Simultaneously, a certain conception of identity was born. In one of his speeches, King Mahendra translated the Western notion of the equality of all citizens into essentially religious (Vaishnavite) terms. In this form of identity, 'all the devotees of Vishnu [have] an identical subtle substance that unites them within the subtle body of Vishnu in the form of Parbrahma.' Thus, all Nepalis are conceived of as identical (*samān*) or 'one and the same' (*ek ra samān*) in their devotion to the nation-state (Burghart 1996: 257).

The efforts to 'build the nation' quickly led to a contradictory situation: in order to avoid ideological conflicts encouraged by political parties, the parties themselves were banned and there was a general repression of the mass media. On the other hand, in order to develop

[3]Some recent work has attempted to qualify this view (see especially Mikesell 1988).
[4]See Gaborieau (1982) for an analysis of the 1962 Constitution.

national identity, schools were established throughout the kingdom.[5] But education played a key role in politicizing the people, who consequently became less and less willing to accept repression from the government. When King Birendra submitted the continuation of the Panchayat regime to a referendum in 1980, his victory over the opposition, which sought the liberalization of political life, was gained only by a narrow margin.

Economic development was another banner waved by the governments of the Panchayat period. But the opening up of the country to a modernity which remained inaccessible to most of its inhabitants[6] only served to provoke frustration among the people who felt themselves to be unfairly neglected. I will return to this point. Thus, even if the revolution of 1990 was also, initially, carried out by an elite of students and city-dwellers, its repercussions were much more profound at all levels of the Nepali population than the first revolution forty years earlier. The revolution was prepared by the gradual development of political awareness in the country; but in its turn the revolution was a key factor in promoting widespread politicization.[7]

Until 1990, rural people were far removed from the centres of power—necessarily so in view of the facts of Nepal's geography. More than two-thirds of the country is made up of mountains where the means of communication are very basic. But, above all, monarchical institutions gave individuals hardly any chance of participating in decisions at the national level. One should not conclude from this that Nepalis passively accepted their lot. The different groups which made up the Nepali population knew how to negotiate the rules that were imposed on them.

Forms of Identity before 1990

Some good examples of the local manipulation of national regulations are provided precisely by the fluctuating identities of ethnic

[5]Whereas literacy stood at 5.3 per cent in 1952, in 1989 it had reached 40 per cent. It should be noted that the population doubled in the same forty-year period (Gurung 1998: 85).
[6]In 1987 the World Bank included Nepal among the seven poorest countries in the world (Gurung 1998: 167).
[7]'This second revolution in Nepal's modern period did not only come as a result of a raised level of political consciousness. The revolution itself made the people politically conscious' (Hoftun, Raeper, and Whelpton 1999: xi).

groups. A national legal code, the Muluki Ain ('law of the country'), was established in 1854. It assigned each group to a very precise position in the hierarchy of castes and regulated the life of the citizens in the smallest details of their life and death. The tribal groups occupy a middle position in this hierarchy, between the Twice-Born or Tāgādhārī who are ritually superior to them, and the Untouchables who are inferior. They form the group of Matwālīs or 'alcohol-drinkers'. Among the latter, there were those who were not permitted to be enslaved, such as Magars and Gurungs, and those who could be enslaved, such as the people of Tibetan origin (known as 'Bhote'), certain groups of Newars, and the Chepang (Höfer 1979: 45).

Each community was granted rights or privileges and duties, which they were quick to use in their relations with the central government. Rights over land and trade were not the same for everyone. Thus, belonging to one group or another had both political and economic consequences. Several studies over the course of the last twenty years have shown how the ethnic identities that can be observed today are the outcome of various processes of mutual accommodation between regional ethnic systems and the policies of a centralizing state.[8]

I was myself able to observe a similar process among a population of miners (*āgrī*) in the Dhaulagiri region. Work in the mines gave individuals of suspect origin (the offspring of intercaste unions, for example) the opportunity to take on a pure identity, and it allowed others to climb in the hierarchy. The government sought to increase the number of miners by giving them various privileges, including that of not being susceptible to enslavement (for example, because of debt). Taking on the status of *āgrī* thus allowed an enslavable alcohol-drinker to be promoted to a more desirable category which included the Magar and the Gurung. Thus, individuals of diverse origin (Magar, Bhote, Chetri) formed communities which were united in the first instance by their occupation and the desire to take advantage of the newly announced rules.

In 1920, the government closed the mines and offered the miners land as compensation. The latter then began to search for a new identity. They took on the name 'Chantyal', and adopted (a) customs from

[8]Cf. Levine (1987) who gives some general reflections on this subject and analyses the case of the Humla region where it is not only individuals but entire villages which have succeeded in changing their ethnic affiliation and their position in the overall Nepalese caste hierarchy. By providing the first analysis of the Muluki Ain of 1854, Höfer (1979) did much to encourage such research in Nepal.

their Magar neighbours, (b) a history that saw them as the descendants of a Rajput clan from west Nepal, and above all (c) a language,
which has become the ultimate defining feature of an ethnic group
(de Sales 1993). The campaigning work of one individual in particular,
Dil Bahadur Chantyal, an emigrant to Kathmandu, was particularly
crucial in arousing this feeling of identity among the villagers to whom
he distributed pamphlets which gave them a summary of their own
culture. He founded an association which had as its primary aim the
acceptance of the Chantyal as a distinct category in the population
census. Only success in establishing the category would legitimate
them as a new ethnic group. It is noticeable that there is a difference
here from the earlier motivations for creating an identity. It is no longer
merely a question of acquiring the means to improve one's political
and economic lot, but also of winning recognition as a Chantyal.

Studies such as these show how individuals have succeeded in
modifying their lot, for all that it was so strictly controlled. They also
show that group attempts to establish identity correspond to given
historical situations. But it is above all the continually changing aspect
of pre-1990 identities that needs to be stressed. Ethnic identities in
this period seem to have been labels that one could change, labels
that had political, economic, and legal reference, rather than a social
or cultural one. Changing a label did not necessarily involve any
existential crisis. It was primarily a question of a more advantageous
adaptation to a given situation.

This frankly instrumentalist vision of identity, seen in the strategic
use of the rules laid down by the 1854 law code, should not cause us
to forget these groups' need for recognition which emerged in the
process of these manipulations, even if such deep-seated sentiments
can easily be exploited for political ends.[9] In Europe this need was
born 'in the middle of the eighteenth century, when the old system of
honours, reserved for a few privileged persons, fell into disuse, and
everyone aspired to his own public recognition, to what one would
come to call one's dignity' (Todorov 1995: 29).

This historical detour through Western thought can help our
understanding of identity in Nepal. In the last hundred years, Nepal
has experienced a profound questioning of the ancient hierarchies
which had provided the taken-for-granted framework of daily life. After

[9]For a discussion, in the Nepalese context, of the debate between primordialists
or essentialists, on the one hand, and instrumentalists or modernists, on the other,
see Gellner (1997a: 6–12).

the conquest of the eighteenth century the different peoples remained attached to their 'countries', from which they drew their 'natural' identity, so to speak, as was suggested above for the Kham Magar—for the old forms of organization were never completely obliterated and can still be seen today. In the 1854 law code all groups are designated as *jāt* or 'species', that is to say, as social units, detached from their territorial base and integrated within the same interdependent system (Burghart 1996: 251–3). Thus, when a new organization was put in place whose aim was the building of a nation, the groups were led to redefine their identity, to find distinguishing elements in their culture, and to establish definitions which were as rigid as they were artificial, in order to achieve recognition. This movement was reinforced after 1990.

THE WARRIOR WHO IS CURSED AND POWERLESS

It is worth considering for a moment this need for recognition as it was expressed by the cultural associations of certain tribal groups even before 1990. The explosion of identity politics which occurred after 1990 may lead one to forget that the first consciousness-raising movements were less concerned with making demands and rather more concerned with self-criticism. One can cite as an example the association for the defence of the language and culture of the Magars, on which we have some fine and valuable observations by a Nepali ethnographer, K.R. Adhikari (1991). This association was formed on the initiative of some Magar soldiers who had retired from the British army. On their return from the Second World War, where many of their fellows died a hero's death, they were struck by the fact that those who had stayed in the village did not seem to appreciate their heroism and continued to have a very low opinion of themselves.

In 1956 the Reform Association of the Magar Society [sic] was formed in 63 districts with the aim of 'root[ing] out the evils that existed in Magar society', i.e. 'over spending and over drinking'. Annual meetings were held in the form of picnics, because the government considered any ethnic meetings to be 'communal propaganda'. During these meetings the Magar accused themselves of being responsible for poverty and 'backwardness' and relied only on their own determination to get out of it. Adhikari was present at a meeting of the association which had become the Nepal Langhali Association (Nepal Langhali Sangh) in April 1989. By this time the issues present at the origin of the movement had developed a political dimension.

Thus in order 'to preserve the language, culture, and identity of the Magars' it was necessary to reconsider

1. Customs of spending on eating and drinking at birth and death rituals beyond limitation of one's means.
2. Excessive belief in ghosts and spirits and the custom of sacrificing animals in the name of gods and goddesses instead of offering just flowers and food ... (Adhikari 1991).

I myself have heard similar proposals from Magars living among other castes who are often better off than they are, or from Kham Magars who, having lived elsewhere, return home with a new perspective on village problems. The image of Magar culture that is revealed here is the negative side of high-caste Hindu values: to tribal excesses, the Brahman opposes his own preference for economizing (to put it at its mildest), his rejection of alcohol, and his worship of pure and vegetarian Hindu divinities. Most important of all, communal rituals—the very activities which are precisely the context in which tribal culture comes into play—are picked out as threatening to it. That which the activists propose to suppress (or weaken) in order to save Magar culture is the very thing that constitutes it.

Other quotations are eloquent. An orator, recalling how the Magars have contributed to the conquest of great Nepal and how they have been praised throughout the world for their courage in the past 100 years, adds that at present, 'The Magars are like those warriors who have forgotten their power and strength because of a curse, and they will remain weak unless they are reminded of their strength for the struggle' (ibid.).

This curse has to be understood as an expression of the Magars' alienation caused by their subordination to the dominant groups in Nepali society, as is proved by the negative image of their own customs reflected in the mirror they hold up to the culture of the high Hindu castes. They are trapped by their contradictory conceptions and this confused feeling paralyses them and ensures that their attempts to participate in the enterprises of modern society usually fail.[10] It is clearly a question of a suffering that is not acknowledged, of a need for recognition. This need can no longer be accommodated within a politics that seeks merely to ameliorate the material conditions

[10]The biographies of villagers who have departed to seek their fortunes make rather depressing reading. Not only are they often the victims of dishonest middlemen, they also have failed to form networks of mutual assistance sufficiently strong to defend themselves.

of life: it needs to be met, in the first place, on the symbolic level. Moreover, it seems as if winning this recognition requires violent means to be employed. The cursed and weak warrior may wish to seek his revitalization in the sacrifices entailed in a revolutionary struggle.

A third and new argument, which was more directly political, made its appearance as a consequence of this discourse in the period leading up to the revolution: 'The Magars are an exploited group. They should no longer tolerate this exploitation, they should struggle for their rights.' It is one thing to play by rules that have been imposed from above, it is quite another to wish to play a part in deciding on new rules. After the revolution of 1990 a new political sensibility, that is to say, the beginnings of a feeling among individuals that they could change the contours of their own social life and participate in the government of the country, penetrated even the most remote villages. This political awareness took several different forms.

Before presenting the different organizations and their ideologies, it is necessary to mention those individuals, who have become increasingly numerous in recent years, who have had experience of realities other than those of the daily life of the village. Whether their personal journeys have been in search of a better education or, more commonly, in search of work, whether they have gone to the flatlands of the Tarai, to the capital, or abroad, they have come into contact with a modernity which, even if it is not viewed as 100 per cent positive, marks a Rubicon. The perception of rural areas like theirs as dead ends, forgotten by the rest of the world, discourages the young people, who are more inclined than in previous times to join a militant project for a society in which they would have a more respected place and a better life. And these projects, whether revolutionary or ethnic, are all about making identity claims.

ETHNIC MOVEMENTS AFTER 1990

A brief glance at the events which followed from 1990 shows that there is a considerable gap between the claims put forward by individuals, their motivations, and the political responses they received. Immediately following the 'People's Movement' and during the six months leading up to the promulgation of the new constitution, ethnic parties multiplied alongside the big national parties. The last national census of 1991 listed 60 *jāt* or 'species': these included 26 ethnic groups, making up 35 per cent of the total population, 30 castes, and 3 religious groups (Tarai Muslim, hill Muslim, and Sikh), and a

Bengali group (Gurung 1998: 43-5). The census also recorded about twenty Tibeto-Burman languages.[11] Many of the ethnic groups have retained their original shamanic or oracular religion to a greater or lesser extent, even if the census classification is not always able to convey this.[12] In the west of Nepal, certain groups, such as the Magars and Tharus, have conserved their own religion while integrating into it Hindu practices such as the cult of Shiva or the Goddess, which means that they are officially classed as Hindus.

In order to build a national identity, which was the principal aim of the 'Panchayat philosophy', the Nepali language was imposed from the beginning of primary school, to the detriment of other languages. Children learned, and still learn, the history of the unification of the country by Prithvi Narayan Shah as a 'unification'—though many today would prefer to describe it as a violent military conquest. Schoolbooks on Nepali culture include the biographies of historical personages who have been designated as national heroes. A good example is Drabya Shah, an ancestor of the reigning dynasty, who is presented as having imposed himself in a Magar and Gurung milieu by means of his wisdom and physical prowess (de Sales 1998). A final element was that Hinduism was presented as the religion of the kingdom. The legal code forbade both sorcery and the specialists who were traditionally charged with combatting it. This proscription did not prevent these traditions from maintaining themselves (sometimes secretly), but it was seen as oppressive. People in Kham Magar villages still remember angrily how for several years their shamans were forbidden to beat their drums or to denounce sorcerers by making them dance.

The 'People's Movement' was the chance for this repressed diversity to come out into the open. The domination of the high castes of the hills (the Parbatiya) in every sphere—economic, political, and religious—was openly criticized. This tendency was already manifest

---

[11]The latter can be placed in six principal groups: Magar, Bhotia, Gurung-Tamang, Newari, Chepang-Thami, Danuwar. The difficulty of distinguishing a language from a dialect means that more than a hundred languages have been identified in Nepal. About fifteen Indo-Aryan languages are recognized in the census, including Nepali (spoken as a mother tongue by 50.3 per cent of the population) and Maithili (Gurung 1998: 59-60).

[12]The first census to record religion was that held in the aftermath of the first revolution, between 1952 and 1954. The census of 1991 is more complete and distinguishes, in addition to Hinduism, Buddhism, and Islam, Christianity, Jainism, and 'Kiranti' (taken from the name of the tribes of east Nepal) (Gurung 1998: 95).

during the 1980 referendum campaign. Ten years later the international context provided indirect support for such claims. It has been suggested that the collapse of Soviet power and the reawakening of the nations of eastern Europe which followed on from it played an important catalytic role in the Nepalese revolution. When the United Nations declared 1993 'International Year of Indigenous Peoples' it provided world backing for local problems.

The first political party to be established after the revolution was the National Front for the Liberation of the People (Nepal Rāstriya Janamukti Morchā), made up basically of Tibeto-Burmans of the hills. The secretary general, Gore Bahadur Khapangi, presented a memorandum demanding a federal government to the commission preparing the new constitution. Another party, the Janajati Party or 'minorities' party', led by Khagendra Jang Gurung, which was more violent in its mode of expression, campaigned for the division of the kingdom into twelve autonomous ethnic states. Alongside these parties, which attempted to organize nationally, each ethnic group formed one or more parties made up only of its own members.[13] These ethnic parties are sometimes old cultural associations founded during the Panchayat period which had to hide their political ambitions, as was the case with the Magar association discussed above.

A simplified map of Nepal reveals, from west to east, several ethnically Tibetan enclaves in the north of the country, whereas the plains in the south are the habitat of various different Tharu groups dotted around a mosaic of very different peoples (Muslims and Chetris in the west, Yadavs and Bahuns in the east) (see p. 23 above). By contrast the hill peoples have a tendency to form solid blocs. The Karnali basin in the west is inhabited predominantly by Chetris (70 per cent) of Khas culture. There is a Magar zone in the mid-western region bordering on an area inhabited by Bahuns. From the Kali Gandaki river eastwards the people of the Parbatiya caste hierarchy form only a half, more or less, of the population. The northern half is the homeland of the Gurungs and further east of the Tamangs. Finally, in the east of the country there are three cultural zones dominated by the Chetri, the Rai, and the Limbu respectively. It is here that ethnic movements are the most active. The Limbus have a strong tradition of opposition to the state, focused on their claims to tribal land-rights (*kipat*), going

[13]The Newars are an exception here. Gellner (1997b) examines the reasons why the Newars, despite being a highly educated and politicized group, were slow to set up an ethnic party.

back to their conquest in the eighteenth century. By contrast, the Gurungs and the Magars were a part of that conquest and provided a large part of the military personnel that carried it out.

The ethnic movements are organized primarily around the three themes of *bhūmi, bhāsā, dharma* ('land, language, and religion'), a phrase which recurs like a ritual formula in the activists' discourse. Protection of the mother tongue, secularization of the state, and, to varying degrees, local autonomy, were the main issues which came to the fore in the spontaneous days following 1990—to the point that people feared the appearance of regional or communal conflicts of the sort seen in India. These were the issues which were thrashed out in tea houses and led to angry fist-shaking during political meetings. These discussions inevitably led to more and more debates over the definition of particular groups, and with them came the fundamentalist notion of pure and unequivocal ethnic affiliation. In this way of thinking, either one is born a 'pure' Magar, or not. This exclusive notion of group belonging defined in terms of blood derives from a concern to erect barriers between categories that previously were permeable. It can even be interpreted as an expression of alienation arising from the domination of the high castes who are well known, as noted above, for their use of purity to exclude and subordinate others.

Shortly after the new constitution was promulgated, those who sympathized with the ethnic organizations held an enormous demonstration in Kathmandu to protest specifically against Nepal's official designation as a 'Hindu kingdom'. Their call for a secular state that would no longer legitimate the superiority of the Tagadhari over the Matwali (not to mention the low castes) went unheard.

Moreover, the national elections which followed did not reflect these priorities: not one single MP was elected from the ethnic organizations, either in 1991 or in 1994. Even in the eastern hills, the region with the strongest presence of organizations fighting for the rights of ethnic groups, and where several neighbouring districts form a bloc dominated by Limbus, the National Front for the Liberation of the People took second place to the communists. These political setbacks have generally been explained not only by the inevitable divisions between those making identity claims that reduce their importance at the national level, but also by the fact that, when people enter the voting booth, they prefer to vote for projects which are likely to improve their everyday life. Everyone is concerned about drinking water, jobs, and education, and national parties, including the communists, win votes with policies on these issues.

None the less, it is interesting that the ideals for which people are willing to be mobilized and risk death in street demonstrations do not appear or are much diluted in the political programmes that succeed in elections. The very same people who carry out a revolution to defend their identity will vote for politicians who promise them clean drinking water. To interpret this gap between the need for recognition and political action as a sign that the former is less important or less urgent than the latter would be to misunderstand individual motivations. Rather, it is a question of different motivations coming into play at different moments. But the very fact that the dominant political process does not take identity claims seriously into account means that these claims are left unsatisfied; they remain full of life, and potentially revolutionary.

Another pole of opposition to the government is formed by the revolutionary communist movements which have figured regularly and prominently on the front pages of the daily newspapers between 1996 and 2001. It is necessary to examine the history of their foundation in order to undestand how they have taken root in particular locales.

THE EMERGENCE OF THE MAOIST MOVEMENT

The Communist Party of Nepal was born towards the end of the Rana period, on 15 September 1949, in Calcutta. Its founder, Pushpa Lal Shrestha, remained a radical republican up to his death in 1978, refusing all compromise with the king and insisting, in line with Maoist tradition, on a mobilization of the peasantry in order to overthrow the 'feudal state'. However, another tendency became apparent early on, which prefigured the emergence of a policy of reconciliation with the constitutional monarchy as a form of transition to the establishment of a republic. This position was taken up, to different degrees depending on the period, by Man Mohan Adhikari, who was elected general secretary of the party in 1953.[14] In the general election of 1959 the communists won only four seats (out of 109), which demonstrated the small significance of the party at that period. Mahendra's coup d'état in 1960 forced the communists to go underground again. Factions multiplied.

[14]This position was taken up above all by Keshar Jang Rayamajhi, who gave his name to a faction of the party in 1963. It was pro-Soviet and hardly exists today.

At the end of the 1960s the peasant revolt in Naxalbari, in the Bengali foothills of east India, encouraged the Nepali revolutionaries to form a fraternal movement. Called after the district of Jhapa, which adjoins Naxalbari, the Jhapalis began 'a campaign to eliminate class enemies', which was forcibly repressed by the Nepalese army in 1973. Around this time another group, calling itself the 'Fourth Convention', emerged. It established itself particularly well in Pyuthan, the natal region of its founder, Mohan Bikram Singh, and also in Gorkha. Just before the 1980 referendum, which the Fourth Convention boycotted, the army was put on a war footing in this region (Hoftun *et al.* 1999: 237). After several internal splits, this faction became the Communist Party of Nepal (Mashal), which is at the forefront of the revolt today.[15]

The Jhapali formed the Communist Party of Nepal (Marxist-Leninist) or 'Mā-lé'. They gradually distanced themselves from their Jhapali origin and gave up terrorism as a means of political action. Eventually they were close to the position adopted by Man Mohan Adhikari and Pushpa Lal Shrestha's widow, Sahana Pradhan, with whom they allied themselves to form the Communist Party of Nepal (United Marxist-Leninist) or UML, which in 1991 became the second-strongest political force in the country after the Congress Party. They even formed a minority government of the country for nine months in 1994. The accession of the communists to power involved them abandoning the very principles which were at the origin of the movement. They accepted the Hindu kingdom and aimed for agrarian reform rather than armed combat against big landlords.

Small groups of revolutionary communists did not accept this tendency and turned their backs on those they accused of having slavishly followed the social-democratic policy of the dominant party 'as a tail follows its dog'. They remained faithful to orthodox Maoism and accused the new Chinese government, which overturned the Gang of Four in 1976, of being counter-revolutionaries. During this period, mainly in the USA but also in Britain, revolutionary international movements were formed which advocated armed revolution against imperialism and revisionism. In March 1984 the CPN (Mashal) was represented at the second international conference of Maoist parties

[15]Hoftun *et al.* (1999: 392) give a useful figure which represents all the numerous splits and regroupings of the various communist factions between 1949 and 1995. On Mashal vs. Masal, see (ibid.: 237).

in London. This conference ended with the delegates of nineteen revolutionary movements, including the Peruvian Shining Path, signing a declaration that saw the birth of the Revolutionary International Movement or RIM.

In 1989–90 Mashal, as a party, did not join other Communists and the Congress in the Movement for the Restoration of Democracy (MRD). None the less, its members were very active in the many demonstrations which began in February 1990. One of the young leaders of the party, Baburam Bhattarai, organized an alliance of extreme leftist groups under the name United People's Front (Samyukta Jan Morchā or SJM). Day after day the SJM pushed forward each stage of the struggle and was quick to criticize the MRD for failing to keep constant vigilance and being incapable of taking advantage of its position of strength to extract real concessions from the king (Nickson 1992: 366–70).

Bhattarai decided to stand for election in 1991 without intending to take his seat in Parliament. His aim was to show that his movement, which remained underground, was not a negligible force: they won nine seats and the status of a national party (with more than 3 per cent of the votes).

The map of the electoral results in 1991 is significant in this regard. It clearly demonstrates the cleavage between the Kathmandu Valley and the east of the country, where the communists won a majority of seats, and the west, dominated by the Congress Party. The regions which were the most politicized, and which returned communists, were also the best off economically, whereas the west contains the poorest districts. The few islands gained by the Maoists were to be found principally in the traditionally conservative west, specifically in the districts of Rukum and Rolpa which are of particular concern here.

The years which followed the first election were marked by extreme governmental instability. Different ministerial teams succeeded one another, alliances between the parties were made and remade in accordance with individual allegiances, which satisfied no one. In this new democratic context, those in power managed to lose their legitimacy in the eyes of a population which, in different forms, seemed to have lost its illusions.

On 4 February 1996, the SJM submitted a list of forty demands to the government, requiring a response within two weeks or it would begin a 'People's War'. The memorandum strongly criticized the Hindu kingdom and demanded a republican constitution drawn up by a constituent assembly elected by universal suffrage. At the same time it evinced a virulent nationalism which criticized all Indian and Western influence.[16]

The government did not consider it wise to respond to this memorandum, and on 13 February the SJM carried out simultaneous raids against police stations in Haleri (Rolpa) and Athbiskot (Rukum). In Haleri the telephone lines were cut and a temple was set on fire. There were no deaths but the Maoist operations became more frequent. Three and a half years later, in 1999, a fortnightly leftist magazine[17] had on its cover a photograph of Musikot, the district headquarters of Rukum, which had become the 'Maoist capital'; the (official) tally of deaths from the People's War had reached more than 1500.

HOW THE MAOISTS ESTABLISHED THEMSELVES IN THE KHAM MAGAR COUNTRY

A Natural Guerilla Site

Numerous newspaper articles have attempted to explain why this region has become a Maoist stronghold. Three factors are usually cited: the presence of the forest which offers a natural opportunity for guerilla operations, the particularly poor economic conditions, and finally a local population, mostly Magars, who are seen as

a naïve people ... easily swayed ... but who, if they can be enlisted for a task, continue in it or die in the attempt. There is irony in the fact that as many Magars have been killed by the Maoists as by the police. According to unofficial statistics half of all victims have been Magars (*Āwāj Weekly Chronicle*, 15 February 1999, Vol. 2, No. 23).

Poverty and the presence of the forest have certainly played their part in the rise of the Maoists, although the same conditions are of course found in many other regions of Nepal. The third point—the presence of the Magars—requires some commentary. The northern part of the area selected by the Maoists is in fact partly covered by the National Park of Dhorpatan, and the communal lands of the villages are still largely wooded: more than half of the districts of Rukum

---

[16]In the first place it demanded that all treaties with India which threaten Nepali sovereignty must be abandoned (on these treaties, see Hoftun *et al.* 1999: 260 and 275). In addition it required Western imperialism to be fought, both as expressed in international development aid, which encourages general corruption, and in the 'pollution' of the media (video and licensed newspapers).

[17]*Naulo Bihāni 2056* (1999, Baisākh-Sāun).

and Rolpa are forested.[18] Furthermore, the extremely primitive state of the communications network keeps the hills in isolation.

These characteristics, which make the region an ideal refuge for fighters, equally impede its development. It is, along with some of the districts further to the north-west, one of the least developed of the country (Gurung 1998: 169, Fig. 30). In the two districts of Rolpa and Rukum there is, for example, not a single hospital nor any industry. Ninety-five per cent of the population depend on agriculture. The most fertile land in the southern parts of the region is inhabited by Chetris, whereas the Kham Magar to the north and north-west live above 2000 metres and supplement agriculture with transhumant animal husbandry and the secret production of hashish.

This configuration is not unique to the region. The districts further to the west are, as just noted, equally isolated and poor and have experienced a very high level of emigration to India: every year hundreds of villagers in the area around Jumla are forced by hunger to leave and seek work of whatever kind. Epidemics also ravage the enfeebled inhabitants. The great majority (more than 70 per cent) are Chetris and they tend to support the Congress Party. The success of the Maoists in establishing themselves in the west-central region does seem to be due, at least in part, to the presence of the Magars, the third frequently invoked factor.

It is easy to recognize in the quotation given above the stereotypes frequently used for those groups which provide recruits for the Gurkhas: naivety, courage, endurance, and loyalty to their leaders (who, one may suspect, are responsible for propagating the stereotypes in the first place). The military qualities of the Magars, Gurungs, and Kirantis have been praised many times—in inverse proportion to the degree to which those in charge have given them a place in running the country. And it may be that the young mountain-dwellers—brought up in harsh surroundings and enrolling at the end of their adolescence in the military (the only way they see of obtaining what they lack: regular income, education, travel)—do in fact correspond to these descriptions. It remains true that these are stereotypes and it would be false to imagine the Magars as a people who go to war blindly, unanimously following their leader.

[18]Cf. HURPES (1999). HURPES is a Nepali human-rights NGO funded by the Norwegian Human Rights Fund. Its report traces the history of the leftist parties since 1990 and the birth of the Maoist movement in Nepal. Much of its information about the districts affected by the People's War is derived from investigations in the field.

Bearing these qualifications in mind, it is necessary to underline the similarities between the Nepalese situation and that which gave birth to the Naxalites. In his famous study of the revolutionary movement in India, Sumanta Banerjee noted that 'a special feature of the peasant rebellions has been the role of the tribal population ... It is significant that Naxalbari, where the first uprising took place in 1967, is inhabited by Santal tribal people who took a prominent part in the movement. In Srikakulam in the south also, where the movement matured in 1968, Girijans or the hill tribals, formed its nucleus' (Banerjee 1980: 33–4). That the tribals should have been the spearhead of the peasant revolts can be explained in the first place by the fact that they were the first to suffer because of continual immigration by peasants from the lowlands. But he also remarks that 'through all these vicissitudes, the tribals have jealously guarded the autonomy of their various social institutions, and have retained a certain amount of militancy ...' (ibid.: 34). If Banerjee had been writing today, no doubt the term 'identity' would have sprung naturally from his pen in connection with the tribal peoples.

The potential of these peoples for activism was well perceived by the leaders of the revolutionary movements. Banerjee (1980: 36) suggests that in the case of Srikakulam 'both the existing economic frustration of the tribal peasants and their past militancy encouraged the leaders of the RCC [Revolutionary Communist Committee] to concentrate their activities in this area' (which was moreover largely forested). One may well suppose that the leaders of the Nepalese Maoist movement followed a similar reasoning when they chose Rukum and Rolpa as the base area of their guerilla movement. The two leading figures of the Maoist movement are both Brahmans, originally from west Nepal and coming to politics during the student movements of the 1980s. Baburam Bhattarai, mentioned above, studied in India and presents himself as the theorist of the movement, whereas P.K. Dahal, better known by his *nom de guerre* Prachanda, is the commander-in-chief of the 'People's Army'.

Certainly the situations in India and Nepal are different, if only because the events compared are separated by thirty years and the world and political forces have changed. It remains true that the Nepali revolutionaries see themselves as continuing the Naxalite heritage. The magazine of RIM, *A World to Win*, celebrated the thirtieth anniversary of the Naxalbari revolt at the same time as the first anniversary of the People's War in Nepal. A selection of writings by Charu Mazumdar, 'the pioneer of Maoism in India', was published in this issue as a source of inspiration for the activists of today. It is very likely that the Nepali leaders based themselves on the analysis of the earlier ideologists in organizing their guerilla campaign. Although many other scenarios may have been conceivable,[19] the Kham Magar country probably appeared as a tempting target.

The Country of the Kham Magar

As we have seen, the term 'country' refers to an entity that is simulta-neously geographical and cultural: those who live there automatically feel attached to it. Each year the Kham Magar migrate south with their flocks of sheep; the southerners call them Shesh and Sheshini, i.e. 'those who live high up, hidden away' (Nep. *shesh*: 'end', 'remainder'). They have long lived far from the centres of power and this distin-guishes them from their cousins, the Magars, who are nowadays scat-tered everywhere throughout the kingdom. The Kham Magar inhabit about thirty compact villages in the higher parts of Rukum and Rolpa districts. All of them are peasant cultivators of land which they them-selves own. They have hereditary relations with low service castes (blacksmiths and tailor-musicians) who live at the edge of their villages; no other caste has settled in their territory. With a history different from that of other Magars, the Kham Magar have conserved or developed many of their own unique cultural practices. They pre-serve a particularly rich and lively shamanic tradition, for example, which leads them to call their land 'the country of the blind' where only shamans can see (cf. Oppitz 1981). Their compact villages have as many as 300 or 400 houses and several thousand inhabitants.

[19]Although geographic and economic criteria would naturally tend to indicate the west of Nepal as the choice for a base, the Tharu groups in the Tarai could also have been susceptible to Maoist propaganda. Far more than the Magars, they are a people who have suffered from the exploitation of large landowners belonging to the high Hindu castes for whom they have to work in a kind of feudal relationship. Perhaps the Tharus' reputation for timidity—they do not share the warlike character attributed to the hill populations—has played a part in the Maoists' not taking this option. But this is not to say that the Tharus have remained unaffected by the movement. By contrast, the Kiranti groups in the east of the country are well known for their tradition of resistance to the state. The Limbus, as noted above, have a long tradition of fighting for their privileged form of tribal land tenure. However, not only are forests rarer in that part of Nepal, and impoverishment less extreme, but these tribal groups also possess a political organization which is perhaps more solid and less easily penetrated by the radicalism of the Maoists. Instead, the communists have been able to establish themselves in this region by skilfully including strong ethnic claims within their programme.

These sizeable communities are endogamous. The Kham Magars marry preferentially with their matrilateral cross cousins: this form of alliance engenders a difference of status between the sons-in-law, the wife-takers, who thereby become inferior, and their maternal uncles, the wife-givers, who are superior to them. Numerous rituals, from weddings to funerals, and including ritual healing, reinforce this fundamental relationship, which defines every individual. Another important relationship exists between the founders of a given site, where a village is established, and later settlers. The former are believed to have a privileged relationship to the earth, which legitimates their dominance, both politically and religiously, in the community. Of course this dominance can be questioned. The analysis of some rituals allows one to surmise that the tensions between the two sides, i.e. the founders and the rest, are in fact at the heart of social dynamics in these communities (de Sales 1996).

These two structuring relationships, between founders and later immigrants on the one side, and between marital allies on the other, once coincided with each other, since the first founders made the later immigrants into their sons-in-law, by giving them both daughters and land. This bipartite schema became ever more complicated with time and the division of clans and lineages, but these social units are still visible in the layout of the village as well as of the cultivated fields which surround it. Behind the unity of these large villages, it is necessary to know how to discern clan-based fragmentation.

Members of the same clan believe that they share a common ancestor and common geographical origin, which, in the last analysis, determines clan exogamy. Thus each of the four Kham Magar clans—Pun, Gharti, Buda, and Rokha—is known by a second geographical designation, which locates its ancient site of residence. Two members of different clans but originally coming from the same village may not marry each other. The conclusion is inevitable that belonging to a clan is not a matter of blood alone, but also of territory. In fact it is territorial attachment that is the ultimate determining factor.

The Lack of Identity Politics Despite the Long-term Presence of Communism

The relative isolation of the Kham Magars may explain why ethnic activists have made little impression on them until recently. Gore Bahadur Khapangi, the founder of the first national ethnic party, is himself a Magar, but he comes from the eastern Tarai. He is also the secretary of the National Magar Association (Nepal Magar Sangh), which did not have a single Kham Magar volunteer or employee working in its office in 1997. Since then the Association has remedied this embarrassing lack, but Khapangi himself, when questioned on this point, argued that the Kham were not yet politicized and were difficult to mobilize because of their 'lack of education'.[20] One may add that very few of them had entered the British army up to the middle 1980s, though their number has increased since then.[21] The role of retired servicemen in the politicization of ethnicity has already been pointed out.

In contrast it seems that the village of Thawang, in the heart of the Kham country (in the north of Rolpa district), had already become communist as early as 1957. It was a bridgehead of the revolutionary movement founded by Mohan Bikram Singh in the neighbouring district of Pyuthan. Later, in 1980, a local with a very strong personality, Barman Budha, was elected the mayor of Thawang. He is known for having boycotted the referendum and burned the portraits of the King and Queen which are supposed to be displayed in every government office. He was imprisoned for five years and his project of establishing a commune in the village failed. But he returned and was elected as a Maoist (SJM) MP in 1991.

Locals relate how, before he went underground, he turned up at the first sessions of the National Assembly dressed as a Kham Magar peasant: around his thighs a short piece of cloth made of woven hemp, which left his legs naked, was held up by a long woollen belt wound several times around his waist, in which was stuck a large dagger (*khukurī*), the symbol of the hill peoples. An upper garment that crossed over his chest and formed a pocket on his back was the distinctive sign of Magar dress. The contrast between this and official Nepali costume was certainly striking. This story, told as a joke against the dominant high castes, shows how the revolutionary Maoist movement learned very quickly how to make skilful use of ethnic symbols.

Although the success of the SJM at the national polls in 1991 was relatively modest, in the following year's local elections it obtained a majority in Rolpa district and in neighbouring Rukum it came a very close second to the Congress Party. This advance of the Maoists was evidently seen as very threatening by the party in power (Congress).

[20]Interview with the author, May 1998.
[21]In 1981, when I began my first fieldwork among the Kham Magar, not one of the 2,500 inhabitants of the village where I lived had joined the British army. Nowadays there are about twelve who have done so.

It was then that the activists of the two rival parties began a merciless war against each other. Amnesty International reported numerous cases of arbitrary arrest by the police, of torture and murders 'including numerous Magars, members of the low Hindu castes, lawyers, teachers, and young people' and, on the other side, murders by Maoist activists of 'class enemies', meaning local politicians who belonged to the Congress Party.[22]

Ancestral Conflicts become Murderous

It is not only crimes: false accusations have also become more common. They enable us to understood how it is that members of the same community have come to the point of killing each other, in the absence of the traditional safeguards that used to prevent conflict from getting out of hand and encouraged compromise between warring parties. Most false accusations are treated as matters of public order. The slightest altercation between two people in public, at a fair (*melā*) for example, is likely to be reported to the police by a witness. The case then becomes the responsibility of the Chief of Police. The accused is put in prison and stays there until his case appears in court, unless he can put up bail of 28,000 rupees. Very few villagers can afford or raise such a sum. Above all, in this context, the accused will doubt that the strength of his case will have any relevance, because the police chief, appointed by the Home Minister, will back up the supporters of the party in power. The majority find that the only solution is to run away 'into the forest', to a city, to the plains, or even to India in the hope of passing time there until their relatives manage to sort out the dispute.

An accusation by a neighbour who supports the Congress Party in power will be much talked about in the village, where all neighbours are relatives to some degree or other. Usually it serves to stir up ancient conflicts which would previously have been dealt with inside the community. The senior men of the clans would hold a meeting at the headman's house in the presence of the parties to the dispute, and the difference would be discussed and settled. Villagers rarely resorted to the state's legal institutions in the district capital. Nowadays disputes of this sort very quickly move out of the control of the protagonists

---

[22]In addition, two SJM activists were assassinated in Rolpa and three communists in Dang during the national election campaign of 1994 (Amnesty International 1997: 3–4).

themselves. The Maoists get hold of it and send their hooded guerillas (*chāpāmār*) to kill the 'class enemy' who has made a 'false accusation'. The 'people's army' is organized in such a way that the fighters in any one district always come from outside it. They are mostly young peasants (all castes mixed up), some of whom have suffered setbacks when attempting to emigrate to the town or abroad. They are led by leaders who are said to have received special training, sometimes in India. It is also said that in order to rise up in the hierarchy of the revolutionary army and to achieve the status of *chāpāmār*, it is necessary to kill a 'class enemy'. The fighters are informed about their victims by their contacts in the village, but they do not know them personally. This is how ancestral conflicts, rarely fatal until now, have become so.

In the past the opposition between 'us' and 'the others' (our clan and our affines, or the founders and the more recent settlers) was counterbalanced by a whole network of relationships which enabled life in common to carry on within the community. Affiliation to national political parties has dissolved the boundaries of the village. The neighbour who makes an accusation is protected by the party in power, the accused is 'defended' by the revolutionaries. The two sides then become pawns who are manipulated by forces outside the community. This type of scenario occurs more easily in a society that has already become fragile, a society whose members are no longer in a position to unite in the face of forces coming from the outside.

It is striking that the opposition between the two parties at the local level makes far more use of a logic of identity reduced to its most basic form than it does of political convictions. The large village of Taka illustrates this phenomenon particularly well. Two clans there marry each other: the Gharti, the founders of the site, and the Budha, who arrived later. If one knows that the Gharti support the Congress Party, it is not hard to guess that the majority of the Budha support the SJM. This should not blind us to other cleavages which are important nowadays, in particular the generational gap between the youth, who are more easily seduced by Maoist propaganda, and their elders who no longer have the right to pronounce on political matters, whatever their clan. None the less, it remains true that the overturning of traditional rules exacerbates the logic of identity and leads to murder.

Khapangi was very quick to denounce a situation in which Kham Magar peasants were fighting a war that was not theirs, but that of the two parties fighting for territory. He emphasized that once again the Magars were the victims of high castes, since the political leaders both of the Congress Party and of the revolutionary movement were equally Brahmans. The Maoist conquest has been made at the cost of Magar blood, just like the conquest of 'great Nepal' by Prithvi Narayan Shah. The founder of the first ethnic party wants to awake the feeling of Magar identity among the Kham. Such ethnic feeling will follow paths that are hard to predict.

The Development of the Situation

The situation which has just been described obtained at the beginning of the 'People's War' in 1996. But it was transformed by the intervention of the police who were supposed to re-establish order. Conflicts were displaced. It was no longer a case of villagers settling scores by using the Maoists as intermediaries. It became a direct confrontation between the Maoists and the state. There is no space here to go into the details of the police procedures which have been denounced for four years by numerous organizations concerned to defend human rights. It is enough to know that, in addition to almost daily cases of arbitrary arrest or murder reported in the national press, three special police operations have been launched. In November 1995 a squadron of 165 policemen, of whom 50 had received special military training, were charged with 'winning the hearts and minds' of the people of Rolpa in an operation dubbed 'Romeo' (an involuntary irony derived from the language of radio transmission: Romeo was the 'R' for Rolpa). In June 1998 there began an operation called 'Kilo Sierra Two' which was to last for more than a year in eighteen districts. The police were charged with finding the Maoists in the most remote villages and in the forest where they were hiding. Finally the last operation appeared in the newspapers under a name that requires no commentary: 'Search and Kill'.

The organization of daily life in the village is paralysed: peasants who leave the village risk being arrested by the police who suspect them of helping the guerillas. Thus taking animals to pasture, departing for summer residences, going to the forest to collect berries and mushrooms, which form a not insubstantial part of the village diet, have become either impossible or extremely problematic. Schools are closed. Young men, those who have not joined the guerillas in the forest, have left to hide in the big cities or in India. It is said that the women plough and the old people keep silent.

All the accounts I have received describe an impossible living situation. The villagers are harassed at night by Maoists who have to be fed and during the day by policemen looking for suspects. But very quickly, and whatever their political inclinations, my informants admit that they prefer the Maoists, who make do with maize and salt, whereas the police demand chicken and alcohol. Above all, the Maoists have shown themselves over time to be predictable in the way they deal with people. They inform the villagers about their activities during programmes that they hold, usually at night. Individuals from whom money is demanded are informed by letter. They have the reputation of never harming poor people, whereas the police, no doubt themselves often under pressure, consider any peasant they meet on the path to be guilty and often beat them without any further investigation.

The villagers view their country as currently being unjustly perse-cuted by the forces of the state. A feeling of revolt has developed that focuses on the defence of their territory, a sentiment that has been cleverly exploited by the revolutionaries who promise the Kham Magars autonomy. Thus the situation has evolved considerably over the first four years of the People's War. It began as intra-communal conflicts which were used by two opposed political parties, and it has become transformed into a struggle for territorial autonomy, an entirely new idea for the Kham Magar. This idea put forward by ethnic activists only caught on among the Kham Magar with the development of the Maoist guerilla movement. The villagers do not notice the paradox of the revolutionaries, fervent defenders of a new nation, becoming activists in favour of ethnic autonomy. Ideological principles, which are in any case rarely made explicit, give way before the necessities of action. The needs of the Maoists (to have a secure base territory for their guerilla action) and those of the villagers (to protect them-selves from a government that has become hostile and dangerous) coincide, even though their projects are not the same. The Maoists' techniques are capable of covering up such ambiguities.

The Symbolic Conquest of Territory and its Revitalization

Despite its overt anti-religious statements, Marxism possesses a hidden religious dimension that has often been remarked upon. The first analysts who were interested in this question in the Nepali context sought to point out the continuity between communism and certain elements of Hindu and particularly Buddhist tradition (Hoftun *et al.* 1999: 215–18). Philippe Ramirez demonstrates how a materialist ideology has been adapted to Nepalese reality, 'a society where religion does not constitute an autonomous domain' (1997: 52), and how the practice of Nepalese Maoism is hardly a secular affair. He mentions

Plate 10.1. A Maoist propaganda poster stuck to a tree in Dolpo district, north of Rukum. Only part of the text is visible in the photograph. It is signed by a Maoist group and announces to passersby that they are entering the territory under its jurisdiction. The authors refer to an assembly of people united in their opposition to hangings carried out by the government. In the foreground of the poster men and women are shown brandishing their weapons against government forces who can be seen running away from explosions in the background. The scene is dominated by a communist flag flying from the summit of a mountain behind which the sun is rising. In line with conventional communist imagery, this symbolizes the dawn of a new era. (I thank Marietta Kind for providing me with this image which dates from 1999; it was taken in lower Dolpo towards Rukum by J.S. Milne and published on www.jmilne.org/mntn.

in particular the cult of 'martyrs' (*shahid*), a term that refers both to the communist victims of repression under the Panchayat regime and to present-day Maoists killed by the police. According to Ramirez, this cult can be traced back to traditional conceptions in which 'the martyr who dies a violent death can only escape from eternal wandering by a recognition of his status, which is the equivalent of reintegrating him into society' (Ramirez 1997: 60). In the region discussed here this fundamental ritual of Maoist propaganda has been adapted in a way that returns us precisely to the discussion of territory.

An article that appeared in a Maoist-aligned magazine in May 1998 contained a balance sheet of two years of the 'People's War' in Rolpa district: 56 civilians killed by the police were declared as martyrs.[23] Their names were combined and given to two gardens set up in their honour, to about a dozen paths, and to five wayside stopping places with stone platforms (often constructed in the shade, they enable travellers to put down their loads).[24] Although the gardens are a new idea (borrowed, presumably, from a communist vision of urban development), the resting platforms and paths are traditionally built in memory of the dead, who then, in Kham Magar belief, become ancestors. Established in a locality where he will receive regular worship, the spirit of the dead person will, it is believed, ensure the prosperity of the place. It seems that the revolutionaries have adopted this reasoning: they seek to neutralize the violent deaths of the victims of the People's War by turning them into benevolent ancestors.

Another example illustrates how the Maoists are willing to follow local traditions. Two commemorative pillars have been erected. One, at the top of a hill, celebrates the second anniversary of the 'People's War' and is called 'Shahid'. The other has been put up exactly on the Jaljala pass, the highest point of the district. It has been baptized 'Sija', from 'Sisne' (a neighbouring pass) and 'Jaljala'. This site is particularly rich in symbolism for the villagers of the valley it overlooks. The god Braha lives there and each year hundreds of rams are sacrificed in his honour. Braha is a local god attached to a specific village territory (there are numerous accounts of conflicts between neighbouring Brahas); he is closely linked to the ancestors (de Sales 1991: 145–6). Establishing a commemorative pillar on his site shows that the revolutionaries do not think that it is sufficient to occupy a place

[23]*Muktiyuddha* (The War of Liberation), no. 1.
[24]Several of the names were represented by the first syllable only, in order to make a single name by running them together.

physically, but that they have to root it in a specific history of events in which the principal actors are locals. The veneration of dead heroes both ties this history to the place and opens it up to the other world.

Alongside this appropriation of space by means of ritual activity, the Maoists take care to eulogize places, just as they exalt the dead. The article cited above finishes with a series of praises in the epic style of communist propaganda:

Rolpa will be immortal in the history of Nepal. Rolpa is not just a district, it is Nepal. It is the source of revolution, the centre of hope. Glory to Jaljala, glory to Sisne! For Jaljala [we feel] an infinite faith and for Sisne a deep love!

Thus the 'country' that was forgotten in its remote fastnesses is placed at the centre of the nation, praised for being the nation itself, and the mountain passes that are so intimately related to the villagers' everyday landscape are recognized by everyone as the source of deep attachments. This need for recognition, the source of the revolt over identity, is expressed most movingly in revolutionary songs. More than a hundred songs are recorded on cassettes that are handed around clandestinely. They deserve a separate study, but it should be noted here that although propaganda rhetoric is present, most of them simply describe the suffering (*dukha*) of the peasant trying to survive in a country where the conditions have become too difficult and which he is often forced to leave to seek his fortune elsewhere. The musical style of the traditional folk songs of west Nepal conveys with nostalgia all 'the love for this country in the shadow of Dhaulagiri, stretched out in the cool of the evening'.

It is difficult to know whether the revolutionaries make use of such traditional techniques for their own ends in full consciousness of what they are doing, or whether such techniques impose themselves as a spontaneous response to a situation of crisis. Or, to put it another way, whether it is a question of a strategic or a traditional use of local tradition. Either way, local tradition continues to live on in their practices. The ethnic movements, by contrast, have set themselves up to defend a tribal heritage which loses its vitality in the very efforts made to define it, when it is represented in cultural programmes or made the instrument of political ambitions.

Another example goes in the same direction. When the Magar activist calls himself a warrior who has been cursed and is without strength, he is certainly the victim of the stereotypes which depict him as a brave and long-suffering fighter. The hill tribes have been trapped by these descriptions by means of a process of 'self-fulfilling prophecy' (Clarke 1995: 114–15). It remains true that the depression and frustration which results cannot find much satisfaction in the contradictions of ethnic revivalism, as expressed in the desire to save Magar society by reforming its 'excessive' or superstitious customs.

In contrast, the revolutionary struggle may seem to offer a solution when it preaches the 'annihilation of class enemies'. Charu Mazumdar, the ideologist of the Naxalite movement which the Nepali Maoist leaders view as a forerunner to their own, conceived of battle (and murders) as the only way in which 'the new man [can] be reborn' (cited in Banerjee 1980: 145). The conception of a 'nation sacrificed by feudals', 'eaters of men', is central to Nepali revolutionary propaganda, as is the necessity of 'taking revenge for the blood of the martyrs'. The conceptual universe revealed by these few key terms of activist discourse is evidently organized around a sacrificial schema, and this suggests that the combatants, by participating in the revolutionary struggle, are seeking some kind of symbolic revitalization.

It was suggested above that there was considerable truth in the remark made by Khapangi, to the effect that the Magars have found themselves fighting a war that is not theirs: they are just cannon-fodder for the two parties struggling over their territory. Perhaps one could go further and suggest that the young people enrolled by the Maoists are fighting precisely in order to revive the strength of the warriors that they suppose their grandfathers to have been, and to free them from the curse that has paralysed them and reduced them to silence in their own territory. This would then be their way of appropriating the war and making it their own.

CONCLUSION

In conclusion let us consider the way in which the Kham Magars have resorted to an intensified sense of identity in relation to their 'country'. Should one see it as a resurgence, in a situation of crisis, of a traditional identity which combines both territorial and cultural ties in one, which fixes on the locality's uniqueness rather than on its differences from the other countries of the kingdom? Richard Burghart expressed this Nepalese notion of 'country' particularly well when he remarked, 'Although a native may claim that his country is best of all, the point ... is not that one's country is better than any other country; it is that one's country is best for oneself' (Burghart 1996: 235). No doubt the villagers caught up in the chaos of the guerilla war feel great nostalgia for their country, either because they have been forced to leave it, or because they have to see it being torn apart by incessant fighting. But their attachment to their country and their efforts to defend it or to claim autonomy for it are about as far as it is possible to be from the projects of the revolutionary leaders. Maoist propaganda is quite clear: when it draws a metonymic link between Rolpa and Nepal ('Rolpa ... is Nepal'), it is attempting to construct a nation out of all these countries, a nation in which all these countries will be united and ultimately dissolved. The Maoist project with respect to the nation is remarkably similar to that of King Mahendra as evident in the discourse, discussed above, in which all subjects were to find their 'identity' in their shared devotion to the newly conscious nation.

Let us note, finally, that the guerilla war is simply accelerating the exodus of the mountain-dwellers for the valleys further south where the dynamism of the nation is located. Thus, the focus of the Kham Magars on their identity in relation to their country has to be viewed as the response of individuals who are caught in a bind. Once the crisis has passed, however that may come about, they will abandon their autonomy and their principal aspiration will be to merge into the wider Nepali population.

REFERENCES

Adhikari, K.R. 1991. 'The Quest for Unity among the Magars of Nepal'. Unpublished ms., AAA meeting, Chicago.
Banerjee, S.1980. *In the Wake of Naxalbari: A History of the Naxalite Movement in India*. Calcutta: Subarnarekha.
Burghart, R. 1996. 'The Formation of the Concept of Nation-State in Nepal'. In R. Burghart *The Conditions of Listening: Essays on Religion, History and Politics in South Asia*. Delhi: OUP, pp. 226–60.
Clarke, G.E. 1995. 'Blood and Territory as Idioms of National Identity in Himalayan States' *Kailash* 17 (3–4): 89–132.
Gaborieau, M. 1982. 'Les rapports de classe dans l'idéologie officielle du Népal' *Purusartha* 6: 251–90.
Gellner, D.N. 1997a. 'Introduction: Ethnicity and Nationalism in the World's Only Hindu State' in Gellner *et al.* (eds.).
—— 1997b. 'Caste, Communalism, and Communism: Newars and the Nepalese State' in Gellner *et al.* (eds).
——, J. Pfaff-Czarnecka, and J. Whelpton (eds) 1997. *Nationalism and Ethnicity in a Hindu Kingdom: The Politics of Culture in Contemporary Nepal*. Amsterdam: Harwood.
Gurung, H. 1998. *Nepal: Social Demography and Expressions*. Kathmandu: New Era.

Höfer, A. 1979. *The Caste Hierarchy and the State in Nepal: A Study of the Muluki Ain of 1854*. Innsbruck: Universitäsverlag Wagner.

Hoftun, M., W. Raeper, and J. Whelpton 1999. *People, Politics, and Ideology: Democracy and Social Change in Nepal*. Kathmandu: Mandala Book Point.

Levine, N.E. 1992. 'Caste, State, and Ethnic Boundaries in Nepal' *Journal of Asian Studies* 46: 71–88.

Mikesell, S.L. 1988. 'Cotton on the Silk Road (or the dialectic of a Merchant Community in Nepal)'. Unpublished PhD dissertation, University of Wisconsin.

Nickson, R.A. 1992. 'Democratisation and the Growth of Communism in Nepal: A Peruvian Scenario in the Making?' *Journal of Commonwealth Studies and Comparative Politics* 30(3): 358–86.

Oppitz, M. 1981. *Schamanen im Blinden Land*. Frankfurt: Syndikat.

Ramirez, P. 1997. 'Pour une anthropologie religieuse du maoïsme népalais' *Archives de Sciences Sociales des Religions* 99: 47–68.

——— 2000. *De la disparition des chefs: Une anthropologie politique népalaise* . Paris: CNRS.

Sales, A. de 1991. *Je suis né.e vos jeux de tambours* . Nanterre: Société d'Ethnologie.

——— 1993. 'When the Miners Came to Light: The Chantel of Dhaulagiri' in G. Toffin (ed.) *Nepal, Past and Present*. New Delhi: Sterling, pp. 91–7.

——— 1996. 'Dieu nourricier et sorcier cannibale: Les esprits des lieux chez les Magar du nord (Nepal)' *Etudes Rurales* 143–4: 45–65.

——— 1998. 'Simarekha: A Historical Borderline?' *European Bulletin of Himalayan Research* 15–16: 78–85.

Todorov, T. 1995. *La vie commune: Essai d'anthropologie générale* . Paris: Le Seuil.

Reports and Brochures

Amnesty International 1997. *Nepal: Human Rights Violations in the Context of a Maoist "People's War"*.

A World to Win 1998. No. 23. London.

Human Rights Bulletin 1994. 6(15). 'Report on the Situation of Human Rights in Rolpa'.

Human Rights Bulletin 1996. 8(18). 'Statement of the Human Rights Fact-Finding Team Regarding the Human Rights Situation in Rolpa and Dang'.

HURPES 2054 (1997). *Sandharbha māobādī janayuddha: himsā ra mānab adhikār ullanghan silsilā* [The context of the People's War: violence and violations of human rights].

Muktiyuddha (War of Liberation) 1998. 1.

Naulo Bihānī (New Morning) 2056 (1999), Baisākh-Sā.

Nepālmā janayuddha [The People's War in Nepal] 2054 (1997). Published by Nepal Rāstrīya Buddhijībi Sangathan (National Organization of Nepalese Intellectuals).

RECENT REFERENCES

Biswokarma, B. et al. 2004. *People in the 'People's War'* (Centre for Investigative Journalism). Lalitpur: Himal Association.

Dixit, K.M. 2002. 'Insurgents and Innocents: The Nepali Army's Battle with the Maobadi' *Himal South Asia* (June issue).

___ & S. Ramachandaran (eds) *State of Nepal*. Kathmandu: Himal Books.

Hutt, M. (ed.) 2004. *Himalayan 'People's War': Nepal's Maoist Rebellion*. London: Hurst & Co; Bloomington: Indian University Press.

Karki, A. & D. Seddon (eds) 2003. *The People's War in Nepal: Left Perspectives*. Delhi: Adroit.

Karki, A. & B. Bhattarai (eds) 2003. *Whose War? Economic and Socio-Cultural Impacts of Nepal's Maoist-Government Conflict*. NGO Federation Nepal.

K.C., S.B. et al. 2003. *Despatches from the Grey Zone* (Centre for Investigative Journalism). Lalitpur: Himal Association.

Lecomte-Tilouine, M. 2004. 'Regicide and Maoist Revolutionary Warfare in Nepal: Modern Incarnations of a Warrior Kingdom' *Anthropology Today* 20(1): 13-19.

Metz, J. (ed.) 2003. *Himalaya: The Journal of the Association for Nepal and Himalayan Studies* 23(1), special issue on Nepal's Maoist Insurgency.

Muni, S.D. 2003. *Maoist Insurgency in Nepal: The Challenge and the Response*. Delhi: Rupa & Co.

Ogura, K. forthcoming. 'Maoists, People, and the State, as Seen from Rolpa and Rukum' in H. Ishi, D.N. Gellner & K. Nawa (eds) *Political and Social Transformations in North India and Nepal*, Delhi: Manohar.

Onesto, Li 2005. *Dispatches from the People's War in Nepal*. London: Pluto.

Shrestha, C.B. 2004. *Nepal: Coping with Maoist Insurgency*. Kathmandu: self-published.

Thapa, D. 2002. 'Erosion of the Nepali World' *Himal South Asia* (April issue).

___ (ed.) 2003. *Understanding the Maoist Movement of Nepal*. Kathmandu: Martin Chautari.

___ with B. Sijapati 2004. *A Kingdom under Siege: Nepal's Maoist Insurgency, 1996 to 2004*. London: Zed.

Verma, A.S. 2001. *Maoist Movement in Nepal*. Noida: Samakaleen Tisri Duniya.

CHAPTER 9 REFERENCES *(continued from page 325)*

Mainali, S. 2004. 'Sexual Violence Against Women' in *People in the 'People's War'* (Centre for Investigative Journalism), pp. 85–91. Kathmandu: Himal Books.

Manchanda, R. 2001, *Women, War and Peace in South Asia: Beyond Victimhood to Agency*. London: Sage.

Parvati, Comrade 2003a. 'The Question of Women's Leadership in People's War in Nepal' *The Worker* 5 (October): 1–16 (also at www.maoism.org).

_____ 2003b. 'Women's Participation in the People's War' in A. Karkii & D. Seddon (eds) *The People's War in Nepal: Left Perspectives*, pp. 165–82. Delhi: Adroit.

Pettigrew, J. 1995. 'Shamanic Dialogue: History, Representation and Landscape in Nepal.' Unpublished PhD thesis, University of Cambridge.

_____ 2004. 'Living Between the Maoists and the Army in Rural Nepal' in M. Hutt (ed) *Himalayan 'People's War': Nepal's Maoist Rebellion*, pp.261–85. London: Hurst.

_____ in press. 'Learning to be Silent: Change, Childhood, Mental Health, and the Maoist Insurgency in Nepal' in H. Ishi, D.N. Gellner, & K. Nawa (eds) *Nepalis Inside and Outside Nepal*. Manohar: Delhi.

_____ & S. Shneiderman 2004. 'Women and the Maobaadi: Ideology and Agency in Nepal's Maoist Movement' *Himal South Asian* 17(1): 19–29.

Shakya, S. 2003. 'The Maoist movement in Nepal: An Analysis from the Women's Perspective' in A. Karki & D. Seddon (eds) *The People's War in Nepal: Left Perspectives*, pp. 375–404. Delhi: Adroit.

Sharma, S. 2004. 'The Maoist Movement: An Evolutionary Perspective' in M. Hutt (ed.) *Himalayan 'People's War,'* pp. 38–57. London: Hurst

Sharma, M. & D. Prasain 2004. 'Gender Dimensions of the People's War: Some Reflections on the Experiences of Rural Women' in M. Hutt (ed.) *Himalayan 'People's War,'* pp. 152–65. London: Hurst.

Shrestha, D.K. 2004. 'Ethnic Autonomy in the East' in *Centre for Investigative Journalism People in the 'People's War,'* pp. 19–40. Kathmandu: Himal Books

Shneiderman, S. & M. Turin 2004. 'The Path to *Jan Sarkar* in Dolakha District: Towards an Ethnography of the Maoist Movement' in M. Hutt (ed.) *Himalayan 'People's War,'* pp. 79–111. London: Hurst.

Thapa, M. 2003. 'Girls in Nepal's Maoist War' *Himal South Asian* 16: 49–55.

Person Index

364 Resistance and the State: Nepalese Experiences

General Index

Italicized entries indicate where the term or acronym is defined and/or substantially discussed.